A LATIN GRAMMAR

A LATIN GRAMMAR:

ADAPTED FOR THE USE OF COLLEGES

DR. F. SCHULTZ

Published by

FacsiMile Publisher
12 Pragati Market
Ashok Vihar, Ph-2
Delhi - 110052, India
Phone: 011-47034999
Email: www.facsimilepublishers.com
info@facsimilepublishers.com

Distribution Network
gyanbooks.com
India, USA, Canada, UK, Australia

ISBN: 978-93-6896-926-6 (PB)

First Published, 1878

2nd Impression 2026

Printed at: Gyan Press, Delhi.

A LATIN GRAMMAR
Author: DR. F. SCHULTZ

A

LATIN GRAMMAR

ADAPTED FOR THE USE OF COLLEGES.

FROM THE FIFTEENTH GERMAN EDITION OF

DR. F. SCHULTZ'S GRAMMAR.

THIRTY-FIFTH EDITION

Frederick Pustet & Co.

Printers to the Holy Apostolic See and the Sacred Congregation of Rites

RATISBON ROME NEW YORK CINCINNATI

PREFACE.

THE Grammar which we here present to the classical public, is arranged according to the German-Latin Grammar of Dr. Ferdinand Schultz. It is no small recommendation of the original, that it has passed through fifteen large editions in as many years.

The great merits of the work, which have made it so much esteemed, are its simplicity, clearness, and conciseness; for, while it does not overburden the learner with that boundless erudition, which is so frequently, in many text-books, a stumbling-block to the student, yet, we are convinced, nothing essential has been omitted.

Some additions have been made in order to render the work better adapted to the curriculum of studies in our American institutions.

All we ask for it is a fair trial in the *practical* work of the schoolroom; for it is there that the true test of a text-book must be sought, and we believe that when it has been so tested, it will be found to be all that it is claimed to be.

CONTENTS.

PART I.

GRAMMATICAL FORMS.

PART II.

SYNTAX.

PART III.

PROSODY.

APPENDIX.

PART I.

GRAMMATICAL FORMS.

CHAPTER I.

VOWELS AND CONSONANTS.

§ 1.

1. **The** Latin alphabet consists of twenty-four letters:

a b c d e f g h i (j) k l m n o p q r s t u v x y z.

A B C D E F G H I (J) K L M N O P Q R S T U V X Y Z.

2. Of these letters six are vowels, namely: *a*, *e*, *i*, *o*, *u*, and *y*; the rest are consonants.

3. The vowels are pronounced either short or long; the short vowel is marked thus ˘, the long vowel ¯; *e. g.*, *contĭnens*, *rosārum*.

a. The vowels are pronounced according to what is called the Continental method:

ă (short *a*),	like *a* in man;
ā (long *a*),	like *a* in far;
ĕ (short *e*),	like *e* in met;
ē (long *e*),	like *a* in mate;
ĭ (short *i*),	like *i* in pin;
ī (long *i*),	like *i* in machine;
ŏ (short *o*),	like *o* in log;
ō (long *o*),	like *o* in throne;
ŭ (short *u*),	like *u* in bull;
ū (long *u*),	like *u* in rule;
y̆ (short *y*),	like *i* in pin;
ȳ (long *y*),	like *i* in machine.

Qu is always pronounced like *kw;* thus *qui*, *quae*, *quod;* *ngu* before vowels, like *ngw;* *lingua*, *anguis*, *languor*, are therefore dissyllables (*argŭo*, on the contrary, is a trisyllable).

Su before vowels is pronounced like *sw* in *suadeo*, *suavis*, *suesco*, in all other words like *su;* *e. g.*, *su-us*, *su-es*, *censu-it.*

b. The consonants are pronounced as in English: but *c* and *g*, when followed by *e*, *i*, *y*, *ae*, or *oe*, have the soft sound; in all other cases, the hard.

Tĭ (short) before vowels is pronounced like *ci*; as, *lectio*, lek-cio; *gratia*, gra-cia; *otium*, o-cium; only after *s* and *x*, and in Greek words, *t* always retains its own sound; as, *osti-um*, *mixti-o*, *Milti-ades;* also *niti-er*, *quati-er*, *toti-us* (*i* being long).

4. There are in Latin the following compound vowels or diphthongs:—*ae*, *au*, *oe;* *e. g.*, *aetas*, *aurum*, *coelum;* *eu* is rare; still more so, *ei*, *oi*, *ui*. The diphthongs are always long.

Eu is diphthong only in *ceu*, *neu*, *seu*, *heu*, *eheu*, *heus*, *neuter*, *neutiquam*, and in foreign proper names; as, *Europa*, *Eurus;* *ei* only in *hei* (with the poets, also in *dein*, *deinde;* likewise, *oi* in *proin* and *proinde*), *ui* only in *hui* (with poets, also in *cui*, *huic*).

Points of separation (*puncta diaereseos*); as, *aër*, *poëta.*

5. The consonants are divided into

a. Semivowels (*semivocales*), to which the liquids (*liquidae*) and the sibilant *s* (*littera sibilans*) belong.

b. Mutes (*mutae*), which include the rest. The mutes are classified with reference to the organ by which they are pronounced; they are, 1, labials (*labiales*), *b*, *p*, *f*, *v;* 2, gutturals (*gutturales*), also called palatals (*palatinae*), *c* (*k*, *q*), *g* (*h*); 3, linguals (*linguales*), also called dentals (*dentales*), *d*, *t.* Another division: *p*, *c*, *t*, smooth (*tenues*); *b*, *g*, *d*, middle (*mediae*); *ph*, *ch*, *th*, aspirate (*aspiratae*). Double consonants are *x* (*cs*, *gs*, *qs*, *hs*) and *z* (*ds*, *ts*); *h* is only an aspiration, not properly a consonant.

6. Every word is written as it is spoken. Capital letters are used, 1, at the beginning of a sentence; 2, for proper names and the adjectives formed from them.

7. The syllables are divided at the end of a line according to pronunciation; *e. g.*, *magi-stri*, *om-nis*, *ig-nis*, *duc-tus*, *rap-tus.* In compound words the division must be made so as to keep the component parts distinct; *ad-ire*, *post-ea*, *dis-tribu-ere*, *di-stare.*

CHAPTER II.

PARTS OF SPEECH.

§ 2.

There are in Latin eight different kinds of words, or parts of speech, namely:

1. **Substantives** (*nomina substantiva*); *e. g., vir*, the man; *rosa*, the rose; *virtus*, virtue; *verbum*, the word. Substantives are divided into:

1. Common nouns (*nomina appellativa*); as, *arbor*, the tree.
2. Proper names (*nomina propria*); as, *Caesar*, Caesar.
3. Collective nouns (*nomina collectiva*); as, *multitudo*, the crowd.
4. Abstract nouns (*nomina abstracta*); as, *mens*, the mind.

The three first classes are called concrete nouns (*nomina concreta*) in contradistinction to abstract nouns.

2. **Adjectives** (*nomina adiectiva*); *e. g., bonus*, good; *pulcher*, beautiful; *amabilis*, amiable.

To the adjectives belong most of the numerals (*numeralia*); *e. g., multi*, many; *unus*, one; *duo*, two; *primus*, the first.

3. **Pronouns** (*pronomina*); *e. g., ego*, I; *tu*, thou; *qui*, who.

These three parts of speech are declined.

4. **Verbs** (*verba*); *e. g., sum*, I am; *amo*, I love; *monere*, to warn; *dormire*, to sleep.

Verbs are conjugated.

5. **Adverbs** (*adverbia*); *e. g., valde*, very; *saepe*, often; *ibi*, there.

To the adverbs belong several numerals; *e. g., semel*, once; *primum*, first.

6. **Prepositions** (*praepositiones*); *e. g., ad*, to; *ab*, from; *ante*, before.

7. **Conjunctions** (*coniunctiones*); *e. g., et*, and; *sed*, but; *si*, if; *quia*, because.

8. **Interjections** (*interiectiones*); *e. g., vae*, woe! *ah*, ah!

These four parts of speech are indeclinable (*indeclinabilia*). The declinable words are called by a common name (*nomina*), the indeclinable words (*particulae*). All words are therefore *nomina*, or *verba*, or *particulae*.

The Latin language has no article, consequently *vir* may be either *the man*, *a man*, or *man*.

CHAPTER III.

GENDER OF WORDS.

§ 3.

ALL nouns have one of three genders (*genera*).

1. The **masculine** gender (*genus masculinum*); *e. g.*, *vir*, man; *rivus*, brook.

2. The **feminine** gender (*genus femininum*); *e. g.*, *femina*, woman; *virtus*, virtue.

3. The **neuter** gender (*genus neutrum*); *e. g.*, *lignum*, wood; *foedus*, alliance.

Some words can be used either in the masculine or feminine gender, they are therefore **common** (*generis communis*).

§ 4.

The gender of substantives is determined partly by their termination, and partly by their meaning.

RULES OF GENDER ACCORDING TO MEANING.

1. The men, the nations, rivers, winds,
   And names of months are masculine.
2. The women, trees, the towns, and lands,
   And islands, all are feminine.
3. The words which cannot be declined
   Are of the neuter gender all.
4. *Commune* call what either man
   Or woman also signifies.

1. Of the masculine gender are therefore *pater*, father; *nauta*, sailor; *Persa*, Persian; *Albis*, the Elbe; *Sequăna*, the Seine; *aquilo*, the northwind; *Aprilis*, April; etc.

Some rivers are feminine, namely: *Albula*, *Allia*, *Matrona*, *Lethe*, and *Styx*. Also *copiae*, troops, remains feminine. *Hadria* (poet.), the Adriatic Sea, is masculine.

2. Of the feminine gender, are *mater*, mother; *pirus*, pear-tree; *Corinthus*, Corinth; *Germania*, Germany; *Aegyptus*, Egypt; *Delus*, the island of Delos; etc.

Of cities and countries are

a. Always masculine, 1, the plurals in **i**; as, *Delphi*, *Veii;* 2, the town *Canopus*, *-i*, and the countries, *Bospŏrus*, *Pontus*, *Hellespontus*, and *Isthmus;* 3, the towns, *Hippo*, *Narbo*, *Sulmo*, *Vesontio*, *-onis*, *Tun-es*, *-etis*.

b. Always neuter: 1, the plurals in **a** (gen. *orum*); as, *Susa*, *Susorum*, *Leuctra*, *Arbela;* 2, all those ending in **um, on, ur,** or **e**; as, *Tusculum*, *Ilion*, *Tibur*, *Praeneste* (*Argos*, indeclinable and neuter, whereas *Argi*, *-orum*, masc.).

3. Of the neuter gender are *nihil* (indecl.), nothing; *fas* (indecl.), right; *vale* (indecl.), the farewell; *valde* (the word *valde*), also *amo*, *ante*, etc.

4. Common are, *adolescens*, the youth, the maiden; *comes*, male or female companion; *dux*, male or female leader; *civis*, male or female citizen; *heres*, heir or heiress; *sacerdos*, priest, priestess; *infans*, male or female child.

These substantives of the common gender denote mostly living beings; as, *bos*, ox or cow.

5. Many names of men and animals have for the masculine and feminine gender a word of the same stem, but with different terminations (**substantiva mobilia**); as, *victor*, conqueror; *victrix*, female conqueror; *dominus*, lord; *domina*, lady; *puer*, boy; *puella*, girl; *magister*, master; *magistra*, mistress; *rex*, king; *regina*, queen; *asinus*, ass; *asina*, female ass; *gallus*, cock; *gallina*, hen. Rarely have the names entirely different roots; as, *servus*, slave; *ancilla*, female slave (seldom *serva*); *taurus*, steer; *vacca*, cow; *aries*, ram; *ovis*, sheep.

6. Many names of animals always keep the same gender (**nomina epicoena**); *corvus*, raven, only masc.; *cornix*, crow, only fem.; *passer*, sparrow, only masc.; *ciconia*, stork, only fem. We find, however, *corvus femina*, the female raven; *cornix mas* or *mascula*, the male crow.

§ 5.

The adjectives also have genders, which we generally recognize by the ending; *e. g.*, *bonus*, good, is masculine; *bona*, good, is feminine; *bonum*, good, is neuter. Thus, *malus*, *mala*, *malum*, bad; *magnus*, *magna*, *magnum*, great; *parvus*, *parva*, *parvum*, small; *carus*, *cara*, *carum*, dear.

§ 6.

The adjective takes, in Latin, always the gender of the substantive to which it belongs, 1, as **attribute**; *bonus pater*, the good father; 2, as **predicate**; *pater est bonus*, the father is good. *Bona mater*, the good mother; *mater est bona*, the mother is good. *Bonum exemplum*, the good example; *exemplum est bonum*, the example is good. *Comes bonus*, the good companion; *comes bona*, the good companion (female). *Dux bonus*, the good leader; *dux bona*, the good leader (female).

CHAPTER IV.

DECLENSION.

§ 7.

In the declension or inflection of nouns, the Latin language has:

1. The **number** (*numerus*). The number is either **singular** (*singularis*) or **plural** (*pluralis*); *e. g.*, the father, the fathers.

2. The **case** (*casus*). In Latin there are six cases, namely, the Nominative, which answers the question, **Who? What?** 2, the Genitive, which answers the question, **Whose? Of whom? Of what?** 3, the Dative, which answers the question, **To whom? For whom?** 4, the Accusative, which answers the question, **Whom? What?** 5, the Vocative, in exclamations; 6, the Ablative, in answer to the question, **by, from, in, with, whom,** or **what?**

The nominative and vocative are called *casus* **recti**; the other, *casus* **obliqui.**

§ 8.

In Latin there are five declensions. The declensions are distinguished by the termination of the genitive singular; the first declension has the genitive singular in **ae,** the second in **i,** the third in **is,** the fourth in **us,** the fifth in **ei.**

§ 9.

The terminations of the five Latin declensions are found in the following tables of case-endings:

SINGULAR.

	First Decl.	Second Decl.		Third Decl.		Fourth Decl.		Fifth Decl.
			Neut.		Neut.		Neut.	
Nom.	ă	ŭs, ĕr;	ŭm	———	———	ŭs;	ū	ēs
Gen.	ae	ī		ĭs		ūs		ēi
Dat.	ae	ō		ī		ŭī;	ū	ēi
Acc.	ăm	ŭm		ĕm, ĭm;	*like Nom.*	ŭm;	ū	ĕm
Voc.	ă	ĕ, ĕr;	ŭm	*like Nom.*		ŭs;	ū	ēs
Abl.	ā	ō		ĕ, ī		ū		ē

PLURAL.

	First Decl.	Second Decl.		Third Decl.		Fourth Decl.		Fifth Decl.
			Neut.		Neut.		Neut.	
Nom.	ae	ī;	ă	ēs;	ă, ĭă	ūs;	ŭă	ēs
Gen.	ārŭm	ōrum		ŭm or ĭŭm		ŭŭm		ērŭm
Dat.	īs	īs		ĭbŭs		ĭbŭs (ŭbŭs)		ēbŭs
Acc.	ās	ōs;	ă	ēs;	ă, ĭă	ūs;	ŭă	ēs
Voc.	ae	ī;	ă	ēs;	ă, ĭă	ūs;	ŭă	ēs
Abl.	īs	īs		ĭbŭs		ĭbŭs (ŭbŭs)		ēbŭs

2. Several cases, as may be seen from the table, have sometimes the same form.

a. The Vocative is everywhere like the Nominative, except in the second declension, where *ĕ* takes the place of *us.*

b. The neuter nouns of all declensions have a common form for the Nom., Acc., and Voc., sing., and another common form for the Nom., Acc., and Voc., plur.

c. The Dat. and Abl., plur., in all declensions, have a common form.

d. In the second decl., Dat. and Abl. sing., are the same.

e. In the third, fourth, and fifth, the Nom. and Acc. plur. are the same.

f. In the first, the Gen. and Dat. sing. and Nom. plur. have the same form.

g. In the fifth also, Gen. and Dat. sing. are alike.

h. In the fifth, Nom. sing. and Nom. plur. are alike.

CHAPTER V.

FIRST DECLENSION.

§ 10.

The nominative case of all Latin nouns of the first declension ends in **a.** This vowel is changed through the different cases; the rest of the word, called the **root,** remains unchanged.

SINGULAR.

Nom.	*rŏs-***ă,** the rose.	*scrībă,* the scribe.
Gen.	*ros-***ae,** of the rose.	*scribae,* of the scribe.
Dat.	*ros-***ae,** to or for the rose.	*scribae,* to or for the scribe.
Acc.	*ros-***ăm,** the rose.	*scribăm,* the scribe.
Voc.	*ros-***ă,** O rose!	*scribă,* O scribe!
Abl.	*ros-***ā,** by, from, with the rose.	*scribā,* by, from, with the scribe.

PLURAL.

Nom.	*ros*-**ae**, the roses.	*scribae*, the scribes.
Gen.	*ros*-**ārum**, of the roses.	*scribarum*, of the scribes.
Dat.	*ros*-**īs**, to or for the roses.	*scribis*, to or for the scribes.
Acc.	*ros*-**ās**, the roses.	*scribas*, the scribes.
Voc.	*ros*-**ae**, O roses!	*scribae*, O scribes!
Abl.	*ros*-**īs**, by, from, with the roses.	*scribis*, by, from, with the scribes.

§ 11.

All adjectives in **a** (the feminine of those in **us** and **er**, § 18) follow the first declension.

SINGULAR.

Nom.	*forma*	*pulchra*,	the beautiful form.
Gen.	*formae*	*pulchrae*,	of the beautiful form.
Dat.	*formae*	*pulchrae*,	to the beautiful form.
Acc.	*formam*	*pulchram*,	the beautiful form.
Voc.	*forma*	*pulchra*,	O beautiful form!
Abl.	*forma*	*pulchra*,	from the beautiful form.

PLURAL.

Nom.	*formae*	*pulchrae*,	the beautiful forms.
Gen.	*formarum*	*pulchrarum*,	of the beautiful forms.
Dat.	*formis*	*pulchris*,	to the beautiful forms.
Acc.	*formas*	*pulchras*,	the beautiful forms.
Voc.	*formae*	*pulchrae*,	O beautiful forms!
Abl.	*formis*	*pulchris*,	by, etc., the beautiful forms.

§ 12.

All words in **a**, of the first declension, are of the feminine gender (*generis feminini*). Only those which denote men, nations, or rivers remain masculine (§ 4).

§ 13.

Words for Exercise.

1. *Alauda*, the lark;
ancilla, the servant-girl;
aura, the air;
bacca, the berry;
catēna, the chain;
causa, the cause;
columba, the dove;
cura, the care;
faba, the bean;
fabula, the fable;
ianua, the door;
lana, the wool;
luscinia, the nightingale;
penna, the feather;
poena, the punishment;
praeda, the prey;
schola, the school;
terra, the earth;
unda, the wave;
uva, the grape;
virga, the rod.

2. *ala*, the wing;
aquĭla, the eagle;
ara, the altar;
barba, the beard;
fama, the fame;
fossa, the ditch;
gloria, the glory;
ira, the wrath;
luna, the moon;
rana, the frog;
sagitta, the arrow;
silva, the forest;
stella, the star;
umbra, the shade;
via, the way.

3. *aqua*, the water;
bestia, the beast;
herba, the herb;
porta, the door;
puella, the girl;
ripa, the bank;
rota, the wheel;
vita, the life.

4. *agricola*, the farmer;
advĕna, the stranger;
aurīga, the driver;
convīva, the guest;
homicīda, the murderer;
incŏla, the inhabitant;
nauta, the sailor;
perfŭga, the deserter;
pirāta, the pirate;
poēta, the poet;
scurra, the jester;
Persa, the Persian;
Scytha, the Scythian;
Mŏsa, the Meuse.

§ 14.

Anĭma divīna, the divine soul;
arānĕa parva, the little spider;
catena firma, the strong chain;

caterva magna,	the large crowd;
cēna lauta,	the exquisite banquet;
formīca sedŭla,	the diligent ant;
regīna bona,	the good queen;
stătua aurĕa,	the golden statue;
tăbŭla nigra,	the black-board;
aula regia,	the royal court;
nĕbŭla densa,	the thick mist;
superbia măla,	the wicked pride;
fortūna dŭbia,	the fickle fortune;
pecunia rotunda,	the round money;
villa ampla,	the spacious country-house.

§ 15.

Observations.

1. Two nouns of the first declension form the dat. and abl. plur. in *abus* instead of *is;* namely, *dea*, goddess, and *filia*, daughter; therefore, *deabus*, *filiabus*. They were thus distinguished from the same cases of *deus* and *filius*, *deis* and *filiis*. The two numeral adjectives, *duae*, two; *ambae*, both; have, in the dat. and abl., only *duabus*, *ambabus* (§ 56, 2).

2. *Amphora*, pitcher, and *drachma*, a drachm, have the gen. plur. sometimes thus, *amphŏrum* and *drachmum*, instead of *amphorarum*, *drachmarum* (cf. § 25, 2). Something similar occurs also in foreign names of nations, and in the compounds of *cŏla* and *gĕna;* as, *Lapithum*, *coelicolum*, *terrigenum*, instead of *Lapitharum*, etc.

3. *Familia*, family, has the gen. sing. *familias*, instead of *familiae*, but only in connection with *pater*, *mater*, *filius*, *filia;* *e. g.*, *pater familias*, the father of the family.

4. Some feminine adjectives, *una*, *sola*, etc., have in the genitive, not *ae*, but *ius*, dative *i* (cf. § 25).

5. Poets sometimes use the antiquated genitive *aï* instead of *ae;* as, *aulaï*, *pictaï*, for *aulae*, *pictae*.

Some Greek words used in Latin are declined after the first declension. They have in the nominative *e*, *as*, or *es*. In the plural they are declined like the Latin words; in the singular, as follows:

Nom.	*epitom*-**ē**, the extract.	*Aenēās*, Aeneas.
Gen.	*epitom*-**ēs**, of the extract.	*Aenēae*, of Aeneas.
Dat.	*epitom*-**ae**, to the extract.	*Aenēae*, to Aeneas.
Acc.	*epitom*-**ēn**, the extract.	*Aenēām* (*an*) Aeneas.
Voc.	*epitom*-**ē**, O extract!	*Aenēā*, O Aeneas!
Abl.	*epitom*-**ē**, by the extract	*Aenēā*, from Aeneas.

Nom. *anagnostès*, the reader.
Gen. *anagnostae*, of the reader.
Dat. *anagnostae*, to the reader.
Acc. *anagnostēn* (*ăm*) the reader.
Voc. *anagnoste* (*ă*) O reader!
Abl. *anagnostā* (*ē*) from the reader.

In the plural *epitomae*, *epitomarum*, &c.; *anagnostae*, *anagnostarum*, &c. Decline in the same manner, *aloe*, aloe; *grammatice*, grammar; *boreas*, Northwind; *tiăras*, turban; *pyrites*, flint; *sophistes*, sophist. Many of these words, however, have in the nominative sing. already the Latin ending *a* for *e* or *es*, as *grammatica* (and *grammatice*), *sophista* (and *sophistes*); then they follow the Latin declension throughout.

1. Rules of Gender according to Termination.

Words of the first declension ending in **a** or **e** are feminine; those ending in **as** or **es** are masculine. (cf. § 12.)

CHAPTER VI.

SECOND DECLENSION.

§ 16.

Nouns of the second declension end in the nom. sing. in **us**, **er** (**ir**, **ur**) or **um**. All the words in **um** are neuter.

The terminations **us** and **um** are the case-endings of the nominative; the ending **er** (**ir**, **ur**) belongs to the root of the word.

Singular.

Nom.	*riv*-**ŭs**, the brook.	*tect*-**um**, the roof.
Gen.	*riv*-**ī**, of the brook.	*tect*-**i**, of the roof.
Dat.	*riv*-**ō**, to the brook.	*tect*-**o**, to the roof.
Acc.	*riv*-**ŭm**, the brook.	*tect*-**um**, the roof.
Voc.	*riv*-**ĕ**, O brook!	*tect*-**um**, O roof!
Abl.	*riv*-**ō**, from the brook.	*tect*-**o**, from the roof.

PLURAL.

Nom.	*riv*-**i**, the brooks.	*tect*-**ă**, the roofs.
Gen.	*riv*-**ōrum**, of the brooks.	*tect*-**orum**, of the roofs.
Dat.	*riv*-**is**, to the brooks.	*tect*-**is**, to the roofs.
Acc.	*riv*-**ōs**, the brooks.	*tect*-**ă**, the roofs.
Voc.	*riv*-**i**, O brooks!	*tect*-**ă**, O roofs!
Abl.	*riv*-**is**, from the brooks.	*tect*-**is**, from the roofs.

§ 17.

The words in **er** (**ir, ur**) have no case-ending in the nom. and voc.; for the rest, they are declined like those in *us*. Be it remarked, however, 1, that the words in *er* (*ir*, *ur*) have the nominative and vocative alike; 2, that the case-ending is appended to the nominative, which either undergoes no change at all, or only drops the *e* before *r*.

SINGULAR.

Nom.	*puĕr*, the boy.	*ăger*, the field.
Gen.	*puĕr*-**i**, of the boy	*agr*-**i**, of the field.
Dat.	*puer*-**o**, to the boy.	*agr*-**o**, to the field.
Acc.	*puer*-**um**, the boy.	*agr*-**um**, the field.
Voc.	*puer*, O boy!	*ager*, O field!
Abl.	*puer*-**o**, with, from the boy.	*agr*-**o**, from the field.

PLURAL.

Nom.	*puer*-**i**, the boys.	*agr*-**i**, the fields.
Gen.	*puer*-**orum**, of the boys.	*agr*-**orum**, of the fields
Dat.	*puer*-**is**, to the boys.	*agr*-**is**, to the fields.
Acc.	*puer*-**os**, the boys.	*agr*-**os**, the fields.
Voc.	*puer*-**i**, O boys!	*agr*-**i**, O fields!
Abl.	*puer*-**is**, from the boys.	*agr*-**is**, from the fields.

3. There is but one noun in *ir*, namely, *vir*, the man, gen. *viri*; in *ur* only an adjective, namely, *satur* (*satŭră*) *satŭrum*, sated. Both are declined like *puer*.

§ 18.

Nearly all adjectives in **us**, **er** and **um** are of the second declension; those in *us* follow *rivus;* those in *er*, *puer* or *ager*; those in *um*, *tectum*.

SINGULAR.

	MASC.	FEM.	NEUT.	MASC.	FEM.	NEUT.
N.	*bonus,*	*bona,*	*bonum,* good;	*niger,*	*nigra,*	*nigrum,* black;
G.	*boni,*	*bonae,*	*boni,*	*nigri,*	*nigrae,*	*nigri,*
D.	*bono,*	*bonae,*	*bono,*	*nigro,*	*nigrae,*	*nigro,*
A.	*bonum,*	*bonam,*	*bonum,*	*nigrum,*	*nigram,*	*nigrum,*
V.	*bone,*	*bona,*	*bonum,*	*niger,*	*nigra,*	*nigrum,*
A.	*bono,*	*bona,*	*bono.*	*nigro,*	*nigra,*	*nigro.*

PLURAL.

N.	*boni,*	*bonae,*	*bona,*	*nigri,*	*nigrae,*	*nigra,*
G.	*bonorum,*	*bonarum,*	*bonorum,*	*nigrorum,*	*nigrarum,*	*nigrorum,*
D.	*bonis,*	*bonis,*	*bonis,*	*nigris,*	*nigris,*	*nigris,*
A.	*bonos,*	*bonas,*	*bona,*	*nigros,*	*nigras,*	*nigra,*
V.	*boni,*	*bonae,*	*bona,*	*nigri,*	*nigrae,*	*nigra.*
A.	*bonis,*	*bonis,*	*bonis.*	*nigris,*	*nigris,*	*nigris.*

§ 19.

(1.) Five nouns, *puer*, *socer*, *vesper*, *gener*, *adulter ;* (2), six adjectives, *asper*, *miser*, *tener*, *lacer*, *prosper*, *liber ;* (3), the compounds of **fer** and **ger** retain the e in the genitive. The rare adjective *gibber*, humpbacked, has *gibberi ; dexter* has *dextri* and *dexteri*, right; *sinister*, only *sinistri*, left.

§ 20.

The words in **us** are all declined like *rivus ;* remark however: (1), the vocative singular sometimes drops the ending **e**, viz.: in the words *filius*, son, *gĕnius*, tutelary deity, and in all proper names in **ius** (or *jus*), thus *fili*, O son! (for *fili-e*); *geni*, O tutelary deity; *Tulli*, O Tullius! *Virgili*, O Virgil! *Pompei*, O Pompey! *Cai*, O Caius! When these proper names are adjectives, they have **e**; *e. g.*, *Cynthie*, O Cynthian.

The other common names in *ius*, as *gladius*, sword, *fluvius*, river, &c., have no vocative. *Darius* has *Darie.* Sometimes the nominative is used for the vocative; thus, by Livy: *tu, populus Albanus*, for *popule Albane.*

2. The voc. sing. of *meus*, my, is *mi*, of *Deus*, God, *Deus*; *e. g.*, *mi Deus*, my God; the voc. fem. of *meus* is *mea*, neuter, *meum*.

3. The word *Deus* is declined in the plural nom. *dii*, *di* (*dei*); gen. *deorum*; dat. *diis*, *dis* (*deis*); acc. *deos*; voc. *dii*, *di*; abl. *diis*, *dis* (also *deis*).

4. The words in *ius* and *ium* regularly form their genitive in *ii*; nouns, however, have it often in i, thus: *filii* and *fili*, *ingenii* and *ingeni*.

§ 21.

Us, er, ir, ur are masculine; **um** is neuter.

Exceptions.

The following are feminine; *alvus*, belly; *colus*, distaff; *humus*, ground; *vannus*, van; the three following which have no plural, are neuter: *virus*, poison; *vulgus*, the rabble; *pelagus*, the sea.

2. All names in **us**, of towns, islands, and trees, are, of course, feminine (§ 4).

Feminine are also *arctus*, *atomus*, *methŏdus*, *periŏdus*, *dialectus*, *diamĕtros*, *perimĕtros*, *paragrăphus*, and a few others. They are properly Greek, and retain the feminine gender which they have in Greek.

§ 22.

Words for Exercise.

1. *Avus*,	grandfather;	3. *agnus*,	lamb;
corvus,	raven;	*annus*,	year;
hircus,	he-goat;	*campus*,	field;
hortus,	garden;	*ĕquus*,	horse;
lŭpus,	wolf;	*lūdus*,	game;
ursus,	bear;	*ŏcŭlus*,	eye;
vicīnus,	neighbor;	*pŏpŭlus*,	people.
ventus,	wind.	4. *cĕrăsus*,	cherry-tree;
2. *cĭbus*,	food;	*mālus*,	apple-tree;
morbus,	sickness;	*prūnus*,	plum-tree;
mundus,	world;	*pōmus*,	fruit-tree;
nāsus,	nose.	*fāgus*,	beech-tree;

fraxĭnus, ash-tree;
pōpŭlus, poplar;
ulmus, elm-tree.
5. *arbiter*, umpire;
făber, artisan;
magister, master;
cŏlŭber, adder;
līber, book.
6. *adulter*, adulterer;
armĭger, armor-bearer;
gĕner, son-in-law;
sŏcer, father-in-law;
vesper, evening.
7. *argentum*, silver;
astrum, star;
aurum, gold;
bŏnum, good;
exemplum, example;
ferrum, iron;
lignum, wood;
ōvum, egg;
verbum, word.
8. *arātrum*, plough;
vallum, rampart;
bellum, war;
coelum, heaven;
ōdium, hatred;
prĕtium, price.
9. *auxĭlium*, help;
dēbĭtum, debt;
factum, fact;
gaudium, joy;
mendacium, lie;
scamnum, bench.

§ 23.

MASC. FEM. NEUT.

1. *Albus*, *alba*, *album*, white;
altus, *alta*, *altum*, high;
aptus, *apta*, *aptum*, fit;
caecus, *caeca*, *caecum*, blind;
clarus, *clara*, *clarum*, bright;
durus, *dura*, *durum*, hard;
fidus, *fida*, *fidum*, trusty;
iustus, *iusta*, *iustum*, just;
laetus, *laeta*, *laetum*, joyful;
longus, *longa*, *longum*, long;
multus, *multa*, *multum*, much;
pius, *pia*, *pium*, pious;
probus, *proba*, *probum*, upright;
stultus, *stulta*, *stultum*, foolish;
tardus, *tarda*, *tardum*, slow;
verus, *vera*, *verum*, true.

MASC. FEM. NEUT.

2. *aeger*, *aegra*, *aegrum*, sick;
integer, *integra*, *integrum*, whole;
niger, *nigra*, *nigrum*, black;
piger, *pigra*, *pigrum*, lazy;
vafer, *vafra*, *vafrum*, crafty.
3. *asper*, *aspera*, *asperum*, rough;
lacer, *lacera*, *lacerum*, torn;
miser, *misera*, *miserum*, wretched;
prosper, *prospera*, *prosperum*, prosperous;
tener, *tenera*, *tenerum*, soft;
frugifer, *frugifera*, *frugiferum*, fruit-bearing.

4. *meus, mea, meum*, mine; *noster, nostra, nostrum*, our;
tuus, tua, tuum, thine; *vester, vestra, vestrum*, your;
suus, sua, suum, his; *suus, sua, suum*, their.

§ 24.

Combination of substantives and adjectives of the first and second declensions:

1. *Amīcus benignus*, the kind friend;
angŭlus rectus, the right angle;
dĭgitus parvus, the little finger;
iŏcus grātus, the pleasant joke;
ăper fĕrus, the wild boar;
vĭr probus, the upright man;
ăsĭnus piger, the lazy ass;
servus vafer, the crafty slave;
dŏlus miser, the wretched trick;
capillus tener, the soft hair.

2. *damnum mŏdĭcum*, a slight loss;
horrĕum plēnum, a full granary;
furtum impĭum, a godless theft;
templum sacrum, the sacred temple;
vinum rubrum, red wine;
vĭtium taetrum, an ugly vice;
praedium frugifĕrum, the fruit-bearing farm;
tēlum mortiferum, a deadly weapon;
verbum līberum, a free word.

3. *alvus plena*, the full belly;
malus onusta, the laden apple-tree;
popŭlus alta, the high poplar;
pirus amoena, the agreeable pear-tree;
poēta clarus, the famous poet;
scriba doctus, the learned scribe;
agricŏla pius, the pious farmer;
nauta laetus, the joyful sailor;
aurīga asper, the rough driver;
convīva aeger, the sick guest;
Persa pĭger, the lazy Persian;
Scytha liber, the free Scythian.

§ 25.

Observations.

1. Nine adjectives of the second declension have the genitive sing., not in **ī**, but in **īus**; the dative, not in **o**, but in **ī**, for the three genders. They form the plural regularly. They are:

Unus, solus, totus, ullus,
uter, alter, neuter, nullus,
alius.

Decline, therefore, as follows.

	Masc.	Fem.	Neut.	
Nom.	*totus,*	*tota,*	*totum,*	whole.
Gen.	*tot-***īus,**	*tot-***īus,**	*tot-***īus,**	
Dat.	*tot-***ī,**	*tot-***ī,**	*tot-***ī,**	
Acc.	*totum,*	*totam,*	*totum,*	
Abl.	*totō,*	*totā,*	*toto,*	

solus, a, um, alone.
unus, one.
ullus, any one.
nullus, none (of all).
uter, tra, trum, which (of two).
neuter, tra, trum, none (of two); neither.
alter, tera, terum, the other (of two); a second.
alius, alia, aliud, another (irregular neuter).

They are declined like *totus;* thus: gen. *solīus*, dat. *solī*, &c.; *alter* retains *e* in the genitive, *alterīus, altĕri*, &c.; *uter* and *neuter* drop it, *utrīus, neutrīus.* Note that *alius* makes in the genitive *alīus* (not *aliīus*), and the dat. *aliī.*

2. In the genitive plur., *um* for *orum* is sometimes found; *e. g., liberum* for *liberorum*, of the children; *deum* for *deorum.* Thus they always said *triumvirum* for *triumvirorum*, of the triumvirs; *praefectus fabrum* for *fabrorum.* Nouns which denote money, measure, weight, often form the gen. plur. in *um* instead of *ōrum*, especially *nummus, sestertius, denarius, modius*, and *talentum*, in connection with numerals; *e. g., duo millia nummum* for *nummorum*, two thousand sesterces; *trium modium*, of three bushels; also *duo millia amphŏrum* for *amphorarum*: *trium drachmum* for *drachmarum*; § 15., 2. In Poetry, *Argivum, Danaum, Pelasgum*, instead of *Argivorum*, etc.

3. Greek proper names in *eus* have the gen. in *ĕi*, dat. *ĕo*, acc. *ĕum*, voc. *eu*, abl. *ĕo*; *e.g.*, *Orpheus* (dissyl.), *Orphĕi* (trissyl.), *Orphĕo*, *Orphĕum*, *Orpheu*, *Orphĕo*. *Orphĕa* sometimes used for *Orpheum*.

4. In other Greek words of the second decl., *ŏs* is sometimes used for *us*, and *ŏn* for *um* (in the nom. and acc.) as *arctŏs* and *arctŏn*, *Delos* and *Delon* for *arctus*, *arctum*, *Delus*, *Delum*. Only *Ilios*, *i*, fem., but *Ilion* and *Ilium*, *i*, neut.

5. In titles of books, the gen. plur. *ŏn*, for *ōrum*, of words taken from the Greek, is used; as, *Georgicon libri*, for *Georgicorum libri*.

CHAPTER VII.

THIRD DECLENSION.

§ 26.

1. The words of the third declension end in the nominative either with a **vowel**, or **l, n, r, s, x**, (besides one in **c**, *lac*; one in **t**, *caput*).

2. The case-endings (§ 9) are added to the root. The root is found by cutting off the case-ending **is** from the genitive

3. Words which have the same number of syllables in the nom. and gen. sing. are called **parisyllabic**; *e. g.*, *nubes*, gen *nubis*.

4. Words which increase in gen. sing. are called **imparisyllabic**; *e. g.*, *dolor*, gen. *dŏlōris*.

I. MASCULINE NOUNS.

SINGULAR.

Nom.	*dŏlor*, the pain.	*mōs*, the custom.
Gen.	*dolōr-***is**, of the pain.	*mōr-***is**, of the custom.
Dat.	*dolōr-***ī**, to the pain.	*mor-***i**, to the custom.
Acc.	*dolōr-***ĕm**, the pain.	*mor-***em**, the custom.
Voc.	*dolōr*, O pain!	*mos*, O custom!
Abl.	*dolōr-***ĕ**, from the pain.	*mor-***e**, from the custom.

PLURAL.

Nom.	*dolŏr*-**ēs**, the pains.	*mōr*-**es**, the customs.
Gen.	*dolōr*-**ŭm**, of the pains.	*mor*-**um**, of the customs.
Dat.	*dolōr*-**ĭbŭs**, to the pains.	*mor*-**ĭbus**, to the customs.
Acc.	*dolōr*-**ēs**, the pains.	*mor*-**es**, the customs.
Voc.	*dolōr*-**ēs**, O pains!	*mor*-**es**, O customs!
Abl.	*dolōr*-**ĭbŭs**, from the pains.	*mor*-**ĭbus**, from the customs.

SINGULAR.

Nom.	*anser*, the goose.	*păter*, the father.
Gen.	*ansĕr-is*, of the goose.	*patr-is*, of the father.
Dat.	*ansĕr-ī*, to the goose.	*patr-ī*, to the father.
Acc.	*ansĕr-em*, the goose.	*patr-em*, the father.
Voc.	*anser*, O goose!	*pater*, O father!
Abl.	*ansĕr-e*, from the goose.	*patr-e*, from the father.

PLURAL.

Nom.	*ansĕr-es*, the geese.	*patr-es*, the fathers.
Gen.	*ansĕr-um*, of the geese.	*patr-um*, of the fathers.
Dat.	*ansĕr-ĭbus*, to the geese.	*patr-ĭbus*, to the fathers.
Acc.	*ansĕr-es*, the geese.	*patr-es*, the fathers.
Voc.	*ansĕr-es*, O geese!	*patr-es*, O fathers!
Abl.	*anser-ĭbus*, from the geese.	*patr-ĭbus*, from the fathers.

II. FEMININE NOUNS.

SINGULAR.

Nom.	*virtus*, virtue.	*cupĭdĭtas*, the desire.
Gen.	*virtūt-is*, of virtue.	*cupiditāt-is*, of the desire.
Dat.	*virtūt-i*, to virtue.	*cupiditāt-i*, to the desire.
Acc.	*virtūt-em*, virtue.	*cupiditāt-em*, the desire.
Voc.	*virtus*, O virtue!	*cupiditas*, O desire!
Abl.	*virtūt-e*, from virtue.	*cupiditāt-e*, from the desire.

PLURAL.

Nom.	*virtut-es*, virtues.	*cupiditat-es*, the desires.
Gen.	*virtut*-**um**, of virtues.	*cupiditat*-**um**, of the desires.
Dat.	*virtut-ĭbus*, to virtues.	*cupiditat-ĭbus*, to the desires.
Acc.	*virtut-es*, virtues.	*cupiditat-es*, the desires.
Voc.	*virtut-es*, O virtues!	*cupiditat-es*, O desires!
Abl.	*virtut-ĭbus*, from virtues.	*cupiditat-ĭbus*, from the desires.

SINGULAR.

Nom.	*pars*, the part.	*nūbes*, the cloud.
Gen.	*part-is*, of the part.	*nub-is*, of the cloud.
Dat.	*part-i*, to the part.	*nub-i*, to the cloud.
Acc.	*part-em*, the part.	*nub-em*, the cloud.
Voc.	*pars*, O part!	*nubes*, O cloud!
Abl.	*part-e*, from the part.	*nub-e*, from the cloud.

PLURAL.

Nom.	*part-es*, the parts.	*nub-es*, the clouds.
Gen.	*part-***ium**, of the parts.	*nub-***ium**, of the clouds.
Dat.	*part-ĭbus*, to the part,	*nub-ĭbus*, to the clouds.
Acc.	*part-es*, the parts.	*nub-es*, the clouds.
Voc.	*part-es*, O parts!	*nub-es*, O clouds.
Abl.	*part-ĭbus*, from the parts.	*nub-ĭbus*, from the clouds.

III. NEUTER NOUNS.

SINGULAR.

Nom.	*ănĭmal*, the animal.	*măre*, the sea.
Gen.	*animāl-is*, of the animal.	*mar-is*, of the sea.
Dat.	*animāl-i*, to the animal.	*mar-i*, to the sea.
Acc.	*animal*, the animal.	*mare*, the sea.
Voc.	*animal*, O animal!	*mare*, O sea!
Abl.	*animāl-***i**, from the animal.	*mar-***i**, from the sea.

PLURAL.

Nom.	*animāl-***ĭă**, the animals.	*mar-***ĭa**, the seas.
Gen.	*animal-***ium**, of the animals.	*mar-***ĭum**, of the seas.
Dat.	*animal-ĭbus*, to the animals.	*mar-ĭbus*, to the seas.
Acc.	*animal-***ia**, the animals.	*mar-***ia**, the seas.
Voc.	*animal-***ia**, O animals!	*mar-***ia**, O seas!
Abl.	*animal-ĭbus*, from the animals.	*mar-ĭbus*, from the seas.

SINGULAR.

Nom.	*guttur*, the throat.	*nōmen*, the name.
Gen.	*guttŭr-is*, of the throat.	*nomĭn-is*, of the name.
Dat.	*guttŭr-i*, to the throat.	*nomĭn-i*, to the name.
Acc.	*guttur*, the throat.	*nomen*, the name.
Voc.	*guttur*, O throat!	*nomen*, O name!
Abl.	*guttŭr-***e**, from the throat.	*nomĭn-***e**, from the name.

PLURAL.

Nom.	*guttŭr-***a**, the throats.	*nomĭn-***a**, the names.
Gen.	*guttur-***um**, of the throats.	*nomĭn-***um**, of the names.
Dat.	*guttur-ĭbus*, to the throats.	*nomin-ĭbus*, to the names
Acc.	*guttur-a*, the throats.	*nomĭn-a*, the names.
Voc.	*guttur-a*, O throats!	*nomĭn-a*, O names!
Abl.	*guttur-ibus*, from the throats.	*nomin-ibus*, from the names

§ 27.

In order to find out whether a word is declined after the third declension, the gen. sing. must be known.

1. Nom. **a**, gen. **ătis**; as, *poēma*, *poēmătis*, the poem; all derived from the Greek. Declined like *guttur*.

2. Nom. **e**, gen. **is**; as, *rete*, *retis*, the net. Like *mare*.

3. Nom. **o**, gen. 1) **inis**; as, *homo*, *hominis*, man; *nemo* (*neminis*), nobody; *turbo*, *turbĭnis*, the whirlwind; *Apollo*, *Appollinis*, and nearly all the words in **do** and **go**; as, *ordo*, *ordinis*, order; *imago*, *imaginis*, image; *caro*, flesh, has *carnis* (instead of *carinis*). Like *anser*.

   2) **ōnis**, all other words; as, *leo*, *leōnis*, the lion; *ratio*, *ratiōnis*, reason; also, a few in **do** and **go**; as, *praedo*, *praedōnis*, robber; *harpăgo*, *harpagōnis*, grappling-hook. Like *dolor*.

4. Nom. **al**, gen. **ālis**; as, *vectigal*, *vectigālis*, tax. Like *animal*. Only *sal*, salt, has *sălis*. Like *anser*.

5. Nom. **l**, gen. **lis**; as, *sol*, *sōlis*, the sun; *exsul*, *exsŭlis*, the exile; *vigil*, *vigilis*, watchful, watchman. Like *anser*.

   Mel, honey, has *mellis*; *fel*, gall, *fellis*. Like *guttur*.

6. Nom. **en**, gen. **ĭnis**; as, *carmen*, *carminis*, poem; *agmen*, *agminis*, army. Like *nomen*.

Ren, kidney, has *rēnis*. Like *dolor*.

7. Nom. **ar**, gen. **āris**; as, *exemplar*, *exemplāris*, pattern: *calcar*, *calcāris*, spur. Like *animal*.

Lar, household god, has *lăris*; *par*, like, and *dispar*, unlike, *păris* and *dispăris*; *Caesar*, *Caesăris*. Like *anser*. *Iubar*, ray, *iubăris*; *nectar*, nectar, *nectăris*. Like *guttur*.

Far, meal, *farris*; *hepar*, liver, *hepătis*. Like *guttur*.

8. Nom. **er**, gen. 1) **ĕris**; as, *agger*, *aggĕris*, mound; *carcer*, *carcĕris*, prison; *mulier*, *muliĕris*, woman; also all names of plants ending in **er**, of the third decl.; as, *acer*, *acĕris*, maple-tree (all neuter, § 34, I, 4); finally, five adjectives, namely, *celer*, swift; *degĕner*, degenerate; *pauper*, poor; *puber*, adult; *uber*, fertile. Like *anser*.

2) **ris**; those in **ter**, beside most of the adjectives of the third declension: thus, *frater*, *fratris*, brother; *mater*, mother; *venter*, belly; *imber*, *imbris*, rain; and the names of months in **ber**; as, *September*. Like *pater*. Adjectives: *acer*, *acris*, sharp; *alăcer*, *alacris*, lively; etc.

NOTE.—*later*, *latĕris*, tile; *ver*, *vēris*, spring; *iter*, *itinĕris*, journey.

9. Nom. **or**, gen. **ōris**; as, *amor*, *amōris*, love; *soror*, sister; *creator*, creator; *viator*, traveler; *auditor*, hearer; *doctor*, teacher. Like *dolor*.

Arbor, tree, makes *arbŏris*; *castor*, beaver, *castŏris*; *rhetor*, rhetorician, *rhetŏris*; *Hector*, *Hectŏris*. Like *anser*. Thus also: *ador*, *adŏris*, spelt; *aequor*, *aequŏris*, sea; *marmor*, *marmŏris*, marble. Like *guttur*. Moreover, *memor*, *memŏris*, mindful; *immemor*, *immemŏris*, unmindful.

Cor, heart, has *cordis*.

10. Nom. **ur**, gen. **ŭris**; as, *fulgur*, *fulgŭris*, lightning. Four have **ŏris**, viz., *ebur*, *ebŏris*, ivory; *femur*, *femŏris*, thigh; *iecur*, *iecŏris*, liver; *robur*, *robŏris*, strength; the oak. Like *guttur*.

Fur, thief, takes *fūris*. Like *dolor*.

11. Nom. **as**, gen. **ātis**; as, *aestas*, *aestātis*, summer; *aetas*, *aetātis*, age; *brevitas*, shortness· *civitas*, citizenship; *libertas*,

freedom; *paupertas*, poverty; *potestas*, power; *veritas*, truth; *voluntas*, will; *nostras*, of our country, our countryman. Like *cupiditas*.

NOTE.—*Anas*, *anătis*, duck; *as*, *assis*, pound; *mas*, *măris*, male; *vas*, *vădis*, bail; *vas*, *văsis*, vase; *gigas*, *gigantis*, giant; *lampas*, *lampădis*, torch. *Fas*, right, *nefas*, wrong, are not declined.

12. Nom. es, gen. 1) is; about thirty words; as, *caedes*, *caedis*, murder; *clades*, *cladis*, defeat; *fames*, hunger; *moles*, load; *sedes*, seat; *vulpes*, fox. Like *nubes*.

2) ĕtis; about ten words; as, *abies*, *abiĕtis*, fir; *aries*, *ariĕtis*, ram; *paries*, wall; *interpres*, interpreter; *seges*, crop; *teges*, mat; *hebes*, *hebĕtis*, dull. Like *anser*.

3) ĭtis; about twenty-five words; as, *ales*, *alĭtis*, bird; *comes*, *comĭtis*, companion; *eques*, rider; *hospes*, host; *miles*, soldier; *pedes*, footman; *caeles*, celestial; *dives*, rich. Like *anser*.

NOTE.—*Obses*, *obsidis*, hostage; *reses*, *resĭdis*, inactive; *pes*, *pĕdis*, foot; *heres*, *herēdis*, heir; *merces*, *mercēdis*, reward; *quies*, *quiētis*, rest; *locŭples*, *locuplētis*, rich; *aes*, *aeris*, ore, bronze; *Ceres*, *Cereris*, Ceres.

13. Nom. is, gen. is; about eighty substantives and all adjectives in **is**; as, *amnis*, river; *collis*, hill; *ignis*, fire; *orbis*, circle; *piscis*, fish; *finis*, end; *mensis*, month; *apis*, bee; *avis*, bird; *clavis*, key; *febris*, fever; *navis*, ship; *ovis*, sheep; *turris*, tower; *vallis*, valley; *brevis*, short; *dulcis*, sweet; *facilis*, easy; *fortis*, brave; *nobilis*, noble; *turpis*, foul. Like *nubes*.

Note the following substantives:

1. *Lapis*, *lapidis*, stone; *tyrannis*, *tyrannidis*, tyranny.
2. *Cinis*, *cinĕris*, ashes; *pulvis*, *pulvĕris*, dust; *vomis*, *vomĕris*, plough-share.
3. *Lis*, *litis*, quarrel; *sanguis*, *sanguinis*, blood; *glis*, *glīris*, dormouse; *vis*, force, strength; plur., *vires* (acc. sing. *vim*; abl. *vi*).

14. Nom. os, gen. ōris; as, *flos*, *flōris*, flower; *ros*, *rōris*, dew; *os*, *ōris*, mouth.

NOTE.—*Os*, *ossis*, bone; *bos*, *bŏvis*, ox; *cos*,

cōtis, whetstone; *dos*, *dotis*, dowry; *nepos*, *nepōtis*, grandson; *sacerdos*, *sacerdōtis*, priest; *custos*, *custōdis*, guardian; *compos*, *compŏtis*, controlling; *impos*, *impŏtis*, powerless. Greek: *heros*, *herōis*; *Minos*, *Minōis*; *Tros*, *Trōis*.

15. Nom. **us**, gen. 1) **ĕris**; as, *Venus*, *Venĕris*, the goddess Venus; *vetus*, *vetĕris*, old; and eighteen neuters, namely, *acus*, *acĕris*, chaff; *rudus*, *rudĕris*, rubbish, which are rare, and

foedus, *genus*, *latus*, *glomus*,
olus, *opus*, *pondus*, *onus*,
scelus, *sidus*, *ulcus*, *funus*,
vellus, *viscus*, *vulnus*, *munus*.

foedus, alliance;	*scelus*, crime;
genus, sex, gender;	*sidus*, star;
latus, side;	*ulcus*, ulcer;
glomus, ball of yarn;	*funus*, funeral;
olus, vegetable;	*vellus*, fleece;
opus, work;	*viscus* (*viscera*), entrails;
pondus, weight;	*vulnus*, wound;
onus, load;	*munus*, office, gift.

Like *guttur*.

2) **ŏris**; as, *lepus*, *lepŏris*, hare; and fourteen neuters, namely:

corpus, *fenus*, *frigus*, *decus*,
litus, *nemus*, *pectus*, *pecus*,
pignus, *stercus*, *facinus*,
tempus, *tergus*, *dedĕcus*;

corpus, body;	*pecus*, a herd;
fenus, rent;	*pignus*, token, pledge;
frigus, cold;	*stercus*, dung;
decus, ornament;	*facinus*, deed;
litus, shore;	*tempus*, time;
nemus, grove;	*tergus*, back;
pectus, breast;	*dedecus*, disgrace.

Like *guttur*.

3) **ūtis**, only five; as, *salus*, *salūtis*, welfare; *servitus*, *servitūtis*, slavery. Like *virtus*.

4) **ūris**, only seven; as, *crus*, *crūris*, leg; *ius*, right; *rus*, country; *mus*, mouse; *tellus*, earth.

NOTE.—*Palus*, *palūdis*, swamp; *incus*, *incū*

dis, anvil; *grus*, *grŭis*, crane; *sus*, *suis*, hog; *fraus*, *fraudis*, deceit; *laus*, *laudis*, praise; *pecus*, *pecŭdis*, a single head of cattle (*pecus*, *pecŏris*, a herd).

16. Nom. **bs**, gen. **bis**; as, *plebs*, *plebis*, the people; *urbs*, *urbis*, the town; *caelebs*, bachelor, has *caelibis*.

17. Nom. **ns**, gen. **ntis**; as, *dens*, *dentis*, tooth; *fons*, *fontis*, spring; *mons*, *montis*, mountain; *constans*, *constantis*, constant; *prudens*, *prudentis*, prudent.

NOTE.—*Frons*, *frondis*, foliage; *glans*, *glandis*, acorn (*frons*, *frontis*, brow). Like *pars*.

18. Nom. **ps**, gen. **pis**; as, *stirps*, *stirpis*, stem, trunk.

NOTE.—*Auceps*, *aucŭpis*, fowler; *princeps*, *princĭpis*, chief; *anceps*, *ancipitis*, twofold, doubtful; (*biceps*, *praeceps*).

19. Nom. **rs**, gen. **rtis**; as, *ars*, *artis*, art; *mors*, *mortis*, death; *sors*, *sortis*, lot; *iners*, *inertis*, indolent. Like *pars*.

Concors, concordant, *discors*, discordant, *misericors*, compassionate, make **rdis** thus, *concordis*, etc.

20. Nom. **ax**, gen. **ācis**; as, *pax*, *pācis*, peace; *audax*, *audācis*, bold; *rapax*, *rapācis*, rapacious; *tenax*, tenacious; *vorax*, greedy. Like *pars*.

Fax, torch, takes *făcis*.

21. Nom. **ex**, gen. **icis**, as, *index*, *indĭcis*, informer; *iudex*, *iudicis*, judge; *vertex*, *verticis*, summit; *duplex*, *duplĭcis*, double; *supplex*, *supplicis*, suppliant.

NOTE.—*Rex*, *rēgis*, king; *lex*, *lēgis*, law; *grex*, *grĕgis*, flock; *nex*, *nĕcis*, death; *prex*, *prĕcis*, prayer; *senex*, *sĕnis*, old man; *suppellex*, *suppellectilis*, furniture; *remex*, *remigis*, rower. Like *anser*.

22. Nom. **ix**, gen. **icis**; as, *cornix*, *cornicis*, crow; *radix*, *radicis*, root; *nutrix*, *nutricis*, nurse; *victrix*, conqueror (fem.); *felix*, happy; *pernix*, swift.

Appendix, addition, *appendicis*; *calix*, chalice, *calicis*; *pix*, pitch, *picis*; *nix*, snow, *nivis*.

23. Nom. **ox**, gen. **ōcis**; only *vox*, *vōcis*, voice; and the adjectives, *atrox*, *atrōcis*, fierce; *ferox*, wild; *velox*, swift; *nox*, night, has *noctis*; *praecox*, mature, has *praecŏcis*.

24. Nom. **ux**, gen. **ŭcis**; as, *crux*, *crŭcis*, cross; *dux*, *dŭcis*, leader; *nux*, *nŭcis*, nut; *trux*, *trŭcis*, savage

NOTE.—*Lux*, *lūcis*, light; *conjux*, *conjŭgis*, spouse; *frux*, *frūgis*, fruit; *faux*, *faucis*, throat, jaw.

25. Nom. **x**, with preceding consonant; gen. **cis**; as, *arx*, *arcis*, stronghold; *falx*, *falcis*, sickle; *lanx*, *lancis*, dish. Like *pars*.

26. Anomalous. *Lac*, *lactis*, milk; *caput*, *capitis*, head; *hiems*, *hiĕmis*, winter.

§ 28.

All adjectives, except those in *us*, *a*, *um*, and *er*, *a*, *um* (§ 18), follow the third declension.

1. **All adjectives of one termination** (cf. § 48); as, *audax*, *audācis*, bold; *praeceps*, *praecipĭtis*, steep; *iners*, *inertis*, slothful; *dives*, *ĭtis*, rich; *mĕmor*, *ŏris*, mindful; *par*, *păris*, equal; *pauper*, *ĕris*, poor; *vetus*, *ĕris*, old (all others in *us* are of the second); moreover, all those in *ns*; as, *prudens*, *ntis*, prudent; *amans*, loving; *constans*, constant.

2. **All adjectives of two terminations**; as, *brĕvis*, neut. *breve*, gen. *brevis*, short; *făcĭlis*, *facile*, gen. *facilis*, easy; *suāvis*, *suave*, gen. *suavis*, sweet; etc. Also the comparatives; as, *brevĭor*, neut. *brevius*, gen. *breviōris*, shorter; *facilior*, neut. *facilius*, gen. *ōris*, easier; *suavior*, neut. *suavius*, gen. *ōris*, sweeter.

3. **Of the adjectives of three terminations**, only thirteen; as, *celer*, *celĕris*, *celere*, gen. *celĕris*, swift. All others drop the **e** of the nom. masc.; as, *acer*, *acris*, *acre*, gen. *acris*, keen.

NOTE.—Six of the adjectives in **er**, that have three terminations, end in **ster** (§ 48, 4). The others are:

salūber, *bris*, *bre*, wholesome;	*acer*, *cris*, *cre*, keen;
volūcer, *cris*, *cre*, winged;	*celer*, *is*, *e*, swift;
cĕlĕber, *bris*, *bre*, renowned;	*puter*, *tris*, *tre*, rotten;
alăcer, *cris*, *cre*, lively.	

The following four have one termination:

puber, (*pubes*,) *ĕris*, adult;	*degĕner*, *ĕris*, degenerate;
pauper, *ĕris*, poor;	*ūber*, *ĕris*, fertile.

All others in **er** are declined after the second decl. (§ 19); also one in **ster**; namely, *sinister*, *sinistra*, *sinistrum*, left.

Singular.

	Masc. Fem.	Neut.	Masc. Fem.	Neut.
Nom.	*audax*, bold.	*audax*.	*brĕvior*,	**brevius**, shorter.
Gen.	*audācis*,		*breviōris*.	
Dat.	*audāci*,		*breviōri*.	
Acc.	*audācem*,	*audax*.	*breviōrem*,	**brevius**.
Voc.	*audax*,	*audax*.	*brevior*,	**brevius**.
Abl.	**audāci** and **audace**.		**breviōre** (*breviori*).	

Plural.

	Masc. Fem.	Neut.	Masc. Fem.	Neut.
Nom.	*audaces*,	**audacia**.	*breviōres*,	**breviōra**.
Gen.	*auda*-**cium**.		*breviorum*.	
Dat.	*audacibus*.		*brevioribus*.	
Acc.	*audaces*,	**audacia**.	*breviores*,	**breviora**.
Voc.	*audaces*,	**audacia**.	*breviores*,	**breviora**.
Abl.	*audacibus*.		*brevioribus*.	

Singular.

	Masc.	Fem.	Neut.	Masc. Fem.	Neut.
Nom.	*ācer*,	*acris*,	*acre*, keen.	*dulcis*,	*dulce*, sweet.
Gen.	*acris*.			*dulcis*,	
Dat.	*acri*.			*dulci*.	
Acc.	*acrem*,		*acre*.	*dulcem*,	*dulce*.
Voc.	*acer*,	*acris*,	*acre*.	*dulcis*,	*dulce*.
Abl.	*acri*.			*dulci*.	

Plural.

	Masc. Fem.	Neut.	Masc. Fem.	Neut.
Nom.	*acres*,	*acria*.	*dulces*,	*dulcia*.
Gen.	*acrium*.		*dulcium*.	
Dat.	*acribus*.		*dulcibus*.	
Acc.	*acres*,	*acria*.	*dulces*,	*dulcia*.
Voc.	*acres*,	*acria*.	*dulces*,	*dulcia*.
Abl.	*acribus*.		*dulcibus*.	

§ 29.

Remarks on Certain Cases.

Three words have always the acc. sing. in ĭm instead of ĕm. They are:

***sĭtis*, thirst; *vīs*, strength; *tussis*, cough.**

Also names of towns and rivers in **is**; as, *Tĭbĕris*, *Neapŏlis.*

The following nine have **im** and **em**:

febris,	fever;	*turris*,	tower;	*messis*,	harvest;
pelvis,	basin;	*restis*,	cord;	*nāvis*,	ship.
puppis,	stern;	*secūris*,	hatchet;	*clāvis*,	key.

NOTE.—The six first have generally **im**, the three last generally **em.**

§ 30.

I. In the abl. sing. have only **i** instead of **e**:

1. All words which have in the acc. only **im**; as, *sitis*, abl., only *siti*; *vis*, only *vi*; *tussis*, only *tussi*; *Tiberis*, only *Tiberi*.

2. The neuters in **e**, **al**, and **ar**, which have the gen. in **ālis** and **āris** (*ā* long); as, *ovīle*, the sheep-fold, *ovili*; *vectīgal*, the tax, *vectigali*; *calcar*, the spur, *calcāri*; (on the contrary, *nectar*, abl., *nectăre*; *iubar*, ray, *iubăre*; *hepar*, liver, *hepăte*; *far*, meal, *farre*).

The names of towns in **e** always keep **e**, in the abl.; as, *Caerĕ*, *Praenestĕ* (they are, properly speaking, indeclinable). The masculine in **al** and **ar** have always **e**; as, *sal*, *săle*; *Caesar*, *Caesăre*.

3. All adjectives, whose neuter ends in **e** (**is**, **is**, **e**, and **er**, **is**, **e**), as well as those substantives in **er** and **is**, which are properly adjectives of this class; as, *facilis*, abl. *facili*; *acer*, abl. *acri*; *September* (sc. *mensis*), abl. *Septembri*; *natālis* (sc. *dies*), birthday, abl. *natāli*; *annālis* (sc. *liber*), annals, abl. *annali*; *aequalis*, contemporary, abl. *aequali*; *affinis*, relative *affini*.

Iuvenis, young man, has *iuvene*; *aedilis*, *aedile*; also the adjectives, when used as proper names; as, *Metellus Celer*, abl. *Metello Celere*; *Iuvenalis*, abl. *Iuvenale*.

II. Ablative in **i** and **e**:

1. Those which have **im** and **em** in the accusative; thus, *puppi* and *puppe*, *turri* and *turre* (but only *reste*, *secūri*, generally *navi*).

Some parisyllables in **is** have also the double termination **e** and **i** in the abl.; as, *amnis*, *avis*, *civis*, *ignis*. It is always *aqua et igni interdicere* (§ 229); otherwise oftener *igne*.

2. All adjectives which form no neuter in **e**: consequently, *felici* and *felice*, *veteri* and *vetere*, *prudenti* and *prudente*, *constanti* and *constante*. The comparative usually takes **e**; as, *maiore* (very seldom *maiori*).

Most adjectives of one termination prefer **i**, in the ablative, especially *memor*, *par*, *concors*, *discors*, *atrox*, *audax*, *ingens*, *recens*, *praeceps*, *inops*, *teres*, *hebes*; hence, *memori*, *pari*, *concordi*, etc. However,

a. The participles in **ns** have only **e**, when used as participles, especially in the abl. absolute; as, *Romulo regnante*. On the contrary, they have mostly **i**, when used as adjectives.

b. The participles and adjectives of one termination have mostly **e** in the ablative, when used as substantives to signify persons (§287, 4, 2); therefore, *multum distat rudis a sapiente*.

The substantive *par*, the pair, has *pare* and *pari*.

c. The following adjectives of one termination have only **e** in the ablative:

Caelebs, *compos*, *impos*, *deses*,
Pauper, *princeps*, *puber*, *reses*,
Those in **es**, **itis**; as, *ales*,
Dives, *sospes*, and *superstes*. (§ 27, 16, 14, 12.)

deses, *desidis*, slothful; *sospes*, *sospitis*, safe;
ales, *alitis*, winged; *superstes*, *superstitis*, surviving.

§ 31.

The nominative plural of neuters ends in **a**, more rarely in **ia**. The following words have the termination **ia**:

1. The neuters in **e**, **al**, and **ar**, which have **ālis** and **āris** in the genitive (§ 30, I, 2); thus, *maria*, seas; *animalia*, animals; *exemplaria*, patterns; (but *farra* from *far*).

2. All adjectives and participles in the positive degree: *facilia*, *brevia*, *dulcia*, *acria*, *salubria*, *celeria*, *felicia*, *prudentia*, *sapientia*, *amantia*; except *vetus*, plur. neut. *vetĕra*.

In the comparative, however, they have always **a**; as, *maiora*, *acriora*, *breviora*, *plura* (likewise *complura*, rarely *compluria*).

Some adjectives of one termination form no nom. and acc. neut. for the plural, namely: 1, those which have in the abl. sing. only **e**, (§ 30 I, 2, *c*); 2, *cicur*, *memor*, *immemor*, *supplex*, *uber*, *particeps*, and *vigil*.

§ 32.

The genitive plural ends in um, more rarely in ium. The following words have *ium:*

1. All parisyllables (§ 26, 3); as, *clades*, defeat, *cladium*, likewise, *brevium*, *omnium*, *carnium*, *imbrium*. The following parisyllables, however, have *um:*

> *Vătes*, *sĕnex*, *păter*, *pānis*,
> With *accĭpĭter* and *cănis*,
> *Frāter*, *māter*, *iŭvenis*,
> Sometimes *ăpis*, *vŏlucris*.

Vates, seer (gen. plur. *vatum*); *canis*, dog;
panis, bread; *apis*, bee;
accipiter, hawk (*accipitrum*); *volucris*, bird.

2. All imparisyllables which have two consonants before the case-ending; as, *ars*, art, *artium; fons*, spring, *fontium;* likewise, *assium*, *noctium*, *ossium*, *urbium*, *amantium*, *inertium*.

Parentes, parents, has *parentum;* often also, *adolescentum*, *clientum*, *prudentum*, *sapientum*, for *adolescentium*, etc.; but then only when the words are used as substantives.

3. The following ten monosyllables:

> *faux*, *fraus*, *glis*, *ius*, *lis*,
> *mas*, *mus*, *nix*, *plus*, *vis*.

Faux, *faucium*, throat;
fraus, *fraudium*, cheat;
glis, *glirium*, dormouse;
ius, *iurium*, right;
lis, *litium*, quarrel;
mas, *marium*, the male;
mus, *murium*, mouse;
nix, *nivium*, snow;
plus, *plurium*, more;
vis, *virium*, strength.
Ops, *opis*, help, has *opum*.

Pes, foot, has *pedum;* likewise *quadrupes*, the quadruped, has *quadrupedum;* but *compes*, fetter, *compedium*. A number of monosyllables have no gen. plur.; as, *aes*, *cos*, *rus*, *sal*, *sol*, *far*, *fel*, *mel*.

4. All words which make the plur. neut. in **ia** (§ 31); as, *marium*, *animalium*, *exemplarium*, *audacium*, *amantium*, (except

veterum, *maiorum*, and all comparatives, except *plurium* and *complurium*).

Those adjectives which form no nom. plur. neut. (§ 31, 2, note) make the gen. plur. in **um**; thus, *caelebs*, gen. plur. *caelibum*; *dives*, gen. plur. *divitum* (but *dis*, *ditis*, plur. neut. *ditia*, gen. *ditium*); etc.

5. The names of nations in **is** and **as**, gen. **itis** and **ātis**; as, *Quiris*, gen. plu. *Quiritium*; *Arpinas*, *Arpinātium*. Likewise *nostras*, *vestras*, *cuias*, have only *nostratium*, etc.; *optimates* and *penates* have *optimatium* and *penatium*, rarely *optimatum* and *penatum*.

6. The neuter names of feasts, only used in the plural, have, instead of **ium**, sometimes **iorum** after the second declension; as, *Saturnalia*, *Saturnalium*, and *Saturnaliorum*.

§ 33.

1. The acc. plur. of the masc. and fem. words which have **ium** in the gen. plur., had anciently the termination **is** (**eis**), instead of **ēs**; thus, *cladis*, *omnis*, *tris*, instead of *cladēs*, *omnes*, *tres*.

2. Note.—*Bōs*, *bŏvis*, ox, cow, is regular; however, it has the gen. plu. *boum* for *bŏvum*, dat. plu. *bōbus* or *būbus* for *bŏvibus*. *Sus*, *suis*, hog, has mostly *sŭbus* for *suibus*. Jupiter has gen. *Jŏvis*, dat. *Jŏvi*, acc. *Jovem*, voc. *Jupiter*, abl. *Jove*.

§ 34.

RULES OF GENDER ACCORDING TO TERMINATION.

I. General Rule.

Masculine are those which end in **o, or, os, e-r,** and those in **e-s** which increase in the genitive.

Exceptions.

1. In **o.** Words ending in **do, go, io,** are feminine, also **caro.** Masculine, however, are the following: *ordo*, *cardo*, *ligo*, *harpăgo*, *margo*, *septentrio*, *vespertilio*, *papilio*, *pugio*, *scipio*.

Căro, *carnis*, flesh;	*margo*, *inis*, border;
ordo, *inis*, order;	*septentrio*, *ōnis*, north;
cardo, *inis*, hinge;	*vespertilio*, bat;
ligo, *ōnis*, hoe;	*pāpilio*, butterfly;
harpăgo, *ōnis*, grappling-hook;	*pūgio*, dagger;

scipio, staff.—(§ 27, 3.) p 32

2. In **or.** Four are neuter: *aequor*, sea; *ădor*, spelt; *marmor*, marble; *cŏr*, heart. *Arbor*, *arbŏris*, tree, is fem. (§ 27, 9)

3. In **os.** Three are feminine; *ĕos*, *cōs*, *dōs*. *Ōs*, mouth, *ŏs*, bone, are always neuter (§ 27, 14).

Eos (indecl.), dawn; *dos*, *dōtis*, dowry; *cos*, *cōtis*, whetstone.

4. In **e-r.** The following are neuter: *cadāvĕr*, *cĭcer*, *ĭter*, *papāver*, *pĭper*, *spinther*, *tŭber*, *ūber*, *vēr*, *verber*. *Linter* is fem.

cadaver, *ĕris*, corpse; *spinther*, *ĕris*, bracelet;
cicer, *ĕris*, a pea; *tuber*, *ĕris*, hump;
iter, *itinĕris*, journey; *uber*, *ĕris*, udder;
papaver, *ĕris*, poppy; *vēr*, *vēris*, spring;
piper, *ĕris*, pepper; *verber*, *ĕris*, blow;
linter, *tris*, skiff.—(§ 27, 8).

5. In **e-s,** increasing in the genitive. One is neuter: *aes*. Eight are feminine: *compes*, *merces*, *merges*, *quies*, *rĕquies*, *inquies*, *sĕges*, *tĕges* (§ 27, 12).

aes, *aeris*, ore, bronze; *merges*, *mergitis*, sheaf;
requies, *requiētis*, rest; *compes*, *compĕdis*, shackle;
quies, *quiētis*, rest; *inquies*, *inquiētis*, restlessness;
merces, *mercēdis*, reward; *seges*, *segĕtis*, crop.

II. General Rule.

Words ending in **as, is, aus,** and **x**; as, *aetas*, *ăvis*, *laus*, and *nix*, as also **s,** preceded by a consonant, are feminine. Parisyllables in **es** are also feminine.

Aetas, *aetatis*, age; *laus*, *laudis*, praise;
avis, *avis*, bird; *nix*, *nivis*, snow.

Exceptions.

1. In **as.** The word *as*, gen. *assis*, a pound, is masculine; *vas*, *vāsis*, a vessel, neut.

Vas, a bail, *vădis*, and *mas*, the male, *măris*, are already masculine from their meaning. The Greek words in **as,** gen. **-antis,** are also masc.; as, *adămas*, *-antis*, the diamond.

2. In **is.** Words in **cis, guis,** and **quis**; in **alis, ollis, mis, nis**; and *axis*, *callis*, *caulis*, *ensis*; and *fustis*, *orbis*, *vectis*, *mensis*; *glis*, *lăpis*, *pulvis*, are masc.; also, *buris*, *scrobis*, *torris*, *postis*; and *sentis*, *cassis*, *vepris*, *hostis*.

Fascis, *is*, bundle; *piscis*, fish; *anguis*, serpent; *sanguis*, *inis*, blood; *unguis*, *is*, claw; *torquis*, *is*, necklace; *annālis*, *is*, annals; *canalis*, *is*, canal; *amnis*, *is*, stream; *cinis*, *ĕris*, ashes; *crinis*, *is*, hair; *axis*, axle; *callis*, path; *caulis*, stalk; *ensis*, sword; *fustis*, club; *orbis*, circle; *vectis*, lever; *mensis*, month; *glis*, *glīris*, dormouse; *natalis*, birthday; *collis*, hill; *follis*, bellows; *pollis*, *inis*, mill-dust; *cucumis*, *ĕris*, cucumber; *vermis*, *is*, worm; *vomis*, *eris*, ploughshare; *finis*, *is*, end; *funis*, cord; *ignis*, fire; *panis*, bread; *lapis*, *idis*, stone; *pulvis*, *ĕris*, dust; *būris*, *is*, part of a plough; *scrŏbis*, ditch; *torris*, firebrand; *postis*, post; *sentis*, briar; *cassis*, snare; *vepris*, thorn-bush; *hostis*, enemy.

Canis, dog, is gen. com.; likewise *tigris*, tiger. The Greek words, *tyrannis*, *-idis*, tyranny; *pyrămis*, *-idis*, pyramid; *proboscis*, *-idis*, trunk; are fem. *Sentis*, *cassis*, *vepris*, are hardly ever used, except in the plural.

3. In **x**. With **x**, those that have **ex** are masculine; as, *cōdex*, *pollex*, *grex;* but *lex*, *nex*, *suppellex*, *forfex*, *faex*, and *prex*, are feminine.

In **ix** and **yx** are masculine: *calix*, *fornix*, *phoenix*, *bombȳx*, *varix;* also *tradux*, *thorax;* and the numbers in **unx**; as, *quincunx*, *deunx* (§ 27, 20–25).

Codex, *icis*, book; *pollex*, *icis*, thumb; *grex*, *grĕgis*, flock; *lex*, *lēgis*, law; *nex*, *nĕcis*, death; *suppellex*, *suppellectilis*, furniture; *forfex*, *icis*, scissors; *faex*, *faecis*, yeast; *prex*, *prĕcis*, prayer; *calix*, *icis*, chalice; *fornix*, *icis*, vault; *phoenix*, *icis*, phoenix (a fabulous bird); *bombyx*, *ȳcis*, silk-worm; *varix*, *icis*, vein; *tradux*, *ūcis*, vine-branch; *thorax*, *ācis*, breast-plate; *quincunx*, *uncis*, $\frac{5}{12}$; *deunx*, *uncis*, $\frac{11}{12}$.

4. In **s**, with preceding consonant:

> All masculine are *fons* and *mons*,
> *Dens*, *rŭdens*, *chălybs*, *hȳdrops*, *pons*,
> With *torrens*, *trĭdens*, *ŏriens*,
> And *dodrans*, *triens*, *occĭdens*.—(§ 27, 17).

dens, *ntis*, tooth; *rudens*, cable; *hydrops*, *ōpis*, dropsy; *chalybs*, *ȳbis*, steel; *pons*, *ntis*, bridge; *torrens*, torrent; *tridens*, trident; *oriens*, *ntis*, east; *dodrans*, $\frac{9}{12}$; *triens*, $\frac{4}{12}$; *occidens*, west.

III. General Rule.

Words in e, l, ur, us, ar, men, ma, are neuter (§ 27; 1, 2, 4–7, 10, 15).

Exceptions.

1. In **l** and **ur.** *Sōl, sāl, turtur*, and *vultur* are masculine; *pectĕn, liēn, rēn*, and *splēn* (not ending in **men**), are also masculine (§ 27; 4, 5, 6, 10).

sol, sōlis, sun;	*pecten, inis*, comb;
sal, sălis, salt;	*lien, ēnis*, milt;
turtur, ŭris, turtle-dove;	*ren, rēnis*, kidney;
vultur, vulture;	*splen, ēnis*, spleen.

2. In **us.** Nine words in **ūs** (long) are feminine; *servitus, senectus, virtus, subscus, sălus, iuventus, incus, tellus, pălus;* likewise, *pĕcus, pecŭdis, sūs*, and *grūs, grŭis* are generally feminine. Masculine are three: *trĭpus, lĕpus, mūs* (§ 27; 15).

Servitus, ūtis, slavery;	*subscus, ūdis*, tongue of a dovetail;	*sus, suis*, hog;
senectus, old age;	*incus, ūdis*, anvil;	*grus, gruis*, crane;
virtus, virtue;	*palus, ūdis*, swamp;	*tripus, ŏdis*, tripod;
salus, welfare;	*tellus, ūris*, earth;	*lepus, lepŏris*, hare;
iuventus, youth;	*pecus, ŭdis*, cattle;	*mus, mūris*, mouse.

3. Separately must be remembered the neuters: *lăc, lactis*, milk; and *căput, capĭtis*, head (*sincĭput, sincipĭtis*, half the head; *occĭput*, back part of the head).

§ 35.

Observations.

1. Some Greek proper names in **es** have the gen. sing. in **i**, besides **is**; as, *Achilles*, gen. *Achillis* and *Achilli;* likewise, *Themistocli, Neocli*, for *Themistoclis, Neoclis*.

2. Greek words in **ma** have the dat. and abl. plur. oftener in **mătis** than **matibus**; *e. g.*, *poēma*, poem; oftener *poēmatis* than *poēmatibus*.

3. Greek words in **is**, gen. **is**, have the acc. in **im** (**in**), abl. **i**; as, *poēsis*, poetry, acc. *poēsim* (rarely *poēsin*), abl. *poēsi;* likewise, *Apis*, gen. *Apis*, acc. *Apim*, abl. *Api*.

4. Greek words in **is** and **as** have, in poetry, instead of **idis, ădis**, sometimes the Greek gen. **idŏs, ădos**; as, *Aenēis, Aenēidos: Pallas,*

Pallădŏs. *Pan* has even in prose only gen. *Panos*, acc. *Pana* (*panis*, bread; gen. *panis*, acc. *panem*).

5. Greek words have sometimes the Greek acc. sing. **a** along with the Latin **em**; as, *Agamemnŏna* and *Agamemnonem*, *Salamina*, *Periclĕa*. *Aër* and *aethĕr* have the acc. always *aëra*, *aethera*, instead of *aërem*, *aethĕrem*. *Paris*, *Paridos*, has, in the acc., *Paridem*, *Parida*, *Parim*, or *Parin*.

6. Proper names of men in **es** make the acc. **em** and **en**, voc. **es** and **ē**; as, acc. *Xerxem*, *Xerxen*, voc. *Xerxes*, *Xerxē*; *Socratem*, *Socraten*, *Socrates*, *Socrate*.

7. Greek proper names in **is**, **ys**, **eus**, form the vocative, as in Greek, by dropping **s**; as, *Alexis*, voc. *Alexi*; *Cotys*, voc. *Coty*; *Perseus*, voc. *Perseu* (cf. § 25; 4).

8. Greek names of men in **as**, gen. **antis**, make the vocative **a**; as, *gigas*, *gigantis*, giant, voc. *gigā*; also, *Atlā*.

9. Foreign proper names sometimes take, in the nom. and acc. plur., the Greek terminations **ĕs** and **ăs** (for **ēs**); as, nom. *Arcădĕs*, acc. *Arcădăs*, *Macedŏnas*, *Allobrŏgas*.

10. The Greek feminine words in **o** have **us**, in the gen.; as, *echo*, the echo, gen. *echūs*; *Sappho*, *Sapphus*, in dat. acc. and abl. they retain **o**, therefore, *echo*, *Sappho*. Of *Io*, we find the dative *Iōni*.

11. The Greek neuters, *melos*, song, and *cetos*, sea-monster, are indeclinable in the singular; in the nom. and acc. plur., they have *melē* and *cetē*. A similar plural is *Tempē*, the valley of Tempe.

12. In titles of books, Greek words often keep the Greek termination **ōn**, in the gen. plur.; as, *Metamorphoseon libri*, the Books of the Metamorphoses (cf. § 25; 5).

§ 36.

Words for Exercise.

1. *Lătro*, *ōnis*, robber;
tīro, beginner;
pāvo, peacock;
carbo, coal;
pulmo, lung;
tēmo, pole (of wagon);
clāmor, *ōris*, cry;
cŏlor, color;
error, mistake;
lăbor, work;
ŏdor, smell;
terror, fright;
tĭmor, fear;
ōrātor, speaker;
peccātor, sinner;
vēnātor, hunter;
condĭtor, builder;
iānĭtor, porter;
audĭtor, hearer;
largītor, briber;
pastor, shepherd;
pictor, painter;
praeceptor, teacher;
scriptor, writer;

victor, conqueror;
dēfensor, defender;
possessor, owner;
rōs, *rōris*, dew;
ūter, *tris*, hose;
caespes, *ĭtis*, turf;
gurges, whirlpool;
līmes, boundary;
satelles, satellite.

2. *Altitūdo*, *ĭnis*, height;
consuētūdo, custom;
fortitūdo, bravery;
multitūdo, crowd;
hirundo, swallow;
hirūdo, leech;
testūdo, turtle;
orīgo, source;
virgo, maiden;
actio, *ōnis*, action;
contio, assembly;
lectio, reading;
mōtio, motion;
mūtatio, change;
narratio, tale;
nōtio, notion;
ōrātio, speech;
quaestio, question;
rătio, reason;
rĕgio, country;
suspīcio, suspicion;

II.

1. *Aequĭtas*, *ātis*, equity;
auctorĭtas, authority;
calămitas, misfortune;
crudelitas, cruelty;
dignitas, dignity;
facultas, faculty;
grăvitas, heaviness;
lĕvitas, lightness;
māiestas, majesty;
piĕtas, piety;
societas, society;
tempestas, weather;
vetustas, antiquity;
voluptas, pleasure;

2. *Auris*, *is*, ear;
classis, fleet;
corbis, basket;
fēlis, cat;
messis, harvest;
pellis, fur, hide;
pestis, pestilence;
vestis, dress;
vītis, vine.

3. *Fraus*, *dis*, deceit;

4. *Cornix*, *īcis*, crow;
rādix, root;
nutrix, nurse;
arx, *cis*, castle;
crux, *crŭcis*, cross;
falx, sickle;
nex, *nĕcis*, murder, death
vox, *vōcis*, voice.

5. *Cohors*, *tis*, troop;
fors, chance;
gens, people;
lens, lentil;
mens, mind;
serpens, snake.

6. *Aedes*, *is*, temple;
fāmes, *is*, hunger;
saepes, fence;
vulpes, fox.

III.

1. *Altāre*, *is*, altar;
bovīle, cattle-stall;
conclāve, room;
cubīle, couch;
sedīle, seat;
tribūnal, *ālis*, tribunal;
vectīgal, tax;
cochlear, *āris*, spoon,
lacūnar, ceiling.
2. *Murmur*, *ŭris*, murmur;
sulfur, sulphur;
funus, *ĕris*, funeral;
glŏmus, ball of yarn;
ŏlus, vegetable;
ŏpus, work;
pondus, weight;
sīdus, star;
ulcus, ulcer;
făcĭnus, *ŏris*, deed;
frīgus, cold;
lītus, shore;
nĕmus, grove;
pignus, token;
stercus, dung;
tergus, back.
4. *Acūmen*, *ĭnis*, point;
certāmen, contest;
crīmen, crime;
exāmen, swarm;
flūmen, river;
fulmen, lightning;
grāmen, grass;
līmen, threshold;
lūmen, light;
nūmen, divinity;
ōmen, foreboding;
sēmen, seed;
specĭmen, sample;
strāmen, straw.

§ 37.

1. *Agrestis*, rustic;
illustris, illustrious;
lēnis, soft;
tristis, sad;
cīvīlis, civil;
hostīlis, hostile;
vĭrīlis, manly;
mortālis, mortal;
fĭdēlis, faithful;
diffĭcĭlis, difficult;
sĭmĭlis, like;
ūtĭlis, useful.
2. *Abstĭnens*, abstemious;
clemens, clement;
dīligens, diligent;
frĕquens, frequent;
ingens, mighty;
innŏcens, innocent;
pŏtens, powerful;
săpiens, wise;
vĕhĕmens, violent;
ēlĕgans, tasty;
expers, devoid;
iners, lazy;
ferox, wild;
mendax, lying;
trux, fierce.

§ 38.

Miles alăcer, the lively soldier; *ăvis celĕris*, the swift bird; *ĭter salūbre*, the wholesome journey; *lăbor difficilis*, the hard work; *aestas brĕvis*, the short summer; *ŏpus ūtile*, a useful work; *cochlear aureum*, the golden spoon; *vectīgal grave*, the heavy tax; *nōmen clārum*, the bright name; *certāmen nōbile*, the noble contest; *leo generōsus*, the generous lion; *arbor frugifĕra*, the fruit-tree; *pignus grātum*, the precious token; *ventus vehĕmens*, the violent wind; *schŏla illustris*, the famous school; *mendacium pertinax*, the stubborn lie.

CHAPTER VIII.

FOURTH DECLENSION.

§ 39.

Words of the fourth declension end, in the nominative either in **us** (masc. and fem.), or in **u** (neut.).

SINGULAR.

Nom.	*sens*-**ŭs**,	the sense.	*corn*-**ū**,	the horn.
Gen.	*sens*-**ūs**,	of the sense.	*corn*-**ūs**,	of the horn.
Dat.	*sens*-**ŭi**,	to the sense.	*corn*-**ū**,	to the horn.
Acc.	*sens*-**ŭm**,	the sense.	*corn*-**ū**,	the horn.
Voc.	*sens*-**ŭs**,	O sense!	*corn*-**ū**,	O horn!
Abl.	*sens*-**ū**,	from the sense.	*corn*-**ū**,	from the horn.

PLURAL.

Nom.	*sens*-**ūs**,	the senses.	*corn*-**ŭa**,	the horns.
Gen.	*sens*-**ŭum**,	of the senses.	*corn*-**ŭum**,	of the horns.
Dat.	*sens*-**ĭbus**,	to the senses.	*corn*-**ĭbus**,	to the horns.
Acc.	*sens*-**ūs**,	the senses.	*corn*-**ŭa**,	the horns.
Voc.	*sens*-**ūs**,	O senses	*corn*-**ŭa**,	O horns!
Abl.	*sens*-**ĭbus**,	from the senses.	*corn*-**ĭbus**,	from the horns.

§ 40.

Twelve words make the dative and ablative plural in **ŭbus**, instead of **ĭbus**; viz., 1, all dissyllables in **cus**; 2, five others.

Quercus, spĕcus, ăcus,
Arcus, pĕcu, lăcus,
Vĕru, trĭbus, artus,
Portus, also *partus.*

Quercus, oak;	***pĕcu***, cattle;	***artus***, member;
spĕcus, cave;	***lăcus***, lake;	***portus***, harbor;
ăcus, needle;	***vĕru***, spit;	***partus***, birth;
arcus, bow;	***trĭbus***, tribe;	

Portus **has *portubus* and *portĭbus*.**

§ 41.

The word *domus*, house, is declined partly after the fourth, partly after the second declension.

	SINGULAR.	PLURAL.
Nom.	*dŏmūs*, the house.	*domūs*, the houses.
Gen.	*domūs*, of the house.	*domŭum* and *domōrum*, of the houses.
Dat.	*domŭi* (rarely *domō*), to the house.	*domĭbus*, to the houses.
Acc.	*domum*, the house.	*domos* (*domūs*), the houses.
Voc.	*domus*, O house!	*domūs*, O houses!
Abl.	*domō* (rarely *domu*), from the house.	*domĭbus*, from the houses.

REMARK.—*Domi* (old genitive) means only, at home; *domum* often means, home (motion towards); *domo*, from home.

§ 42.

Remark the following singularities:

1. *Tonitrus* (masc.), thunder, makes the plural, *tonitrua* (neuter).

2. The words *colus*, *cupressus*, *ficus*, *laurus* and *pinus* are of the second declension, but take also the cases in *us* and *u* of the fourth, thus: *colūs* with *coli* and *colos*, *colu* with *colo*.

3. The dative-ending *ui* is sometimes contracted into *u*; thus: *equitatus*, dat. *equitatui* and sometimes *equitatu*.

4. The gen. sing. *senati* instead of *senatus* is not in use.

§ 43.

RULES OF GENDER ACCORDING TO TERMINATION.

Principal Rule.

Words in us are masculine; those in u are neuter.

Exceptions.

Nine words in us are feminine:

Porticus, hall; *Quinquatrus*, *uum*, a Roman feast; *ăcus*, needle; *fīcus*, fig; *Idus*, *uum*, the Ides (middle of month); *dŏmus*, house; *mănus*, hand; *ănus*, an old woman; *trĭbus*, tribe.

§ 44.

Words for Exercise.

1. *Adventus*, arrival;
aestus, heat;
audītus, hearing;
cantus, singing;
cāsus, fall, case;
currus, wagon;
cursus, course, race;
equitatus, cavalry;
exercĭtus, army;
fructus, fruit;
gustus, taste;
impĕtus, attack;
luctus, mourning;
lūsus, play, game;
magistratus, magistrate;
mĕtus, fear;
morsus, bite;
mōtus, motion;
olfactus, smell;
ornātus, ornament;
principatus, leadership;
quaestus, gain;
rĕdĭtus, return;
rīsus, laughter;
saltus, leap;
senātus, senate;
sĭnus, bosom;
sŏnĭtus, sound;
spirĭtus, spirit;
tactus, touch;
transĭtus, crossing;
ūsus, use;
versus, verse;
vīsus, sight;
vultus, mien;
gĕlu, cold;
gĕnu, knee.

2. *fructus mātūrus*, ripe fruit;
cursus cĕler, swift race;
arcus intentus, bent bow;
cantus dulcis, sweet song;
mănus pura, clean hand;
lăcus magnus, great lake;
ornatus insŏlens, unusual ornament;
ăcus aurea, golden needle.

CHAPTER IX.

FIFTH DECLENSION.

§ 45.

THE nominative of the fifth declension ends in **ēs.**

SINGULAR.

Nom.	*r***ēs,**	the thing.	*di*-**ēs,**	the day.
Gen.	*r***ĕi,**	of the thing.	*di*-**ēī,**	of the day
Dat.	*r***ĕi,**	to the thing.	*di*-**ēī,**	to the day.
Acc.	*r***em,**	the thing.	*di*-**em,**	the day.
Voc.	*r***ēs,**	O thing!	*di*-**ēs,**	O day!
Abl.	*r***ē,**	from the thing.	*di*-**ē,**	from the day.

PLURAL.

Nom.	*r***ēs,**	the things.	*di*-**ēs,**	the days.
Gen.	*r***ērum,**	of the things.	*di*-**ērum,**	of the days.
Dat.	*r***ēbus,**	to the things.	*di*-**ēbus,**	to the days.
Acc.	*r***ēs,**	the things.	*di*-**ēs,**	the days.
Voc.	*r***ēs,**	O things!	*di*-**ēs,**	O days!
Abl.	*r***ēbus,**	from the things.	*di*-**ēbus,**	from the days.

1. The other words of the fifth declension have no plural; only the nom., acc., and voc. of some are found, especially of *species* and *spes*; also of *acies*, *effigies*, *facies*, and *series*.

2. The genitive and dative **ēi** is sometimes contracted into **ē** or **i**; as, *perniciē* or *pernicii*, instead of *perniciei*.

3. Some words of the fifth have a secondary form of the first declension; as, *barbaries*, *ei*, and *barbaria*, *ae*, barbarity; likewise *luxuries* and *luxuria*, luxury; *segnities* and *segnitia*, sloth.

4. For the quantity in *rĕi* and *diēi*, compare § 324, 2, note 1

§ 46.

Rules of Genders.

Words of the fifth declension in e-s are feminine.

Exceptions.

Merīdies is masculine. *Dies* is masculine in the plural; in the singular, it is used in the masculine and feminine.

Meridies, noon; *dies*, day.

Dies is feminine, especially in the meaning of time or term; as, *quod allatura est dies; praestituta die.*

Words for Exercise.

1. *Acies*, *ēi*, point, battle array;
effĭgies, image;
măcies, leanness;
pernĭcies, bane;
răbies, rage;
făcies, face;
fĭdes, *ĕi*, faith;
glăcies, ice;
sĕries, row;
spĕcies, form, shape;
spēs, *ĕi*, hope.

2. *Planĭties magna*, great plain;
effigies pulchra, beautiful image;
spes fallax, deceitful hope;
dies festus, feast-day.

CHAPTER X.

OBSERVATIONS ON THE DECLENSIONS.

§ 47.

Defective and Redundant Nouns.

(*Defectiva and Abundantia.*)

Many words have no declension at all, or an incomplete one only; they are, therefore, called *defectiva* or defectives.

I. Words that are not declined at all, are called *indeclinabilia*. Indeclinables are:

1. Substantives: *fas*, right; *nefas*, wrong; *nihil*, nothing; *instar*, likeness; *mane*, dawn; *pondo*, weight.

Corona aurea libram pondo, a pound in weight; *corona pondo ducentum* (instead of *ducentorum*), of 200 pounds; *clarum mane*, bright morn; *multo mane* (as ablative) at early dawn; *mane*, early. *Instar veris*, like spring;

unus Plato mihi est millium instar, has with me the weight of thousands. Besides a few foreign words; as, *alpha*, *beta*, *gummi*, *epos*, *pascha*, *Bethlehem*, *Abraham* (also *Abrahamus*, *i*, *o*, etc.).

2. Adjectives: *frugi*, honest; *nequam*, worthless; *quot*, how many (*tot*, *aliquot*); besides most of the cardinal numerals (§ 55). *Homo frugi*, an honest man; *frugi servum* (acc.), an honest slave; *homines nequam*, *hominum nequam*, *hominibus nequam*. Others are used only in connection with *esse*; as, *necesse est* and *opus est*, it is necessary; *praesto sum*, I am ready.

II. Words which have not all the cases, or only one case, are called *defectiva casibus*, defective in case.

1. Words with but one case (*monoptōta*): *dicis* and *nauci*, in *dicis causa*, for form's sake; *nauci non esse*, not to be worth a cent. *Derisui*, *despicatui esse*, to be an object of derision, of contempt (with *esse*, § 208). *Venum*, for sale; and *pessum*, to destruction (with *ire* and *dare*, § 110; 1); *infitias ire*, to deny. *Natu*, by birth; as, *natu maior*, greater by birth, older; *noctu*, by night; *sponte*, freely, of one's own accord; as, *mea sponte feci*, I did it of my own accord; *tua sponte*, of thy own accord. *Iussu*, by order; as *iussu populi*, by order of the people; *iusso meo*, by my order; likewise *iniussu*, *monitu*, *rogatu* (§ 221; 2, 1).

2. *Diptōta* (with two cases) are *foras*, out (motion), and *foris*, without (place); *fors*, chance; and *forte*, by chance. *Triptōta* (three cases) are *nemo*, *nemini*, *neminem* (instead of the genitive, use *nullius*; instead of the ablative, *nullo*); also, *lues*, *luem*, *lue*, pestilence. *Tetraptōton* (four cases) is *dicionis*, *i*, *em*, *e* (from *dicio*, sway). Some are defective in the singular only; as, *compede*, *fauce*, *prece*, *verbere*; *opis*, *opem*, *ope*; *vis*, *vim*, *vi* (with gen. and dat.), all with complete plural; *vicis*, *vicem*, *vice*, has only *vices*, *vicibus*, in the plural. Without nom. sing., otherwise complete, are *dapis* and *frugis* (*daps* and *frux* are wanting); single cases of other words do not occur; thus the gen. plur. of *lux*, *ōs* (*ōris*), *sol*. The genitive of *plerique*, most, is also wanting; instead of it, use *plurimorum*, *plurimarum*.

III. Some defectives have no plural, but only a singular (*singularia tantum*); as, *letum*, death; *meridies*, noon; *vesper*, evening; *ver*, spring; *virus*, poison; *vulgus*, people. As in English, a great many abstract and material nouns have no plural; as, *iuventus*, youth; *sapientia*, wisdom; *scientia*, science; *aurum*, gold; *sabulum*, sand; *cicer*, pease; *lac*, milk. *Faba abstinere*, to abstain from beans.

IV. Some defectives have no singular, but only the plural (*pluralia tantum*), especially:

1. *Deliciae*, delight;
divitiae, wealth;
indutiae, truce;
inimicitiae, enmity;
insidiae, ambush;
minae, threats;
nundinae, market-day;
nuptiae, wedding;

reliquiae, relics;
tenĕbrae, darkness;
valvae, folding-door;
Athēnae, Athens;
Thebae, Thebes.
2. *Gemini*, twins;
liběri, children;
infĕri, the dead;
supĕri, the gods;
postĕri, descendants;
Fasti, calendar;
Delphi, Delphi;
Veii, Veji;
arma, *ōrum*, arms;

exta, bowels;
spolia, spoils;
Leuctra, Leuctra;
Susa, Susa.
3. *Maiores*, ancestors;
optimātes, the aristocrats;
penātes, the household gods;
moenia, the walls;
Saturnalia, the Saturnalia;
Alpes, *ium*, the Alps;
Gades, Cadiz;
Sardes, Sardis;
4. *artus*, *uum*, limbs.

V. Some words take a new meaning in the plural.

SINGULAR.	PLURAL.
aedes, temple;	*aedes*, *ium*, (1) temple, (2) house.
aqua, water;	*aquae*, (1) waters, (2) baths.
auxilium, help;	*auxilia*, (1) resources, (2) auxiliary troops.
carcer, prison;	*carceres*, (1) prisons, (2) goal.
castrum, castle, fort;	*castra*, camp.
copia, abundance, provision;	*copiae*, (1) provisions, (2) troops.
finis, end, limit;	*fines*, (1) limits, (2) territory.
fortuna, luck;	*fortunae*, goods, possessions.
impedimentum, obstacle;	*impedimenta*, (1) obstacles, (2) baggage.
littera, letter (of alphabet);	*litterae*, (1) letters, (2) writing, epistle.
(*ops*), help;	*opes*, resources, wealth, influence.
rostrum, beak;	*rostra*, (1) beaks, (2) tribune.
sal, salt.	*sales*, wit.

Opposed to the defectives (*defectiva*) are those which have an abundance of forms (*abundantia*), viz.:

VI. Words which follow partly one declension, partly another (*heteroclita*—cf. § 32, 6; § 41 and 42, 2); thus, *vesper*, evening, is declined after the second; but the abl. is *vespere* and *vesperi*, in the evening; *vas*, vase, follows the third in the sing.; *vasis*, *vasi*, *vas*, *vase*, whilst in the plural, it is of the second, *vasa*, *vasorum*, *vasis*. *Requies* (§ 34, 5) makes the acc. *requiētem* and *requiem*, abl. *requiētĕ* and *requiĕ*.

VII. Words which, in the plural, take a new gender (*heterogenĕa*); as, *iocus*, jest, plur. *ioci* (masc.) and *ioca* (neut.), jests; *locus*, place, plur. *loci*, passages (in books), and *loca*, places; *frenum*, bridle, plur. *freni* and *frena*, bit; *Tartărus*, *i*, (masc.); plur. *Tartăra*, *orum*, (neut.), hell.

VIII. A number of words have, in the nom. sing., already, different forms, and are partly *heteroclita*, partly *heterogenea*, partly both at the same time.

1. Only *heteroclita* (the first form used in prose, the second in poetry): *colluvio, onis*, and *colluvies, ei*, f., offscourings; *elephantus, i*, and *elephas, antis*, m., elephant; *iuventus, utis*, and *iuventa, ae*, f., youth; *paupertas, atis*, and *pauperies, ei*, f., poverty; *senectus, utis*, and *senecta, ae*, old age (cf. § 45, 3).

2. Only *heterogenea: baculum, i*, n., stick, (rarely *baculus*); *clipeus*, shield (rarely *clipeum*); *cubitus* and *cubitum*, elbow, ell; *pilleus* and *pilleum*, hat.

3. Both *heteroclita* and *heterogenea: alimonia, ae*, f., and *alimonium, i*, n., food; *pecus, ŭdis*, f., a head of cattle, and *pecu*, n., from which *pecua* and *pecubus* (§ 40), also *pecus, ŏris*, n., a herd of cattle; *conatus, us*, m., and *conatum, i*, n., undertaking; *praetextus, us*, m., and *praetextum, i*, n., pretext. Sometimes the meaning also changes: *epŭlŭm, i*, n., a (religious) banquet; *epulae, arum*, f., meal; *balneum, i*, n., bath; *balneae, arum*, f., baths, bath-house.

CHAPTER XI.

THE ADJECTIVE (ADJECTIVUM).

Comparison of Adjectives.

§ 48.

The adjectives (and participles) have either, 1, for each of the three genders a special termination (adjectives of three terminations); or, 2, for the masculine and feminine, one, and for the neuter, another termination (adjectives of two terminations); or, 3, for all three genders, only one termination (adjectives of one termination).

I. The adjectives of three terminations have the following endings:

1. **Us, a, um**; as, *bon***us**, *bon***a**, *bon***um**,
*amat***us**, *amat***a**, *amat***um**.
2. **Er, a, um**; as, *rub***er**, *rub***ra**, *rub***rum**,
*asp***er**, *asp***era**, *asp***erum**.

The latter, except those mentioned in § 19, drop the **e** before **r**.

3. One adjective in **ur**, viz., *satur*, *satŭra*, *satŭrum*, sated, filled.

4. **Er, is, e**; as, *acer*, *acris*, *acre*;
celer, *celĕris*, *celĕre*.

Of this last kind there are thirteen altogether, six of them in **ster**;

campester, *campestris*, *e*, belonging to the field, flat;
equester, belonging to cavalry, on horseback;
paluster, belonging to a swamp, swampy;
pedester, belonging to the infantry, on foot;
silvester, belonging to the wood, woody;
terrestor, belonging to the earth, earthy.

For the others, see § 28, 3, note.

The names of the months, September, October, November, and December, are also used as adjectives of three terminations of the third declension.

Some of the adjectives just mentioned have, in the masculine gender, sometimes the termination **is**; as, *equestris tumultus* and *equester tumultus*.

II. The adjectives of two terminations have the following endings:

1. **Is** (masc. and fem.); **e** (neut.); as,

facilis, *facilis*, *facile*;
suavis, *suavis*, *suave*.

2. **Or** (masc. and fem.); **us** (neut.); as,

clarior, *clarior*, *clarius*;
maior, *maior*, *maius*;

and all comparative forms (§ 50).

Some adjectives have a double form, in **us, a, um**, and in **is, is, e**; as, *hilărus*, *a*, *um*, and *hilăris*, *is*, *e*, cheerful. Likewise some compound adjectives; as, *semiermus* and *semiermis*, half-armed; *exanimus* and *exanimis*, lifeless. They are consequently *abundantia* and *heteroclita* (§ 47, vi.).

III. The adjectives of one termination have the following endings:

1. In **s**, with a consonant preceding (and omitted *t*), as *constans*, constant; *prudens*, wise; *iners*, slothful; *biceps*, two-headed. (§ 27, 17 to 19), and all participles in **ns**.

2. In **x**, (i. e., *cs*), as *audax*, bold; *supplex*, suppliant; *felix*, happy; *atrox*, fierce; *trux*, savage, (§27, 20 to 23).

3. In **es**, (*t* or *d* having been rejected); as *sospes*, *sospĭtis*, safe; *teres*, *terĕtis*, round, cylindrical; *deses*, *desĭdis*, inactive, (§ 27, 12). In **os**: *compos*, (*impos*), *compŏtis*, (§ 27, 14).

4. In **us**, only *vetus*, § 27, 15; all other adjectives in *us* have *us*, *a*, *um*.

5. In **er**, only four: *degener* (*congener*), *pauper*, *puber* and *uber*, (§ 28); in **or**, only one, *memor*, (*immemor*, § 27, 9); in **ar**, only one, *par* (*impar*, *dispar*, § 27, 7); in **ur**, only one, *cicur*, tame; in **l**, only one, *vigil*, watchful.

1. *Victor* may be used as an adjective; as, *victor exercitus*, the victorious army; *victrices litterae*, tidings of victory; *victricia arma*, victorious arms.

2. Besides the indeclinable adjectives (§ 47, I, 2), some others are defective. Thus, the nom. sing. mas. of *cetera*, *ceterum*; of *ludicra*, *ludicrum*; of *pleraque*, *plerumque*, is wanting. Of *exspes*, only the nom. sing. is found; of *pernox*, only nom. and abl. sing. (*pernocte*). Of some, the nom. plur. neut. (§ 32, 4, note) is wanting, others are *pluralia tantum*; as, *singuli*, *bini*; generally, also *pauci* and *plerique*.

§ 49.

The adjectives, in Latin as in English, are compared by means of three degrees (*gradus*).

1. Positive degree (*gradus positīvus*); fair, strong, fast.

2. Comparative degree (*gradus comparatīvus*); fairer, stronger, faster.

3. Superlative degree (*gradus superlatīvus*); fairest, strongest, fastest.

§ 50.

General Rule.

The comparative degree is formed by adding the termination **ĭor**, neut. **ius**, to the root of the adjective; the superlative is formed by adding **issĭmus** to the root.

The root of the adjective is found by dropping the case-ending of the genitive; thus, *clarus*, gen. *clar-i*, root *clar*; comp. *clar*-**ior**, *clar*-**ius**; sup. *clar*-**issimus** (*a*, *um*); *prudens*, gen. *prudent*-**is**, root *prudent*, comp. *prudent*-**ior**, sup. *prudent*-**issimus**.

POSITIVE.	COMPARATIVE.	SUPERLATIVE.
aptus, fit;	*aptior*, fitter;	*aptissimus*, fittest;
dignus, worthy;	*dignior*, worthier;	*dignissimus*, worthiest.
firmus, fast;	*firmior*, faster;	*firmissimus*, fastest.
grăvis, heavy;	*gravior*, heavier;	*gravissimus*, heaviest.
nobĭlis, noble;	*nobilior*, nobler;	*nobilissimus*, noblest.
audax, bold;	*audacior*, bolder;	*audacissimus*, boldest.
fĕrox, wild;	*ferocior*, wilder;	*ferocissimus*, wildest.
dilĭgens, diligent;	*diligentior*, more diligent;	*diligentissimus*, most diligent.
locŭples, rich;	*locupletior*, richer;	*locupletissimus*, richest.
dīves, (*dis*), } rich.	*divĭtior*, *ditior*, } richer.	*divitissimus*, *ditissimus*, } richest.

§ 51.

To the above principal rule remark the following exceptions:

1. The adjectives in **er** form the comparative according to the general rule; but the superlative, by adding the ending **rimus** to the nominative sing. masc.

POSITIVE.	COMPARATIVE.	SUPERLATIVE.
*crĕb***er**, frequent;	*creb***rior,** more frequent;	*creber***rimus,** most frequent.
nĭger, black;	*nigrior*, blacker;	*nigerrimus*, blackest.
asper, rough;	*aspĕrior*, rougher;	*asperrimus*, roughest.
lĭber, free;	*libĕrior*, freer;	*liberrimus*, freest.
acer, sharp;	*acrior*, sharper;	*acerrimus*, sharpest.
cĕler, swift.	*celĕrior*, swifter.	*celerrimus*, swiftest.

In like manner *vetus* forms the superlative *veterrimus*; moreover, *nuper*, lately, adv., *nuperrime*. *Matūrus*, ripe, makes *maturrimus* and *maturissimus*.

Of *dexter*, a comparative *dexterior*, more right, is found; likewise, of *sinister*, *sinisterior* (retaining the *e*, though it is dropped in the gen.), more left.

2. Six adjectives in **ilis**, viz.:

Dissĭmilis, sĭmilis, făcilis,
Diffĭcilis, hŭmilis, grăcilis,

form the comparative after the general rule; the superlative, by changing the termination **ĭlis** into **illĭmus.**

Dissimilis, unlike;	*dissimilior*, more unlike;	*dissim***illĭmus**, most unlike.
similis, like;	*similior*, more like;	*simillĭmus*, most like.
facĭlis, easy;	*facilior*, easier;	*facillimus*, easiest.
diffĭcĭlis, difficult;	*difficilior*, more difficult;	*difficillimus*, most difficult.
humĭlis, low;	*humilior*, lower;	*humillimus*, lowest.
gracĭlis, slender.	*gracilior*, more slender.	*gracillimus*, most slender.

3. The compound adjectives in **dĭcus, fĭcus,** and **vŏlus,** make the comparative in **entior,** the superlative in **entissimus.**

Maledĭcus, slanderous;	*maledĭcentior*,	*maledĭcentissimus*,
magnĭfĭcus, magnificent;	*magnificentior*,	*magnificentissimus*,
benĕvŏlus, benevolent;	*benevolentior*,	*benevolentissimus.*

These forms must be traced from the words *maledicens*, *benevŏlens*, and an imaginary form, *magnificens* (*faciens*). Compare in the same way *beneficus*, *maleficus*, *honorificus*, *malevolus*. *Egēnus*, needy, makes *egentior*, *egentissimus*; *providus*, provident, *providentior*, *providentissimus*; *validus*, strong, *valentior*, *valentissimus* (from *egens*, *providens*, *valens*).

§ 52.

The following adjectives contain greater irregularities:

1. Degrees from various stems.

bŏnus, good;	**mĕlior**, better;	**optĭmus**, best.
mălus, bad;	**pēior**, worse;	**pessimus**, worst.
magnus, great;	**māior**, greater;	**maximus**, greatest.
parvus, small;	**mĭnor**, smaller;	**mĭnimus**, smallest.
multus, much.	**plūs**, more;	**plūrimus**, most.

Plus is in the sing. always a substantive, neuter and defective, as the dat. and abl. are wanting. In the plur., *plures*, *plura*, *plurium*, *pluribus* are used as substantive and adjective. *Plures* has also a comparative meaning: *i. e.*, more than: the compound *complures* means several; it is never used in a comparative sense, and hence it can never be followed by *quam*.

2. Degrees from indeclinable words:

frūgi, (indecl.), honest; *frugalior*, *frugalissimus*;
nēquam, (indecl.), worthless; *nequior*, *nequissimus*.

3. Local adjectives with two irregular superlatives:

extĕrus, outward;	*extĕrior*, exterior;	*extrēmus* (rarely *extimus*), extreme;
infĕrus, below;	*inferior*, inferior;	*infĭmus* or *imus*, lowermost;
postĕrus, following;	*posterior*, posterior;	*postrēmus*, (*postŭmus*), last, latest;
sŭpĕrus, above;	*superior*, superior;	*suprēmus*, supreme, and *summus*, highest.

4. Degrees which have for their positive a preposition:

citra, on this side;	*citĕrior*, more on this side;	*citimus*, most on this side,
intra, inside;	*intĕrior*, inner;	*intĭmus*, innermost, intimate.
prae, before;	*prior*, prior, former;	*primus*, foremost, first.
prŏpe, near;	*prŏpior*, nearer;	*proximus*, nearest.
ultra, beyond;	*ultĕrior*, ulterior, further;	*ultĭmus*, furthest, last.

5. Degrees with obsolete positive:

detĕrior, worse;	*deterrimus*, worst;	(positive *deter*).
ōcior, swifter;	*ocissimus*, swiftest;	(positive *ocys*).
pŏtior, preferable;	*potissimus*, most important;	(positive *potis*).

Instead of the superlative ending **imus**, we find **ŭmus**; as, *aptissumus*, *optumus*, etc. (cf. § 1, 6).

§ 53.

The adjectives in which the termination **us** is preceded by a vowel, form their degrees of comparison by means of the adverbs *magis*, more, and *maxime*, most, placed before the adjective.

idonĕus, apt;	**magis** *idoneus*, more apt;	**maxime** *idoneus*, most apt.
dŭbĭus, doubtful;	*magis dubius*,	*maxime dubius*.
văcŭus, empty;	*magis vacuus*,	*maxime vacuus*.

Those in **quus**, however, remain regular; as, *aequus*, just, *aequior*, *aequissimus*; *antīquus*, old, *antiquior*, *antiquissimus*.

As an exceptional case, note *assiduus*, *assiduior*, *assiduissimus*; also, *piissimus*, from *pius*.

1. Some adjectives have a superlative, but no comparative; as, *diversus*, different, *diversissimus*; *falsus*, false, *falsissimus*; *inclitus*, illustrious, *inclitissimus*; *meritus*, deserving, *meritissimus*; *novus*, new, *novissimus*, last; *sacer*, sacred, *sacerrimus*; *vetus*, old, *veterrimus*.

2. The substantive *senex*, old man, makes a comparative, *senior*, older; *adolescens*, young, and *iuvenis*, young man, *adolescentior* and *iunior* (from *iuvenior*); these have no superlative.

3. Many adjectives have neither comparative nor superlative, partly on account of their meaning; as, *Latinus*, *aureus*, *peregrinus*; partly for other reasons; as, in the compounds of **fer** and **ger** (§ 19), also, *vicus*, *merus*, *claudus*, *praeditus*, *inops*, *magnanimus*, *modicus*, *sonorus*, *crinitus*, etc. However, these also, when necessary, can be compared by means of *magis* and *maxime*; as, *magis Latinus*, more Latin; *maxime Latinus*, most Latin. Thus also, *magis diversus*, *magis falsus*, etc.

§ 54.

1. The comparative may be rendered by the positive with *too*; or sometimes by *somewhat*, *rather*, and the positive; in which latter instance *paulo* may be prefixed or omitted. Thus, *maior*, *greater*, and *too great*. *Senectus est paulo morosior*, old age is *somewhat* (*rather*) peevish. The superlative may be translated by the positive with *very*; as, *doctissimus*, *most* learned, *very* learned.

2. The English *than*, after the comparative, is expressed by *quam*; *e. g.*, *praeceptor doctior est*, *quam discipulus*, than the pupil.

3. The English *still*, before the comparative, is omitted in Latin; as, *filius maior est*, *quam pater*, the son is still greater than the father. Sometimes it is translated by *etiam*.

4. *Much*, *far*, *by far*, before the comparative, is *multo*; *e. g.*, *multo melior*, much better, by far better, far better.

5. *By far*, before the superlative, is *longe*, sometimes *multo*; as, *longe minimus* (*multo minimus*), by far the smallest.

6. *Even*, with the comparative and superlative, is translated by *vel*; as, *vel maior*, even greater, still greater even; *vel maximus*, even the greatest, the very greatest.

7. *As much as possible*, with the positive (*much*), is expressed in Latin by *quam*, with the superlative; as, *quam maximus*, as great as possible.

CHAPTER XII.

THE NUMERAL (NUMERALE).

§ 55.

		I. CARDINAL NUMBERS. *Numeralia cardinalia.* (How many? *Quot?*)	II. ORDINAL NUMBERS. *Numeralia ordinalia.* (Which, or what in number, order? *Quotus, a, um?*)
1.	I.	*ūnus, a, um,* one.	*prīmus, a, um,* first.
2.	II.	*duo, duae, duo,* two.	*secundus,* second.
3.	III.	*trēs, tria,* three.	*tertius,* third.
4.	IV.	*quattuor* (*quatuor*), four.	*quartus,* fourth.
5.	V.	*quinque,* five.	*quintus,* fifth.
6.	VI.	*sex,* six.	*sextus,* sixth.
7.	VII.	*septem,* seven.	*septĭmus,* seventh.
8.	VIII.	*octo,* eight.	*octāvus,* eighth.
9.	IX.	*nŏvem,* nine.	*nōnus,* ninth.
10.	X.	*dĕcem,* ten.	*dĕcĭmus,* tenth.
11.	XI.	*undĕcim,* eleven.	*undĕcĭmus,* eleventh.
12.	XII.	*duŏdĕcim,* twelve.	*duodecĭmus,* twelfth.
13.	XIII.	*trēdĕcim,* thirteen.	*tertius decimus,* thirteenth.
14.	XIV.	*quattuordĕcim,* fourteen.	*quartus decimus,* fourteenth.
15.	XV.	*quindĕcim,* fifteen.	*quintus decimus,* fifteenth.
16.	XVI.	*sēdĕcim,* sixteen.	*sextus decimus,* sixteenth.
17.	XVII.	*septemdĕcim,* seventeen.	*septimus decimus,* seventeenth.
18.	XVIII.	*duodeviginti,* eighteen.	*duodevicēsĭmus,* eighteenth.
19.	XIX.	*undeviginti,* nineteen.	*undevicesĭmus,* nineteenth.
20.	XX.	*vīginti,* twenty.	*vicesimus* (*vigesimus*), twentieth.
21.	XXI.	*viginti unus,* or *unus et viginti,* twenty-one.	*unus et vicesimus,* or *vicesimus primus,* twenty-first.

22.	XXII.	*viginti duo*, or *duo et viginti*.	*alter et vicesimus*, or *vicesimus alter*.
23.	XXIII.	*viginti tres* (*tria*), etc.	*tertius et vicesimus*, etc.
28.	XXVIII.	*duodetriginta*.	*duodetricesimus*.
29.	XXIX.	*undetriginta*.	*undetricesimus*.
30.	XXX.	*trīginta*.	*tricesimus* (*trigesimus*).
31.	XXXI	*triginta unus* or *unus et triginta*, etc.	*unus et tricesimus*, or *tricesimus primus*.
40.	XL.	*quadrāginta*.	*quadragesimus*.
50.	L.	*quinquāginta*.	*quinquagesimus*.
60.	LX.	*sexāginta*.	*sexagesimus*.
70.	LXX.	*septuāginta*.	*septuagesimus*.
80.	LXXX.	*octōginta*.	*octogesimus*.
90.	XC.	*nonāginta*.	*nonagesimus*.
98.	XCVIII.	*octo et nonaginta*, or *nonaginta octo*.	*nonagesimus octavus*.
99.	XCIX.	*novem et nonaginta*, or *nonaginta novem*.	*nonagesimus nonus*, or *undecentesimus*.
100.	C.	*centum*.	*centesimus*.
101.	CI.	*centum et unus*, or *centum unus*.	*centesimus primus*.
102.	CII.	*centum et duo* (*ae*, *o*), etc.	*centesimus secundus*, etc.
200.	CC.	*dūcenti, ae, a*.	*ducentesimus*.
300.	CCC.	*trĕcenti, ae, a*.	*trecentesimus*.
400.	CCCC.	*quadringenti, ae, a*.	*quadringentesimus*.
500.	IƆ or D.	*quingenti, ae, a*.	*quingentesimus*.
600.	DC.	*sexcenti, ae, a* (*sescenti*).	*sexcentesimus*.
700.	DCC.	*septingenti, ae, a*.	*septingentesimus*.
800.	DCCC.	*octingenti, ae, a*.	*octingentesimus*.
900.	DCCCC.	*nongenti, ae, a*.	*nongentesimus*.
1000.	M.	*mille*.	*millesimus*.
2000.	MM.	*duo millia* (*milia*).	*bis millesimus*.
3000.	MMM.	*tria millia*, etc.	*ter millesimus*.
100000.	CCCIƆƆƆ.	*centum millia*.	*centies millesimus*.

1. *Decem et sex* is sometimes used instead of *sedecim*; likewise, *decem et septem*, *decem et octo*, *decem et novem*, etc.

2. Higher numbers are: *ducenta millia*, etc. A million is *decies centena millia*; 1,100,000, *undecies centena millia*: 2.000.000. *vicies centena millia*.

§ 56.

All these numerals are adjectives. All the ordinal numbers are declined; of the cardinal numbers, only the first three are declined, and from *ducenti, trecenti*, etc., to *nongenti*.

1.	Nom.	*unus*,	*ūna*,	*unum*,	one.
	Gen.	**unīus**,	**unius**,	**unius**,	of one.
	Dat.	**uni**,	**uni**,	**uni**,	to one.
	Acc.	*unum*,	*unam*,	*unum*,	one.
	Abl.	*unō*,	*unā*,	*unō*,	from, by, with one (cfr. § 25, 1).
2.	Nom.	*du***o**,	*du***ae**,	*du***o**,	two.
	Gen.	*duōrum*,	*duārum*,	*duōrum*,	(*duum*, § 25, 2), of two.
	Dat.	*du***ōbus**,	*du***ābus**,	*du***ōbus**,	to two.
	Acc.	*duos* (*duo*),	*duas*,	*duo*,	two.
	Abl.	*du***ōbus**,	*du***ābus**,	*du***ōbus**,	from, by, with two.

Thus decline *ambo, ambae, ambo*, both.

3.	Nom.	*trēs*,	*tres*,	*tria*,	three.
	Gen.		*trium*,		of three.
	Dat.		*tribus*,		to three.
	Acc.	*tres*,	*tres*,	*tria*,	three.
	Abl.		*tribus*,		from, by, with three.

(After the third decl.)

4. *Ducenti, ae, a*, etc., are regularly declined (after the second and first decl.).

§ 57.

1. *Mille* in the singular, is mostly used as an indeclinable adjective; as, nom. *mille equites*; gen. *mille equitum*; dat. *mille equitibus*; etc. The plural *millia* (after *maria*) is always a substantive and governs a genitive; as, *duo millia equitum*, two thousands of horsemen, 2,000 horsemen; *duobus millibus equitum*, to two thousands of horsemen, to 2.000 horsemen; but, *duo millia equitum et trecenti*, or *duo millia trecenti equites*, 2,300 horsemen.

NOTE 1.—From 20 to 100, either the smaller number with *et* is prefixed, or the larger without *et*. Above 100 the larger always precedes without *et*, or is followed immediately by *et*. But *et* is never put twice.

NOTE 2.—*Hundreds* or *thousands* is often used in English for *a great many;* in Latin, it is expressed by *sexcenti*, not *centum* or *mille*. *Sexcenti ceciderunt*, hundreds fell. When the ordinal number or the numeral adverb is used, *millesimus* and *millies* (not *sexcentesimus*, *sexcenties*) are the proper expressions.

2. Dates of years and hours of the day are, in Latin, expressed by ordinal numbers ; *e. g.*, the year 1851 after the birth of Christ, *annus millesimus octingentesimus quinquagesimus primus post Christum natum.* In answer to the question, *When?* the ablative is used; in the year 1851, *anno millesimo octingentesimo quinquagesimo primo. Nonā horā*, at the ninth hour, at nine o'clock. *Quota hora est?* what o'clock is it? *Hora tertia*, three o'clock.

3. Twenty-one men is expressed by *unus et viginti homines*, or *homines viginti et unus* (very rarely *viginti unus homines* or *homo*).

§ 58.

	III. DISTRIBUTIVE NUMBERS. *Numeralia distributiva.* (How many each time? *Quotēni?*)	IV. MULTIPLICATIVE NUMBERS. *Numeralia multiplicantia.* (Numeral adverbs. How often? *Quoties?*)
1.	*Singŭli, ae, a*, one by one.	*sĕmel*, once.
2.	*bīni, ae, a*, two apiece, two by two.	*bĭs*, twice.
3.	*terni, ae, a*, three apiece, three by three.	*tĕr*, thrice.
4.	*quăterni.*	*quăter.*
5.	*quīni.*	*quinquiēs* (*quinquiens*).
6.	*sēni.*	*sexiēs.*
7.	*septēni.*	*septies.*
8.	*octōni.*	*octies.*
9.	*novēni.*	*nŏvies.*
10.	*dēni.*	*dĕcies.*
11.	*undēni.*	*undecies.*
12.	*duodeni.*	*duodecies.*
13.	*terni deni.*	*ter decies*, or *tredecies.*
14.	*quaterni deni*, etc.	*quater decies*, etc.
20.	*vicēni, ae, a.*	*vicies.*
21.	*viceni singŭli.*	*semel et vicies*, or *vicies semel*

22.	*viceni bini.*	*bis et vicies*, or *vicies bis*, etc.
30.	*triceni.*	*tricies.*
40.	*quadrageni.*	*quadragies.*
50.	*quinquageni.*	*quinquagies.*
60.	*sexageni.*	*sexagies.*
70.	*septuageni.*	*septuagies.*
80.	*octogeni.*	*octogies.*
90.	*nonageni.*	*nonagies.*
100.	*centeni, ae, a.*	*centies.*
101.	*centeni singuli.*	*semel et centies.*
200.	*duceni, ae, a.*	*ducenties.*
300.	*treceni.*	*trecenties.*
400.	*quadringeni.*	*quadringenties.*
500.	*quingeni.*	*quingenties.*
600.	*sexceni.*	*sexcenties.*
700.	*septingeni.*	*septingenties.*
800.	*octingeni.*	*octingenties.*
900.	*nongeni.*	*nongenties.*
1000.	*singula millia.*	*millies.*
2000.	*bina millia.*	*bis millies.*
3000.	*terna millia*, etc.	*ter millies*, etc.
100,000.	*centena millia.*	*centies millies.*

§ 59.

1. Form the Latin multiplication table thus: *bis bina sunt quattuor*, twice two are four; *bis terna sunt sex*, twice three are six; *septies novena sunt sexaginta tria.*

2. *Caesar et Ariovistus* **denos** *comites adduxerunt*, means Caesar and Ariovistus brought with them each ten companions. *Decem comites* would mean ten altogether.

3. Distributive numbers are further used with words that in Latin have no singular at all (§ 47, IV), or else have a different meaning in the singular. In English all such words are expressed in the singular, as *nuptiae, a*, the wedding; *castra, a*, the camp; hence, *binae nuptiae*, two weddings, (not *duae*). Instead of *singuli* and *terni*, however, the Romans used, in this case, only *uni* (plural of *unus*) and *trini;* thus, *unae litterae*, one epistle (*singulae litterae*, single letters of the alphabet); *trinae aedes*, three houses (*tres aedes*, three temples). However, *duo liberi*, two children, because children is also plural in English (*bini liberi*, two children each; *terni liberi*, three children each).

4. The plural *binum*, *sen...*, *denum*, is often used instead of *binorum*, etc. (§ 25, 2).

§ 60.

1. Multiplicatives (*multiplicativa*), answering to the question, *Quotŭplex?* how many fold? *Simplex*, single; *duplex*, double; *triplex*, threefold; *quadrŭplex*, fourfold; *multiplex*, manifold. Used always as adjectives and refer to numbers.

2. Proportionals (*proportionalia*), answering to the question, *Quotŭplus?* how many times greater? *Simplum*, simple; *duplum*, twice as great; *triplum*, three times as great; *quadruplum*, four times as great. Used mostly as substantives, and only in reference to the size.

Dimidius, *a*, *um*, half; *dimidia pars*, the half; *tertia pars*, one-third; *duae quintae*, two-fifths; *quattuor partes*, four-fifths (the denominator is not expressed, when it exceeds the numerator only by a unit).

§ 61.

1. *Primānus*, of the first division (class, legion); *secundānus*, of the second; *tertianus*, of the third. *Senarius*, containing six; *sexagenarius*, containing sixty (sixty years old).

2. *Primum*, first, for the first time; *secundo*, secondly; *itĕrum*, the second time; *tertium*, thirdly, the third time; *quartum*, *quintum*, *sextum*, etc. More rare are *primo*, *tertio*, etc.

3. Remark also, 1) *bimus*, two years old; *trimus*, three years old: *quadrimus*, four years old. 2) Compounded with *annus*: *biennis*, of two years' continuance; likewise, *triennis*, *quadriennis*, *quinquennis*, (or rather *quinquennālis*), *sexennis*, *septennis*, and *decennis*; hence the substantives *biennium*, a period of two years; *triennium*, etc. 3) Compounded with *dies*: *biduum*, a period of two days; thus, *triduum* and *quadriduum*, and compounded with *mensis*: *bimestris*, of two months' duration; *trimestris*, *quadrimestris*, *quinquemestris*, *semestris*.

CHAPTER XIII.

THE PRONOUN (PRONOMEN).

§ 62.

I. PERSONAL PRONOUNS.
(*Pronomina personalia.*)

SINGULAR.

Nom.	*ĕgo*, I;	*tū*, thou;	——
Gen.	*meī*, of me;	*tuī*, of thee;	*suī*, of himself.
Dat.	*mĭhi*, to me;	*tĭbi*, to thee;	*sĭbi*, to himself (herself, itself.
Acc.	*mē*, me;	*tē*, thee;	*sē*, himself.
Abl.	*mē*, with, from, &c., me.	*tē*, with thee.	*sē*, with himself (herself, itself).

PLURAL.

Nom.	*nōs*, we;	*vōs* you;	——
Gen.	*nostrī*, of us; *nostrum*, among us;	*vestrī*, of you; *vestrum*, among you;	*sui*, of themselves.
Dat.	*nōbīs*, to us;	*vōbīs*, to you;	*sibi*, to themselves.
Acc.	*nōs*, us;	*vōs*, you;	*sē*, themselves.
Abl.	*nōbīs*, with us;	*vōbis*, with you;	*sē*, with themselves.

Nostrum, *vestrum* are the partitive genit. (§ 212) of *nos*, *vos*, and very rarely used for *nostri*, *vestri*.

§ 63.

1. The preposition *cum*, with, which governs the ablative, always follows the personal pronoun; thus, *mecum*, with me (not *cum me*); *tecum*, with thee; *secum*, with himself; *nobiscum*, with us; *vobiscum*, with you.

2. The syllable **met** may be joined for the sake of emphasis to all these forms, except *tu* and the gen. plur.; thus, *egomet*, *vosmet*, *sibimet* (*egomet ipse*, *vosmet ipsi*, *sibimet ipsi*), etc. *Tu* is strengthened by appending the syllable **te**, therefore, *tute;* but *tuimet*, *tibimet*, etc. In like manner,

the form *se* is often reduplicated for the sake of emphasis; *sese* for *se* (rarely *tete*, *meme*).

3. The poets often say *mi* instead of *mihi* (like *nil* instead of *nihil*).

4. The pronoun *sui*, *sibi*, *se*, is also called reflexive pronoun, because it *points back* to the subject of the sentence.

§ 64.

II. DEMONSTRATIVE PRONOUNS.

(*Pronomina demonstrativa.*)

SINGULAR.

	MASC.	FEM.	NEUT.	
Nom.	*hĭc*,	*haec*,	*hŏc*,	this.
Gen.		*hūius*,		of this.
Dat.		*hŭic*,		to this.
Acc.	*hunc*,	*hanc*,	*hŏc*,	this.
Abl.	*hōc*,	*hāc*,	*hōc*,	with, by, from this.

PLURAL.

Nom.	*hī*,	*hae*,	*haec*,	these.
Gen.	*hōrum*,	*hārum*,	*hōrum*,	of these.
Dat.		*hīs*,		to these.
Acc.	*hōs*,	*hās*,	*haec*,	these.
Abl.		*hīs*,		with, by, from these.

Hice is sometimes used instead of *hic*; likewise *hosce*, *hasce*, *hisce*, *huiusce*, rarely *haece*, *horumce*, etc.; with the interrogative particle *ne* joined to it, *Hicine?* this here?

SINGULAR.

		MASC.	FEM.	NEUT.	
1.	Nom.	*istĕ*,	*istă*,	*istŭd*,	that.
	Gen.		*istīus*,		of that.
	Dat.		*istī*,		to that.
	Acc.	*istum*,	*istam*,	*istud*,	that.
	Abl.	*istō*,	*istā*,	*istō*,	with, from, by that.

PLURAL.

Nom.	*istī*,	*istae*,	*istă*,	those.
Gen.	*istōrum*,	*istārum*,	*istōrum*,	of those.
Dat.		*istīs*,		to those.
Acc.	*istōs*,	*istās*,	*istă*,	those.
Abl.		*istīs*.		with, by, from those.

3. *Ille, illa, illud*, that, is exactly declined like *iste, ista, istud; olli* for *illi*, in Virgil.

1. The demonstrative *hic* mostly points to the speaker or the first person, and whatever is connected with it; *iste* to the second person, *ille* to the third.

2. From a combination of *iste* and *ille* with *hic*, are formed the compounds *istic, istaec, istoc*, or *istuc*, and *illic, illaec, illoc*, or *illuc*. They are declined like *hic*, with the exception of the gen. and dat., which are wanting; thus, acc. *istunc, istanc, istoc*, or *istuc;* abl. *istoc, istac, istoc;* in the plur. only *istaec* and *illaec*. Most of those forms are rarely used.

SINGULAR.

		Masc.	Fem.	Neut.	
4.	Nom.	*ipsĕ*,	*ipsă*,	*ipsum*,	I myself, thou thyself, he, himself, she herself, itself.
	Gen.		*ipsīus*,		of myself, thyself, &c.
	Dat.		*ipsī*,		to myself, thyself, &c.
	Acc.	*ipsum*,	*ipsam*,	*ipsum*,	myself, thyself, &c.
	Abl.	*ipsō*,	*ipsā*,	*ipsō*,	by, with myself, thyself, &c.

PLURAL.

	Nom.	*ipsī*,	*ipsae*,	*ipsă*.
	Gen.	*ipsōrum*,	*ipsārum*,	*ipsōrum*.
	Dat		*ipsīs*.	
	Acc.	*ipsōs*,	*ipsās*,	*ipsă*.
	Abl.		*ipsīs*.	

§ 65.

SINGULAR.

		Masc.	Fem.	Neut.	
5.	Nom.	*ĭs*,	*ĕă*,	*ĭd*,	he, she, it, or that.
	Gen.		*ĕiŭs*,		of him, his, her, its, &c.
	Dat.		*ĕī*,		to him, &c.
	Acc.	*eum*,	*eam*,	*id*,	him, &c.
	Abl.	*eō*,	*eā*,	*eō*,	by, with him, &c.

PLURAL.

	Nom.	*ii* (*ei*),	*eae*,	*eă*,	they, those.
	Gen.	*eōrum*,	*eārum*,	*eōrum*,	of them, their.
	Dat.		*iīs* or *eīs*,		to them.
	Acc.	*eōs*,	*eās*,	*eă*,	them, those.
	Abl.		*iīs* or *eīs*,		by, with them.

SINGULAR.

		MASC.	FEM.	NEUT.	
6.	Nom.	*īdem,*	*eădem,*	*ĭdem,*	the same.
	Gen.		*eiusdem,*		of the same.
	Dat.		*eīdem,*		to the same.
	Acc.	*eundem,*	*eandem,*	*ĭdem,*	the same.
	Abl.	*eōdem,*	*eādem,*	*eōdem,*	with, by, from the same.

PLURAL.

Nom.	*iīdem,*	*eaedem,*	*eădem,*	the same.
Gen.	*eorundem,*	*earundem,*	*eorundem,*	of the same.
Dat.		*iisdem* or *eisdem,*		to the same.
Acc.	*eōsdem,*	*eāsdem,*	*eădem,*	the same.
Abl.		*iisdem* or *eisdem,*		with, by, from the same.

Idem is formed from *is* and the strengthening suffix *dem.*

§ 66.

III. RELATIVE PRONOUN.

(*Pronomen relativum.*)

SINGULAR.

Nom.	*quī,*	*quae,*	*quŏd,*	who, which, that.
Gen.		*cūius,*		of whom, whose.
Dat.		*cŭi,*		to whom.
Acc.	*quem,*	*quam,*	*quŏd,*	whom, which.
Abl.	*quō,*	*quā,*	*quō,*	by, with, from whom

PLURAL.

Nom.	*qui,*	*quae,*	*quae,*	who, which.
Gen.	*quōrum,*	*quārum,*	*quōrum,*	of whom.
Dat.		*quĭbus,*		to whom.
Acc.	*quōs,*	*quās,*	*quae,*	whom.
Abl.		*quĭbus,*		by, from, with whom.

1. *Quocum,* with whom, is generally used instead of *cum quo* (cfr., § 68); likewise *quacum, quibuscum;* however, *cum quo, cum qua, cum quibus,* are also used.

2. An old abl. sing. is *qui*; it is used 1) as interrogative adverb; *e. g.*, *Qui fit?* how does it happen? 2) In *quicum*, instead of *quocum*. An old abl. plur. is *quis* for *quibus* (*quoius* and *quoi*, for *cuius* and *cui*, are antiquated).

§ 67.

IV. INTERROGATIVE PRONOUNS.

(*Pronomina interrogativa.*)

1. Masc. *Quis?* who? which? what? *Qui?* who? what? Fem. *Quae?* Neut. *Quid? Quod?*

Quis is mostly substantive, *quid* always; *quod* is adjective. *Quis* inquires for the name, *qui* for the character or quality. *Quis vir? Caesar.* What is the man's name? Caesar. *Qui vir?* what kind of a man? *Bonus vir*, the good man.

They are declined like the relative; hence, gen. *cuius?* dat. *cui?* acc. *quem? quam? quid?* and *quod?* abl. *quo? qua? quo?* (*qui?*).

2. Also *numquis?* who? *numqui*, *numquae*, *numquid? numquod?* Moreover, *quisnam?* who? *quinam? quaenam? quidnam? quodnam?* Also *ecquis?* who? *ecquid?* what? They are declined like *quis*; *num*, *nam*, and *ec*, remaining unchanged; therefore, gen. *numcuius*, *cuiusnam*, *eccuius*, dat. *numcui*, *cuinam*, *eccui*, etc.

3. *Uter*, *utra*, *utrum?* which of the two? (§ 25, 1.) *e. g.*, *uter oculus?* which eye? *utra manus?* which hand? but *quis discipulorum?*

§ 68.

V. INDEFINITE PRONOUNS.

(*Pronomina indefinita.*)

1. *Quicunque*, *quaecunque*, *quodcunque*, whatsoever. It is declined like *qui*, *quae*, *quod*; *cunque* is invariable; in the plural, *all who.*

2. *Quisquis*, whosoever; *quidquid*, whatsoever. Besides these two forms, only the abl. *quoquo* is used; as, *quoquo modo*, in whatsoever manner.

Quicunque is mostly adjective, *quisquis* is substantive.

3. *Quis* (*qui*), *quae* (*qua*), *quid* and *quod*, some one, something, any one; declined like *quis?* Plur. neut. mostly *qua.*

4. *Aliquis* (*aliqui*), *aliqua*, *aliquid*, and *aliquod*, some one, something; like *quis*, except sing. fem. *aliqua*, and plur. neut. only *aliqua*.

5. *Quispiam*, *quaepiam*, *quidpiam*, and *quodpiam*, some one, something; like *quis*.

6. *Quidam*, *quaedam*, *quiddam*, and *quoddam*, a certain one; like *quis*, but before **d**, an **n** instead of an **m**; hence, *quendam*, *quandam*, *quorundam*.

7. *Quisquam*, neut. *quidquam* (*quicquam*), some one, something; without feminine or plural, otherwise like *quis*.

8. *Quisque*, *quaeque*, *quidque*, and *quodque*, each one (among many).

9. *Quivis*, *quaevis*, *quidvis*, and *quodvis*, any one you please.

10. *Quilibet*, *quaelibet*, *quidlibet*, and *quodlibet*, any one you please.

11. *Unusquisque*, *unaquaeque*, *unumquidque*, and *unumquodque*, each one.

Both parts of the words are declined; hence, gen. *uniuscuiusque*, dat. *unicuique*, acc. *unumquemque*, *unamquamque*, *unumquidque*, or *unumquodque*, abl. *unoquoque*, *unaquaque*.

12. *Ullus*, *a*, *um*, any, any one (§ 25, 1).

13. *Uterque*, *utrăque*, *utrumque*, both one and the other, each of two.

14. *Utervis*, *utrăvis*, *utrumvis*, either one of the two, which you please.

15. *Uterlibet*, *utrălibet*, *utrumlibet*, either of the two.

16. *Utercunque*, *utracunque*, *utrumcunque*, whichever of the two.

17. *Altĕrŭter*, *alterautra*, *alterumutrum*, one of the two, either.

Alter and *uter* are both declined; however, *alter* remains sometimes undeclined; hence, gen. *alteriusutrius* or *alterutrius*, etc.

18. Negative pronouns are *nemo* (§ 47, II, 2), nobody, opposed to *aliquis*, some one; *nihil*, nothing, opposed to *aliquid*, something; *nullus*, *a*, *um*, not any, opposed to *ullus*, any; *neuter*, *tra*, *trum*, neither of two, opposed to *alteruter* and *uterque*.

NOTES.—1. The neuters formed with *quid* are all substantives; those with *quod*, adjectives; thus, *aliquid ingenii*, but *aliquod ingenium*. The masculines formed with *quis* are mostly substantives; those with *qui*, adjectives. *Nemo* and *quisquam* are substantives; *nullus* and *ullus*, adjectives.

2. *Quis, qua, quid* (also *qui, quae, quod*), are mostly used instead of *aliquis* and *quisquam*, after *ne, num, si, nisi, quo* (§ 171, etc.), and sometimes also after other relatives; hence, *nequid nimis; si quis dubitat; num quae te vexat cura?* With emphasis, *si quisquam, num aliquid.*

3. *Aliquis, quispiam*, and *quidam*, are mostly used in affirmative sentences; *quisquam* and *ullus*, in negative sentences. *Dicet aliquis.* Yes, some one will say. *Quisquam hoc dicet?* requiring the answer, No one will say this. Hence, only *sine ulla spe*, without any hope, not *aliqua* (still less *omni*); *sine* has a negative power. Nevertheless, *non sine aliqua spe = cum aliqua spe.*

4. *Quisque* always follows an emphasized word as enclitic. This word is generally either, 1) a reflexive; *suum cuique* tribue; or 2) a relative; *quo quisque* est ingeniosior, eo docet laboriosius; or 3) a superlative; *optimus quisque* gloria maxime ducitur; or 4) an ordinal numeral; *decimum quemque* securi percuti iussit. *Quarto quoque anno*, every fourth year, every four years.

§ 69.

VI. ADJECTIVE PRONOUNS.

(*Adiectiva pronominalia.*)

1. The possessive pronouns, *pronomina possessīva: Meus, a, um*, my; *tuus, a, um*, thy; *suus, a, um*, his; *noster, nostra, nostrum*, our; *vester, vestra, vestrum*, your; *suus, a, um*, their.

1. From *noster* and *vester* are formed the *pronomina gentilicia; nostras*, of our country; *vestras*, of your country; as, *nostrātes*, our countrymen; *nostratia verba*, words in use with us. From the gen. *cuius* is likewise formed *cuias*, from what country? The possessive, *cuius, cuia, cuium*, whose? is rare.

b. To *suo* and *sua* (abl.) is sometimes added, for the sake of emphasis, the syllable **pte**; as, *suopte pondere*, by his own weight; *suapte manu*. In like manner, but rarely, *meamet, suamet* (neut. plur.).

2. THE CORRELATIVE PRONOUNS (*pronomina correlativa*):

INTERROGATORY AND RELATIVE.	DEMONSTRATIVE.	INDEFINITE.
a. *Quālis, e,* of which (what) kind? such as.	*tālis, e,* of such kind.	
b. *Quantus, a, um,* (so great) how great.	*tantus, a, um,* so great.	*aliquantus, a, um,* of considerable size.
c. *Quŏt* (indecl.), (so many) as, how many?	*tŏt* (indecl.), so many.	*ălĭquot* (indecl.), a certain number, some.

1. Moreover, *qualiscunque*, of whatsoever kind; *quantuscunque*, how great soever; *quotcunque* and *quotquot*, how many soever; *totidem*, just as many; *quotus* and *quotusquisque*, which one, in number or rank?

2. The interrogative correlatives are at the same time relatives, and then correspond to the English *as*. *Vir talis qualis Africanus*, a man such *as* Africanus; *exercitus tantus, quantus nunquam antea fuit*, such as; *tot victoriae, quot pugnae*, as many victories *as* battles (in such cases, never *ut* or *quam*).

CHAPTER XIV.

§ 70.

THE VERB (VERBUM).

I. THE Latin language has three forms of the verb, *genera verbi*, viz.:

1. The **active form,** *genus activum*, which signifies an action; as, *laudo*, I praise.
2. The **passive form,** *genus passīvum*, which signifies suffering; as, *laudor*, I am praised.
3. The **deponent form,** *genus depōnens*, a middle form, a verb with passive form and active meaning; as, *hortor*, I exhort.

1. The expression, *genera verbi*, suggests the analogy with the genders of nouns; the active corresponds to the masculine, the passive to the feminine, the deponent (laying aside) to the neuter.

II. *Active* and *deponent* verbs are either:

1. Transitive (*transitīva*); as, *laudo* and *hortor; e. g., discipulum*, I praise or exhort the pupil; or,
2. Intransitive or Neuter (*intransitīva, neutra*); as, *dormio*, I sleep; *orior*, I rise. Transitive verbs can form a complete passive; not so, intransitives.

The semi-deponent (*semideponentia*), *vide* § 115; the neuter-passive (*neutropassiva*), § 144, 2, note 1.

§ 71.

To the conjugation or inflection of the verb belong:

I. THE MOODS (MODI) AND THE PARTICIPIALS.

A. 1. The Indicative Mood (*modus indicatīvus*), asserts a fact; as, *laudat*, he praises.

2. The Subjunctive Mood (*modus coniunctīvus*) is the conditional or dependent mood; *laudet*, he may praise.

3. The Imperative Mood (*modus imperatīvus*) is the mood of command; *lauda*, praise thou.

B. Middle forms or participials (being partly verb, partly noun):

1. Infinitive (*infinitīvus*); as, *laudare*, to praise.
2. Gerund (*gerundium*); as, *laudandi*, of praising.
3. Supine (*supīnum*); as, *laudātu*, to praise, to be praised.
4. Participle (*participium*); as, *laudans*, praising.

Indicative, subjunctive, and imperative are moods, and express a limited or finite action or condition of a subject (finite verb, *verbum finitum*); infinitive, gerund, supine, and participle are participials, and express no definite action or condition of the subject (*verbum infinitum*).

II. TENSES.

(*Tempora.*)

1. Present (*praesens*); *laudo*, I praise (now).
2. Imperfect (*imperfectum*); as, *laudābam*, I praised (then).

3. Future (*futurum*); as, *laudābo*, I shall praise (hereafter).
4. Perfect (*perfectum*); *laudāvi*, I have praised.
5. Pluperfect (*plusquamperfectum*); as, *laudavĕram*, I had praised.
6. Future perfect (*futurum exactum*); as, *laudavĕro*, I shall have praised.

The imperfect, perfect, and pluperfect are called past tenses (*tempora praetĕrita*).

III. NUMBER.

(*Numĕrus.*)

The number is either singular or plural. In each number the verb has three persons, the first (the person who speaks); the second (the person spoken to); the third (the person spoken of).

The tense of the Latin verbs has personal terminations to express the different persons, sing. and plur., thus avoiding the use of the pronouns. In this point it differs from all modern languages; *laudo*, I praise; *laudas*, thou praisest, etc.

CHAPTER XV.

THE AUXILIARY VERB ESSE, TO BE.

§ 72.

		A. INDICATIVE.	B. SUBJUNCTIVE.
		PRESENT.	
		Am.	***May or can be, that I be.***
S.	1st pers.	*sum*, I am.	*Sim*, I may or can be.
	2d "	*ĕs*, thou art (you are).	*sīs*, thou mayest be (you may be).
	3d "	*est*, he, she, it is.	*sĭt*, he may be.
P.	1st "	*sŭmus*, we are.	*sīmus*, we can be.
	2d "	*estis*, you are.	*sītis*, you may be.
	3d "	*sunt*, they are.	*sint*, they may be.

Imperfect.

	Was, used to be.	***Might be, that I were.***
S. 1.	*Eram*, I was.	*Essem*, I might be.
2.	**ĕrās,** thou wast (you were).	*essēs*, thou mightst be.
3.	*ĕrăt*, he, she, it was.	*essĕt*, he might be.
P. 1.	*erāmus*, we were.	*essēmus*, we might be.
2.	*erātis*, you were.	*essētis*, you might be.
3.	**ĕrant,** they were.	*essent*, they might be.

Future.

	Shall or ***will be.***	***May be about to be.***
S. 1.	*Ero*, I shall be.	*futūrus* (*a*, *um*), *sim*, I may be about to be.
2.	**ĕris,** thou wilt be (you will be).	*futurus sis*, thou mayest, &c.
3.	*ĕrĭt*, he, she, it will be.	*futurus sit*, he may, &c.
P. 1.	*ĕrĭmus*, we shall be.	*futuri* (*ae*, *a*) *simus*, we, &c.
2.	*ĕrĭtis*, you will be.	*futuri sitis*, you may, &c.
3.	**ĕrunt,** they will be.	*futuri sint*, they may, &c.

Perfect.

	Have been, was.	***May have been, that I have been.***
S. 1.	*Fuī*, I have been.	*Fuĕrim*, I may have been.
2.	*fuistī*, thou hast been (you have been).	*fuĕrĭs*, thou mayst have been.
3.	*fuĭt*, he, she, it has been.	*fuĕrĭt*, he may have been.
P. 1.	*fuĭmus*, we have been.	*fuĕrĭmus*, we may have been.
2.	*fuistis*, you have been.	*fuĕrĭtis*, you may have been.
3.	**fuērunt** (*fuēre*), they have been.	**fuĕrint,** they may have been.

Pluperfect.

	Had been.	***Might have, that I had, been.***
S. 1.	*Fuĕram*, I had been.	*fuissem*, I might have been.
2.	*fuĕrās*, thou hadst been.	*fuissēs*, thou mightst have been.
3.	*fuĕrăt*, he had been.	*fuissĕt*, he might have been.

P. 1.	*fuerāmus*, we had been.	*fuissēmus*, we might have been.
2.	*fuerātis*, you had been.	*fuissētis*, you might have been.
3.	**fuĕrant,** they had been.	*fuissent*, they might have been.

FUTURE PERFECT.

Shall have been.

S. 1.	*Fuĕro*, I shall have been.	
2.	*fuĕris*, thou wilt have been.	
3.	*fuĕrit*, he will have been.	
P. 1.	*fuĕrimus*, we shall have been.	Wanting.
2.	*fuĕritis*, you will have been.	
3.	**fuĕrint,** they will have been.	

§ 73.

C. IMPERATIVE.

PRESENT.		FUTURE.	
SING. 2.	*Es*, be thou.	SING. 2.	*Esto*, thou shalt be.
— —		3.	*esto*, he shall be.
PLUR. 2.	*este*, be ye.	PLUR. 2.	*estōte*, ye shall be.
— —		3.	*sunto*, they shall be.

D. INFINITIVE.

PRESENT.	FUTURE.	
Esse, to be.	SING. *Futūrum*, (*am*, *um*) *esse*, PLUR. *futūros* (*as*, *a*), *esse*,	or *fore*, to be about to be.

PERFECT.

Fuisse, to have been.

E. PARTICIPLE.

PRESENT.	FUTURE.
(*Ens*), being.	*Futurus* (*a*, *um*), about to be.

F. SUPINE and **G.** GERUND of *esse* are wanting.

§ 74.

1. Like *sum* are conjugated its compounds, viz.:

de*sum*, I am wanting in.
in*sum*, I am in.
inter*sum*, I am in the midst of.
prae*sum*, I am at the head of.
sub*sum*, I am under.
super*sum*, I am above.

The following have a slight change in the prefix:

ab*sum*, **af***ui* (**a***futurus*, **a***fore*), **ab***esse*, I am away, absent.
ad*sum*, **ad***fui*, and **af***fui*, **ad***esse*, I am present.
ob*sum*, **of***fui*, **ob***esse*, I am in the way, hurtful.
pro*sum*, **pro***fui*, **prod***esse*, I am useful.

Wherever, in *prosum*, the verb *sum* begins with a vowel, the letter **d** is prefixed to the verb (§ 185, note, *a*); as,

Pro*sum*, **prod***es*, **prod***est*, **pro***sumus*, **prod***estis*, **pro***sunt*; also, **prod***eram*, **prod***essem*, **prod***ero*, **prod***es*, **prod***esse*; but **pro***fui*, **pro** *futurus*.

For *possum*, *vide* § 138.

2. Neither *sum* nor any of its compounds has a present participle, except *praesens*, present, and *absens*, absent.

3. The personal pronouns, I, thou (you), he, she, it, we, you, they, are expressed in Latin, or joined to the verb, only when they are emphasized; as, thou hast been present, not I, **tu** *adfuisti*, *non* **ego**.

Fore and *forem*, *vide* § 153. Antiquated forms, ***siem***, ***sies***, ***siet***, ***sient***, for *sim*, *sis*, etc. They may be used in the solemn style.

CHAPTER XVI.

THE REGULAR CONJUGATIONS.

§ 75.

There are in Latin four conjugations, distinguished by the endings of the infinitive present. They are:

First Conj.	Second Conj.	Third Conj.	Fourth Conj.
āre, *laud*-**āre,** to praise.	**ēre,** *mon*-**ēre,** to advise.	**ĕre,** *leg*-**ĕre,** to read.	**īre,** *aud*-**īre,** to hear.

2. In order to conjugate a verb, the four roots or principal parts of the verb must be known. These are, *Present Indicative*, *Perfect Indicative*, *Supine* and *Present Infinitive*. From these all the other tenses are formed.

The four endings are as follows:

Present Ind.	Perfect Ind.	Supine.	Present Inf.
I. **ō** (from *ao*), *laud*-**o.**	**āvi,** *laud*-**āvi.**	**ātum,** *laud*-**ātum.**	**āre,** *laud*-**āre.**
II. **eo,** *mŏn*-**eo.**	**ui,** *mon*-**ui.**	**ĭtum,** *mon*-**ĭtum.**	**ēre,** *mon*-**ēre.**
III. **o,** *lĕg*-**o.**	**i,** *lēg*-**i.**	**tum,** *lec*-**tum.**	**ĕre,** *leg*-**ĕre.**
IV. **io,** *aud*-**io.**	**īvi,** *aud*-**īvi.**	**ītum,** *aud*-**ītum.**	**īre,** *aud*-**īre.**

Note.—The first conjugation contains over 1000 verbs; the second about 150, the third 800, and the fourth 100.

§ 76.

I. There are four methods or rules for obtaining the perfect:

1. Formation by the *characteristic* **v** or **u** (**v** wherever a vowel, and **u** wherever a consonant precedes); as, *lauda-***v***-i; dele-***v***-i; audi-***v***-i; dom-***u***-i; doc-***u***-i; col-***u***-i.*

2. Formation by the *characteristic* **s**, (besides modifications produced on the consonants preceding; *cfr.*, Note 2); as, *man-***s***-i; ar-***s***-i* (for *ard-***s***-i*); *di-***x***-i* (for *dic-***s***-i*); *te-***x***-i* (for *teg-***s***-i*); *mul-***s***-i* (for *mulc-***s***-i*).

3. Formation by lengthening the *root-vowel;* as, *adi-***ū***-vi*, from *adiŭvo; vīdi* from *vĭdeo; lēgi* from *lĕgo; vēni* from *vĕnio.*

4. Formation by *reduplication; i. e.*, repeating the first consonant and the vowel which follows it, (if this is **a** or **ae** then **e** is substituted); as, **tŏ***-tondi* from *tondeo;* **cŭ***-curri* from *curro;* **cĕ***-cīdi* from *cado.*

Spondeo has *spo-pondi; disco, didici; sto, stĕti* (the last from *sta-o*, like *dĕdi* from *da-o;* § 78, note 1, *d*). In the compounds, however, the reduplication disappears; as, *detondeo*, perf. *detondi;* but it is retained in the compounds of *do, sto, sisto, posco*, and *disco;* sometimes also in those of *curro.*

II. The supines formerly had only the ending **tum**, which has often been changed into **sum**.

1. The supines in all the conjugations end mostly, (and in the first without a single exception), in **tum**.

2. In the second and third conjugation, the supine usually ends in **sum**, when the verbal root terminates with **d, t, rg**; as, *ar-***sum** from *ard-eo; mis-***sum** from *mitt-o; ter-***sum** from *terg-eo; mer-***sum** from *merg-o.*

Changes from the *present-root* in the perfect and supine·

NOTE 1. In the perfects, with **v** or **u**, the verbal root remains unchanged; the *characteristic* of the conjugation is sometimes kept, sometimes rejected; as, *am-***ā***-vi, mon-***ui**.

NOTE 2. The following *consonant*-modifications take place in the perfects in **si**, and the supines in **sum** and **tum**:

1. The letter **b** before *s* or *t* becomes **p**; as, *scribo, scri-***p***-si, scri-***p***-tum, scrĭbere.*

2. A guttural, followed by **s** becomes **x**; followed by **t**, it becomes **c**; as, *dico, di-***x***-i, dictum, dicere; te-g-o, te-***x***-i, te-***c***-tum, tegere; co-***qu***-o, co-***x***-i, co-***c***-tum, coquere;* so, also, *traho, tra-***x***-i, tra-***c***-tum, trahere;* and *veho, ve-***x***-i, ve-***c***-tum, vehere.* The same occurs in *vivo, vixi, victum, vivere; struo (struvo), struxi, structum, struere; fluo (fluvo), fluxi, fluxum, fluere.* But if the guttural **c** or **g** is preceded by **l** or **r**, then the guttural is dropped before **si**, **sum**, and **tum**; as, *fulcio,* **fulsi, fultum,** *fulcire; mergo, mersi, mersum, mergere.*

3. A dental is rejected before **s**; as, *claudo,* **clausi,** *clausum, claudere;* the preceding vowel becomes long; as, *divido, divisi, divisum, dividere;* sometimes the **s** is doubled; as, *concutio,* **concussi, concussum,** *concutere.*

4. The letter **p** is often inserted after **m**, before **si** and **tum**; as, *sumo,* **sumpsi, sumptum,** *sumere.*

Note 3. When the present has been strengthened by the insertion of **n** (**m**), the perfect and the supine reject this letter which does not really belong to the root of the verb; as, *vinco,* **vici, victum,** *vincere; frango,* **fregi, fractum,** *frangere; fundo,* **fudi, fusum,** *fundere; relinquo,* **reliqui, relictum,** *relinquere;* (*rumpo,* **rupi, ruptum,** *rumpere*).

§ 77.

From the four principal parts (primary tenses) all the other tenses are formed in the following manner:

I. From the present indicative are formed five tenses:

	I.	II.	III. IV.
	by changing ō into		
1) Imperfect indicative,	**ābam,**	**bam,**	**ēbam.**
2) First future indicative,	**ābo,**	**bo,**	**am.**
3) Present subjunctive,	**em,**	**am,**	**am.**
4) Present participle,	**ans,**	**ns,**	**ens.**
5) Gerund (fut. part. pass.),	**andi,**	**ndi,**	**endi.**

	I.	II.	III.	IV.
Thus, 1)	*laud*-**ābam,**	*monē*-**bam,**	*leg*-**ēbam,**	*audi*-**ēbam.**
2)	*laud*-**ābo,**	*monē*-**bo,**	*leg*-**am,**	*audi*-**am.**
3)	*laud*-**em,**	*monĕ*-**am,**	*leg*-**am,**	*audi*-**am.**
4)	*laud*-**ans,**	*mone*-**ns,**	*leg*-**ens,**	*audi*-**ens.**
5)	*laud*-**andi** (**andus**),	*mone*-**ndi** (**ndus**),	*leg*-**endi** (**endus**),	*audi*-**endi** (**endus**)

II. From the perfect indicative active are formed five tenses:

1) Pluperfect indicative active, by changing **i** into **ĕram.**
2) Future perfect, " " **ĕro.**
3) Perfect subjunctive, " " **ĕrim.**
4) Pluperfect subjunctive, " " **issem.**
5) Perfect infinitive, " " **isse.**

	I.	II.	III.	IV.
Thus, 1)	*laudav*-**eram,**	*monu*-**eram,**	*leg*-**eram,**	*audiv*-**eram.**
2)	*laudav*-**ero,**	*monu*-**ero,**	*leg*-**ero,**	*audiv*-**ero.**
3)	*laudav*-**erim,**	*monu*-**erim,**	*leg*-**erim,**	*audiv*-**erim.**
4)	*laudav*-**issem,**	*monu*-**issem,**	*leg*-**issem,**	*audiv*-**issem.**
5)	*laudav*-**isse,**	*monu*-**isse,**	*leg*-**isse,**	*audiv*-**isse.**

III. From the supine are formed three tenses:

1. The future participle active by changing **m** into **rus**; as, *laudatū*-**rus** (*a, um*), *monitū*-**rus,** *lectū*-**rus,** *auditū*-**rus.**

NOTE.—The following future participles are formed not from the existing, but from a supposed *regular* supine: as, **iuvaturus,** *secaturus, sonaturus, luiturus, abnuiturus, pariturus, ruiturus,* **moriturus, nasciturus,** and **oriturus**; from *lavo* only **lavaturus,** and *fruor, fruiturus;* cfr. § 108.

2. The perfect participle by changing **m** into **s**; as, *laudātus, a, um, monĭtus, lectus, audītus.*

NOTE.—The perf. and pluper. ind. and subj. and fut. perf. are formed by adding to the perfect participle the tenses of **esse**; as, *laudatus* (*a, um*) *sum, sim, eram, essem, ero,* etc.

3. The future infinitive passive is formed by adding to the supine **iri** [pass. inf. of *ire*, to go]; as, *laudatum iri, monitum iri, lectum iri, auditum iri.*

IV. From the pres. infinitive are formed four tenses:

1. The present imperative active by dropping **re**; as *laudā, monē, legĕ, audī.*

2. The imperfect subjunctive active by adding **m**; as, *laudārem, monērem, legĕrem, audīrem.*

3. The present infinitive passive by changing **e** into **i**, except for the third conjugation, where **ĕre** is changed into **i**; as, *laudāri, monēri, legi, audīri.*

4. The imperative present passive, which is simply the form of the present infinitive active; as, *laudāre*, *monēre*, *legĕre*, *audīre*.

V. The active tenses, ending in **o**, become passive by adding **r**, those in **m** by changing this letter into **r**. The compound tenses are excepted.

Synopsis.

*Laud***o** (*laud***or**),	*laudav***i**,	*laudat***um**,	*laud***are**.
*laud***em** (*laud***er**),	*laudav***erim**,	*laudat***urus**,	*laud***a**.
*laud***abam** (*laud***abar**),	*laudav***eram**,	*laudat***us**,	*laud***arem**.
*laud***abo** (*laud***abor**),	*laudav***issem**,	*laudat***us sum**,	(*laud***arer**.)
*laud***ans**,	*laudav***ero**,	(*eram*, *ero*),	*laud***ari**.
*laud***andus**,	*laudav***isse**,	*laudat***um iri**,	*laud***are**.

§78.

PERSONAL TERMINATIONS.

I. Indicative and Subjunctive Active.

	First Person.	Second Person.	Third Person.
Sing.	**o, m, i,**	**(i)s (sti),**	**(i)t.**
Plur.	**(ĭ)mus,**	**(ĭ)tis (stis),**	**(u)nt (ērunt).**

II. Indicative and Subjunctive Passive.

	First Person.	Second Person.	Third Person.
Sing.	**r,**	**(ĕ)ris,**	**(ĭ)tur.**
Plur.	**(ĭ)mur,**	**(ĭ)mĭni,**	**(u)ntur.**

III. Imperative.

		A. Active.		B. Passive.	
		Second Per.	Third Per.	Second Per.	Third Per.
Sing.	Pres.,	**ā, ē, ĕ, ī,**	——	**(ĕ)re,**	——
	Fut.,	**(ĭ)to,**	**(ĭ)to,**	**(ĭ)tor,**	**(ĭ)tor.**
Plur.	Pres.,	**(ĭ)te,**	——	**(ĭ)mĭni,**	——
	Fut.,	**(ĭ)tōte,**	**(u)nto,**	——	**(u)ntor.**

1. In the inflection of the verb, distinguish the following elements or parts:

a) The *root* of the verb; **laud**, root of *laudo;* **mon**, root of *moneo*.

b) The *characteristic* of the verb, which in the first conjugation is **a**; in the second, **e**; in the fourth, **i**; the third has none.

c) The *connecting vowel* is a short vowel which serves as a link between the root and the termination. It is mostly **i**, sometimes **ĕ**; and before **nt, u**. This is pointed out above in the paradigm by the parentheses.

d) The *termination*. The termination and connecting vowel remain unchanged only in the third conjugation. In *leg-ĕ-re*, the root is **leg**; the connecting-vowel, **ĕ**; and the termination, **re**. In the other conjugations, the connecting-vowel is blended with the characteristic, except the **u** after **i**. Thus, *amāre* from *ama-ĕre*, *amo* from *ama-o*, *amas* from *ama-is*, *amăt* from *ama-it*, etc.; likewise, *monēmus* from *mone-imus*, *audimus* from *audi-imus*, *monent* from *mone-unt;* but *audiunt*, *legunt*.

e) The *tense-sign*, by which the tense is known. Thus *laudabam* is recognized as the imperfect indicative from **ba**; *laudavi* as perfect from **v**.

Hence in *aud-i-v-i-t*, the root is **aud**; the characteristic of the fourth conj., **i**; the tense-sign of the perfect, **v**; the connecting vowel, **i**; and the third personal ending **t**.

2. In parsing a verb, proceed in this manner: 1, person; 2, number; 3, tense; 4, mood; 5, voice; as, *laudaremini*, second person, plural, imperfect, subjunctive, passive.

CHAP.

VIEW OF THE FOUR

I. AC-

§

A. INDI.

PRESENT.

	First Conjugation.	*Second Conjugation.*
S. 1.	*laud*-**o,** I praise.	*mŏn*-**ĕo,** I advise.
2.	*laud*-**ās,**	*mŏn*-**ēs,**
3.	*laud*-**at,**	*mŏn*-**et,**
P. 1.	*laud*-**āmus,**	*mon*-**ēmus,**
2.	*laud*-**ātis,**	*mon*-**ētis,**
3.	*laud*-**ant.**	*mŏn*-**ent.**

IMPERFECT.

S. 1.	*laud*-**ābam,** I was praising, I praised.	*mŏn*-**ēbam,** I was advising, I advised.
2.	*laud*-**ābas,**	*mon*-**ēbas,**
3.	*laud*-**ābat,**	*mon*-**ēbat,**
P. 1.	*laud*-**abāmus,**	*mon*-**ebāmus,**
2.	*laud*-**abātis,**	*mon*-**ebātis,**
3.	*laud*-**ābant.**	*mon*-**ēbant.**

FUTURE.

S. 1.	*laud*-**ābo,** I shall praise.	*mŏn*-**ēbo,** I shall advise.
2.	*laud*-**ābis,**	*mon*-**ēbis,**
3.	*laud*-**ābit,**	*mon*-**ēbit,**
P. 1.	*laud*-**ābĭmus,**	*mon*-**ēbĭmus,**
2.	*laud*-**ābĭtis,**	*mon*-**ēbĭtis,**
3.	*laud*-**ābunt.**	*mon*-**ēbunt.**

PERFECT.

S. 1.	*laud*-**āvi,** I have praised.	*mŏn*-**ŭi,** I have advised.
2.	*laud*-**āvisti,**	*mon*-**uisti,**
3.	*laud*-**āvit,**	*mŏn*-**ŭit,**
P. 1.	*laud*-**āvĭmus,**	*mon*-**uĭmus,**
2.	*laud*-**āvistis,**	*mon*-**uistis,**
3.	*laud*-**āvērunt.**	*mon*-**uērunt.**

TER XVII.

CONJUGATIONS.

TIVE.

79.

CATIVE.

PRESENT.

Third Conjugation.	*Fourth Conjugation.*
lĕg-**o**, I read.	*aud*-**ĭo**, I hear.
lĕg-**ĭs**,	*aud*-**īs**,
lĕg-**it**,	*aud*-**it**,
lĕg-**ĭmus**,	*aud*-**īmus**,
lĕg-**ĭtis**,	*aud*-**ītis**,
lĕg-**unt**.	*aud*-**ĭunt**.

IMPERFECT.

lĕg-**ēbam**, I was reading, I read.	*aud*-**iēbam**, I was hearing, I heard.
leg-**ēbas**,	*aud*-**iēbas**,
leg-**ēbat**,	*aud*-**iēbat**,
leg-**ebāmus**,	*aud*-**iebāmus**,
leg-**ebātis**,	*aud*-**iebātis**,
leg-**ēbant**.	*aud*-**iēbant**.

FUTURE.

lĕg-**am**, I shall read.	*aud*-**ĭam**, I shall hear.
lĕg-**ēs**,	*aud*-**ĭēs**,
lĕg-**ĕt**,	*aud*-**ĭet**,
leg-**ēmus**,	*aud*-**iēmus**,
leg-**ētis**,	*aud*-**iētis**,
lĕg-**ent**.	*aud*-**ĭent**.

PERFECT.

lēg-**i**, I have read.	*aud*-**īvi**, I have heard.
lēg-**isti**,	*aud*-**īvisti**,
lēg-**it**,	*aud*-**īvit**,
lēg-**ĭmus**,	*aud*-**īvĭmus**,
lēg-**istis**,	*aud*-**īvistis**,
lēg-**ērunt**.	*aud*-**ivērunt**.

Pluperfect.

S. 1.	*laud*-**āvĕram**, I had [praised.	*mon*-**uĕram**, I had advised.
2.	*laud*-**āvĕras**,	*mon*-**uĕras**,
3.	*laud*-**āvĕrat**,	*mon*-**uĕrat**,
P. 1.	*laud*-**avĕrāmus**,	*mon*-**uĕrāmus**,
2.	*laud*-**avĕrātis**,	*mon*-**uĕrātis**,
3.	*laud*-**āvĕrant**.	*mon*-**uĕrant**.

Future Perfect.

S. 1.	*laud*-**āvĕro**, I shall have [praised.	*mon*-**uĕro**, I shall have ad- [vised.
2.	*laud*-**āvĕris**,	*mon*-**uĕris**,
3.	*laud*-**āvĕrit**,	*mon*-**uĕrit**,
P. 1.	*laud*-**avĕrĭmus**,	*mon*-**uĕrĭmus**,
2.	*laud*-**avĕrĭtis**,	*mon*-**uĕrĭtis**,
3.	*laud*-**āvĕrint**.	*mon*-**uĕrint**.

§

B. SUB-

Present.

S. 1.	*laud*-**em**, I may praise.	*mŏn*-**ĕam**, I may advise.
2.	*laud*-**ēs**,	*mŏn*-**eās**,
3.	*laud*-**et**,	*mŏn*-**ĕat**,
P. 1.	*laud*-**ēmus**,	*mon*-**eāmus**,
2.	*laud*-**ētis**,	*mon*-**eātis**,
3.	*laud*-**ent**.	*mŏn*-**ĕant**.

Imperfect.

S. 1.	*laud*-**ārem**, I might praise.	*mŏn*-**ērem**, I might advise.
2.	*laud*-**āres**,	*mon*-**ēres**,
3.	*laud*-**āret**,	*mon*-**ēret**,
P. 1.	*laud*-**arēmus**,	*mon*-**erēmus**,
2.	*laud*-**arētis**,	*mon*-**erētis**,
3.	*laud*-**ārent**.	*mon*-**ērent**.

Perfect.

S. 1.	*laud*-**āvĕrim**, I may have [praised.	*mŏn*-**uĕrim**, I may have ad [vised
2.	*laud*-**āvĕris**,	*mon*-**uĕris**,
3.	*laud*-**āvĕrit**,	*mon*-**uĕrit**,
P. 1.	*laud*-**avĕrĭmus**,	*mon*-**uĕrĭmus**,
2.	*laud*-**avĕrĭtis**,	*mon*-**uĕrĭtis**,
3.	*laud*-**āvĕrint**.	*mon*-**uĕrint**.

PLUPERFECT.

lēg-**ĕram**, I had read.	*aud*-**īvĕram**, I had heard.
lēg-**ĕras**,	*aud*-**īvĕras**,
lēg-**ĕrat**,	*aud*-**īvĕrat**,
lēg-**erāmus**,	*aud*-**iverāmus**,
lēg-**erātis**,	*aud*-**iverātis**,
lēg-**ĕrant**.	*aud*-**īvĕrant**.

FUTURE PERFECT.

lēg-**ĕro**, I shall have read.	*aud*-**īvĕro**, I shall have heard.
lēg-**ĕris**,	*aud*-**īvĕris**,
lēg-**ĕrit**,	*aud*-**īvĕrit**,
lēg-**ĕrĭmus**,	*aud*-**ivĕrĭmus**,
lēg-**ĕrĭtis**,	*aud*-**ivĕrĭtis**,
lēg-**ĕrint**.	*aud*-**īvĕrint**.

80.

JUNCTIVE.

PRESENT.

lĕg-**am**, I may read.	*aud*-**ĭam**, I may hear.
lĕg-**ās**,	*aud*-**iās**,
lĕg-**at**,	*aud*-**iat**,
leg-**āmus**,	*aud*-**iāmus**,
leg-**ātis**,	*aud*-**iātis**,
lĕg-**ant**.	*aud*-**ĭant**.

IMPERFECT.

lĕg-**ĕrem**, I might read.	*aud*-**īrem**, I might hear.
lĕg-**ĕres**,	*aud*-**īres**,
lĕg-**ĕret**,	*aud*-**īret**,
leg-**erēmus**,	*aud*-**irēmus**,
leg-**erētis**,	*aud*-**irētis**,
lĕg-**ĕrent**.	*aud*-**īrent**,

PERFECT.

lēg-**ĕrim**, I may have read.	*aud*-**īvĕrim**, I may have heard.
leg-**ĕris**,	*aud*-**īvĕris**,
leg-**ĕrit**,	*aud*-**īvĕrit**,
leg-**ĕrĭmus**,	*aud*-**ivĕrĭmus**,
leg-**ĕrĭtis**,	*aud*-**ivĕrĭtis**,
leg-**ĕrint**.	*aud*-**īvĕrint**.

PLUPERFECT.

S. 1.	*laud*-**āvissem,** I might have [praised.	*mŏn*-**uissem,** I might have [advised.
2.	*laud*-**avissēs,**	*mon*-**uissēs,**
3.	*laud*-**avisset,**	*mon*-**uisset,**
P. 1.	*laud*-**avissēmus,**	*mon*-**uissēmus,**
2.	*laud*-**avissētis,**	*mon*-**uissētis,**
3.	*laud*-**avissent.**	*mon*-**uissent.**

FUTURE.

S. 1. 2. 3.	*laud*-**ātūrus** (*a, um*)	*sim*, I may be *sis*, [about to *sit*, [praise.	*mŏn*-**ītūrus** (*a, um*)	*sim*, I may be *sis*, [about to *sit*, [advise.
P. 1. 2. 3.	*laud*-**ātūri** (*ae, a*)	*simus*, *sitis*, *sint*.	*mon*-**itūri** (*ae, a*)	*simus*, *sitis*, *sint*.

FUTURE PERFECT

§

C. IMPER-

PRESENT.

S. 2.	*laud*-**ā,** praise thou.	*mŏn*-**ē,** advise thou.
P. 2.	*laud*-**āte,** praise ye.	*mon*-**ēte,** advise ye.

FUTURE.

S. 2.	*laud*-**āto,** thou shalt pr.	*mon*-**ēto,** thou shalt advise.
3.	*laud*-**āto,** he shall praise.	*mon*-**ēto,** he shall advise.
P. 2.	*laud*-**atōte,** ye shall pr.	*mon*-**etōte,** ye shall advise.
3.	*laud*-**anto,** they shall pr.	*mon*-**ento,** they shall advise.

§

D. INFIN-

PRESENT.

aud-**āre,** to praise. *mŏn*-**ēre,** to advise.

PERFECT.

aud-**āvisse,** to have praised. *mon*-**uisse,** to have advised.

FUTURE.

S. *laud*-**ātūrum** (*am, um*) **esse,** to be about to praise. *mon*-**ītūrum** (*am, um*) **esse,** to be about to advise.

P. *laud*-**aturos** (*as, a*) **esse.** *mon*-**ituros** (*as, a*) **esse.**

PLUPERFECT.

lĕg-**issem**, I might have read.	*aud*-**īvissem**, I might have heard.
leg-**issēs**,	*aud*-**īvissēs**,
leg-**isset**,	*aud*-**īvisset**,
leg-**issēmus**,	*aud*-**īvissēmus**,
leg-**issētis**,	*aud*-**īvissētis**,
leg-**issent**.	*aud*-**īvissent**.

FUTURE.

lec-**tūrus** (*a*, *um*)	*sim*, I may be about read. *sis*, *sit*,	*aud*-**ītūrus** (*a*, *um*)	*sim*, I may be about to hear. *sis*, *sit*,
lec-**tūri** (*ae*, *a*)	*simus*, *sitis*, *sint*.	*aud*-**itūri** (*ae*, *a*)	*simus*, *sitis*, *sint*.

is wanting.

81.

ATIVE.

PRESENT.

lĕg-**ĕ**, read thou.	*aud*-**ī**, hear thou.
leg-**ĭte**, read ye.	*aud*-**īte**, hear ye.

FUTURE.

leg-**ĭto**, thou shalt read.	*aud*-**īto**, thou shalt hear.
leg-**ĭto**, he shall read.	*aud*-**īto**, he shall hear.
leg-**ĭtōte**, ye shall read.	*aud*-**ītōte**, ye shall hear.
leg-**unto**, they shall read.	*aud*-**iunto**, they shall hear.

82.

ITIVE.

PRESENT.

lĕg-**ĕre**, to read.	*aud*-**īre**, to hear.

PERFECT.

lēg-**isse**, to have read.	*aud*-**īvisse**, to have heard.

FUTURE.

lec-**tūrum** (*am*, *um*) **esse**, to be about to read.	*aud*-**ītūrum** (*am*, *um*) **esse**, to be about to hear.
lec-**turos** (*as*, *a*) **esse**,	*aud*-**ituros** (*as*, *a*) **esse**.

§

E. PAR-

PRESENT.

laud-**ans**, praising. *mŏn*-**ens**, advising.

FUTURE.

laud-**ātūrus** (*a*, *um*), about to praise. *mŏn*-**ītūrus** (*a*, *um*), about to advise.

§

F. GE-

Nom. *laud*-**andum** *est*, it must be praised, it is necessary to praise

Gen.	*laud*-**andi**, of praising.	*mon*-**endi**, of advising.
Dat.	*laud*-**ando**, to praising.	*mon*-**endo**, to advising.
Acc.	(*ad*) *laud*-**andum**, praising.	(*ad*) *mon*-**endum**, advising.
Abl.	*laud*-**ando**, by praising.	*mon*-**endo**, by advising.

§

G. SU-

laud-**ātum**, to praise. *mŏn*-**ĭtum**, to advise.
laud-**ātu**, to praise, to be praised. *mŏn*-**ĭtu**, to advise, to be adv.

II. PAS-

§

A. INDI-

PRESENT.

	First Conjugation.	***Second Conjugation.***
S. 1.	*laud*-**or**, I am praised.	*mŏn*-**ĕor**, I am advised.
2.	*laud*-**āris**,	*mon*-**ēris**,
3.	*laud*-**ātur**,	*mon*-**ētur**,
P. 1.	*laud*-**āmur**,	*mon*-**ēmur**,
2.	*laud*-**āmĭni**,	*mon*-**ēmĭni**,
3.	*laud*-**antur**.	*mon*-**entur**.

83.

TICIPLES.

PRESENT.

lĕg-**ēns**, reading.	*aud*-**iēns**, hearing.

FUTURE.

lec-**tūrus** (*a*, *um*), about to read.	*aud*-**ītūrus** (*a*, *um*), about to hear.

84.

RUND.

(§ 107, note 1).

leg-**endi**, of reading.	*aud*-**iendi**, of hearing.
leg-**endo**, to reading.	*aud*-**iendo**, to hearing.
(*ad*) *leg*-**endum**, reading.	(*ad*) *aud*-**iendum**, hearing.
leg-**endo**, by reading.	*aud*-**iendo**, by hearing.

85.

PINE.

lec-**tum**, to read.	*aud*-**ītum**, to hear.
lec-**tu**, to read, to be read.	*aud*-**ītu**, to hear, to be heard.

SIVE.

86.

CATIVE.

PRESENT.

Third Conjugation.	***Fourth Conjugation.***
lĕg-**or**, I am read.	*aud*-**ior**, I am heard
lĕg-**ĕris**,	*aud*-**īris**,
lĕg-**ĭtur**,	*aud*-**ītur**,
lĕg-**ĭmur**,	*aud*-**īmur**,
leg-**ĭmĭni**,	*aud*-**īmīni**,
leg-**untur**.	*aud*-**iuntur**.

Imperfect.

S. 1.	*laud*-**ābar**, I was praised.	*mon*-**ēbar**, I was advised.
2.	*laud*-**abāris**,	*mon*-**ebāris**,
3.	*laud*-**abātur**,	*mon*-**ebātur**,
P. 1.	*laud*-**abāmur**,	*mon*-**ebāmur**,
2.	*laud*-**abāmĭni**,	*mon*-**ebāmĭni**,
3.	*laud*-**abantur**.	*mon*-**ebantur**.

Future.

S. 1.	*laud*-**ābor**, I shall be praised.	*mon*-**ēbor**, I shall be advised.
2.	*laud*-**āběris**,	*mon*-**ēběris**,
3.	*laud*-**ābĭtur**,	*mon*-**ēbĭtur**,
P. 1.	*laud*-**ābĭmur**,	*mon*-**ēbĭmur**,
2.	*laud*-**abĭmĭni**,	*mon*-**ebĭmĭni**,
3.	*laud*-**abuntur**.	*mon*-**ebuntur**.

Perfect.

S. 1.	*laud*-**ātus**	*sum*, I have been praised.	*mŏn*-**ĭtus**	*sum*, I have been advised.
2.	(*a*, *um*)	*es*,	(*a*, *um*)	*es*,
3.		*est*,		*est*,
P. 1.	*laud*-**āti**	*sumus*,	*mŏn*-**ĭti**	*sumus*,
2.	(*ae*, *a*)	*estis*,	(*ae*, *a*)	*estis*,
3.		*sunt*,		*sunt*.

Pluperfect.

S. 1.	*laud*-**ātus**	*eram*, I had been praised.	*mŏn*-**ĭtus**	*eram*, I had been advised.
2.	(*a*, *um*)	*eras*,	(*a*, *um*)	*eras*,
3.		*erat*,		*erat*,
P. 1.	*laud*-**āti**	*eramus*,	*mŏn*-**ĭti**	*eramus*,
2.	(*ae*, *a*)	*eratis*,	(*ae*, *a*)	*eratis*,
3.		*erant*.		*erant*,

Future Perfect.

S. 1.	*laud*-**ātus**	*ero*, I shall have been praised.	*mŏn*-**ĭtus**	*ero*, I shall have been advised.
2.	(*a*, *um*)	*eris*,	(*a*, *um*)	*eris*,
3.		*erit*,		*erit*,
P. 1.	*laud*-**āti**	*erimus*,	*mŏn*-**ĭti**	*erimus*,
2.	(*ae*, *a*)	*eritis*,	(*ae*, *a*)	*eritis*,
3.		*erunt*.		*erunt*.

IMPERFECT.

leg-**ēbar**, I was read.	*aud*-**iēbar**, I was heard.
leg-**ebāris**,	*aud*-**iebāris**,
leg-**ebātur**,	*aud*-**iebātur**,
leg-**ebāmur**,	*aud*-**iebāmur**,
leg-**ebāmĭni**,	*aud*-**iebāmĭni**,
leg-**ebantur**.	*aud*-**iebantur**.

FUTURE.

lĕg-**ar**, I shall be read.	*aud*-**iar**, I shall be heard.
leg-**ēris**,	*aud*-**iēris**,
leg-**ētur**,	*aud*-**iētur**,
leg-**ēmur**,	*aud*-**iēmur**,
leg-**ēmĭni**,	*aud*-**iēmĭni**,
leg-**entur**.	*aud*-**ientur**.

PERFECT.

lec-**tus**	*sum*, I have been read.	*aud*-**ītus**	*sum*, I have been heard.
(*a*, *um*)	*es*,	(*a*, *um*)	*es*,
	est,		*est*,
lec-**ti**	*sumus*,	*aud*-**īti**	*sumus*,
(*ae*, *a*)	*estis*,	(*ae*, *a*)	*estis*,
	sunt.		*sunt*.

PLUPERFECT.

lec-**tus**	*eram*, I had been read.	*aud*-**ītus**	*eram*, I had been heard.
(*a*, *um*)	*eras*,	(*a*, *um*)	*eras*,
	erat,		*erat*.
lec-**ti**	*eramus*,	*aud*-**īti**	*eramus*,
(*ae*, *a*)	*eratis*,	(*ae*, *a*)	*eratis*,
	erant.		*erant*.

FUTURE PERFECT.

lec-**tus**	*ero*, I shall have been read.	*aud*-**ītus**	*ero*, I shall have been heard.
(*a*, *um*)	*eris*,	(*a*, *um*)	*eris*,
	erit,		*erit*,
lec-**ti**	*erimus*,	*aud*-**īti**	*erimus*,
(*ae*, *a*)	*eritis*,	(*ae*, *a*)	*eritis*,
	erunt.		*erunt*.

§

B. SUB-

PRESENT.

S. 1.	*laud*-**er**, I may be praised	*mon*-**ĕar**, I may be advised.
2.	*laud*-**ēris**,	*mon*-**eāris**,
3.	*laud*-**ētur**,	*mon*-**eātur**,
P. 1.	*laud*-**ēmur**,	*mon*-**eāmur**,
2.	*laud*-**ēmĭni**,	*mon*-**eāmĭni**,
3.	*laud*-**entur**.	*mon*-**eantur**.

IMPERFECT.

S. 1.	*laud*-**ārer**, I might be [praised.	*mon*-**ērer**, I might be advised.
2.	*laud*-**arēris**,	*mon*-**erēris**,
3.	*laud*-**arētur**,	*mon*-**erētur**,
P. 1.	*laud*-**arēmur**,	*mon*-**erēmur**,
2.	*laud*-**arēmĭni**,	*mon*-**erēmĭni**,
3.	*laud*-**arentur**.	*mon*-**erentur**.

PERFECT.

S. 1. 2. 3.	*laud*-**ātus** (*a*, *um*)	*sim*, I may have *sis*, [been *sit*, [praised.	*mŏn*-**ĭtus** (*a*, *um*)	*sim*, I may have *sis*, [been advised. *sit*,
P. 1. 2. 3.	*laud*-**āti** (*ae*, *a*)	*simus*, *sitis*, *sint*,	*mŏn*-**ĭti** (*ae*, *a*)	*simus*, *sitis*, *sint*.

PLUPERFECT.

S. 1. 2. 3.	*laud*-**ātus** (*a*, *um*)	*essem*, I might *esses*, [have been *esset*, [praised.	*mŏn*-**ĭtus** (*a*, *um*)	*essem*, I might have *esses*, [been ad- *esset*, [vised.
P. 1. 2. 3.	*laud*-**āti** (*ae*, *a*)	*essemus*, *essetis*, *essent*.	*mŏn*-**ĭti** (*ae*, *a*)	*essemus*, *essetis*, *essent*.

FUTURE and FUTURE

87.

JUNCTIVE.

PRESENT.

lĕg-**ar**, I may be read.	*aud*-**iar**, I may be heard.
leg-**āris**,	*aud*-**iāris**,
leg-**ātur**,	*aud*-**iātur**,
leg-**āmur**,	*aud*-**iāmur**,
leg-**āmĭni**,	*aud*-**iāmĭni**,
leg-**antur**.	*aud*-**iantur**.

IMPERFECT.

lĕg-**ĕrer**, I might be read.	*aud*-**īrer**, I might be heard.
leg-**erēris**,	*aud*-**irēris**,
leg-**erētur**,	*aud*-**irētur**,
leg-**erēmur**,	*aud*-**irēmur**,
leg-**erēmĭni**,	*aud*-**irēmĭni**,
leg-**erentur**.	*aud*-**irentur**.

PERFECT.

lec-**tus** (*a*, *um*)	*sim*, I may have been read. *sis*, *sit*,	*aud*-**ītus** (*a*, *um*)	*sim*, I may have been heard. *sis*, *sit*,
lec-**ti** (*ae*, *a*)	*simus*, *sitis*, *sint*.	*aud*-**īti** (*ae*, *a*)	*simus*, *sitis*, *sint*.

PLUPERFECT.

lec-**tus** (*a*, *um*)	*essem*, I might have been read. *esses*, *esset*,	*aud*-**ītus** (*a*, *um*)	*essem*, I might have been heard. *esses*, *esset*,
lec-**ti** (*ae*, *a*)	*essemus*, *essetis*, *essent*.	*aud*-**īti** (*ae*, *a*)	*essemus*, *essetis*, *essent*.

PERFECT are wanting.

§

C. IMPER

PRESENT.

S. 2.	*laud*-**āre**, be thou praised.	*mon*-**ēre**, be thou advised.
P. 2.	*laud*-**āmĭni**, be ye praised.	*mon*-**ēmĭni**, be ye advised.

FUTURE.

S. 2.	*laud*-**ātor**, thou shalt be praised.	*mon*-**ētor**, thou shalt be advised.
3.	*laud*-**ātor**, he shall be praised.	*mon*-**ētor**, he shall be advised.
P. 2.	—— instead: *laudabĭmini.*	—— instead: *monebĭmĭni.*
3.	*laud*-**antor**, they shall be praised.	*mon*-**entor**, they shall be advised.

§

D. INFIN-

PRESENT.

laud-**āri**, to be praised.	*mon*-**ēri**, to be advised.

PERFECT.

S.	*laud*-**ātum** (*am*, *um*) **esse**, to have been praised.	*mon*-**ĭtum** (*am*, *um*) **esse**, to have been advised.
P.	*laud*-**ātos** (*as*, *a*) **esse**.	*mon*-**ĭtos** (*as*, *a*) **esse**.

FUTURE.

laud-**ātum iri**, to be about to be praised.	*mon*-**ĭtum iri**, to be about to be advised.

§

E. PARTI-

PERFECT.

laud-**ātus** (*a*, *um*), praised, having been praised.	*mŏn*-**ĭtus** (*a*, *um*), advised, having been advised.

FUTURE.

laud-**andus** (*a*, *um*), to be praised.	*mon*-**endus** (*a*, *um*), to be advised.

88.

ATIVE.

PRESENT.

lĕg-**ĕre**, be thou read. *aud*-**īre**, be thou heard.

leg-**imini**, be ye read. *aud*-**imini**, be ye heard.

FUTURE.

lĕg-**ĭtor**, thou shalt be read. *aud*-**ītor**, thou shalt be heard.

leg-**itor**, he shall be read. *aud*-**ītor**, he shall be heard.

—— instead: *legĕmini*. —— instead: *audiēmini*.

leg-**untor**, they shall be read. *aud*-**iuntor**, they shall be heard.

89.

ITIVE.

PRESENT.

lĕg-**ī**, to be read. *aud*-**īri**, to be heard.

PERFECT.

lec-**tum** (*am*, *um*) **esse**, to have been read. *aud*-**ītum** (*am*, *um*) **esse**, to have been heard.

lec-**tos** (*as*, *a*) **esse**. *aud*-**ītos** (*as*, *a*) **esse**.

FUTURE.

lec-**tum iri**, to be about to be read. *aud*-**ītum iri**, to be about to be heard.

90.

CIPLES.

PERFECT.

lec-**tus** (*a*, *um*), read, having been read. *aud*-**ītus** (*a*, *um*), heard, having been heard.

FUTURE.

leg-**endus** (*a*, *um*), to be read. *aud*-**iendus** (*a*, *um*), to be heard.

§ 91.

Words for Exercise.

First Conjugation.

1. *Aestimo*, I value.
ămo, love.
ăro, plough.
certo, struggle.
clāmo, shout.
creo, create, elect.
dico, dedicate.
erro, mistake, err.
flagro, burn.
flo, blow.
lănio, mangle.
lātro, bark.
lēgo, send.
mando, enjoin.
migro, wander.
narro, tell, relate.
nĕgo, deny, refuse.
no, swim.
opto, desire.
orno, adorn.
păro, prepare.
pecco, sin, fail.
plōro, weep.
porto, carry.
pŭto, think, judge.
rŏgo, ask, beseech.
servo, save, protect, observe.
sūdo, sweat.
vŏlo, fly.
vŏro, devour.

2. *Accūso*, I accuse.
armo, arm, equip.
consīdĕro, look at carefully.
cŏrōno, crown, wreathe.
crŭcio, torment.
cūro, take care of, care.
damno, condemn.
dōno, present.
ēmendo, improve.
formo, shape, prepare.
fŭgo, put to flight.
hŏnōro, honor.
hŭmo, inter.
indĭco, disclose, show.
iūdico, decide, hold.
iūro, swear, take an oath.
lăbōro, toil, suffer.
lăcrimo, weep, lament.
lŏco, place, put.
măcŭlo, stain.
mendico, beg.
mīlito, am a soldier.
ministro, serve, provide.
monstro, show, point out.
nĕco, kill.
nōmino, call, name.
nŭmĕro, count.
nuntio, report, announce.
ordino, arrange.
ŏnĕro, burden, load.
ōro, pray, beseech.
pugno, fight, combat.
regno, reign.
sălūto, greet.
spēro, hope.
tempĕro, govern, moderate.
vēlo, cover, veil.
vŏco, call, name.
vulgo, publish, make known.
vulnĕro, wound.

3. *Aegrōto*, I am sick.
aequo, make equal, compare.
caeco, blind, make dark.
cĕlĕbro, celebrate.
dēbilito, weaken, maim.
declāro, declare.
dŭbito, doubt, hesitate.
dūro, harden, last.
exacerbo, provoke.
festino, hasten.
firmo, strengthen.
foedo, deform, disfigure.
frequento, visit often.
gĕmino, double, pair.
ignōro, am ignorant.
lăcĕro, tear in pieces.
lībĕro, set free.
mātūro, make ripe, hasten.
nūdo, bare, uncover.
orbo, bereave, rob.
prŏbo, examine, approve.
purgo, clean.
sacro, devote.
sāno, cure.
sollicito, disturb.
sŭpĕro, surpass, overtop.
vasto, devastate.
vigilo, watch.

4. *Appello*, address, call.
canto, sing.

cōgito, think.
consulto, consult.
delecto, amuse.
edŭco, educate.
exercito, exercise diligently.
iacto, throw, hurl.
mūto, change, barter.
năto, swim.
occŭpo, occupy, seize.
salto, dance.
sēdo, quiet, calm.
specto, behold, gaze at.
tento, attempt, instigate.
tŏlĕro, tolerate.
tracto, manage.
vexo, torment, injure.

§ 92.

Second Conjugation.

1. *Coërceo*, I restrain, check.
exerceo, exercise, drill.
hăbeo, have, hold.
dēbeo, owe, am bound, must.
praebeo, offer, grant.

2. *Căleo*, I am warm.
căreo, am deprived of.
dŏleo, feel pain, grieve over.
iăceo, lie down,
mĕreo, gain, deserve.
nŏceo, hurt.
păreo, obey, submit to.
plăceo, please.
tăceo, am silent.
terreo, frighten.
văleo, am strong, well, able.

(Chap. xx.)

§ 93.

Third Conjugation.

Emo, ēmi, emptum, emĕre, I buy.
ăgo, ēgi, actum, agĕre, drive, lead, do.
dico, dixi, dictum, dicĕre, say, proclaim.
tĕgo, texi, tectum, tegĕre, cover.

(Chap. xxi.)

§ 94.

Fourth Conjugation.

1. *Condio*, I season, embalm.
custōdio, watch over, protect.
erŭdio, educate, instruct.
impĕdio, hinder.
finio, end, finish.
irrētio, ensnare.
lēnio, render gentle.
mollio, soften.
mūnio, fortify.
nutrio, nourish.
pŏlio, polish.
pūnio, punish.
scio, know.
vestio, dress, clothe.
ēsŭrio, am hungry.
grunnio, grunt.
hinnio, neigh.
mūgio, low, bellow.
servio, serve, am subject to.
tinnio, jingle, tinkle.
vagio, whine, bleat.

2. *Dormio*, I sleep.

(Chap. xxii.)

§

III. DEPO-

The DEPONENT VERB has the *passive form*, but everywhere an *active* like the passive verb. It has, however, besides these 2) the *supine;* 3) the

A. INDI-

PRESENT.

	First Conjugation. *Hortor*, exactly like *laudor*.	Second Conjugation. *Vereor*, exactly like *moneor*
S. 1.	*hort-***or**, I exhort.	*vĕr-***ĕor**, I fear.
2.	*hort-***āris**,	*ver-***ēris**,
3.	*hort-***ātur**,	*ver-***ētur**,
P. 1.	*hort-***āmur**,	*ver-***ēmur**,
2.	*hort-***āmĭni**,	*ver-***ēmĭni**,
3.	*hort-***antur**.	*ver-***entur**.

IMPERFECT.

S. 1.	*hort-***ābar**, I was exhorting, I exhorted.	*ver-***ēbar**, I was fearing, I feared.
2.	*hort-***abāris**,	*ver-***ebāris**,
3.	*hort-***abātur**,	*ver-***ebātur**,
P. 1.	*hort-***abāmur**,	*ver-***ebāmur**,
2.	*hort-***abāmĭni**,	*ver-***ebāmĭni**,
3.	*hort-***abantur**.	*ver-***ebantur**.

FUTURE.

S. 1.	*hort-***ābor**, I shall exhort.	*ver-***ēbor**, I shall fear.
2.	*hort-***abĕris**,	*ver-***ebĕris**,
3.	*hort-***abĭtur**,	*ver-***ebĭtur**,
P. 1.	*hort-***abĭmur**,	*ver-***ebĭmur**,
2.	*hort-***abĭmĭni**,	*ver-***ebĭmĭni**,
3.	*hort-***abuntur**.	*ver-***ebuntur**.

PERFECT.

S. 1.	*hort-***ātus** (*a, um*) **sum**, I have exhorted.	*vĕr-***ĭtus** (*a, um*) **sum**, I have feared.
P. 1.	*hortati* (*ae, a*) *sumus*, we have exhorted.	*veriti*, (*ae, a*) *sumus*, we have feared.

95.

NENT VERBS.

meaning, except for the *participle* in **ndus** (§ 99); it is conjugated exactly forms, 1) the *participles* of the *active* in **ns** and **urus**; *gerund* (cfr. § 104).

CATIVE.

Present.

Third Conjugation.	*Fourth Conjugation.*
Fungor, exactly like *legor.*	*Partior*, exactly like *audior.*
fung-**or**, I perform.	*part*-**ĭor**, I divide.
fung-**ĕris**,	*part*-**īris**,
fung-**ĭtur**,	*part*-**ītur**,
fung-**ĭmur**,	*part*-**īmur**,
fung-**ĭmĭni**,	*part*-**īmĭni**,
fung-**untur.**	*part*-**iuntur.**

Imperfect.

fung-**ēbar**, I was performing, I performed.	*part*-**iēbar**, I was dividing, I divided.
fung-**ebāris**,	*part*-**iebāris**,
fung-**ebātur**,	*part*-**iebātur**,
fung-**ebāmur**,	*part*-**iebāmur**,
fung-**ebāmĭni**,	*part*-**iebāmĭni**,
fung-**ebantur.**	*part*-**iebantur.**

Future.

fung-**ar**, I shall perform.	*part*-**ĭar**, I shall divide.
fung-**ēris**,	*part*-**iēris**,
fung-**ētur**,	*part*-**iētur**,
fung-**ēmur**,	*part*-**iēmur**,
fung-**ēmĭni**,	*part*-**iēmĭni**,
fung-**entur.**	*part*-**ientur.**

Perfect.

func-**tus** (*a*, *um*) **sum**, I have performed.	*part*-**ītus** (*a*, *um*) **sum**, I have divided.
functi (*ae*, *a*) *sumus*, we have performed.	*partiti* (*ae*, *a*) *sumus*, we have divided.

PLUPERFECT.

S. 1. *hort*-**ātus** (*a, um*) **eram,** I had exhorted, etc.	*ver*-**ĭtus** (*a, um*) **eram,** I had feared, etc.

FUTURE PERFECT.

S. 1. *hort*-**ātus** (*a, um*) **ero,** I shall have exhorted, etc.	*ver*-**ĭtus** (*a, um*) **ero,** I shall have feared, etc.

§

B. SUB-

PRESENT.

S. 1. *hort*-**er,** I may exhort.	*ver*-**ĕar,** I may fear.
2. *hort*-**ēris,**	*ver*-**eāris,**
3. *hort*-**ētur,** etc.	*ver*-**eātur,** etc.

IMPERFECT.

S. 1. *hort*-**ārer,** I might ex., etc.	*ver*-**ērer,** I might fear, etc.

PERFECT.

S. 1. *hort*-**ātus** (*a, um*) **sim,** *sis, sit,* I may have exhorted, etc.	*ver*-**ĭtus** (*a, um*) **sim,** *sis, sit,* I may have feared, etc.

PLUPERFECT.

S. 1. *hort*-**ātus** (*a, um*) **essem,** I might have exhorted, etc.	*ver*-**ĭtus** (*a, um*) **essem,** I might have feared, etc.

FUTURE.

S. 1. *hort*-**atūrus** (*a, um*) **sim,** I may be about to exhort, etc.	*ver*-**ĭturus** (*a, um*) **sim,** I may be about to fear, etc.

§

C. IMPER-

PRESENT.

S. 2. *hort*-**āre,** exhort thou.	*ver*-**ēre,** fear thou.
P. 2. *hort*-**āmĭni,** exhort ye.	*ver*-**ēmĭni,** fear ye.

FUTURE.

S. 2. *hort*-**ātor,** thou shalt exh.	*ver*-**ētor,** thou shalt fear.
3. *hort*-**ātor,** he shall exhort.	*ver*-**ētor,** he shall fear.
P. 2. —— instead: *hortabĭmĭni.*	—— instead: *verebĭmĭni.*
3. *hort*-**antor,** they shall exhort.	*ver*-**entor,** they shall fear.

Pluperfect.

func-**tus** (*a, um*) **eram,** I had performed, etc.	*part*-**ītus** (*a, um*) **eram,** I had divided, etc.

Future Perfect.

func-**tus** (*a, um*) **ero,** I shall have performed, etc.	*part*-**ītus** (*a, um*) **ero,** I shall have divided, etc.

96.

JUNCTIVE.

Present.

fung-**ar,** I may perform.	*part*-**iar,** I may divide.
fung-**āris,**	*part*-**iāris,**
fung-**ātur.**	*part*-**iātur.**

Imperfect.

fung-**ĕrer,** I might perform, etc.	*part*-**īrer,** I might divide, etc.

Perfect.

func-**tus** (*a, um*) **sim,** *sis, sit,* I may have performed, etc.	*part*-**ītus** (*a, um*) **sim,** *sis, sit,* I may have divided, etc.

Pluperfect.

func-**tus** (*a, um*) **essem,** I might have performed, etc.	*part*-**ītus** (*a, um*) **essem,** I might have divided, etc.

Future.

func-**tūrus** (*a, um*) **sim,** I may be about to perform, etc.	*part*-**itūrus** (*a, um*) **sim,** I may be about to divide, etc.

97.

ATIVE.

Present.

fung-**ĕre,** perform thou.	*part*-**īre,** divide thou.
fung-**ĭmini,** perform ye.	*part*-**īmini,** divide ye.

Future.

fung-**ĭtor,** thou shalt perform.	*part*-**ītor,** thou shalt divide.
fung-**ĭtor,** he shall perform.	*part*-**ītor,** he shall divide.
—— instead: *fungĭmĭnī.*	—— instead: *partīmĭnī.*
fung-**untor,** they shall perform.	*part*-**iuntor,** they shall divide.

§

D. INFIN-

PRESENT.

hort-**āri**, to exhort. *ver*-**ēri**, to fear.

PERFECT.

S. *hort*-**ātum** (*am*, *um*) **esse**, to have exhorted. *ver*-**ĭtum** (*am*, *um*) **esse, to** have feared.

P. *hort*-**ātos** (*as*, *a*) **esse**. *ver*-**ĭtos** (*as*, *a*) **esse**.

FUTURE.

S. *hort*-**atūrum** (*am*, *um*) **esse**, to be about to exhort. *ver*-**itūrum** (*am*, *um*) **esse, to** be about to fear.

P. *hort*-**aturos** (*as*, *a*) **esse**. *ver*-**ituros** (*as*, *a*) **esse**.

§

E. PARTI

PRESENT.

hort-**ans**, exhorting. *vĕr*-**ens**, fearing.

PERFECT.

hort-**ātus** (*a*, *um*), having exhorted. *vĕr*-**ĭtus** (*a*, *um*), having feared.

FUTURE (ACTIVE).

hort-**atūrus** (*a*, *um*), about to exhort. *ver*-**itūrus** (*a*, *um*), about to fear.

FUTURE (PASSIVE).

hort-**andus** (*a*, *um*), to be exhorted. *ver*-**endus** (*a*, *um*), to be feared.

§

F. GE-

Nom. ***hortandum est***, **it must be exhorted, it is necessary to exhort.**

Gen. *hort*-**andi**, of exhorting. *ver*-**endi**, of fearing.

Dat. *hort*-**ando**, to exhorting. *ver*-**endo**, to fearing.

Acc. (*ad*) *hort*-**andum**, exhorting. (*ad*) *ver*-**endum**, fearing.

Abl. *hort*-**ando**, by exhorting. *ver*-**endo**, by fearing.

§

G. SU-

hort-**ātum**, to exhort. *vĕr*-**ĭtum**, to fear.

hort-**ātu**, to exhort. *vĕr*-**ĭtu**, to fear.

98.

ITIVE.

PRESENT.

fung-**i**, to perform. *part*-**īri**, to divide.

PERFECT.

func-**tum** (*am*, *um*) **esse**, to have performed. *part*-**ītum** (*am*, *um*) **esse**, to have divided.

func-**tos** (*as*, *a*) **esse**. *part*-**ītos** (*as*, *a*) **esse**.

FUTURE.

func-**tūrum** (*am*, *um*) **esse**, to be about to perform. *part*-**itūrum** (*am*, *um*) **esse**, to be about to divide.

func-**turos** (*as*, *a*) **esse**. *part*-**ituros** (*as*, *a*) **esse**.

99.

CIPLES.

PRESENT.

fung-**ens**, performing. *part*-**iens**, dividing.

PERFECT.

func-**tus** (*a*, *um*), having performed. *part*-**ītus** (*a*, *um*), having divided.

FUTURE (ACTIVE).

func-**tūrus** (*a*, *um*), about to perform. *part*-**itūrus** (*a*, *um*), about to divide.

FUTURE (PASSIVE).

fung-**endus** (*a*, *um*), to be performed. *part*-**iendus** (*a*, *um*), to be divided.

100.

RUND.

fung-**endi**, of performing. *part*-**iendi**, of dividing.

fung-**endo**, to performing. *part*-**iendo**, to dividing.

(*ad*) *fung*-**endum**, performing. (*ad*) *part*-**iendum**, dividing.

fung-**endo**, by performing. *part*-**iendo**, by dividing.

101.

PINE.

func-**tum**, to perform. *part*-**ītum**, to divide.

func-**tu**, to perform. *part*-**ītu**, to divide.

§ 102.

Words for Exercise.

First Conjugation.

Adūlor, I flatter.
aemūlor, emulate, am envious of.
arbitror, think, suppose.
calumnior, slander.
cōmitor, accompany.
cōnor, venture, dare.
consōlor, comfort.
conspicor, descry.
contemplor, consider.
cunctor, linger, hesitate.
frustror, deceive.
fūror, steal.
glōrior, glory, boast.
grātūlor, congratulate.
imitor, imitate.
interprĕtor, explain.
iŏcor, jest.
laetor, rejoice.
lāmentor, moan.
lucror, gain.
luctor, wrestle.
mĕdicor, heal.
mĕditor, reflect, muse.
minor, threaten.
miror, admire, wonder.
misĕror, deplore.
mŏror, delay, wait.
opinor, conjecture, think.
pālor, struggle.
piscor, fish.
pŏpūlor, ravage.
praedor, plunder.
precor, ask, pray.
rĕcordor, call to mind.
rixor, wrangle.
suspicor, mistrust, suspect.
testor, witness, prove.
tūtor, guard, watch.
vāgor, ramble about.
vĕnĕror, revere, venerate.
vēnor, hunt.
versor, dwell.

§ 103.

Second Conjugation.

Pollĭceor, promise.
tueor, protect. (§ 134).

Third Conjugation.

Fruor, ***fructus sum***, enjoy.
lŏquor, ***locūtus sum***, speak, talk.
nascor, ***nātus sum***, am born (§ 135).

Fourth Conjugation.

Blandior, flatter.
largior, bestow, grant.
mentior, tell a lie.
mōlior, undertake.
sortior, cast lots.
pŏtior, take possession of. (§ 136).

§ 104.

The deponent verb is originally always a passive verb.

This appears sometimes very clearly; as, in *nascor*, I am born; sometimes the active form of the deponent is still used; as, *veho* (trans.), I ride; *vehor* (intrans.), I ride; *pasco*, I drive to the pasture; *pascor*, I feed, graze (cfr. § 135). Both the passive and the deponent often partake of the reflexive meaning, like the Middle in Greek; *e. g.*, *nitor*, I rest upon; *vescor*, I feed on something, I eat; *proficiscor*, I set out, I travel. In the same manner, the passives: *delector*, I am pleased (= *me delecto*); *accingor*, I gird myself; *fallor*, I am mistaken; *moveor*, I bestir myself; *inclinor*, I am disposed; *mutor*, I am changed; *recreor*, I become refreshed. But the present participle is *me recreans*, *me delectans*, etc.

CHAPTER XVIII.

REMARKS ON THE FOUR CONJUGATIONS.

§ 105.

VERBS IN **io** OF THE THIRD CONJUGATION.

1. In the third conjugation there are fifteen verbs (with their compounds) that have a short **ĭ** before the termination. This **i** is dropped whenever followed by a second **i**, or by a syllable beginning with a short **ĕ**.

1) *căpio*, § 120, 2.	2) *cŭpio*, § 118, 47.	3) *făcio*, § 120, 3.
4) *fŏdio*, § 120, 15.	5) *fŭgio*, § 120, 6.	6) *iăcio*, § 120, 4.
7) (*lăcio*), § 119, 16.	8) *părio*, § 121, 2.	9) *răpio*, § 118, 6.
10) *quătio*, § 119, 54.	11) (*spĕcio*) § 119, 17.	12) *săpio*, § 118, 58.
13) *grădior*, § 135, 9.	14) *pătior*, § 135, 13.	15) *mŏrior*, § 135, 5.

and partly, also *ŏrior*, § 136, 11.

2. **ACTIVE.** **PASSIVE.**

PRESENT.

căp-**i-o**,	*căp*-**i-am**,	*căp*-**i-or**,	*căp*-**i-ar**,
căpis,	*căp*-**i-as**,	*căpĕris*,	*căp*-**i-aris**,
căpit,	etc.	*căpĭtur*,	etc.
căpĭmus,		*căpĭmur*,	
căpĭtis,		*căpĭmini*,	
căp-**i-unt**,		*căp*-**i-untur**,	

IMPERFECT.

căp-**i**-*ēbam*,	*căp***ĕrem**,	*căp*-**i**-*ēbar*,	*căp***ĕrer**,
căp-**i**-*ēbas*,	*căp***eres**,	*căp*-**i**-*ēbaris*,	*căp***ereris**,
etc.	etc.	etc.	etc.

FUTURE.

căp-**i**-*am*,	*căp*-**i**-*ar*,
căp-**i**-*es*,	*căp*-**i**-*ēris*.

IMPERATIVE. INFINITIVE.

ACT.	PASS.	ACT.	PASS.
*căp***e**,	*căp***ĕre**,	*căp***ĕre**.	*căp***i**.
căpĭte,	*căpimini*,		
căpĭto,	*căpitor*,	PARTICIPLE.	GERUND.
căpĭto,	*căpitor*,	*căpiēns*.	*căpiendi*.
căpĭtote,	———		
căp-**i-unto**,	*căp*-**i-untor**.		

The deponents are conjugated like the passive of *capio;* thus, *morior*, *mor-***ĕris**, *morĭtur*, *morimur*, *morimini*, *moriuntur; moriar*, *moriaris*, &c.; *moriebar; morĕrer*; *moriar*, *moriēris; morĕre*, die; *mori*, to die; *moriens*, *moriendi*.

§ 106.

Twofold Forms of Conjugations.

1. In the perfects in **avi** of the first conjugation, and the tenses formed from them, **avi** when followed by **s**, and **ave** followed by **r**, are contracted into **ā**; as, *laud-***āsti**, *laud-***āssem**, *laud-***āsse**; *laud-***ārunt**, *laud-***ārim**, *laud-***āram**, *laud-***āro**, for *laudavisti*, *laudaverunt*, etc.

2. Perfects in **īvi** and the tenses derived from them, may always drop the **v**; as, *aud-***iisti**, *aud-***iisse**, *aud-***iissem**, and more frequently still, be contracted thus: *aud***isti**, *aud***isse**, *aud***issem**: similarly, *aud-***iĕrunt**, *audiĕrim*, *audieram*, *audiero*. But the uncontracted forms *audivi*, *audivit*, and *audivimus* are more usual than *audii*, *audiit*, *audiimus*.

3. Perfects in **ēvi** and **ōvi** of the second and third conjugations, sometimes admit a like contraction: thus, *quievērunt*, *quiē***runt**, they have reposed; *consuēvĕram*, and *consuē***ram**, I had been accustomed; *nōveram*, and **noram**, I knew; *consuevissem*, and *consue***ssem**; *novisti*, and **nosti**; *movisti*, though rarely *mosti*, thou hast moved.

4. In the third pers. plur. perf. ind. act. the abbreviated form **ēre** for **ērunt** is common; as *laudav***ēre** for *laudavērunt*; *monu***ēre**, *leg***ēre**, *audiv***ēre**. The form in **ēre** does not drop the **v**, hence never *audi***ēre** for *audivēre*.

5. In the second pers. sing. pass. the form **rĕ** is often used for **ris**; thus, *laud***ēre** for *laudēris*; *monebĕ***re** for *monebĕris; leg***āre** for *legāris; audieb***āre** for *audiebāris*. But **re** for **ris** in the pres. ind. is rare: *laudāris*, rarely *laudāre*.

6. **Undus** for **endus** occurs as ending of the fut. part. pass. in the third and fourth conj. Always write *eundus* and *oriundus*. You may say *potiundus* or *potiendus* (*potiri*). Technical expressions: *in jure dicundo* for *dicendo; repet-***undarum** or *de repet***undis**, on account of extortions, instead of *repetendarum* (*pecuniarum*.)

7. Four verbs, *dīcĕre*, *dūcĕre*, *făcĕre* and *ferre* (for *ferĕre*) have the imperative **dīc**, say; **dūc**, lead; **fac**, do; **fer**, bear.

The compounds follow the same rule, except those of *facio*, which have **ficio** instead of *facio*: as, *benedic*, *calefac*, *educ*, *refer*; *confi*, *perfice*. (§ 144, 2.)

8. Some ancient forms of conjugation occur in a few verbs; a) the subjunctive **im**: *duim*, *duint*, for *dem*, *dent*; *edim* for *edam* (*cfr.* § 141). *b*) the infinitive passive **ier**: *laudarier*, *viderier*, *dicier*, *mollirier*; also *labier*, *nitier*; *c*) the imperfect, **ibam**, and future, **ibo**, of the fourth conj. instead of *iebam*, and *iam*; as, *audibam*, *audibo*, for *audiebam*, *audiam*, (§ 142); *d*) the future perfect **asso** and **esso**, for *avero* and *uero* as *levasso*, *prohibesso*, in place of *levavero*, *prohibuero*; *e*) syncopation (rejection of syllables); as, *dixti* for *dixisti*; likewise *faxim* for *fecerim*; *ausim* for *ausus sim*.

§ 107.

Periphrastic Conjugation.

The participles joined to the tenses of **sum** give rise to the periphrastic conjugation. Some of these forms are used in the regular inflection of the verb, to supply the tenses wanting there. Only those formed with the future part. act. and pass. (**rus** and **dus**) are considered really periphrastic.

2. The future part. in this conjugation always retains its native meaning; thus, *laudaturus sum*, I am about to praise, I am on the point of praising; *i. e.*, I will praise; *laudaturus eram*, I was about to praise. Pass. *laudandus sum*, I am to be praised, *i. e.*, I must be praised; *laudandus eram*, I was to be praised.

3. Conjugate thus:

ACTIVE.

	INDICATIVE.		SUBJUNCTIVE.	
		Present.		
S.	*Laudaturus* (*a*, *um*)	{ *sum*, I will praise. *es*, thou wilt praise. *est*, he will praise,	*laudaturus* (*a*, *um*),	{ *sim*, I may be about to [praise. *sis*, *sit*,
P.	*laudaturi* (*ae*, *a*)	{ *sumus*, we will praise. *estis*, ye will praise. *sunt*, they will praise.	*laudaturi* (*ae*, *a*).	{ *simus*, *sitis*, *sint*.

Imperfect.

S. *laudaturus eram*, I was about to praise. — *laudaturus essem*, I might be about to praise.

P. *laudaturi eramus*. — *laudaturi essemus*.

INDICATIVE.	SUBJUNCTIVE.
Future.	
S. *laudaturus ero*, I shall be about to praise.	wanting.
Perfect.	
S. *laudaturus fui*, I have been about to praise.	*laudaturus fuerim*, I may have been about to praise.
Pluperfect.	
S. *laudaturus fueram*, I had been about to praise.	*laudaturus fuissem*, I might have been about to praise.
Future Perfect.	
S. *laudaturus fuero* (rare) I shall have been about to praise.	wanting.

INFINITIVE.

Pres. *laudaturum (am, um) esse*, to be about to praise.
Perf. *laudaturum (am, um) fuisse*, to have been about to praise.

PASSIVE.

INDICATIVE.	SUBJUNCTIVE.
Present.	
S. *laudandus sum*, I am to be praised. I must be praised.	*laudandus sim*, if I must be praised.
Imperfect.	
S. *laudandus eram*, I was to be praised.	*laudandus essem*, if I were to be praised.
Future.	
S. *laudandus ero*, I shall be about to be praised.	wanting.
Perfect.	
S. *laudandus fui*, I have to be praised.	*laudandus fuerim*, I may have to be praised.
Pluperfect.	
S. *laudandus fueram*, I had to be praised.	*laudandus fuissem*, I might have to be praised.
Future Perfect.	
S. *laudandus fuero*, I shall have been about to be praised.	wanting.

INFINITIVE.

Pres. *laudandum (am, um) esse*, necessary to be praised.
Perf. *laudandum (am, um) fuisse*, necessary to have been praised.

NOTE 1.—*Laudandum est*, it must be praised, it is necessary to praise. In like manner the deponents: *hortandum est*, it must be exhorted. *Virtus colenda est*, virtue must be cherished. *Maiores natu verendi sunt*, elders must be respected. *Mihi laudandum est*, I must praise (it must be praised by me); *tibi laudandum est*, you must praise; *ei laudandum est*, he must praise; *nobis*, *vobis*, *patri laudandum est*. *Virtus nobis colenda est*, we must cherish virtue. Cfr. § 209.

NOTE 2.—The part. in **ndus** of the periphrastic conj. expresses necessity (must): *Hoc non ferendum est*, this must not be suffered. It must not be confounded with *can*: *Hoc ferri non potest*, this cannot be suffered.

CHAPTER XIX.

IRREGULAR PERFECTS AND SUPINES.

First Conjugation.

§ 108.

PERFECTS WITH THE CHARACTERISTIC u, (v), 11.

I. SUPINE IN **itum**, 6:

1. *Crĕpo*, *crepui*, *crepĭtum*, *crepāre*, I creak.
   Compounds: *discrĕpo*, *avi*, *ui*, jar, differ; *incrĕpo*, chide.
2. *cŭbo*, *cubui*, *cubĭtum*, *cubāre*, lie.
   accŭbo, lie near; *incŭbo*, lie upon (cfr. § 118, 20.)
3. *dŏmo*, *domui*, *domĭtum*, *domāre*, tame, check.
   edŏmo, *perdomo*, subdue.
4. *sŏno*, *sonui*, *sonĭtum*, *sonāre*, sound, ring (§ 77, note).
   consŏno, resound, accord, (*resono*, *resonavi*.)
5. *tŏno*, *tonui*, *tonĭtum*, *tonāre*, thunder.
   attŏno, thunder at, stun.
6. *vĕto*, *vetui*, *vetĭtum*, *vetāre*, forbid.

II. VARIOUS SUPINES, 4:

7. *Frĭco*, *fricui*, *frictum* (for *fricĭtum*), and *fricātum*, *fricāre*, rub.
   infrico, rub in; *perfrico*, rub through.
8. *sĕco*, *secui*, *sectum* (for *secĭtum*), *secāre*, cut (§ 77, note).
   desĕco, cut off; *insĕco*, cut into.
9. *enĕco*, *enecui*, *enectum*, *enecāre*, kill.
   nĕco, kill, has always, and *enĕco* sometimes, *āvi*, *ātum*.
10. *mĭco*, *micui* (no supine), *micāre*, shine forth.
    emico, *emicui*, *emicātum*, shine forth.
    dimico, *āvi*, *ātum*, *āre*, fight, struggle, (regular).

III. Perfects in āvi and ui, Supines in ātum and ĭtum, 1:

11. *Plico, plicāvi, plicātum*, and *plicui, plicitum, plicāre*, fold.

applĭco, attach; *explĭco*, unfold;
complĭco, fold together; *implĭco*, involve.

The others in *plico* are derived from the adjectives in *plex*, and have only *avi, atum;* as, *multiplico, duplico, supplico.*

§ 109.

PERFECTS WITH LENGTHENED ROOT-VOWELS.

Supines in tum, 2:

1. *Iŭvo, iūvi, iūtum, iuvāre*, help, assist (§ 97, note).

adiŭvo, adiūvi, adiūtum, adiuvāre, help.

2. *lăvo, lāvi, lavātum, lautum* or *lōtum, lavāre* (obsolete, *lavĕre* after the third), wash, bathe (§ 77, note).

The compounds have *luo* (cfr. § 118, 28).

§ 110.

PERFECTS WITH REDUPLICATION; SUPINES IN tum, 2:

1. *Do, dĕdi, dătum, dăre*, give.

circumdo, surround; *satisdo*, I give bail;
pessumdo, ruin; *venumdo*, sell.

The other compounds of **do**, all dissyllables, belong to the third conjugation, and have *didi, ditum* (cfr. § 121, 17).

2. *sto, stĕti, stătum, stāre*, stand.

Of the compounds of **sto**, the trisyllables have, in the perfect, *stĕti;* the dissyllables, *stiti*. *Praesto* alone has a supine. However, the future part. act. of several occurs; as, *constāturus, instaturus, obstaturus*, and only *praestaturus.*

antesto, antestĕti, antestāre, excel.
circumsto, circumstĕti, circumstāre, stand around.
praesto, praestiti, praestitum, praestāre, execute, surpass.
consto, constiti, constāre, consist, cost.
insto, urge, press upon; *obsto*, hinder, stand against;
persto, persist; *resto*, remain, am left.

Disto, am distant, and *exsto*, exist, want also the perfect.

NOTE.—*Iuro*, I swear; *ceno*, I dine; *poto*, I drink, are regular. But the perfect part. pass. has also an active meaning; thus, *iuratus*, one who has sworn; *cenatus*, having dined, one who has dined; for *potatus*, the form *potus* is used, having drunk (§ 114, 5).

CHAPTER XX.

IRREGULAR PERFECTS AND SUPINES.

Second Conjugation.

§ 111.

PERFECTS WITH CHARACTERISTIC v, 5.

I. SUPINES IN **ētum**, 4:

1. *Dēleo*, *delēvi*, *delētum*, *delēre*, destroy, blot out.
2. *fleo*, *flēvi*, *flētum*, *flēre*, weep (*defleo*, weep over).
3. *neo*, *nēvi*, *nētum*, *nēre*, spin.
4. From the obsolete *pleo*, *plēvi*, *plētum*, *plēre*, fill:

compleo, fill up;	*impleo*, fill in;
expleo, fill out;	*suppleo*, supply.

II. SUPINE IN **ĭtum**, 1:

5. *Abŏleo*, *abolēvi*, *abolitum*, *abolēre*, utterly remove (§ 129).

§ 112.

PERFECTS WITH THE CHARACTERISTIC s, 20.

I. SUPINES IN **tum**, 3:

1. *Indulgeo*, *indulsi*, *indultum*, *indulgēre*, yield.
2. *torqueo*, *torsi*, *tortum*, *torquēre*, twist, torture.
   contorqueo, turn round; *extorqueo*, wrest away.
3. *Augeo*, *auxi* (for *augsi*), *auctum*, *augēre*, enlarge.

II. SUPINES IN **sum**, 9:

4. *Ardeo*, *arsi*, *arsum*, *ardēre*, burn.
5. *haereo*, *haesi*, *haesum*, *haerēre*, cling, hang.
   adhaereo, cleave to; *cohaereo*, hold together.
6. *iŭbeo*, *iussi*, *iussum*, *iubēre*, command, bid.

7. *măneo, mansi, mansum, manēre*, remain.
permăneo, hold out; *remaneo*, stay behind.
8. *mulceo, mulsi, mulsum, mulcēre*, caress, fondle.
9. *mulgeo, mulsi, mulsum, mulgēre*, milk (§ 76, note 2).
10. *rīdeo, rīsi, rīsum, ridēre*, laugh.
arrideo, smile at; *irrideo*, laugh at; *subrideo*, smile.
11. *suādeo, suāsi, suāsum, suadēre*, advise.
dissuādeo, advise against; *persuadeo*, induce, convince.
12. *tergeo, tersi, tersum, tergēre*, wipe (also *tergo*, § 119, 57).
abstergeo, wipe off; *detergeo*, wipe away.

III. No Supine, 8:

13. *Algeo, alsi, algēre*, feel cold.
14. *fulgeo, fulsi, fulgēre*, shine.
15. *turgeo, tursi, turgēre*, swell.
16. *urgeo, ursi, urgēre*, urge.
17. *frīgeo, frixi, frigēre*, am cold.
18. *lūceo, luxi, lucēre*, light (*elūceo*, shine forth).
19. *lūgeo, luxi, lugēre*, mourn, bewail.
20. *conniveo, connixi* (and *connivi*), *connivēre*, wink at.

§ 113.

PERFECTS BY LENGTHENING THE ROOT-VOWELS, 8:

I. Supines in **tum**, 5:

1. *Căveo, cāvi, cautum, cavēre*, take care.
2. *făveo, fāvi, fautum, favēre*, favor.
3. *fŏveo, fōvi, fōtum, fovēre*, warm, cherish.
4. *mŏveo, mōvi, mōtum, movēre*, move.
admŏveo, bring to; *commoveo*, stir up.
5. *vŏveo, vōvi, vōtum, vovēre*, vow.
devŏveo, curse, consecrate.
Cieo, civi, citum, ciēre, rouse (§ 127).

II. Supines in **sum**, 2:

6. *Sĕdeo, sēdi, sessum, sedēre*, sit.
assideo, assēdi, assessum, assidēre, sit by.
obsideo, besiege; *possideo*, possess; *circumsĕdeo*, invest.
supersĕdeo, forbear.
7. *vĭdeo, vīdi, vīsum, vidēre*, see.
invideo, envy; *provideo*, foresee, provide.

III. No Supine, 1:

8. *Păveo*, *pāvi*, *pavēre*, tremble, am afraid.

§ 114.

PERFECTS WITH REDUPLICATION, SUPINES IN **sum**, 5 (6):

I. The Compounds do not take the Reduplication, 4:

1. *Mordeo*, *mŏmordi*, *morsum*, *mordēre*, bite.
2. *pendeo*, *pĕpendi* (*pensum*), *pendēre*, hang.
   dependeo (neither perfect nor supine), hang down.
   impendeo (neither perfect nor supine), overhang, threaten.
3. *spondeo*, *spŏpondi*, *sponsum*, *spondēre*, promise.
   respondeo, *respondi*, *responsum*, *respondēre*, answer.
4. *tondeo*, *tŏtondi*, *tonsum*, *tondēre*, shear.
   attondeo, clip, shorten.

II. Without Reduplication, 2:

5. *Prandeo*, *prandi*, *pransum*, *prandēre*, breakfast.

The perf. part. pass. *pransus* also has an active meaning: having breakfasted, one who has breakfasted (§ 110, 2, note).

6. *strīdeo*, *strīdi*, (no supine), *stridēre*, hiss.

§ 115.

PERFECTS WITH PASSIVE FORM, 3:

1. *Audeo*, *ausus sum*, *audēre*, dare (*ausim* = *audeam*).
2. *gaudeo*, *gavīsus sum*, *gaudēre*, rejoice.
3. *sŏleo*, *solĭtus sum*, *solēre*, am used (to do).

These three verbs, as also *fido* (§ 122, 20), on account of their partial passive inflection and active meaning, are called semi-deponents.

§ 116.

PERFECTS REGULAR IN **ui**, SUPINE SHORTENED (BY THROWING OUT THE SHORT **i**, &c.), 5:

1. *Dŏceo*, *docui*, *doctum*, *docēre*, teach.
   dedoceo, unteach; *edoceo*, teach thoroughly.
2. *misceo*, *miscui*, *mixtum* and *mistum*, *miscēre*, mix.
   admisceo, mix with: *permisceo*, confound.

3. *tĕneo*, *tenui*, *tentum*, *tenēre*, hold.
 abstineo, ***abstinui***, ***abstentum***, ***abstinēre***, **refrain.**
 attineo, **pertain;** ***contineo***, **keep together;** ***obtineo***, **maintain;**
 retineo, **keep back;** ***pertineo***, **belong to;** ***sustineo***, **bear up.**

4. *torreo*, *torrui*, *tostum*, *torrēre*, scorch, roast.

5. *censeo*, *censui*, *censum*, *censēre*, value, deem.
 recenseo, **review, (supine:** ***recensum*** **and** ***recensitum*****).**
 succenseo, **am angry (for** ***suscenseo*****).**

§ 117.

1. Perfects Regular, no Supine.

Arceo, keep off.
 coërceo, ***ui***, ***itum***, **restrain.**
 exerceo, ***ui***, ***itum***, **exercise.**
ĕgeo, am destitute.
 indigeo, **need.**
emĭneo, stand out.
flōreo, blossom.
horreo, shudder.
 abhorreo, **shudder at.**
lăteo, am concealed.
nĭteo, glisten.
păteo, am open.
sĭleo, am silent.
sorbeo, swallow.
splendeo, glitter.
stŭdeo, apply oneself.
tĭmeo, fear.
vĭgeo, am vigorous.
vĭreo, am fresh, etc.

2. Neither Perfect nor Supine.

Aveo, crave.
calveo, am bald.
cāneo, am gray.
immĭneo, hang over, menace.
langueo, am faint.
maereo, am in mourning.
polleo, am powerful.
squaleo, am filthy.

3. Double Perfect, no Supine.

Ferveo, ***fervi*** **and** ***ferbui***, ***fervēre***, **boil, glow.**
liqueo, ***liqui*** **and** ***licui***, ***liquēre***, **am liquid, clear.**

CHAPTER XXI.

PERFECTS AND SUPINES.

Third Conjugation.

§ 118.

PERFECTS WITH THE CHARACTERISTIC u or v, 59:

I. Supines in **tum**, 8:

1. *Alo*, *alui*, *altum*, (also *alĭtum*), *alĕre*, nourish.
2. *cŏlo*, *colui*, *cultum*, *colĕre*, honor, till (the soil).
   excŏlo, perfect; *incolo*, dwell in.
3. *consŭlo*, *consului*, *consultum*, *consulĕre*, consult, take counsel, care for (with dative).
4. *depso*, *depsui*, *depstum*, *depsĕre*, knead.
5. *occŭlo*, *occului*, *occultum*, *occulĕre*, conceal.
6. *răpio*, *rapui*, *raptum*, *rapĕre*, seize, rob.
   abripio, *abripui*, *abreptum*, *abripĕre*, tear away.
   arripio, snatch; *diripio*, tear asunder, plunder.
   corripio, carry off; *eripio*, pull out.
7. *sĕro*, *serui*, *sertum*, *serĕre*, contrive, bind, entwine (§ 118, 56).
   consĕro, connect; *dissĕro*, discourse, speak about;
   desĕro, abandon; *insĕro*, engraft.
8. *texo*, *texui*, *textum*, *texĕre*, weave.
   contexo, braid; *retexo*, reverse, unweave.

II. Supines in **ĭtum**, 7:

9. *Elĭcio*, *elicui*, *elicĭtum*, *elicĕre*, lure forth.
   compound of *lacio* (cfr. § 119, 16).
10. *frĕmo*, *fremui*, *fremĭtum*, *fremĕre*, growl, grumble.
11. *gĕmo*, *gemui*, *gemĭtum*, *gemĕre*, sigh.
12. *mŏlo*, *molui*, *molĭtum*, *molĕre*, grind.
13. *pinso*, *pinsui*, *pinsitum* (also *pinsi*, *pinsum* and *pistum*), *pinsĕre*, crush, pound.
14. *strĕpo*, *strepui*, *strepĭtum*, *strepĕre*, make noise, roar.
15. *vŏmo*, *vomui*, *vomĭtum*, *vomĕre*, spew.

III. No Supine, 4:

16. *Compesco, compescui, compescĕre*, curb, repress.
17. *sterto, stertui, stertĕre*, snore.
18. *tremo, tremui, tremĕre*, tremble.
19. *vŏlo, volui, velle*, will (§ 141).
    mālo, mālui, malle, choose rather (§ 141).
    nōlo, nōlui, nolle, will not (§ 141).

Note.—The compounds of *cano* belong to this class; cfr. § 121, 1.

IV. Change of the Present Stem; Supines in ĭtum, 3:

20. *Accumbo, accubui, accubĭtum, accumbĕre*, lay myself down.
    incumbo, lie upon; *occumbo*, yield, die (§ 108, 2).
21. *gigno, gĕnui, genĭtum, gignĕre*, beget.
22. *pōno, pŏsui, pŏsĭtum, pōnĕre*, place, put.
    antepōno, prefer; *expōno*, explain; *compōno*, bring together; *oppōno*, set against; *dispōno*, set in order; *propōno*, set forth.

V. Supine in ūtum, 14:

23. *Acŭo, ăcui* (for *acuvi*), *acūtum, acuĕre*, sharpen.
24. *arguo, argui, argūtum, arguĕre*, charge with.
    evarguo, convict; *redarguo*, disprove.
25. *exuo, exui, exūtum, exuĕre*, pull off.
26. *imbuo, imbui, imbūtum, imbuĕre*, soak.
27. *induo, indui, indūtum, induĕre*, put on.
28. *luo, lui, lūtum, luĕre*, expiate (wash, § 109, 2, and 77, note).
    abluo, wash away; *eluo*, wash out; *diluo*, dissolve; *polluo*, soil.
29. *mĭnuo, minui, minūtum, minuĕre*, diminish.
30. *nuo, nui, nūtum, nuĕre*, nod (§ 77, note).
    abnuo, refuse; *adnuo*, nod to.
31. *spuo, spui, spūtum, spuĕre*, spit.
32. *stătuo, statui, statūtum, statuĕre*, fix, determine.
    constituo, constitui, constitūtum, constituĕre, arrange, resolve.
    instituo, establish; *destituo*, forsake; *restituo*, restore.
33. *suo, sui, sūtum, suĕre*, sew.
34. *tribuo, tribui, tribūtum, tribuĕre*, grant.
    contribuo, contribute; *distribuo*, divide.
35. *solvo, solvi* (for *solvui*), *solūtum, solvĕre*, loose.
    absolvo, acquit; *dissolvo*, dissolve.

36. *volvo, volvi, volūtum, volvĕre*, roll.
convolvo, roll up; *involvo*, wrap up.

VI. No Supine, 5:

37. *Batuo, batui, batuĕre*, fence, strike.
38. *congruo, congrui, congruĕre*, coincide.
39. *mĕtuo, metui, metuĕre*, fear.
40. *pluo*, (*pluit*, it rains), *plui* (and *plūvi*), *pluĕre*, rain.
41. *sternuo, sternui, sternuĕre*, sneeze.

VII. Supine in **ŭtum**, 1:

42. *Ruo, rui, rŭtum, ruĕre*, fall (§ 77, note).
corruo, fall down; *irruo*, rush into;
diruo, destroy; *obruo*, overwhelm.

VIII. Perfects in **īvi**, Supines in **ītum**, 9:

43. *Arcesso, arcessīvi, arcessītum, arcessĕre*, summon.
44. *capesso, capessīvi, capessītum, capessĕre*, seize.
45. *facesso, facessīvi, facessītum, facessĕre*, execute, perform.
46. *lacesso, lacessīvi, lacessītum, lacessĕre*, excite, provoke.
47. *cŭpio, cupīvi, cupītum, cupĕre*, long for, desire.
48. *pĕto, petīvi, petītum, petĕre*, seek after, attack.
appĕto, strive; *repĕto*, demand back.
49. *quaero* (*quaeso*, § 152), *quaesīvi, quaesītum, quaerĕre*, ask.
acquiro, acquisivi, acquisitum, acquirĕre, acquire.
inquiro, search into; *requiro*, inquire, miss.
50. *rŭdo, rudīvi, rudītum, rudĕre*, bray.
51. *tĕro, trīvi* (for *terīvi*, syncope), *trītum, terĕre*, rub.
contĕro, grind; *detĕro*, rub away.

IX. Perfects in **īvi**, no Supine, 2:

52. *Incesso, incessīvi* and *incessi, incessĕre*, assail.
53. *săpio* (*sapīvi* and *sapui*), *sapĕre*, taste, am wise.

X. Perfects in **vi**, by Rejecting a Consonant from the Present, Supines in **tum**, 6:

54. *Lĭno, lēvi*, and *līvi, lĭtum, linĕre*, rub over, besmear.
55. *sĭno, sīvi, sĭtum, sinĕre*, allow.
desino, cease; *desivi* or *desii, desitum, desinĕre* (*desitum est*, only with the infinitive passive, instead of *desiit*, § 146, note).

56. *sĕro*, *sēvi*, *sătum*, *serĕre*, sow, plant (§ 118, 7).
insero, *insēvi*, *insitum*, *inserĕre*, put in, implant; *obsĕro*, sow about.

57. *cerno* (*crēvi*, *crētum*), *cernĕre*, see, separate.
decerno, decide; *discerno*, distinguish.

58. *sperno*, *sprēvi*, *sprētum*, *spernĕre*, despise.

59. *sterno*, *strāvi*, *strātum*, *sternĕre*, spread out stretch out.
consterno, cover; *prosterno*, overthrow.

XI. Inchoatives in sco (cfr. § 129).

§ 119.

PERFECTS WITH THE CHARACTERISTIC s, 68.

I. Supines in tum, 41:

a. Present in po, 5:

1. *Carpo*, *carpsi*, *carptum*, *carpĕre*, pluck.
concerpo, *cerpsi*, *cerptum*, *cerpĕre*, tear in pieces, *decerpo*, pluck off; *discerpo*, rend.

2. *rēpo*, *repsi*, *reptum*, *repĕre*, creep.
arrēpo, creep to; *obrēpo*, steal upon.

3. *serpo*, *serpsi*, *serptum*, *serpĕre*, glide, crawl.

4. *scalpo*, *scalpsi*, *scalptum*, *scalpĕre*, scrape, scratch.

5. *sculpo*, *sculpsi*, *sculptum*, *sculpĕre*, carve, chisel.

b. Present in bo, 3:

6. *Glūbo*, *glupsi* (for *glubsi*), *gluptum*, *glubĕre*, peel.

7. *nūbo*, *nupsi*, *nuptum*, *nubĕre*, take a husband (*viro*, marry a husband).

8. *scrībo*, *scripsi*, *scriptum*, *scribĕre*, write.
adscribo, ascribe; *praescribo*, dictate;
inscribo, write in; *proscribo*, outlaw.

c. Present in mo (mno), 4 (5):

9. *Cōmo*, *compsi*, *comptum* (§ 76, note 2), *comĕre*, adorn.

10. *dēmo*, *dempsi*, *demptum*, *demĕre*, take away.

11. *prōmo*, *prompsi*, *promptum*, *promĕre*, take out.

12. *sūmo*, *sumpsi*, *sumptum*, *sumĕre*, take.
absūmo, waste; *consūmo*, spend.

13. *contemno*, *contempsi*, *contemptum*, *contemnĕre*, despise.

d. Present in co (cio, quo), 2 (5):

14. *Dīco, dixi* (for *dicsi*), *dictum, dicĕre*, **say.**
edico, declare; *praedico*, foretell.

15. *dūco, duxi, ductum, ducĕre*, lead.
addūco, lead to; *obdūco*, veil;
edūco, lead forth; *subduco*, withdraw.

16. (*lacio, laxi, lactum, lacĕre*, entice, is obsolete).

The compounds have *licio, lexi, lectum;* as,
allĭcio, allure; *pellicio*, decoy;
illicio, seduce; (*elicio* has **ui, itum,** § 118, 9).

17 (*spĕcio, spexi, spectum, specĕre*, catch a sight of).
adspĭcio, adspexi, adspectum, adspicĕre, look on;
conspicio, look at; *prospicio*, look forward;
respicio, look back; *despicio*, disdain;
perspicio, see through; *suspicio*, look upward.

18. *Cŏquo, coxi, coctum, coquĕre*, cook.
concŏquo, digest; *decŏquo*, boil down.

e. Present in go, 14:

19. *Cingo, cinxi, cinctum, cingĕre*, gird, surround.

20. (*fligo, flixi, flictum, fligĕre*, strike).
afflīgo, strike down; *conflīgo*, combat; *inflīgo*, inflict.
(*proflīgo*, cast down; like *laudo*).

21. *frīgo, frixi, frictum, frigĕre*, roast.

22. *iungo, iunxi, iunctum, iungĕre*, join, unite.
adiungo, add; *disiungo*, part;
coniungo, join together; *subiungo*, annex.

23. *lingo, linxi, linctum, lingĕre*, lick.

24. *mungo* (*emungo*), *munxi, munctum, mungĕre*, blow the nose.

25. *plango, planxi, planctum, plangĕre*, strike, lament.

26. *rĕgo, rexi, rectum, regĕre*, govern, guide.
arrigo, arrexi, arrectum, arrigĕre, raise.
corrigo, improve; *erigo*, erect;
dirigo, direct; *porrigo*, stretch out.
Pergo (for *perrigo*,), *perrexi, perrectum, pergĕre*, pass on.
surgo (for *surrigo*) *surrexi, surrectum, surgĕre*, rise.

27. *Dīlĭgo, dilexi, dilectum, diligĕre*, love.
intellĭgo (*intelligo*), understand; *neglĭgo*, neglect.

These are compounds of *lego;* cfr. § 120, 7.

28. (*stinguo, stinxi, stinctum, stinguĕre*, quench).
distinguo, distinguish; *extinguo*, put out.
29. *sūgo, suxi, suctum, sugĕre*, suck.
30. *tĕgo, texi, tectum, tegĕre*, cover.
contĕgo, cover up; *obtĕgo*, screen;
detĕgo, reveal; *protĕgo*, defend.
31. *tingo, tinxi, tinctum, tingĕre*, soak, dye.
32. *ungo, unxi, unctum, ungĕre*, anoint.
The compounds of *pungo* belong to this class; § 121, 5.

f. Present in ho, 2:

33. *Trăho, traxi, tractum, trahĕre*, draw.
contrăho, draw together; *distrăho*, pull asunder.
34. *vĕho, vexi, vectum, vehĕre*, carry (transitive).
advĕho, carry to; *transvĕho*, carry across.
(*Vehor*, I am carried, I ride; neuter (cfr. § 104), *invĕhor*, I scold.)

g. Present ngo; Supine rejects the n, 3:

35. *Fingo, finxi, fictum, fingĕre*, frame, imagine.
36. *pingo, pinxi, pictum, pingĕre*, paint.
37. *stringo, strinxi, strictum, stringĕre*, pull, graze.
adstringo, tighten; *obstringo*, pledge;
destringo, strip; *perstringo*, draw through, reprove.

h. Present in uo (vo), 2:

38. *Struo, struxi, structum, struĕre*, build, pile up.
construo, construct; *exstruo*, build up;
destruo, destroy, pull down; *instruo*, arrange, teach.
39. *vīvo, vixi, victum, vivĕre*, live.

i. Present in ro, 2:

40. *Gĕro, gessi, gestum, gerĕre*, bear, conduct.
congĕro, carry on; *digĕro*, dispose.
41. *ūro, ussi, ustum, urĕre*, burn (transitive).
combūro, consume; *inuro*, brand.

II. Supines in sum, 27:

a. Present in do, 10:

42. *Claudo, clausi, clausum, claudĕre*, close.
conclūdo, conclūsi, conclūsum, conclūdĕre, shut up.
inclūdo, confine; *reclūdo*, unlock.
43. *dīvĭdo, divīsi, divīsum, dividĕre*, divide.

44. *laedo*, *laesi*, *laesum*, *laedĕre*, dash against, hurt.
allīdo, *allīsi*, *allīsum*, *allidĕre*, strike against.
collīdo, strike together; *elīdo*, strike out.

45. *lūdo*, *lūsi*, *lūsum*, *ludĕre*, play.
allūdo, sport with; *illudo*, jeer.

46. *plaudo*, *plausi*, *plausum*, *plaudĕre*, clap.
applaudo, applaud; *explōdo*, hoot off.

47. *rādo*, *rāsi*, *rāsum*, *radĕre*, scrape, shave.

48. *rōdo*, *rōsi*, *rōsum*, *rodĕre*, gnaw.
arrōdo, nibble; *corrōdo*, eat away.

49. *trūdo*, *trūsi*, *trūsum*, *trudĕre*, jostle, push.
abstrūdo, conceal; *intrūdo*, obtrude.

50. *vādo* (*vāsi*, *vāsum*), *vadĕre*, go.
evādo, escape; *invādo*, assault.

51. *cēdo*, *cessi*, *cessum*, *cedĕre*, give way.
accēdo, approach; *praecēdo*, go before; *antecēdo*, excel; *procēdo*, advance; *concēdo*, yield; *recēdo*, retreat.

b. Present in to *(tio), 3:*

52. *Mĕto*, *messui*, *messum*, *metĕre*, mow.
demĕto, cut, reap.

53. *mitto*, *mīsi*, *missum*, *mittĕre*, send.
admitto, allow; *omitto*, pass over; *amitto*, lose; *permitto*, let; *committo*, trust, commit; *promitto*, promise; *intermitto*, leave off; *remitto*, send back.

54. *quătio*, *quassi*, *quassum*, *quatĕre*, shake.
concŭtio, *concussi*, *concussum*, *concutĕre*, shake violently; *excŭtio*, shake out, search; *percutio*, pierce.

c. Present in rgo, *3:*

55. *Mergo*, *mersi*, *mersum*, *mergere*, plunge (§ 76, note 2).
demergo, sink down; *submergo*, plunge under.

56. *spargo*, *sparsi*, *sparsum*, *spargĕre*, scatter.
aspergo, *aspersi*, *aspersum*, *aspergĕre*, sprinkle.
conspergo, besprinkle; *dispergo*, scatter about.

57. *tergo*, *tersi*, *tersum*, *tergĕre*, wipe.
(The compounds fall under the second conjugation, § 112, 9).

d. Perfects in xi, *Supines in* xum, *5:*

58. *Figo*, *fixi*, *fixum*, *figĕre*, fasten.
affigo, attach; *transfigo*, pierce through.

59. *fluo*, *fluxi*, *fluxum*, *fluĕre*, flow.
confluo, flow together; *praeterfluo*, flow by.

60. *flecto*, *flexi*, *flexum*, *flectĕre*, bend.
deflecto, turn aside; *reflecto*, turn back.

61. *pecto*, *pexi*, *pexum*, *pectĕre*, comb.

62. *necto*, *nexi* and *nexui*, *nexum*, *nectĕre*, tie, bind.
The compounds have always **ui** in the perfect; thus,
annecto, *annexui*, *annexum*, *annectĕre*, tie to.
connecto, *connexui*, *connexum*, *connectĕre*, tie together.

e. Anomalous, 2:

63. *Prĕmo*, *pressi*, *pressum*, *premĕre*, press, squeeze.
comprimo, *compressi*, *compressum*, *comprimĕre*, press together.
exprimo, squeeze out; *opprimo*, bear down.

64. *Vello*, *vulsi* (*velli* is preferable, § 122, 13), *vulsum*, *vellĕre*, pluck.

f. Defectives, without Supine or without Perfect, 4:

65. *Ango*, *anxi*, *angĕre*, alarm.

66. *ningo* (*ningit*, it snows), *ninxi*, *ningĕre*, snow.

67. *Frendo*, sup. *frēsum* or *fressum*, *frendĕre*, gnash, bruise.

68. *Plecto*, sup. *plexum*, *plectĕre*, braid (cfr. § 135, 12).

§ 120.

PERFECTS BY LENGTHENING THE ROOT-VOWEL, 16:

I. Supines in **tum**, 12:

a. Changing ă into ē, 4:

1. *Ago*, *ēgi*, *actum*, *ăgĕre*, drive, do.
circumăgo, drive round; *perăgo*, to lead through.
Abigo, *abēgi*, *abactum*, *abigĕre*, drive away;
adigo, drive to; *redigo*, drive back;
exigo, complete, pass by; *subigo*, subject.
Cōgo (*coigo*), *coēgi*, *coactum*, *cogĕre*, collect, force.
dēgo, *dēgi*, no supine, *degĕre*, spend (*vitam*).

2. *căpio*, *cēpi*, *captum*, *capĕre*, take, seize, catch.
accipio, *accēpi*, *acceptum*, *accipĕre*, get;
decipio, cheat; *percipio*, conceive;
incipio, begin; *praecipio*, enjoin, order.

3. *făcio*, *fēci*, *factum*, *facĕre*, do, make.
patefăcio, open; *satisfăcio*, satisfy.
Afficio, *affēci*, *affectum*, *afficĕre*, affect.
conficio, accomplish; *interficio*, kill.
deficio, forsake; *proficio*, contribute;
efficio, bring about; *reficio*, mend, cfr. § 144, 2.

4. *iăcio*, *iēci*, *iactum*, *iacĕre*, throw;
abiicio, *abiēci*, *abiectum*, *abiicĕre*, throw away;
adiicio, add; *subiicio*, subject;
deiicio, cast down; *traiicio*, cross.

b Retaining the Vowel of the Present, 3:

5. *Emo*, *ēmi*, *emptum*, *ĕmĕre*, buy (originally, take);
adimo, *adēmi*, *ademptum*, *adimĕre*, take away;
dirimo, part; *interimo*, slay.

6. *fŭgio*, *fūgi*, *fugĭtum*, *fugĕre*, flee.
aufŭgio, fly from; *confugio*, take refuge.
effugio, escape; *profugio*, run away.

7 *lĕgo*, *lēgi*, *lectum*, *legĕre*, read.
perlĕgo, read through; *relĕgo*, read again.
Colligo, *collēgi*, *collectum*, *colligĕre*, gather.
deligo, choose; *eligo*, select.

(Three compounds of *lĕgo* have the perfect in **exi**, § 119, 27.)

c. Dropping the n (m) of the Present, 5:

8. *Frango*, *frēgi*, *fractum*, *frangĕre*, break.
defringo, *defrēgi*, *defractum*, *defringĕre*, break off.
infringo, impair; *refringo*, break open.

9. *linquo*, *liqui*, *lictum*, *linquĕre*, leave.
relinquo, leave behind, abandon.

10. *pango*, *pēgi*, *pactum*, *pangĕre*, fasten (§ 121, 4).
compingo, *pēgi*, *pactum*, *compingĕre*, compose.

11. *vinco*, *vīci*, *victum*, *vincĕre*, conquer, vanquish.
convinco, prove; *devinco*, subdue.

12. *rumpo*, *rūpi*, *ruptum*, *rumpĕre*, rend, break.
corrumpo, spoil; *erumpo*, burst forth.

II. Supines in **sum**, 3:

13. *Fundo*, *fūdi*, *fūsum*, *fundĕre*, pour.
confundo, disturb; *profundo*, spill.

14. *ĕdo*, *ēdi*, *ēsum*, *edĕre*, eat (cfr. § 139).

15. *fŏdio*, *fōdi*, *fossum*, *fodĕre*, dig.
confŏdio, stab; *effŏdio*, dig out.

No Supine:

16. *Scăbo*, *scābi*, *scabĕre*, scrape, scratch.

§ 121.

PERFECTS FORMED BY REDUPLICATION, 20:

I. SUPINES IN tum, 6:

1. *Căno*, *cĕcĭni*, *cantum*, *canĕre*, sing.
(*concino*, agree, *concinui*, *concentum*).
2. *părio*, *pĕpĕri*, *partum*, *parĕre*, bear, bring forth (§ 77, note).
3. *tendo*, *tetendi*, *tentum* (*tensum*), *tendĕre*, stretch.
(The compounds take no reduplication):
attendo, *attendi*, *attentum*, *attendĕre*, apply, give heed.
contendo, exert; *ostendo*, show.
4. *pango*, *pĕpĭgi*, *pactum*, *pangĕre*, contract (cfr. § 120, 10, and 135, 24).
5. *tango*, *tĕtĭgi*, *tactum*, *tangĕre*, touch.
(Compounds without reduplication):
attingo, *attigi*, *attactum*, *attingĕre*, touch upon.
(*Contingit*, *contigit* and *obtingit*, *obtigit*, it happens.)
6. *pungo*, *pŭpŭgi*, *punctum*, *pungĕre*, sting.
The compounds have only *punxi* in the perfect:
compungo, *compunxi*, *compunctum*, *compungĕre*, sting sharply.
interpungo, *interpunxi*, *interpunctum*, *interpungĕre*, punctuate

II. SUPINES IN sum, 10:

7. *Cădo*, *cĕcĭdi*, *cāsum*, *cadĕre*, fall.
(Compounds without reduplication):
occido, *occidi*, *occāsum*, *occidĕre*, go down, perish.
incido, fall into; *recido*, fall back;
accidit, it happens.
8. *caedo*, *cĕcīdi*, *caesum*, *caedĕre*, hew.
(Compounds without reduplication, supine *isum*):
abscido, *abscidi*, *abscisum*, *abscidĕre*, cut off;
concido, cut to pieces; *incido*, cut into;
occido, kill; *praecido*, cut away.
9. (*cello*, *cecŭli*, *culsum*, *cellĕre*, impel);
percello, *percŭli*, *perculsum*, *percellĕre*, smite, beat down.
antecello and *praecello*, surpass, and *excello*, am eminent, have no perfect nor supine.
10. *curro*, *cucurri*, *cursum*, *currĕre*, run.
(The compounds have generally no reduplication):
concurro, run together; *occurro*, meet;
discurro, run about; *succurro*, aid.

11. *fallo, fĕfelli, falsum, fallĕre,* deceive.
refello, refelli, no supine, *refellĕre,* rebut.

12. *pello, pĕpŭli, pulsum, pellĕre,* drive, rout.
(The compounds without reduplication):
compello, compŭli, compulsum, compellĕre, force;
expello, drive out; *repello,* drive back.

13. *pendo, pĕpendi, pensum, pendĕre,* hang, weigh, pay.
(Compounds without reduplication):
expendo, expendi, expensum, expendĕre, spend;
impendo, devote; *rependo,* repay;
perpendo, consider; *suspendo,* hang up;

14. *parco, pĕperci, parsum, parcĕre,* spare.

15. *tundo, tŭtŭdi, tūsum (tunsum), tundĕre,* beat, bruise.
(Compounds without reduplication):
contundo, contŭdi, contūsum, contundĕre, grind.
obtundo, blunt; *retundo,* beat back.

16. (*fendo, fefendi, fensum, fendĕre,* strike, is found only in the compounds; the perfects admit no reduplication).
defendo, defendi, defensum, defendĕre, protect;
offendo, offendi, offensum, offendĕre, strike against, displease.

III. PERFECTS WHICH DOUBLE THE FINAL SYLLABLE; SUPINES IN tum, 2:

17. *Crēdo, crēdĭdi, credĭtum, credĕre,* believe, trust.
Thus all dissyllables derived from *dare* (110, 1):
abdo, remove, hide; *prōdo,* betray;
addo, add; *reddo,* return, render;
condo, found, build; *trādo,* surrender;
perdo, destroy; *vendo,* sell.

18. *Sisto, stĭti* (for *sistĭti*), *stătum, sistĕre,* place.
(The compounds have *stiti* in the perfect, *stitum* in the supine).
desisto, leave off; *persisto,* persevere.
exsisto, come forth; *resisto,* oppose.
circumsisto, surround, has *circumstĕti* in the perfect, from *circumsto*; but no supine.

IV. PERFECTS BY REDUPLICATION; SUPINE WANTING, 2:

19. *Disco, dĭdĭci, discĕre,* learn.
(The compounds keep the reduplication);
addisco, addĭdĭci, addiscĕre, learn more;
dedisco, unlearn; *edisco,* learn by heart.

20. *posco, pŏposci, poscĕre*, demand.
(Compounds keep the reduplication);
deposco, depoposci, deposcĕre, require;
exposco, entreat; *reposco*, claim.

§ 122.

PERFECTS WITHOUT definite TENSE CHARACTERISTIC, 19

I. Supines in tum, 4:

1. *Bĭbo, bĭbi, pōtum, bibĕre*, drink.
Instead of *bibitum*, etc., *potum, potus* and *poturus* are used.
ebibo, drain; *imbibo*, drink in.
2. *īco, īci, ictum, icĕre*, strike (*icere foedus*, strike a bargain).
3. *lambo, lambi, lambĭtum, lambĕre*, lick.
4. *fĕro, tŭli* (for *tetuli*), *lātum, ferre*, carry (§ 140).

II. Supines in sum, 12:

5. *Findo, fĭdi, fissum, findĕre*, split.
diffindo, diffidi, diffissum, diffindĕre, divide.
6. *scindo, scĭdi, scissum, scindĕre*, tear, cut,
abscindo, abscidi, abscissum, abscindĕre, cut off;
conscindo, tear to pieces; *rescindo*, tear away, annul.
7. *Accendo, accendi, accensum. accendĕre*, kindle.
incendo, fire; *succendo*, kindle.
8. *cūdo, cūdi, cūsum, cudĕre*, beat, forge, stamp.
9. *mando, mandi, mansum, mandĕre*, chew.
10. *pando, pandi, passum* (*pansum*), *pandĕre*, spread out.
11. *prĕhendo, prehendi, prehensum, prehendĕre*, seize, catch
comprehendo, understand; *reprehendo*, rebuke.
12. *scando, scandi, scansum, scandĕre*, climb.
ascendo, ascendi, ascensum, ascendĕre, mount;
conscendo, embark; *transcendo*, overstep.
13. *Vello, velli, vulsum, vellĕre*, pluck (§ 119, 64).
divello, tear asunder; *evello*, pluck out.
14. *verro, verri, versum, verrĕre*, scour, sweep.
15. *verto, verti, versum, vertĕre*, turn.
averto, turn away; *everto*, destroy;
converto, turn to; *reverto*, turn round (§ 135, 15).
16. *sīdo, sēdi* (*sīdi*), *sessum, sidĕre*, sit down (§ 113, 6).
consido, settle; *subsido*, abide.

III. No Supine, 3:

17. *Strīdo, strīdi, stridĕre*, hiss (§ 114, 6).
18. *vīso, vīsi, visere*, visit (§ 113, 7).
19. *psallo, psalli, psallĕre*, play on the lyre.

V. Semideponent (cfr. § 115).

Fīdo, fīsus sum, fidĕre, trust.
confīdo, rely upon; *diffīdo*, mistrust.

Note.—Without perfect and supine: *ambigo, ambigĕre*, I doubt; *clango*, I sound; *furo*, I rave; *glisco*, I glow; *hisco*, I yawn; *vergo*, I am turned towards.

CHAPTER XXII.

IRREGULAR PERFECTS AND SUPINES.

Fourth Conjugation.

§ 123.

PERFECTS IN ui, SUPINES IN tum, 4:

1. *Apĕrio, aperui, apertum, aperīre*, open.
2. *ŏpĕrio, operui, opertum, operīre*, cover, hide.
3. *sălio, salui (salii), (saltum), salīre*, spring, leap.
   assilio, assilui (assilii), assultum, assilire, spring upon.
   desilio, leap down; *transilio*, leap over.
4. *sărio, sarui* (or *sarīvi*), *sarītum, sarīre*, hoe, weed.

§ 124.

PERFECTS WITH THE CHARACTERISTIC s, 9:

I. Supines in **tum**, 8:

1. *Farcio, farsi, fartum, farcīre*, stuff (§ 76, note 2).
   refercio, refersi, refertum, refercire, fill up.
2. *fulcio, fulsi, fultum, fulcīre*, prop.
3. *sarcio, sarsi, sartum, sarcīre*, patch, mend.
4. *haurio, hausi, haustum, haurīre*, draw.
5. *saepio, saepsi, saeptum, saepīre*, fence in.
6. *sancio, sanxi*, (*sanctum* and) *sancītum, sancīre*, enact, ratify.

7. *vincio, vinxi, vinctum, vincīre*, bind.
8. *amicio* (*amixi*), *amictum, amicīre*, clothe.

II. Supine in **sum**, 1:

9. *Sentio, sensi, sensum, sentīre*, feel, think.
consentio, agree; *dissentio*, differ.

§ 125.

PERFECTS LENGTHENING THE ROOT-VOWEL:

Supine in **tum**, 1:

Vĕnio, vēni, ventum, venīre, come.
advenio, arrive; *invenio*, find,
evenio, result; *subvenio*, assist.

§ 126.

PERFECTS WITH SUPPRESSED REDUPLICATIONS.

Supines in **tum**, 2:

1. *Compĕrio* (*pario*, § 121, 2), *compĕri, compertum, comperīre*, ascertain.
2. *rĕpĕrio, repĕri* (*reppĕri*), *repertum, reperīre*, find, discover.

§ 127.

REGULAR PERFECTS, BUT VARYING SUPINES, 4:

1. *Cio, cīvi, cĭtum, cīre*, rouse (mostly *cieo, ciēre*, § 113, 5).
concio, stir up, assemble (participle, *concitus* and *concĭtus*).
2. *eo, īvi, ĭtum, īre*, go (irregular, § 142).
3. *queo, quīvi, quĭtum, quīre*, can (§ 143).
4. *sĕpĕlio, sepelīvi, sepultum, sepelīre*, bury.

§ 128.

Some have neither perfect nor supine.

1. *fĕrio, ferīre*, smite, form (as *foedus*, an alliance).
2. *superbio, superbire*, am haughty.
3. *partŭrio*, am in labor. Thus all desideratives in **ŭrio** (§ 188, 2).

CHAPTER XXIII.

PERFECTS AND SUPINES OF THE INCHOATIVE VERBS.

§ 129.

The inchoative verbs (*i. e.*, such as denote a beginning or growing, § 183, 3) end in **sco**. This syllable however always vanishes in the perfect and supine.

VERBAL INCHOATIVES FROM OBSOLETE ROOT-VERBS, 10:

1. *Adŏlesco, adolēvi, adultum, adolescĕre*, grow up.
2. *abolesco, abolēvi* (*abolitum*), *abolescĕre*, vanish (cfr. 111, 5).
3. *exolesco, exolēvi, exolētum, exolescĕre*, grow out of use.
4. *obsolesco, obsolēvi, obsolētum, obsolescĕre*, grow out of use.
5. *cresco, crēvi, crētum, crescĕre*, grow.
   decresco, wane; *incresco*, increase.
6. *nosco, nōvi, nōtum, noscĕre*, learn to know (§ 146).
   ignosco, forgive.
   agnosco, agnōvi, agnitum, agnoscĕre, acknowledge.
   cognosco, cognōvi, cognitum, cognoscĕre, perceive.
7. *quiesco, quiēvi, quiētum, quiescĕre*, repose.
8. (*suesco, suēvi*), *suētum* (*suescĕre*) am used to.
   assuesco, have the habit; *consuesco*, am wont.
9. *Pasco, pāvi, pastum, pascĕre*, pasture (as shepherd),
   (*pascor*, browse, intransitive, § 104); *depasco*, feed on.
10. *Conquinisco, conquexi* (no Supine), cower down.

§ 130.

VERBAL INCHOATIVES WITH THE PERFECT (AND SUPINE) OF THEIR STILL CURRENT PRIMITIVES, 8 (14):

1. *Inveterasco, inveterāvi, inveterātum, inveterascĕre* (*inveterāre*), grow old (*inveterātus*, rooted).
2. *convalesco, convălui, convălĭtum, convalescĕre* (*valēre*), grow strong, healthy.
3. *exardesco, exarsi, exarsum, exardescĕre* (*ardēre*), am inflamed.
4. *coalesco, coălui, coalĭtum, coalescĕre* (*alĕre*), grow together, become firm.

5. *concupisco, concupīvi, concupītum, concupiscĕre* (*cupĕre*), strive after, long for.
6. *revivisco, revixi, revictum, reviviscĕre*, (*vivĕre*), to come to life again, awake.
7. *obdormisco, obdormīvi, obdormītum, obdormiscĕre*, (*dormīre*), fall asleep.
8. *scisco, scīvi, scītum, sciscĕre* (*scire*), decree.
   conscisco, inflict, *e. g.*, *mihi mortem*; *descisco*, fall away; *rescisco*, find out.

WITHOUT SUPINE.

9. *āresco, arui, arescĕre* (*arēre*), to dry.
   exaresco, dry up.
10. *indŏlesco, indolui, indolescĕre* (*dolēre*), feel pain.
11. *pūtesco, putui, putescĕre* (*pūtēre*), decay.
12. *rŭbesco, rubui, rubescĕre* (*rubēre*), redden.
   erubesco, blush.
13. *ingĕmisco, ingemui, ingemiscĕre* (*gemĕre*), sigh.
14. *resipisco, resipīvi*, and *resipui, resipiscere* (*sapĕre*), become reasonable again.

§ 131.

DENOMINATIVE INCHOATIVES FROM ADJECTIVES; PERFECTS IN ui, NO SUPINE.

1. *Crēbresco, crebrui, crebrescĕre* (*creber*), become frequent.
   increbresco and *percrebresco*, spread abroad (rumors).
2. *evānesco, evanui, evanescĕre* (*vanus*, vain), vanish.
3. *innōtesco, innotui, innotescĕre* (*notus*), become known.
4. *mātūresco, maturui, maturescĕre* (*maturus*), ripen.
5. *obdūresco, obdurui, obdurescĕre* (*durus*), harden.
6. *obmūtesco, obmutui, obmutescĕre* (*mutus*, dumb), grow dumb.
7. *recrūdesco, recrudui, recrudescĕre* (*crudus*), bleed afresh, break out again.

Other substantive inchoatives have neither perfect nor supine; as, *ditesco*, I grow rich; *puerasco*, I become a boy; etc.

§ 132.

I. THE FOLLOWING FIVE VERBS HAVE THE PERFECT AND SUPINE ALIKE:

1. *Cerno*, see, and *cresco*, grow (§ 118, 57, and 129, 5).
2. *cubo*, lie, and *cumbo*, lay myself (§ 108, 2, and 118, 20).

3. *mulceo*, caress, and *mulgeo*, milk (§ 112, 8 and 9).
4. *pendeo*, hang, and *pendo*, hang (§114, 2, and 121, 13).
5. *sedeo*, sit, and *sido*, sit down (§ 113, 6, and 122, 16).

II. THE FOLLOWING FOUR VERBS HAVE THE PERFECT ALIKE:

1. *Frigeo*, am cold, and *frigo*, roast (§ 112, 17, and 119, 21).
2. *fulgeo*, shine, and *fulcio*, prop (§ 112, 14, and 124, 2).
3. *luceo*, light, and *lugeo*, mourn (§ 112, 18 and 19).
4. *paveo*, am afraid, and *pasco*, pasture (§ 113, 8, and 129, 9).

III. THE FOLLOWING EIGHT VERBS HAVE THE SUPINE ALIKE:

1. *Frico*, rub, *frigo*, roast (§ 108, 7, and 119, 21).
2. *maneo*, remain, and *mando*, chew (§ 112, 7, and 122, 9).
3. *pando*, spread out, and *patior*, suffer (§ 122, 10, and 135, 18).
4. *pango*, fasten, and *paciscor*, bargain (§ 120, 10, and 135, 24).
5. *succenseo*, am angry, and *succendo*, kindle (§ 116, 5, and 122, 7).
6. *teneo*, hold, and *tendo*, stretch (§ 116, 3, and 121, 8).
7. *verro*, sweep, and *verto*, turn (§ 122, 14 and 15).
8. *vivo*, live, and *vinco*, conquer (§ 119, 39, and 120, 11).

IV. THE FOLLOWING TWELVE HAVE THE PRESENT ALIKE, BUT BELONG TO DIFFERENT CONJUGATIONS:

1. *aggĕro*, 1. heap; *aggĕro*, 3. convey.
2. *appello*, 1. call; *appello*, 3. land.
3. *compello*, 1. address; *compello*, 3. force.
4. *colligo*, 1. tie together; *colligo*, 3. gather.
5. *consterno*, 1. startle; *consterno*, 3. cover.
6. *effĕro*, 1. make wild; *effĕro*, 3. carry out.
7. *fundo*, 1. found; *fundo*, 3. pour.
8. *mando*, 1. charge; *mando*, 3. chew.
9. *obsĕro*, 1. bar; *obsĕro*, 3. sow about.
10. *pando*, 1. curve; *pando*, 3. spread out.
11. *resĕro*, 1. unbolt; *resĕro*, 3. sow again.
12. *volo*, 1. fly; *volo*, irreg., will.

V. THE EIGHT FOLLOWING HAVE THE PRESENT ALIKE BUT DIFFERENT QUANTITY AND CONJUGATION:

1. *Cōlo*, 1. filter; *cŏlo*, 3. till, honor.
2. *dico*, 1. dedicate; *dico*, 3. say.
3. *indico*, 1. inform; *indico*, 3. proclaim.
4. *praedico*, 1. praise; *praedico*, 3. foretell.
5. *edūco*, 1. rear; *edūco*, 3. lead out.
6. *lēgo*, 1. send, bequeath; *lĕgo*, 3. read.
7. *allēgo*, 1. despatch; *allĕgo*, 3. choose.
8. *relēgo*, 1. banish; *relĕgo*, 3. read again.

CHAPTER XXIV.

PERFECTS AND SUPINES OF DEPONENT VERBS.

§ 133.

1. The perfect of a deponent verb contains the form of the supine; *e. g.*, perf., *hortātus sum;* supine, therefore, is *hortātum.*

2. All the deponents of the first conjugation form the perfect and supine regularly. There is not a single exception in 170 deponents which belong to this conjugation (*vide* § 102).

§ 134.

The second conjugation embraces eight deponents; five are regular; two have the perfect irregular; and one has no perfect:

1. *Lĭcĕor*, *licĭtus sum*, *licēri*, bid on.
    polliceor, promise.
2. *mĕrĕor*, *merĭtus sum*, *merēri*, deserve (also *mereo*, § 92, 2).
3. *misĕreor*, *miserĭtus sum*, *miserēri*, pity (§ 154, 2).
4. *tueor*, *tuĭtus sum*, *tuēri* (see), defend.
    contueor, survey; *intueor*, look at.
5. *vĕreor*, *verĭtus sum*, *verēri*, fear, dread.
    revereor, fear, respect.
6. *Făteor*, *fassus sum*, *fatēri*, avow, own.
    confiteor, *confessus sum*, *confitēri*, acknowledge.
    profiteor, avow openly.
7. *reor*, *rătus sum*, *rēri*, deem, believe.
8. *mĕdeor* (no perf.) *medēri*, heal.

§ 135.

The third conjugation has twenty-nine deponents:

1. *Fruor*, *fruĭtus* (*fructus*) *sum*, *frui*, enjoy (§ 77, note).
    perfruor, enjoy fully.
2. *fungor*, *functus sum*, *fungi*, execute, administer.
    defungor, acquit; *perfungor*, fulfill.

3. *vĕhor*, *vectus sum*, *vehi*, ride (intrans., § 119, 34).
   invĕhor, scold, upbraid.
4. *lŏquor*, *locūtus sum*, *loqui*, speak.
   allŏquor, address; *collŏquor*, converse.
5. *mŏrior*, *mortuus sum*, *mori*, die (§ 77, note).
   demorior, die off; *emorior*, pass away.
6. *pascor*, *pastus sum*, *pasci*, browse (intrans., § 129, 9).
7. *quĕror*, *questus sum*, *queri*, complain.
   conquĕror, bewail.
8. *sĕquor*, *secūtus sum*, *sequi*, follow.
   assĕquor, obtain; *exsĕquor*, carry out;
   consĕquor, reach; *persĕquor*, pursue.
9. *Grădior* (*gressus sum*), *gradi*, step.
   aggredior, *aggressus sum*, *aggrĕdi*, attack;
   congredior, meet; *ingredior*, enter.
10. *lābor*, *lapsus sum*, *lābi*, slip, waver, fall.
   collābor, fall to ruins; *elābor*, slip away.
11. *nītor*, *nīsus* or *nixus sum*, *niti*, rely upon.
   adnitor, strive after; *renitor*, struggle against.
12. (*plector*, *plexus sum*, *plecti*, entwine, cfr. § 119, 68).
   amplector, encircle; *complector*, embrace.
13. *pătior*, *passus sum*, *pati*, suffer.
   perpetior, *perpessus sum*, *perpĕti*, abide, endure.
14. *ūtor*, *ūsus sum*, *ūti*, use.
   abūtor, misuse, consume.
15. (*vertor*, *versus sum*, *verti*, turn; intrans., § 122, 15.)
   devertor, lodge; *revertor*, return (perf. only, *reverti*).

INCHOATIVES.

16. (*apiscor*, *aptus sum*, *apisci*, reach after.)
   adĭpiscor, *adeptus sum*, *adipisci*, obtain.
17. *defetiscor*, *defessus sum*, *defetisci*, weary.
18. *expergiscor*, *experrectus sum*, *expergisci*, awake.
19. *īrascor* (*irātus sum*), *irasci*, am angry.
20. (*meniscor*, *mentus sum*, *menisci*, think.)
   commĭniscor, *commentus sum*, *comminisci*, contrive.
   reminiscor, no perf., *reminisci*, recall.
21. *nanciscor*, *nactus sum*, *nancisci*, meet with.
22. *nascor*, *nātus sum*, *nasci*, am born (§ 77, note).
   innascor, am born in; *renascor*, grow again.
23. *oblīviscor*, *oblītus sum*, *oblivisci*, forget.

24. *păciscor*, *pactus sum*, *pacisci*, contract, bargain (§ 121, 4).
25. *prŏficiscor*, *profectus sum*, *proficisci*, travel.
26. *ulciscor*, *ultus sum*, *ulcisci*, avenge.

No Perfect.

27. *vescor*, *vesci*, subsist upon, enjoy, eat.
28. *liquor*, *liqui*, am fluid, melt.
29. *ringor*, *ringi*, snarl, show the teeth.

§ 136.

The fourth conjugation has fourteen deponents. The perfect in eight is regular; in the remainder, irregular.

1. *Blandior*, *blandītus sum*, *blandīri*, flatter.
2. *largior*, *largītus sum*, *largīri*, give largely.
3. *mentior*, *mentītus sum*, *mentīri*, lie.
   ementior, feign.
4. *mōlior*, *molītus sum*, *molīri*, plan, undertake.
   amolior, remove; *demolior*, tear down.
5. *partior*, *partītus sum*, *partīri*, share.
6. *pŏtior*, *potītus sum*, *potīri*, become master of.
7. *pūnior*, *punītus sum*, *punīri*, avenge (really the passive of *punio*, *punīvi*, *punītum*, *punīre*, punish).
8. *sortior*, *sortītus sum*, *sortīri*, allot, draw lots.
9. *Experior*, *expertus sum*, *experīri*, experience, try.
10. *opperior*, *oppertus* (and *opperītus*) *sum*, *opperīri*, await.
11. *ŏrior*, *ortus sum*, *orīri*, rise, spring from (§ 77, note).
    (Fut. pass. part., *oriundus*, descended from; *orior* follows the third conjugation in the present ind. and imperat., thus: *orĕris*, *orĭtur*, *orĭmur*; *orĕre*, *orĭtor*, *orĭmini*; in the imperf. subj. it usually follows the fourth, *orīrer*; however *orĕrer* occurs).
    The present of *adorior*, attack, is regular and belongs to the fourth; as, *adorīris*, *adorītur*; but *exorior*, spring up, is like *orior*; as, *exorĕris*, *exorĭtur*.
12. *Assentior*, *assensus sum*, *assentīri*, approve.
13. *mētior*, *mensus sum*, *metīri*, measure.
    dimetior, and *emetior*, measure out.
14. *ordior*, *orsus sum*, *ordīri*, undertake.
    exordior, begin.

CHAPTER XXV.

IRREGULAR VERBS.

§ 137.

Irregular verbs are those which depart from the rules laid down for the formation of tenses and persons. There are besides *sum*, ten others; as follows: *possum*, *edo*, *fero*, *volo*, *nolo*, *malo*, *eo*, *queo*, *nequeo*, *fio*.

§ 138.

Possum, I am able, I can. The word is *pot-sum* (composed of *potis*, have the power, and *sum*, I am; hence, I have the power, am able). It is conjugated altogether like *sum*; but remember: 1. the syllable **pot** becomes **pos**, before an **s**; thus: *possum* for *potsum*; 2. the forms *potessem* and *potesse* are contracted into *possem* and *posse*; 3. in *fui*, *fueram*, &c., the **f** is dropped, as *potui* for *pot-fui*; *potueram*.

	INDICATIVE.	SUBJUNCTIVE.
	Present.	
S. 1.	*pos*-**sum**, I am able, I can.	*pos*-**sim**, I may be able.
2.	*pŏt*-**ĕs**, thou art able.	*pos*-**sis**, thou mayst be able.
3.	*pŏt*-**est**, he is able.	*pos*-**sit**, he may be able.
P. 1.	*pos*-**sŭmus**, we are able.	*pos*-**sīmus**, we may be able.
2.	*pŏt*-**estis**, you are able.	*pos*-**sītis**, you may be able.
3.	*pos*-**sunt**, they are able.	*pos*-**sint**, they may be able.

Imperfect.

S. 1.	*pŏt*-**ĕram**, I was able, I could.	*pos*-**sem**, I might be able.
2.	*pot*-**ĕrās**, thou wast able.	*pos*-**sēs**, thou mightst be able.
3.	*pot*-**ĕrat**, he was able.	*pos*-**set**, he might be able.
P. 1.	*pot*-**erāmus**, we were able.	*pos*-**sēmus**, we might be able.
2.	*pot*-**erātis**, you were able.	*pos*-**sētis**, you might be able
3.	*pot*-**ĕrant**, they were able.	*pos*-**sent**, they might be able.

	INDICATIVE.	SUBJUNCTIVE.
	FUTURE.	
S. 1.	*pŏt*-**ĕro,** I shall be able;	Wanting.
2.	*pot*-**ĕris,** thou wilt be able;	
3.	*pot*-**ĕrit,** he will be able;	
P. 1.	*pot*-**erĭmus,** we shall be able;	
2.	*pot*-**erĭtis,** you will be able;	
3.	*pot*-**ĕrunt,** they will be able.	
	PERFECT.	
S. 1.	*pŏt*-**ui,** I have been able.	*pŏt*-**uĕrim,** I may have been able.
2.	*pot*-**uisti,** thou hast been able.	*pot*-**uĕris,** thou mayst have been able.
3.	*pot*-**uit,** he has been able.	*pot*-**uĕrit,** he may have been able.
P. 1.	*pot*-**uĭmus,** we have been able.	*pot*-**uerĭmus,** we may have been able.
2.	*pot*-**uistis,** you have been able.	*pot*-**uerĭtis,** you may have been able.
3.	*pot*-**uĕrunt,** they have been able.	*pot*-**uĕrint,** they may have been able.
	PLUPERFECT.	
S. 1.	*pŏt*-**uĕram,** I had been able.	*pŏt*-**uissem,** I might have been able.
2.	*pot*-**uĕras,** thou hadst been able.	*pot*-**uisses,** thou mightst have been able.
3.	*pot*-**uĕrat,** he had been able.	*pot*-**uisset,** he might have been able.
P. 1.	*pot*-**uerāmus,** we had been able.	*pot*-**uissēmus,** we might have been able.
2.	*pot*-**uerātis,** you had been able.	*pot*-**uissētis,** you might have been able.
3.	*pot*-**uĕrant,** they had been able.	*pot*-**uissent,** they might have been able.
	FUTURE PERFECT.	
S. 1.	*pŏt*-**uĕro,** I shall have been able.	Wanting.
2.	*pot*-**uĕris,** thou wilt have been able.	
3.	*pot*-**uĕrit,** he will have been able.	
P. 1.	*pot*-**uerĭmus,** we shall have been able.	
2.	*pot*-**uerĭtis,** you will have been able.	
3.	*pot*-**uĕrint,** they will have been able.	

INFINITIVE.

PRESENT.	PERFECT.
pos-**se,** to be able.	*pot*-**uisse,** to have been able.

PARTICIPLE.

Wanting.—*Pŏtens*, mighty, is a simple adjective.

IMPERATIVE and GERUND are also wanting.

Instances in early Latin are found, of *potis es* for *potes*, *potis sunt* for *possunt*, *pote* for *potest*. Likewise the subjunctive *possiem* for *possim* (cfr. § 74, note).

§ 139.

Edo, *ēdi*, *ēsum*, *ĕdĕre*, I eat, is conjugated regularly after the third conjugation; but here and there it has abridged forms, which are like those of *sum*, except that the *e* is pronounced long, wherever the tenses of *sum* begins with this vowel.

Pres. Ind. Act.		Imperf. Subj. Act.
S. *ĕdo*,	*edis*, *edit*, **ēs**, **ēst**.	*ĕdĕrem*, *ederes*, *ederet*, **ēssem**, **ēsses**, **ēsset**.
P. *edĭmus*,	*edĭtis*, *edunt*, **ēstis**.	*ederēmus*, *ederētis*, *edĕrent*, **ēssēmus**, **ēssētis**, **ēssent**.

Imperative.		Infinitive Present.
Present,	*ede*, *edĭte*, **ēs**, **ēste**,	*edĕre*, **ēsse**.
Future,	*edĭto*, *edĭto*, *editōte*, **ēsto**, **ēsto**, **ēstote**. *edunto*.	[In the passive, however, also **ēstur** and **essētur** for *editur* and *ederetur*.]

The other tenses are regular. In the same way the compounds, *comĕdo*, I consume, *comedĕre* and *comēsse*; *comederem* and *comēssem*; supine, *comēsum* and *comestum*. Early Latin, subj. *edim*, *edis*, *edit*, cfr. § 105, 8.

§ 140.

Fĕro, *tŭli*, *lātum*, *ferre*, I carry, is conjugated regularly according to the third conjug. with this single exception, that the connecting vowel **i**, before **s**, **t**, is rejected. The same occurs when **ĕ** is between two **r's**; and also in the second sing. pres. imperative. The infinitive pass. is *ferri* (from the old *ferĕri*, instead of *feri*).

ACTIVE.	PASSIVE.
Present Indicative.	
S. *fĕro*, **fers**, **fert**.	*fĕror*, **ferris**, **fertur**,
P. *ferĭmus*, **fertis**, *ferunt*.	*ferĭmur*, *ferimĭni*, *feruntur*.

IMPERFECT SUBJUNCTIVE.

S.	*ferrem, ferres, ferret.*	*ferrer, ferrēris, ferrētur.*
P.	*ferrēmus, ferrētis, ferrent.*	*ferrēmur, ferremĭni, ferrentur.*

IMPERATIVE.

PRES.,	S.	*fer.*	*ferre.*
	P.	**ferte.**	*ferimĭni.*
FUT.,	S.	**ferto, ferto.**	**fertor, fertor.**
	P.	**fertote,** *ferunto.*	*feruntor.*

INFINITIVE PRESENT.

Ferre. **ferri.**

The rest is regular; as, *ferēbam, ferēbas*, etc.; pres. subj., *feram, feras*; pass., *ferar, ferāris*, etc.; fut., *feram, feres*; pass., *ferar, ferēris*. *Tuli* and *latum* are the forms from which are derived *tuleram, tulero, tulerim*, etc.; *latus sum*, etc.

The compounds are conjugated like the primitive verb:

antefĕro, prefer;
circumfĕro, carry about;
defĕro, confer upon, denounce;
perfĕro, endure;
praefĕro, prefer;
profĕro, bring forward, defer;
rĕfĕro (perf. *retuli* and *rettuli*), carry back, relate, report:
transfĕro, carry over.

The following have a slight change in the prefix:

1. **af***fĕro*, **at***tŭli*, **al***lātum*, **af***ferre*, bring to;
2. **au***fĕro*, **abs***tuli*, **ab***latum*, **au***ferre*, carry away;
3. *confĕro, contuli*, **col***latum*, *conferre*, contribute;
4. **dif***fĕro*, **dis***tuli*, **di***latum*, **dif***ferre*, postpone;
5. **ef***fĕro*, **ex***tuli*, **e***latum*, **ef***ferre*, carry out, inter;
6. *infĕro, intuli*, **il***latum*, *inferre*, carry in;
7. **of***fĕro*, **ob***tuli*, **ob***latum*, **of***ferre*, present;
8. **suf***fĕro*, **sus***tuli*, **sub***latum*, **suf***ferre*, endure.

Add, in the perfect and supine,

tollo, sustŭli, sublatum, tollĕre, lift.

attollo, raise; *extollo*, magnify (both without perf. and sup.).

§ 141.

Vŏlo, volui, velle, I will; *nōlo, nolui, nolle*, I am unwilling (from *ne*, instead of *non*, and *volo*); *mālo, malui, malle*, I am more willing (from *ma-volo*, for *mage* or *magis volo*).

INDICATIVE.

Present.

S. 1.	*vŏlo*, I will.	*nōlo*, I am unwilling.	*mālo*, I am more willing.
2.	**vis**, thou willest.	**non vis.**	**māvis.**
3.	**vult**, he will.	**non vult.**	**māvult.**
P. 1.	**volŭmus**, we will.	**nolŭmus.**	**malŭmus.**
2.	**vultis**, you will.	**non vultis.**	**mavultis.**
3.	*volunt*, they will.	*nolunt.*	*malunt.*

Imperfect.

S.	*volēbam, as, at.*	*nolēbam, as, at.*	*malēbam, as, at.*
P.	*volebāmus*, etc.	*nolebāmus*, etc.	*malebāmus*, etc.

Future.

S.	*volam, es, et.*	*nolam, es, et.*	*malam, es, et.*
P.	*volēmus*, etc.	*nolēmus*, etc.	*malēmus*, etc.

Perfect.

S.	*volui, isti*, etc.	*nolui, isti*, etc.	*malui, isti*, etc.

Pluperfect.

S.	*voluĕram, as*, etc.	*noluĕram, as*, etc.	*maluĕram, as*, etc.

Future Perfect.

S.	*voluĕro, is*, etc.	*noluĕro, is*, etc.	*maluĕro, is*, etc.

SUBJUNCTIVE.

Present.

S.	**vĕlim**, I may will.	**nōlim**, I may be	**mālim**, I may
	velis,	**nolis**, [unwilling.	**malis**, [be more
	velit,	**nolit,**	**malit**, [willing.
P.	**velīmus,**	**nolimus,**	**malīmus,**
	velītis,	**nolītis,**	**malītis,**
	velint.	**nolint.**	**malint.**

Imperfect.

S.	**vellem**, *es, et.*	**nollem**, *es, et.*	**mallem**, *es, et.*
P.	*vellēmus*, etc.	*nollēmus*, etc.	*mallēmus*, etc.

Perfect.

S.	*voluĕrim.*	*noluĕrim.*	*maluĕrim.*
P.	*voluerĭmus.*	*noluerĭmus.*	*maluerĭmus.*

PLUPERFECT.

S. *voluissem.*	*noluissem.*	*maluissem.*
P. *voluissēmus.*	*noluissēmus.*	*maluissēmus.*

IMPERATIVE.

PRESENT.

Wanting.	S. **noli,** be unwilling. P. **nolite,** be ye unwilling.	Wanting.

FUTURE.

S. *nolīto,* thou shalt be unwilling.
nolīto, he shall be unwilling.
P. *nolītōte,* you shall be unwilling.
nolunto, they shall be unwilling.

INFINITIVE.

PRESENT.

velle, to will.	**nolle,** to be unwilling.	**malle,** to be more willing.

PERFECT.

voluisse, to have willed.	*noluisse.*	*maluisse.*

PARTICIPLE.

vŏlens, willing.	*nōlens.*	wanting.

GERUND.

volendi, of willing.	*nolendi.*	wanting.

NOTE 1.—Instead of *si vis,* if you will, *sis* is met with; for *si vultis,* rarely *sultis;* for *visne,* will you, *vin'* sometimes.

NOTE 2.—For *vult* and *vultis, volt* and *voltis* are sometimes found.

§ 142.

1. **Eo,** *ivi,* **itum,** *ire,* I go, follows the fourth conjugation, with these variations: 1. before **a, o,** and **u,** the vowel **e** replaces the **i** of the fourth conjugation; thus **eo** instead of **io.** 2. The imperfect is **ibam** instead of *iebam*; the future **ibo** instead of *iam* (§ 106, 8). 3. In the participles, **unt** and **und** are always used instead of **ent, end.**

INDICATIVE.	SUBJUNCTIVE.
	Present.
S. **eo,** *is*, *it*, I go.	**eam, eas, eat,** he may go.
P. *īmus*, *ītis*, **eunt.**	**eamus, eatis, eant.**
	Imperfect.
S. **ībam,** *as*, *at*, I went.	*īrem*, *ires*, *iret.*
P. **ibāmus,** *atis*, *ant.*	*irēmus*, *irētis*, *irent.*
	Future.
S. **ībo, ibis, ibit.**	*itūrus* (*a*, *um*) *sim*, *sis*, *sit.*
P. **ibĭmus, ibĭtis, ibunt.**	*ituri* (*ae*, *a*) *simus*, *sitis*, *sint.*

IMPERATIVE.	INFINITIVE.
Pres. *ī*, go thou; *īte*, go ye.	Pres. *īre*, to go.
Fut. *īto*, thou shalt go.	Perf. *ivisse* or *isse*, to have gone.
īto, he shall go.	
ītōte, ye shall go.	Fut. S. *iturum* (*am*, *um*) *esse.*
eunto, they shall go.	P. *ituros* (*as*, *a*) *esse*, to be about to go.

PARTICIPLE.	GERUND.
Pres. *iens*, gen. **euntis, eunti,** *euntem*, etc.	**eundi,** of going.
	eundo.
Fut. *itūrus*, *a*, *um*.	(*ad*) **eundum.**
Fut. Pass. **eundus,** *a*, *um*.	**eundo.**

SUPINE.

ĭtum, to go. **ĭtu,** to go.

2. The perfect, with all the tenses formed from it, is regular. The passive, also, is regularly formed from the active; thus, *itur*, *eātur*, *ibātur*, *itum est*, *eundum est*, all used impersonally, *i. e.*, only in the third sing.; because *eo* is an intransitive verb. The transitive compounds have a complete passive.

3. The compounds of *eo* are conjugated in the same manner. Remark, however, that the past tenses always drop the **v**; as, *redeo*, perf. *redĭi*, not *redīvi.*

abĕo, go away;
adeo, set about (full passive);
obeo, perform, die;
pereo, perish, decay;
praetereo, pass over (full passive);
prodeo, appear;
redeo, return;
subeo, undertake;
vēneo, go to sale (§ 47, II, 1), be sold: (wants Imperat., Ger., Sup., Part.)

4. *Ambio, ambīvi, ambītum, ambīre*, go around, solicit, is a regular verb of the fourth conj., like *audio*.

§ 143.

Queo, quivi, quitum, quire, I can, and *nequĕo, nequivi, nequitum, nequire*, I cannot, are inflected like *eo;* thus,

INDICATIVE.	SUBJUNCTIVE.
PRESENT.	
S. *nĕqueo, nequis, nequit.*	*nequeam, nequeas, nequeat.*
P. *nequīmus, nequītis, nequeunt.*	*nequeāmus, nequeātis, nequeant.*
IMPERFECT.	
S. *nequībam, as, at,* etc.	*nequīrem, es, et,* etc.

So all the other forms, though they were not in use.

We also meet with the passive, *nequitur* and *quitur*, *nequitum est* and *quita est*, but only when joined to an infinitive passive; (§ 146, note). *Forma in tenebris* **nosci** *non* **quita est.**

§ 144.

Fio, factus sum, fĭĕri, I become, am made, done, is regular according to the fourth conjugation: an irregularity occurs only in the imperf. subj. and pres. inf. where the **i** is shortened and **ĕ** inserted.

PRES. IND.	PRES. SUBJ.
S. *fīo, fīs, fīt.*	*fīam, fīas, fīat.*
P. *fīmus, fītis, fīunt.*	*fīāmus, fīātis, fīant.*
IMPERF. IND.	IMPERF. SUBJ.
S. *fīēbam, as, at.*	*fĭĕrem, fĭĕres, fĭĕret.*
P. *fīebāmus, ātis, ant.*	*fĭĕrēmus, ētis, ent.*
FUT. IND.	IMPERATIVE.
S. *fīam, fīes, fīet.*	PRES. S. *fī*, become; P. *fīte*, become ye.
P. *fīēmus, fīētis, fīent.*	FUT. not used.

INFINITIVE.

PRES. *fĭĕri*, to become.	FUT. *fŏre* or *futurum (am, um) esse.*
PERF. *factum (am, um) esse.*	(*factum iri* is the passive of *facio.*)

From the perfect, *factus sum*, I have become, the other compound tenses are formed regularly: thus, *factus sim, factus eram, factus essem.*

The fut. subj., which is wanting, is supplied by *futurus sim.* Instead of the fut. imperative, *fito, fitote, fiunto*, the pres. subj. form is used; as, *fias, fiat, fiatis, fiunt*, or else *esto, estote, sunto.*

2. *Fio* is likwise the passive of **facio,** I make, do (never *facior*): hence *fio*, I am made, done.

3. The compounds of **facio,** which are composed of a preposition, or of the prefix **re,** have in the active, **ficio,** and in the passive, **ficior:** the conjugation is then regular. Thus, *interficio*, I kill; pass., *interficior, interficĕris, interficĭtur*, I am killed, &c.

4. The other compounds of **facio** have, in the active, **facio,** and in the passive, **fio:** *ārĕ***făcio,** I dry (*areo*, I am dry); pass., *arĕ***fio,** *arĕ***fis,** *arĕ***fit:** *lābĕ***facio,** to shake; *labe***fio,** *labĕ***fis,** *labĕ***fit,** I am caused to shake; *labefiebam, labefierem, labefiam, labefieri* (cfr. § 120, 3).

5. *Fio* has no participles. It borrows *factus* and *faciendus* from *facio;* hence also, *arefaciendus*, (but *interficiendus*.)

NOTE 1.—*Fio, vēneo* (§ 142) and *vāpŭlo* (*avi, atum, are*), I am whipped, are the only verbs which have an active form with passive meaning; they are sometimes called neuter-passive.

NOTE 2.—A few defective compounds of *fio* are sometimes met with; as, *defit*, it is wanting; *infit*, it begins, and some forms of *confieri.*

CHAPTER XXVI.

DEFECTIVE VERBS (VERBA DEFECTIVA).

§ 145.

Some verbs lack many and important tenses, hence they are called defective verbs. They are, 1, the four perfects, **coepi, mĕmĭni, nōvi, ōdi**; 2. **aio**; 3. **inquam**; 4. **fāri**; 5. the imperatives, **ăge, ăpăge, ăve, salve, văle**; 6. **cĕdo**; 7. **quaeso**; 8. **forem.**

§ 146.

Coepi, I have begun; **mĕmĭni,** I remember; **nōvi,** I know; and **ōdi,** I hate, are perfects of an obsolete present. The last three have the meaning of the *present;* **nōvi,** in reality the perfect of *nosco* (§ 129, 6), means, I have learned to know; hence, I know. They are conjugated regularly, as follows:

1. Coepi, I HAVE BEGUN.

Perf. Ind.	Perf. Subj.
S. *coepi, coepisti, coepit.*	*coepĕrim, coeperis, coeperit.*
P. *coepĭmus, coepistis, coepērunt.*	*coeperĭmus, coeperĭtis, coepĕrint.*
Plup. Ind.	**Plup. Subj.**
S. *coepĕram, as, at,* etc.	*coepissem, es, et,* etc.
Fut. Perf.	**Perf. Part. Pass.**
S. *coepĕro, is, it,* etc.	*coeptus, a, um,* begun.
Inf.	**Fut. Part. Act.**
coepisse, to have begun.	*coepturus, a, um,* about to begin.

2. Mĕmini, I REMEMBER.

Perf. Ind.	Perf. Subj.
S. *mĕmĭni, meministi, meminit,* etc.	*meminĕrim, ris, rit,* etc.
Plup. Ind.	**Plup. Subj.**
S. *meminĕram, as, at,* etc., I remembered.	*meminissem, es, et,* etc., I might remember.
Fut. Perf.	**Imp.**
S. *meminĕro, is, it,* etc.	*memento,* remember.
Inf.	*mementōte.*
meminisse, to remember.	

3. Novi, I KNOW.

Perf. Ind.	Perf. Subj.
S. *nōvi, novisti* or *nosti, novit,*	*novĕrim* (*norim*) *is it,*
P. *novĭmus, novistis* (*nostis*), *novērunt* (*nōrunt*).	*novĕrĭmus, novĕrĭtis, novĕrint.*
Plup. Ind.	**Plup. Subj.**
S. *novĕram* or *nōram, as, at,* I knew.	*novissem* or *nossem, es, et,* I might know.
Fut. Perf.	**Inf.**
S. *novĕro, is, it,* etc.	*novisse* or *nosse,* to know.

4. Odi, I HATE.

Perf. Ind.	Perf. Subj.
S. *ōdi, odisti, odit*, etc.	*odĕrim, oderis, oderit*, etc.
Plup. Ind.	**Plup. Subj.**
S. *odĕram, as, at*, etc., I hated.	*odissem, es, et*, etc., I might hate.
Fut. Perf.	**Inf.**
S. *odĕro, is, it*, etc.	*odisse*, to hate.

Perf. part. pass., *osus*, usual only in composition; as, *exōsus, perōsus*, greatly hated; however it is generally used in an active sense, hating very much.

Note.—The best writers do not join *coepi* with a passive infinitive, but they employ *coeptus sum*. *Nos de republica consuli coepti sumus*, we began to be consulted about the republic (They began to consult.) *Armis disceptari coeptum est*. However, when the infinitive has a neuter or middle meaning, *coepi* is used; as, *judicia fieri coeperunt; augeri coepit*, began to grow; *moveri coepit*, to move. In the same manner, do we find *desitus sum* used for *desii* (§ 118, 55); *orationes legi desitae sunt*, have ceased to be read. *Disputari desitum est* (cfr. § 148, note).

§ 147.

Aio, I SAY, I SAY YES.

Pres. Ind.	Pres. Subj.
S. *āio, āis, āit.*	— *āias, āiat.*
P. — — *aiunt.*	— — *aiant.*
Imperf. Ind.	**Perf. Ind.**
S. *āiēbam, as, at.*	— — *āit.*
P. *aiebamus, ātis, ant.*	**Part. Pres.**
Imperative.	*āiens* (affirming).
S. (*ai*). Rest wanting.	(*Ain'* for *aisne*, as in § 141, note).

§ 148.

Inquam, I SAY.

Pres. Ind.	Imperf. Ind.
S. *inquam, inquis, inquit.*	— — *inquiēbat* (*inquibat*).
P. *inquĭmus, inquĭtis, inquiunt.*	

Fut.	Perf. Ind.
S. — *inquies, inquiet.*	— *inquisti, inquit.*

Imperative.

Pres. *inque*, say thou. Fut. *inquito*, let him say.

Note.—*Inquam* is used, as in English, when a conversation is repeated, or for quotation: I said, or said I; while *aio* is only employed in indirect narration, *oratio obliqua.* *Est vero, inquam, notum signum:* It is truly, said I, a seal. *Themistocles universos esse pares aiebat*, Themistocles said that all are equals.

§ 149.

Fari, SAY, SPEAK.

Pres. Ind.

S. — — *fātur.*

P. (*fāmur, fāmĭni, fantur*).

Imperf.

Ind.	Subj.
(*fābar*).	(*fārer*).

Future.

S. *fābor* (*fabĕris*), *fabĭtur.*

Perfect and Pluperfect entire.

fātus sum, sim, eram, essem.

Imperative.	Inf.	Supine.
fāre, speak thou.	*fāri.*	*fātu.*

PARTICIPLE.

Pres. *fans.*

Perf. *fātus*, (having spoken).

Fut. Pass. *fandus, a, um*, about to speak. (*nefandus*, not to be said, heinous).

Gerund.

Gen. *fandi;* Abl. *fando* (*fando audivi*, I know it by hearsay)

Compounds: *affatur, affatus, affari, effabimur, effari;* they however are more or less obselete.

§ 150.

1. *Age*, come! well! Plur. *agĭte.*

2. *Apăge* (=*abige*, take away), begone; *apăge istum hominem!* away with this man! This is the only expression in which it occurs.

3. *Ave* and *salve!* hail! good day! greeting! *văle!* good-bye!

	IMPERATIVE PRESENT.	
S. *ave*, hail!	*salve*, *salveto*, hail!	*vale*, good-bye.
P. *avēte*, hail!	*salvēte*.	*valēte*.
	INDICATIVE FUTURE.	
	salvēbis.	*valēbis*.
	SUBJUNCTIVE PRESENT.	
		valeas, good-bye.
	INFINITIVE.	
avēre, to be greeted.	*salvēre*.	*valēre*.

These three infinitives are used only with *iubeo; valēre te iubeo*, farewell.

§ 151.

Cĕdo, give, say, let's see. *Cĕdo aquam manibus!* Say, give me water for my hands. *Cĕdo dextram*, Your right hand. *Cĕdo, quid faciam!* Say, let's see, what shall I do! The plural *cette* (for *cedite*) may also be used.

§ 152.

Quaeso, I beseech; *quaesŭmus*, we beseech; the rest wanting (cfr. *quaero*, § 118, 49). *Quid, quaeso, faciam?*

§ 153.

Fŏrem, I should be, has *fores*, *foret*, *forent* and *fore*, like *futurum* (*am*, *um; os*, *as*, *a*), *esse*, to be about to be (cfr. § 78, D).

CHAPTER XXVII.

IMPERSONAL VERBS (VERBA IMPERSONALIA).

§ 154.

Impersonal verbs, are those which do not present to the mind a definite person as acting subject; they are, therefore, used only in the third person singular of the indicative and subjunctive, and in the infinitive, never in the imperative, and rarely in the participle.

Among them are:

1. Verbs which denote changes of the weather; as,

fulgŭrat, it lightens:	*gĕlat*, it freezes:
fulminat, it lightens;	*grandinat*, it hails;

lăpidat, it rains stones;
illūcescit, *illuxit*, it dawns;
ningit, it snows;
pluit, it rains;
rōrat, the dew falls;
tŏnat, it thunders;
vesperascit (*advesperascit*, *advesperāvit*), it grows evening.

However, *Jupiter tonat*, *fulminat*, *pluit*.

2. The following verbs of the second conjugation:

piget (*me*), I dislike;
pŭdet (*me*), I am ashamed;
poenitet (*me*), I regret;
taedet (*me*), I am weary, disgusted;
misĕret (*me*; rarely *miseretur me*), pity;
dĕcet (*me*), it becomes;
dēdĕcet (*me*), it is unbecoming;
ŏportet, it behooves;
libet or *lubet* (*mihi*), it pleases;
licet (*mihi*) it is lawful, allowed.

NOTE 1.—The imperative of these verbs is supplied by the subjunctive; as, **pudeat** *te*, be ashamed of; **liceat** *mihi*, let me be allowed. The following participles occur, *dĕcens*, becoming; *libens*, willing; *licens*, unbridled; *poenitens*, repentant; *pŭdens*, modest; also *poenitendus*, *pudendus*. *Mihi poenitendum est*, I must regret (**mihi** not **me**).

NOTE 2.—*Miseret* and *taedet* have, as perfect, *miseritum est* and *pertaesum est*: the rest have a regular perfect; as, *piguit*, *puduit*, *libuit*, *licuit*. However, *pigitum est*, *puditum est*, *libitum est*, *licitum est*, also occur.

NOTE 3.—The following expressions also may be used: *Hoc licet* or *libet*; *non omnia licent*. Poets even make a noun the subject of *decet*; the prose writers, however, only use a neuter adjective or pronoun (§ 196, 2).

3. The following verbs, used personally in their usual acceptations, become impersonal with a slight change in their meaning:

accēdit, in addition to;
accidit, *contingit*, *evĕnit*, it happens;
condūcit, it is useful;
convĕnit, it suits;
expĕdit, it is expedient;
iŭvat, it delights;
constat, it is evident;
restat, it remains;
sŭperest, it remains;
praestat, it is better;
interest, *rēfert* (never pers.) it concerns, it is of importance.
appāret, it appears;
liquet, it is clear;
pătet, it is plain;
fallit (*me*), *fŭgit* (*me*), *praetĕrit* (*me*), it escapes me; I do not know.

4. The third pers. sing. passive of intransitive verbs which otherwise are never used passively (§ 70, II, 2):

curritur, they (people) run.
concursum est, they (people) run together;
vivitur, people live;
itur, they go;
dormitur, they sleep;
dormiētur, people will sleep;
conandum est, it must be tried;
eundum est, people must go;
mihi eundum est, I must go;
vobis eundum est, you must go;
omnibus eundum est, all must go, etc.

CHAPTER XXVIII.

ADVERBS (ADVERBIA).

§ 155.

Adverbs are joined to verbs (*ad-verbia*), and also to adjectives, to limit or modify their meaning. They are divided into adverbs of time, place and manner.

§ 156.

Adverbs of time; in answer to the questions, **Quando?** when? **Quamdiu?** how long? and **Quoties?** how often?

ōlim, once;
quondam, once;
aliquando, once;
unquam, ever;
nunquam, never;
iam, already;
interdum, sometimes;
saepe, often;
semper, always;
pridem, long since;
dūdum, previously;
mox, soon;
brĕvi, shortly;
tandem, at last;
dĕmum, not until, only;
deinde, then;
dēnique, at last;
diū, long;
interdiu, by day;
noctu, by night;
vesperi, in the evening;
māne, early (morning);
nūper, the other day;

hŏdie, to-day;
quŏtidie, daily;
postridie, the day after;
pridie, the day before;
nudiustertius, the day before yesterday;
propĕdiem, one of these days;
hĕri, yesterday;
crās, to-morrow;
tum, then;
tunc, at that time;
nunc, now;
quŏtannis, yearly;
initio, *principio*, } in the beginning; first;
rĕpente, *sŭbito*, } suddenly.
(*rĕcens* lately.)
mŏdo, recently, just now;

ăliās, at other times;
prōtinus, directly;
extemplo, in a moment;
illico, on the spot;
stătim, immediately;
intĕrea, in the meanwhile;
antea, before;
postea, afterwards;
simul, at the same time;
adhūc, yet;
nōndum, not yet;
multo ante, long ago;
paulo post, soon after;
paulisper, a little while;
tantisper, so long;
dēnuo, anew;
plērumque, generally;
tŏties, so often;
aliquŏties, sometimes;
identidem, repeatedly;
rursus (*rursum*), again.

§ 157.

1. Adverbs of place, in answer to the question, **Ubi?** where? **Unde?** whence? **Quo?** whither? **Qua?** by what way?

ibi, there;	*inde*, thence;	*eō*, thither.
hic, here;	*hinc*, hence;	*hūc*, hither.
illic, *istic*, } there;	*illinc*, *istinc*, } thence.	*illūc*, *istūc*, } thither.
ibidem, in the same place;	*indidem*, from the same place;	*eōdem*, to the same place.
ălibi, elsewhere;	*aliunde*, from another place;	*ăliō*, to another place.
ubicunque, wheresoever;	*undecunque*, whencesoever;	*quōcunque*, whithersoever.
alicŭbi, somewhere;	*alicunde*, from somewhere;	*ăliquo*, somewhere.
usquam, somewhere;		*quōquam*, anywhere.
nusquam, nowhere;		
ŭbivis, in any place;		*quōvis*, in any direction you please.
ubique, everywhere;	*undique*, from all sides.	
fŏris, outside;		*fŏrās*, out.
prŏcul, far;	*utrimque*, from either side; on either side;	*obviam*, toward.
prŏpe, near;		*intro*, into.
comminus, close by;		*porro*, forward.
ēminus, at a distance;		*rĕtro*, backward.
pĕrĕgre, abroad;		

2. *Quā?* by, in what way? in what direction? *Eā*, by that way; *quăquam*, in any way; *nequăquam*, in no way; *rectā*, straightway; *dextrā*, to the right; *sinistrā*, to the left; *unā*, in one way, together; *quătĕnus*, how far, in as far as; *hāctĕnus*, so far; *quorsum?* whitherward? *horsum*, hitherward; *aliorsum*, toward another side; *prorsum*, forward; *introrsum*, toward the inside, inward; *deorsum*, downward; *retrorsum*, backward; *dextrorsum*, to the right; *rursum*, again; *sursum*, upward.

§ 158.

1. Adverbs of manner (cause or motive), in answer to the question: **Qui?** how? **Quōmŏdo? Quemadmŏdum?** how? **Cūr? Quare?** why?

Ita, so;	*quăsi*, just as, as if;	*idcirco*, therefore;
sic, so;	*frustra*, vainly;	*ultro*, voluntarily;
ŭt, as;	*nequidquam*, in vain;	*sponte*, freely;
vĕlut, as, like;	*ideō*, therefore;	*quam*, how, how much;

tam, so, so much;
ădeo, so much;
valde, very;
quantŏpĕre, how greatly;
tantŏpĕre, so greatly;
magnŏpere, very;
admŏdum, very much;
nimis, too much;
fĕre, *paene*, nearly, almost;
ferme, *prŏpe*, nearly, almost;
mŏdo, *sŏlum*, only, solely;
tantum, only, solely;
tantummŏdo, only;
sătis, enough;
forte, perchance;
fortasse, *forsitan*, perhaps;
praecipue, especially.

2. Most of the adverbs of manner are derived from adjectives and other parts of speech.

a. Adverbs are formed from participles and adjectives in **us** and **er** by changing the **i** of the gen. into **e**; thus,

ADJECTIVE.	ADVERB.	ADJECTIVE.	ADVERB.
longus, long;	*longē*.	*pulcher*, beautiful;	*pulchrē*.
doctus, learned;	*doctē*.	*prŏbus*, upright;	*prŏbē*.
asper, rough;	*aspĕrē*.	*ornātus*, adorned;	*ornatē*.

Bonus makes *bĕnĕ*, well; *mălus* makes *mălĕ*, ill, badly. *Durus*, hard, *durē* and *duriter*; *firmus*, firm, *firmē* and *firmiter*; *alius* has only *aliter*, otherwise; *violentus*, *violenter*, violently.

b. From adjectives and participles of the third declension, the adverb in **ter** is always formed by changing the genitive ending **is** into **ĭter** and **ntis** into **nter**.

ADJECTIVES.	ADVERBS.	ADJECTIVES.	ADVERBS.
ūtĭlis, useful;	*utĭliter*.	*ăcer*, sharp;	*acriter*.
păr, like;	*părĭter*.	*cĕler*, swift;	*celĕriter*.
fĕrox, fierce;	*ferocĭter*.	*simplex*, simple;	*simplĭcĭter*.
ēlĕgans, fine;	*eleganter*.	*ămans*, loving;	*amanter*.
săpiens, wise;	*sapienter*.	*prūdens*, prudent;	*prudenter*.

NOTE.—*Facilis*, easy; adverb, *facile*. *Rĕcens*, new, recent; adverb, (*recens*). *Difficilis*, difficult; adverb, *difficulter*. *Audax*, bold; adverb, *audacter*. Moreover, *nēquiter* from *nequam*, worthless; *ŏbiter* from *obire*, in passing (by the way).

c. Some adverbs are merely the abl. sing. neut.; others, the acc. sing. neut. of the adjective in **er, us**; as,

certō, surely;
cito, quickly;
crēbro, often;
continuo, instantly;
falso, falsely;
fortuito, accidentally;
improviso, unexpectedly;
mănifesto, manifestly;
mĕrito, justly;
mūtuo, mutually;
necessario, necessarily;
necopinato, unexpectedly;
optato, desirably;
perpĕtuo, unceasingly;

rāro, rarely; *sēdūlo*, industriously; *sērio*, earnestly; *sēro*, too late. *sūbito*, suddenly; *tūto*, securely. *cētērum*, moreover; *multum*, much; *paulum*, little; *nimium*, too much; *pārum*, too little; *potissimum*, the most; *postrēmum* and *postremo*, lastly.

ultimum and *ultimo*, for the last time (cfr. § 61, 2).

§ 159.

Other kinds of adverbs are:

1. In **itus**; as, *coelitus*, from heaven.

Funditus, utterly; *radicitus*, radically, by the root; *antiquitus*, of old; *divinitus*, divinely; (*penitus*, from within, thoroughly; *intus*, within).

2. In **im**, partly verbal adverbs from the supine; as, *certātim*, emulously; partly denominative from nouns; as, *catervātim*, in troops.

From the supine: *contemptim*, scornfully; *nominatim*, expressly; *praesertim*, particularly; *statim*, steadily; *caesim*, by cutting; *passim*, here and there; *sensim*, little by little. From nouns (only **ātim**): *catervatim*, in troops; *gradatim*, by steps; *paulatim*, by degrees; *privatim*, privately; (singly: *furtim*, by stealth; *viritim*, man by man; *tributim*, by tribes; and in **sim**: *vicissim*, in turn). For *partim*, partly, *partem* is also used, both acc. sing. of *pars*.

§ 160.

1. Only such adverbs are compared as are derived from adjectives having a comparative.

2. The comparative of the adverb is always the nom. sing. neut. of the adjective in the comparative; the superlative changes the ending **us** into **ē**.

doctē, learnedly;	*doctius*, more learnedly;	*doctissimē*, most learnedly.
rectē, rightly;	*rectius*, more rightly;	*rectissimē*.
amanter, lovingly;	*amantius*, more lovingly;	*amantissimē*.
certo, surely;	*certius*;	*certissimē*.
crēbro, often;	*crebrius*;	*creberrimē*.
běnĕ, well;	*mĕlius*;	*optimē*.
mălĕ, ill;	*pĕius*;	*pessimē*.
prŏpĕ, nearly;	*prŏpius*;	*proximē*.

3. Of other adverbs, the following only have the three degrees of comparison:

diu, long.	*diutius*, longer.	*diutissimē*, longest.
impūne, with impunity.	*impunius*.	*impunissimē*.
saepe, often.	*saepius*.	*saepissimē*.

Note moreover: *sătius*, better (used nearly always as an adjective and joined to *est*), from *satis*, enough; *sētius* (*secius*), less, only used negatively; as, *nihilo setius*, *neque eo setius*, nevertheless, none the less, perhaps from *sĕcus*, otherwise; *nuperrimē*, quite recently, from *nūper*. Moreover, *prius*, sooner; *primum*, first; *minus*, less; *minime*, least, not at all (cfr. § 51, 1).

Of adverbs in o (§ 158, *c*), only *meritissimo* and *tutissimo* retain o in the superlative; all the others have ē.

CHAPTER XXIX.

PREPOSITIONS.

§ 161.

Prepositions Governing the Accusative.

antĕ, ăpud, ăd, adversus,
circum, circā, citra, cĭs,
erga, contra, inter, extra,
infra, intra, iuxta, ŏb,
pĕnes, pōnĕ, post, and *praeter,*
prŏpĕ, proptĕr, pĕr, secundum,
sŭpra, versus, ultra, trans.

ad, to, at, towards.
adversus, against, towards.
ante, before.
apud, at, near, with, by.
circa, *circum*, around, about.
cis, *citra*, on this side.
contra, against.
erga, towards.
extra, beyond, without.
infra, beneath, below.
inter, between, among.
intra, within.
iuxta, near, beside.
ob, on account of, before.
pĕnes, in the power of.
per, through, by, during.
pone, behind.
post, behind, after.
praeter, beside, except, by.
prope, near.
propter, close by, on account of.
secundum, along, according to.
supra, above.
trans, over, on the other side.
versus, towards.
ultra, beyond.

In compounds *ob* also signifies against; *per*, very, entirely; (cfr. § 186).

§ 162.

Prepositions Governing the Ablative.

absque, ā, ăb, abs and *dē;*
cōram, clam, cum, ex and *ē;*
sĭne, tĕnus, prō and *prae.*

ā, ăb, abs, from; (*a*, only before consonants; *ab*, before vowels and *h;* sometimes, also, before consonants; *abs*, before *te*).
absque, without (obsolete).
clam, without the knowledge of, secretly.
coram, in presence of, before.
cum, with, § 220 and 224.
de, out from, about, of.
e, ex, out of (*e*, only before consonants; *ex*, before any letter).
prae, before, owing to.
pro, for, before, instead of.
sine, without.
tenus, as far as, up to.

§ 163.

Prepositions Governing sometimes the Accusative, sometimes the Ablative.

ĭn, sŭb, sŭper, subter.

1. *In*, in, upon, (**acc.**, in answer to the question, Whither? **abl.**, in answer to the question, Where?) towards, against (only **acc.**)

2. *Sŭb*, under (**acc.**, whither? **abl.**, where?) about (indicating time, only **acc.**)

3. *Sŭper*, over, above (place, always with **acc.**; when it means *de*, over, upon, **abl.**)

4. *Subter*, under, is rare, and always with **acc.** in prose; in poetry, also with the **abl.**

§ 164.

Observations on the Use of some Prepositions.

1. *Ad* is used: 1) of place; as, *ad urbem*, to, up to, near, the city; *ad Rhenum*, on the Rhine; 2) of time; *ad vespĕram*, toward evening; *ad senectutem*, till old age; *ad diem*, on the day fixed; 3) of approximate numbers; *ad ducentos*, about two hundred; 4) of purpose, object; *ad*

2. *Adversus montes*, over against the mountains; *contra*, against, in a hostile sense; *erga*, toward, in a friendly sense; *adversus* and *in*, in either sense; *contra naturam; contra* (*adversus* or *in*) *aliquem bellum gerere; meus erga* (*adversus* or *in*) *te amor.*

3. *Ob; quam ob causam*, wherefore; *ob eam rem*, therefore. —*Ob oculos versari*, to appear before one's eyes.

4. *Penes regem summa potestas est*, with the king, in the king's possession; *apud regem*, near the king.

5. *Per flumen*, through the river; *per orbem terrarum*, over the earth; *per noctem*, through the night, during the night: *si per valetudinem licet*, on account of thy health; *per legatos*, through the ambassadors; *per deos iurare*, by the gods; (cfr. § 220, 1. § 224, 3, 1).

6. *Praeter castra copias duxit*, by, beside the camp; *nemo praeter patrem*, except the father; *praeter ceteros iustus*, beyond the others; *praeter consuetudinem, praeter modum*, contrary to custom, beyond measure.

7. *A* and *ab* are used of place, of time, and with the passive; *ab urbe venit*, from the city; *a muro; a primis temporibus, ab initio; a deo amamur;* (§ 198, 2, 220, 3).

8. *De*, of place; *de coelo*, down from heaven; *de muro*, from the wall (like *a*); very often = on: *de officiis*, on the duties; *de contemnenda morte. Qua de causa*, wherefore; *de industria*, on purpose.

9. *Prae se agere*, to drive before one's self, like *ante se agere;* of time only, *ante* (never *prae*); *prae se ferre*, to make a show of; *prae lacrimis*, for tears; *omnes prae se contemnit*, in comparison with himself.

10. *Pro patria mori*, for one's country; *pro consulibus*, in place of the consuls; *pro castris*, in front of the camp; *pro viribus*, with all your might, according to your strength.

11. *Clam vobis*, without your knowledge.

12. *In patriam redire*, into one's country; *in patria esse*, in one's country; *in diem vivere*, to live only for the day (regardless of the future); *bis in die*, twice a day; *in posterum*, for the future; *in tres annos*, for three years; *amor, odium, merita in patriam*, for one's country; *hostilem in modum*, in a hostile manner; *magna in eo erat modestia*, in him was, *i. e.*, he had; *in oculis omnium*, before the eyes of all, obvious to all; *in his*, among these.

13. *Sub potestatem redigere*, to bring under the power; *nihil novi sub luna est*, under the moon; *sub lucem*, toward morning; *sub divo*, in the open air.

14. *Super aspidem assidere*, to sit on a snake; *super Sunium navigare*, to sail beyond Sunium; *novus luctus super veterem*, new grief added to the old.

15. Prepositions always stand before the case which they govern; the following, however, are put after their case: 1) **cum**, with certain words (*mecum, tecum, secum, nobiscum, vobiscum, quicum*, and mostly *quocum, qua-*

cum, quibuscum); 2) **versus**, with names of towns only; as, *Romam versus*, toward Rome (sometimes **ad** or **in** is put before the case; as, *Italiam versus, ad Oceănum versus*); 3) **tenus**; as, *Tauro tenus*, as far as Mount Taurus; *tenus* sometimes with the genitive; as, *crurum tenus*; 4) the words *causā, gratiā, ergō* = for the sake of; as, *animi causa*, for recreation; *venandi gratia*, for the sake of hunting; *hujus victoriae ergo*, on account of this victory. However, these words are not properly prepositions, but substantives. Instead of the genitive of the personal pronoun, the possessive, with *causa* and *gratia*, is used; as, *meā causā*, for my sake, on my account (§ 221, 2, 1).

16. Several prepositions are sometimes used as adverbs, without any case; as, *ante* for *antea*, *post* for *postea*, etc. On the other hand, several adverbs are sometimes used as prepositions; as, *circiter meridiem*, towards noon; but also *circiter quadringenti; eadem circiter hora;* likewise, *pălam populo*, publicly before the people; *prŏcul dubio*, without doubt, etc. Instead of *prope urbem*, we sometimes find *prope ab urbe; also propius* and *proxime ab urbe*, and *urbem;* or with dat., *propius Tiberi, propius periculo; proxime castris.* § 203, 2, 1.

CHAPTER XXX.

CONJUNCTIONS.

§ 165.

Conjunctions, according to the grammatical nature of the sentences which they connect, are divided into two classes:

A. *Coördinate conjunctions*, or conjunctions which connect coördinate sentences; *i. e.*, sentences of equal independence, as principal sentences with principal, dependent clauses with dependent.

B. *Subordinate conjunctions*, or conjunctions which connect subordinate clauses; *i. e.*, secondary sentences with principal sentences.

These two classes are, according to the logical relation of the connected sentences, subdivided into ten kinds, of which three contain only coördinate conjunctions, two partly coördinate, partly subordinate, five only subordinate conjunctions. To the conjunctions must be added the interrogative and negative particles.

The logical relation of the connected sentences gives the name both to the sentences themselves and to the corresponding conjunctions.

A. Only Coördinate:

I. COPULATIVE CONJUNCTION
(*Coniunctiones copulativae*),

IN COPULATIVE SENTENCES.

Et, *atque*, *ac*, *quĕ*,	and.	*ĕtiam*, *quŏque*,	also.
		nĕque, *nec*,	and **not**.

ĕt — *et*, both — and.
cum (*quum*) — *tum*, both — **and**.
tam — *quam*, as well — as.
tum — *tum*, now — now.
nĕque — *nĕque*, *nec* — *nec*, neither — nor.

1. **Et** and **atque** can always be used, but **ac** only before consonants; **que** is appended to the word; hence, *parentes liberi***que**, parents and children; *parentes* **et** (*atque*, *ac*) *liberi*.

2. **Etiam** is nearly always placed before, **quoque**, after, the word to which it refers; *etiam pater*, the father also, but *pater quoque*.

3. **Et** — **et**, both — and: **et** *parentes* **et** *liberi*, both parents and children.

4. **Neque** — **neque**; **nec** — **nec**, neither — nor; **nec** *parentes* **nec** *liberi*, neither the parents nor the children.

Note 1.—When three or more words are connected, either no conjunction is used in Latin, as: *divitiae*, *honor*, *gloria fortuita sunt* (asyndeton); or **et** is put before every word that is added; as, *stultitiam* **et** *temeritatem* **et** *iniustitiam* **et** *intemperantiam dicimus esse fugienda* (polysyndeton).

Note 2.—**Que** (as well as **ve** and **nĕ**) is not easily appended to prepositions; the Latin says, *in* **eoque** (not so well, **inque**), *de tota***que** *re*, *ab omnibus***que** (*ex ea***ve** *re*, *ad eam***ne** *rem*).

Note 3.—**Etiam** is more emphatic than *quoque;* it has a strengthening force and means *even*, with the comparative. Before pronouns **et** sometimes stands for *etiam*, as: *et ipse*, he himself also; otherwise rare.

Note. 4.—**Neque** joins a negative sentence: when the negative *and not* refers to a single word only, **et non** or **ac non** is used, and when the opposition is marked, simply **non**. *Hoc longum est* **et non** *neces-*

sarium. A gravibus philosophis medicina petenda est, **non** *ab his voluptariis.*

NOTE 5.—**Neque quisquam,** *neque quidquam, neque ullus,* &c., are used in the same manner as *neque;* but when the negation is to be emphatic, use **et nemo, et nihil, et nullus,** &c.

NOTE 6.—In a transition, **neque enim, neque vero, neque tamen** are generally used, where in English we frequently say only: *for not, but not, still not,* without the *and.*

NOTE 7.—The combination **neque — et** occurs also in English, *not — and,* as: *homo* **nec** *meo iudicio stultus,* **et** *suo valde prudens,* in my opinion *not* foolish, *and* in his own very prudent. Vice versa, **et — nec,** in which *et* need not be translated; as, *via* **et** *certa* **nec** *longa,* a road sure *and not* long. Sometimes it may be translated by: On the the one hand — on the other, not. Rare and mostly poetical, are the combinations: *et — que; que — et; que — que.*

§ 166.

II. DISJUNCTIVE CONJUNCTIONS
(*Coniunctiones disiunctivae*),

IN DISJUNCTIVE SENTENCES.

Aut, } or.
vĕl, }

vĕ, } or.
sīve, }

aut — aut, } either — or.
vel — vel, }

sive — sive, whether — or; be it — or.

Aut, or, excludes; **vel** equalizes, corrects, graduates; **ve** (enclitic), like *que,* is appended (§ 165, 2); **sive** (unusual *seu* for *vel si*), when the choice is indifferent.

Plus minusve, more or less; also *plus minus.*

§ 167.

III. ADVERSATIVE CONJUNCTIONS
(*Coniunctiones adversativae*),

IN ADVERSATIVE SENTENCES.

Sĕd, } but.
vērum, }
vēro, }
autem, }
at, }

at vēro, but.

tămen, still, yet.

atqui, but still, but yet.

cētĕrum, for the rest.

ĕnimvēro, truly.

sedtămen, } but yet.
verumtămen, }

attămen, but yet.

non solum — sed etiam,
non modo — sed etiam,
non tantum — sed etiam, } not only — but also.

Sed and **verum** are corrective and affirming; **vero,** advancing; **autem** (atonic) marks transition; **at** objects, brings in an objection.

Sed, verum, at, are placed at the beginning of the sentence; **vero, autem,** only after one or more words.

NOTE.—*Sed enim, at enim,* but forsooth, are often used elliptically; as, *at enim viri clarissimi dissentiunt,* but forsooth (there is still another point; for), the most illustrious men are of a different opinion.

B. PARTLY COÖRDINATE, PARTLY SUBORDINATE.

§ 168.

IV. ILLATIVE CONJUNCTIONS.

a. Coördinate, *coni. conclusivae,* to denote an inference or conclusion, in conclusive sentences:

Igĭtur,
ĭtăque, } therefore.

ergō, consequently.

ĭdeo,
ĭdcirco,
proptĕrea, } therefore, on this account.

proinde, hence.

b. Subordinate, *coni. consecutivae,* to denote consequence, result, in consecutive sentences:

ut, so that, § 249.

ut non, so that not, § 250, 2.

quin, that not, § 252.

1. **Igitur** is always *atonic,* and is placed after another word; as, *omnes* **igitur** *adsunt;* but **itaque** or **ergo** *omnes adsunt.* **Proinde** stands only in sentences with the imperative or subjunctive. Distinguish *ităque,* therefore, from *itāque,* and thus.

2.—Here may be placed the compound expressions, *ob eam rem, ob eam causam, hanc ob rem, hanc ob causam, ea de re, ea de causa,* therefore; also *quocirca, quapropter, quam ob rem, quam ob causam,* wherefore, therefore.

§ 169.

V. CAUSAL CONJUNCTIONS
(*Coniunctiones causales*).

A. Coördinate.	B. Subordinate.
Nam, *namque*, *ĕnim*, *ĕtĕnim*, } for.	*quĭa*, *quod*, } because.
	cum (*quum*), as, because, § 256.
	quŏniam, because indeed.
quippe, for, of course.	*quando*, as indeed.

Nam, namque, etenim are emphatic and stand at the beginning of the sentence: **enim** is atonic and always stands in the second place: thus, **nam** *ipse dixit*, but *ipse* **enim** *dixit*. *Quando*, *quandoquidem* denote a reason implied in a circumstance previously mentioned. Concerning *enimvēro*, *at enim*, cfr. § 167 and note.

C. Only Subordinate.

§ 170.

VI. COMPARATIVE CONJUNCTIONS
(*Coniunctiones comparativae*),

IN COMPARATIVE SENTENCES.

Ut, *ŭti*, } as.	*tanquam*, *quăsi*, *ut si*, *ac si*, } as if.
quam, than, as,	
sīcut, such as,	
vĕlut, as if, for example.	*prout*, according as.

1. **Ut** is the relative corresponding to **ita** and **sic** (§ 158, 1); the three are adjuncts to the verb; as, *ut dixi*, as I said; *ita dixi*, *sic dixi*, thus have I said. **Quam,** how, is relative to **tam,** and both are joined to the adjective; as, *quam bonus est deus!* How good is God! *tam bonus est*, so good is he!

2. As great as, **tantus, quantus**; as many as, **tot quot**; as often as, **toties quoties.** However, the following are also allowable: *tam magnus quam*, *tam multi quam*, *tam saepe quam*. After *idem*, *par*, *similis* and usually after *aeque*, *iuxta*, *perinde* (just), *alius* and *contra* (opposite), the words *to*, *as*, *than*, are rendered by **atque** or **ac:** *e. g.*, *peccasti* **eodem** *modo* **atque** *ego*, thou hast failed in the same manner as I; **aliter atque** *tu*, otherwise than thou.

§ 171.

VII. CONDITIONAL CONJUNCTIONS
(*Coniunctiones conditionales* or *hypotheticae*),

IN CONDITIONAL SENTENCES.

Si, if.	*si nōn*, *nĭsi*, *ni*, } if not, unless.
sin, but if.	
si quĭdem, if indeed.	*si mĭnus*, if not.
quodsi, even if, nay if.	*dummodo*, if only, § 173.

After a negative, **nisi** means except, but; as, *nemo nisi improbissimus*, none but the most shameless. Here **quam** is not admissible.

NOTE 1.—**Sin** is used after a preceding conditional sentence. *Si verum dicis, laudaberis; sin mentiris, punieris;* also, *sin autem*, rarely *si autem*. Instead of **nisi**, you must say **si non**, when the negation refers to *one* word only; *si non omnes tamen aliquot.* In connection with **si minus**, if not, the verb is *not* repeated; *si dabis, accipiam, si minus, abibo.*

NOTE 2.—Concerning the mood with conditional conjunctions, see § 248, 3, *a*.

§ 172.

VIII. CONCESSIVE CONJUNCTIONS
(*Coniunctiones concessivae*),

IN CONCESSIVE SENTENCES.

Etsi, *tametsi*, *etiamsi*, *quamquam*, } even if, even though, although.	*quamvīs*, however much, although.
	lĭcet, although.
	cum (*quum*), although, § 254, 5; 256.
	ut, supposing that, § 249, 3.

Quidem, however, indeed, it is true, may also be reckoned among the concessive conjunctions. It is coördinate, and always leans on another word, being itself atonic; as, *multi quidem dicunt*, many, indeed, say. Likewise, **quamquam** and **etsi** are sometimes coördinates; they then approach the adversatives and have no apodosis; as, *Quamquam quid loquor?* Yet, why do I speak? *Tu ut unquam te corrigas?* Concerning the mood, see § 254, 5.

§ 173.

IX. FINAL CONJUNCTIONS
(*Coniunctiones finales*),

IN FINAL SENTENCES.

Ut (*uti*), in order that, that, § 249.
nē, in order that not, lest, § 250.
nēve, and lest.
quō, in order that, § 251.
quōminus, in order that not, § 253.
mŏdo, *dum*, *dummŏdo*, } in order that, if only, § 254, 3.

§ 174.

TEMPORAL CONJUNCTIONS
(*Coniunctiones temporales*),

IN TEMPORAL SENTENCES.

cum (*quum*) when, § 256.
ŭt, when, as § 245, 2.
ŭbi, when.
antĕquam, *priusquam*, } before that.
dum, *dōnec*, *quoad*, } while, until, as long as.
postquam, *posteaquam*, } after that, § 245, 2.

cum (*quum*) *primum*, *ut primum*, *ubi primum*;
simulatque, *simulac*, as soon as, § 245:
quando, when.

§ 175.

NEGATIVE PARTICLES
(*Particulae Negativae*).

Non, not, no.
haud, not.
nē, not.
et nōn, and not.
nē — quĭdem, not even.
părum, *mĭnus*, } too little, not quite.
vix, scarcely.
nĕque, *nĕve*, } and not.
mĭnĭme, by no means, not at all.
neutĭquam, *nequāquam*, } by no means, not at all.

With **ne — quidem**, the emphasized word is placed in the middle; as, *ne unus quidem*, not even one.

NOTE 1.—**Non (haud)** and **neque** (= *et non*) are negative, **ne** and **neve**, prohibiting; hence the two latter only with imperative and subjunctive. *Haud* is weaker and less frequent than *non;* it occurs chiefly in certain phrases; as, *haud ita facilis*, not so easy. Especially, *haud scio an*, properly, I know not whether; but only used in affirming. It may be translated by *perhaps* (§ 176, note 3, *d.*).

NOTE 2.—**Non** means *no* (adj.) when it refers to an adjective; as, *non inutilis opera*, no useless trouble, *i. e.*, not a useless trouble. *Non magna virtus*, is, a no great virtue, not a great virtue, small virtue; on the contrary, *nulla magna virtus*, is, no great virtue.

NOTE 3.—As *neque quisquam*, *neque ullus*, is said instead of *et nemo*, *et nullus*, so also *ne quis* (rarely *quisquam*), *ne ullus*, *ne quid*, *ne unquam*, etc., is used instead of *ut nemo*, *ut nullus*, *ut nihil*, *ut nunquam*, etc., in every case in which **ne** must be used for **ut non** (§ 250, 2).

NOTE 4.—Two negations within the same sentence destroy each other and form an affirmation. **Non** *potui* **non** *mirari*, I was forced to admire. Remark that the position of the negations often produces a great difference:

non*nemo*, somebody.	*nemo* — **non**, everybody.
non*nullus* (mostly plur. *nonnulli*, some).	*nullus* — **non**, all, each.
non*nihil*, something.	*nihil* — **non**, all.
non*nunquam*, sometimes.	*nunquam* — **non**, always.

Thus also *nusquam* — **non**, everywhere (*alicŭbi*, somewhere), and *nec* — **non** for *and.* However, the latter negation must always stand immediately before the verb. **Nemo** *in hac re tibi* **non** *studuit*, everybody favored thee in this affair (not, *nemo* **non** *in hac re*, etc.). In like manner, *non* — *nisi* used in the sense of *only.* **Non** *loquimur* **nisi** *de te. Vera amicitia* **nisi** *in bonis esse* **non** *potest.*

Two negations do not destroy each other when *nec* — *nec* or *ne* — *quidem* follows a general negation. **Nihil** *est Attico mihi* **nec** *carius* **nec** *iucundius. Nusquam hoc ne apud barbaros quidem auditum est.*

NOTE 5.—*Not even* is **ne quidem** (not *etiam non*); as, *Superbia* **ne** *regem* **quidem** *decet*, is, not becoming even in the king. *Qui sua negligit, is* **ne** *aliena* **quidem** *tuebitur.*

NOTE 6.—The English *not only not*, followed by *but not even*, *but also not*, *but scarcely*, is generally rendered in Latin by **non modo** (*solum*), **non, sed ne — quidem**, or **sed vix.** *Ego* **non modo** *tibi* **non** *irascor*, **sed ne** *reprehendo* **quidem** *factum tuum. Obscoenitas* **non solum non** *foro digna*, **sed vix** *convivio liberorum.* But if both members of the sentence have a common predicate which is in the last member, then it is rendered (one *non* being omitted) by **non modo, sed**

ne — quidem or **sed vix.** *Regnum video*, **non modo** *Romano homini*, **sed ne** *Persae* **quidem** *cuiquam tolerabile, i. e.*, properly, not only to a Roman, but even to a Persian, intolerable. *Haec genera virtutum* **non solum** *in moribus nostris*, **sed vix** *iam in libris reperiuntur.*

NOTE 7.—**Non modo** can often be translated by *I will not say* (for which *non dico, non dicam* sometimes stand); the following **sed** means then, *but only.* *Qua in re* **non modo** *ceteris specimen aliquod dedisti*, **sed** *tute tui periculum fecisti?* **Non modo** means also, *not to say, much less*, when preceded by *ne — quidem* (like *nedum*, § 254, 4). *Apollinis operta nunquam ne mediocri quidem cuiquam*, **non modo** *prudenti, probata sunt.*

NOTE 8.—The expression, **non magis quam** (*non plus quam*), not more than, is equivalent to the English, *just as much as*, when both members of the sentence form an affirmation; to the English, *as little as*, when both members form a negation. *Domus erat* **non** *domino* **magis** *ornamento*, **quam** *civitati* (with inverted order; as much to the state, as to its owner). **Non** *nascitur ex malo bonum*, **non magis, quam** *ficus ex olea* (as little as). The expression **non minus quam,** not less than, is also often equivalent to the English, *as much as.* *Patria hominibus* **non minus** *cara esse debet*, **quam** *liberi*, not less dear, or, as dear as. With **non magis quam,** the more important idea must be in the member beginning with **quam**; with **non minus quam,** in the member beginning with **non minus.** Hence the last example may, without any material change of sense, be expressed thus: *Liberi hominibus* **non magis** *cari esse debent*, **quam** *patria.*

§ 176.

INTERROGATIVE PARTICLES

(*Particulae interrogativae*).

Num, *nĕ,* *nonne,*	a simple question.	*utrum — an,* *nĕ — an,* — *— an* or *nĕ,*	double questions.

The reply to *num* is no, to *nonne*, yes; the question introduced by *ne* implies an uncertainty as to the answer; it is annexed to the most emphatic word (§ 165, note 2).

1. **Num** *vides?* Seest thou? Ans. **non** *video*, no.—**Nonne** *vides?* Dost thou not see? Ans. **ita, ĕtiam,** yes; **sāne,** of course; **omnino,** by all means; **certe,** to be sure.—*Vides***ne** (*vides*)? Dost thou see? Ans., *video*, yes; *non video*, no.—**Utrum** *domi fuisti* **an** *in schola?* Hast thou been at home or at school?

Interrŏgo te, **num videas**, or **videasne**; I ask thee, whether thou seest. *Interrogo te*, **nonne** *videas*; I ask thee, whether thou dost not see. *Interrogo te*, **utrum** *domi fueris*, **an** *in schola*; I ask thee whether thou hast been at home or at school.

2. In disjunctive or double questions, in which it is asked, which of several cases, that exclude one another, will take place; the first member has **utrum** or **ne** or *no interrogative* particle; but in all the following members **an** is used. If the question has only two members, the former can be introduced without a particle, the latter with the annexed particle **ne**.

Utrum *haec syllaba brevis* **an** *longa est?* *Brevis***ne** **an** *longa est?* *Brevis* **an** *longa est?* *Quaero ex te, haec syllaba brevis longa***ne** *sit.* If *or not* occur in the second member, it is expressed by **annon** or **necne**. **Utrum** *domi fuisti* **annon**? *Interrogo te*, **utrum** *domi fueris*, **necne**.

NOTE 1. The above-mentioned interrogative particles are mere forms, without any other meaning than to make the sentence interrogative; they only inquire, Whether, or Whether not. Whereas, the interrogatives, properly speaking, direct the question to some definite point, as: *quis?* who? *ubi?* where? *quando*, when? *cur?* why?

Questions as to form; questions as to contents, cfr. § 67, 156, &c.

NOTE 2.—Questions are direct or indirect. A direct question is one which, by virtue of its form, demands an answer; it is always independent. An indirect question is one which, by virtue of its form, does not require an answer; it is always dependent on another word. **Quid dicis?** what sayest thou? is direct, independent, and requires an answer; likewise, **num dormis?** dost thou sleep? Whereas, in the sentence, *Non intelligo, quid dicas*, the question, **quid dicas,** is indirect, dependent on the verb *intelligo*, and requires no answer. Likewise, *Ista interrogatio*, **num dormiam,** *otiosa est. Incertus sum*, **quid** *optimum* **sit.**

NOTE 3.—Concerning the interrogative particle, **an,** note especially:

a. In the disjunctive (double) interrogation, **an** may only be used in the second and subsequent members; English, *or* (never *whether*).

b. In the simple direct question, **an** is often placed at the beginning of the question, when in English also we say *or*, viz., in oppositions. *Oratorem irasci minime decet.* **An** *tibi irasci tum videmur, quum acrius et vehementius dicimus?* With **an vero** sometimes, for the sake of emphasis. Frequently, **an vero** *dubitamus*, *or* do we perhaps doubt? *Or* could we have the least doubt?

c. Without opposition, an affirmative question is often begun with **an**, nearly in the sense of *nonne*. *Quidnam beneficio provocati facere debemus?* **An** *imitari agros fertiles, qui multo plus efferunt, quam acceperunt?* *Quando autem ista vis (oraculi) evanuit?* **An** *postquam homines minus creduli esse coeperunt?* not perchance when? etc.

d. In the simple indirect question, **an** stands only with expressions of uncertainty; as, **dubito an, nescio an, incertum est an**, etc., and these expressions then always incline towards an affirmation; **an** is equal to *whether not* in this case, and the whole expression to *forsitan*. *Si per se virtus sine fortuna ponderanda sit,* **dubito an** *hunc primum omnium ponam* (I should perhaps place, *forsitan ponam*). *Contigit tibi, quod* **haud scio an** *nemini.* *Moriendum certe est, et id* **incertum, an** *eo ipso die* (perhaps this very day). *I doubt whether*, is always **dubito num.**

§ 177.

Interjections also are particles, incapable of inflection. They are, 1) expressive of joy: *io, euoe, euax;* 2) of grief: *heu, eheu, pro* (*proh*), *vae* (*au, hei, ohe*); 3) of wonder: *o, en,* and *ecce,* lo! *hem, ehem, hui!* 4) of disgust: *phui! apage!* (§ 150); 5) of address: *heus, eho, ehodum!* 6) of flattery · *eia* and *euge!* behold!

As oaths, were used: *nae*, truly; also *hercule* or *mehercule*, by Hercules! (*hercle, mehercle; mehercules*); *medius fidius, mecastor, edepol, per deum*, by God! *pro deum fidem!*

CHAPTER XXXI.

FORMATION OF WORDS.

§ 178.

The simplest element of a word is called the **root**. This is only rarely found, in its root-form, as a current word; *e. g.*, *sol*, the sun. The root generally undergoes various changes before it becomes a word of the language. The word least modified is called **root-word**; thus, *rego*, is root-word from the root *reg*. Words which have the same root are called **derivative**; as, *rego, rex, regnum, erigere,* &c., all formed from the root *reg*. A word which serves as stem from which other words spring forth, is called the (proximate) **stem-word**; thus *facio*, (ro · *fac*) is the stem-word to *facilis*, and the latter in turn to *facilitas*.

New words are formed

I. By *derivation;*

II. By *composition.*

The stem-words are called **primitives** (*primitiva*); those formed by derivation, **derivatives** (*derivāta*); words formed by composition, **compounds** (*composita*); those not thus formed, **simple words** (*simplicia*). Words derived from a verb, **verbals** (*verbalia*); those derived from a noun, **denominatives** (*denominativa*).

By Derivation.

Verbal Substantives (*substantiva verbalia*) are formed:

a). From a verbal-stem by the addition of the following endings:

1. **or,** to denote a *disposition* or *state;* as, *amor*, love; *timor*, fear; *dolor*, pain; *decor*, decency, gen. *decōris:* (but *decus*, ornament, *decŏris*).

Note.—A rare ending, with the same force of meaning, is **us**; as, *decus, ŏris*, the ornament; *frigus*, cold; *genus, ĕris*, race (*gigno*).

2. **ium**; as, *gaudium*, joy; *odium*, hatred.

3. **igo**; as, *origo*, source (*orior*); *vertigo*, dizziness.

4. **ido**; as, *libido*, passion (*libet*); *cupido*, desire.

5. **men** and **mentum,** to denote the *means;* as, *medicāmen* and *medicamentum*, a means of cure, remedy; *tegŭmen* (*tegimen*) and *tegumentum*, a covering; *nomen* (from *no-sco*, a means of knowing), a name; *flumen*, river; *lumen* (for *luc-men*), light; *agmen*, train, troop; *alimentum*, food; *ornamentum*, ornament; *monumentum*, memorial.

6. **bŭlum** and **cŭlum,** to denote the *instrument;* as, *vocabŭlum*, word (means of calling, *vocare*); *pabŭlum*, fodder (*pa-sco*); *venabŭlum*, hunter's spear; *fercŭlum*, bier; *gubernacŭlum*, helm; *iacŭlum*, dart; *vincŭlum*, band (*fulcrum*, support, for *fulcŭlum; latibŭlum* and *latĕbra*, hiding-place).

7. **trum,** to denote an *implement, tool;* as, *arātrum*, plough; *claustrum* (for *claudtrum*), lock; *rostrum* (*rodĕre*), beak.

b. From the **supine-stem** with the endings:

1. **or,** to denote the *person acting*, performing or doing; as, *amātor*, lover; *doctor*, teacher; *cursor*, runner; *audĭtor*, hearer. Most of these have also a feminine form in **trix**; as, *victor*, the conqueror; *victrix*, the female conqueror; *tonsor*, barber, *tonstrix; expulsor, expultrix*, expeller. *Viātor*, from *via*, traveler; *ianitor*, from *ianua*, doorkeeper; *funditor*, from *funda*, slinger, are denominatives; perhaps, also, *gladiator*, from *gladius*, swordsman.

Note.—The person doing (agent) is also sometimes denoted by the ending **a,** added to the stem of the verb; as, *scriba*, the writer (as an official, or clerk); but *scriptor*, one who is engaged in the act of writing; likewise *incŏla, advĕna, conviva*.

2. **io** denotes the *act* itself while *in progress;* as *actio*, deed; *oppugnatio*, storming; *defensio*, defence; *motio*, movement. *Opinio*, belief; *oblivio*, forgetfulness, &c., are formed directly from the verbal stem. *Obsidio*, blockade, *obsessio*, siege.

3. **us**, gen., *ūs*, denotes the *act* as *existing;* thus, *motus*, movement *adventus*, arrival; *auditus*, hearing.

4. **ūra**; as, *pictūra*, painting; *mercatura*, commerce; *censura*, censorship; *praetura*, *quaestura*.

5. **ēla**; as, *tutēla*, guardianship; *corruptēla*, corrupting: the ending is often added to the verbal-stem; as, *querela*, complaint; *candela*, candle.

§ 179.

DENOMINATIVE SUBSTANTIVES (*substantiva denominativa*) are formed partly from nouns, partly from adjectives. The former end in:

1. **a**, forming a feminine for words in **us** and **er** of the second declension; thus, *asina*, she-ass; *dea*, goddess; *magistra*, mistress; *capra*, she-goat (*caper*, he-goat).

2. **ius, ia, ium**, forming diminutives (*diminutiva*), in:

a. **ŭlus, a, um**, for stem-words of the first and second decl., and a few of the third; as, *lunŭla*, small moon; *virgula*, small branch; *hortulus*, small garden; *puerulus*, small boy; *oppidŭlum*, small town. *Vocula*, *regulus*, *adolescentulus*.

b. **ŏlus, a, um**, which is used for *ŭlus*, when a vowel precedes; as, *gloriŏla*, small glory; *filiŏlus*, little son: *malleŏlus*, little hammer; *ingeniŏlum*, small mind (jokingly).

c. **cŭlus, a, um**, found only with root-words of the third, fourth, and fifth declensions; as, *flosculus*, floweret; *matercula*, little mother; *corculum*, little heart; *homunculus*, mannikin, little man; *oratiuncula*, short speech; *igniculus*, small fire; *vulpecula*, little fox; *denticulus*, small tooth; *particula*, little bit, particle; *ossiculum*, small bone; *articulus*, small joint; *corniculum*, little horn; *diecula*, short day.

d. **ellus, a, um**, used with some root-words of the first and second declensions; *ocellus*, little eye, eyelet; *agellus*, small field; *tabella*, small slate; *sacellum*, small sanctuary, chapel (*corolla*, the little wreath).

e. **illus, a, um**, is rare; *lapillus*, little stone, pebble; *anguilla*, eel (*anguis*, serpent); *sigillum*, little picture, seal (*signum*).

Sometimes other diminutives are again formed from diminutives; as, *cista*, a box; *cistula*, a little box; *cistella*, a very small box; *cistellula*, the tiniest little box.

The diminutive usually retains the gender of its stem-word.

3. **ium**, joined to personal nouns, denotes the condition or collection of the persons; as, *sacerdotium*, priesthood; *servitium*, slavery. *Auditorium*, the audience, the lecture-hall, is a verbal word from the supine-stem.

4. **ātus**. gen. *us*, expresses the *office;* as, *consulatus*, the office of consul, the consulship; *tribunatus*, *decemviratus*.

5. **ārium,** denotes a *receptacle; columbarium*, dove-cote; *plantarium*, nursery-garden; *granarium*, granary (*granum*, grain).

6. **ētum,** joined to names of *plants*, points out the *place* where they abound; *quercētum*, a plantation of oaks; *vinētum*, vineyard.

7. **ile** appended to names of *animals* designates their *stall* or *fold: ovile*, sheep-cot; *equile, caprile, bubile* (or *bovile*), &c. (*sedile*, seat; *cubile*, couch, lair).

8. **ina,** usually with the *personal nouns*, denotes both an *occupation* and the *place* where it is exercised; *medicina*, the art of medicine; *sutrina*, shoemaker's shop (*sutor*, shoemaker); *gallina*, hen, from *gallus*; *regina*, queen, from *rex;* here it is only the feminine.

9. Names of *descent* (*patronymica*), to indicate a son or daughter, or descendants in general, are formed from the name of the father or ancestor:

a. **Ides**; as, *Priamides*, Priam's son, descendants of Priam.

b. **ides,** from names in *eus* and *cles; Atrides*, Atrides, the son of Atreus; *Heraclides*, the Heraclide.

c. **ădes** and **iădes,** *Aeneădes*, the son of Aeneas; *Laërtiădes*, the son of Laertes.

d. **is,** gen., **idis** (fem.); *Danăis, Danaidis*, daughter of Danaus; *Nerēis*, daughter of Nereus, Nereid.

§ 180.

Substantives derived from adjectives are mostly ABSTRACT (*abstracta*), and denote a quality.

1. **tas,** mostly **itas**; as, *bonitas*, goodness; *suavitas*, sweetness; *atrocitas*, hideousness; **ietas,** in words ending with *ius;* as, *anxiĕtas*, anguish; *piĕtas*, piety; **stas** from words in *stus;* as, *vetustas*, age (from *vetustus*, old); *libertas*, freedom; *paupertas*, poverty; *difficultas*, difficulty; *simultas*, rivalry; *facultas*, ability; *facilitas*, readiness.

2. **tūdo**; *altitūdo*, height; *fortitūdo*, bravery; *consuetūdo*, custom; (*dulcēdo*, sweetness).

3. **ia**; as, *audacia*, boldness; *concordia*, concord; *prudentia*, prudence; *elegantia*, neatness.

4. **itia**; as, *avaritia*, avarice; *pigritia*, laziness.

5. **mōnia**; *castimōnia*, purity. *Parsimonia*, frugality, and *querimonia*, complaint, are verbals.

§ 181.

VERBAL ADJECTIVES end in:

1. **bundus** and **cundus,** and have the meaning of the present par-

ticiple (somewhat intensified); *errabundus* (= *errans*), wandering; *moribundus*, dying; *iracundus*, passionate (*irascor*); *verecundus*, bashful (*vereor*). *Iūcundus*, pleasing, stands for *iūvicundus* from *iūvo*.

2. **idus** expresses the same as the pres. part., but implies a continued state, from verbs of the second conj.; as, *timidus* (*timens*), fearful; *avidus*, greedy; *placidus*, obliging; *lucidus*, bright; rarely in **idis**, as *viridis* (*virens*), green.

3. **ilis** and **bilis** denote possibility or capability in a passive sense; as, *amabilis*, worthy of love; *facilis*, easy to do; *utilis*, useful; *mobilis* (for *mŏvibilis*) movable. Only a few have an active meaning, such as, *terribilis*, terrible; *fertilis*, fruitful.

4. **ax** denotes a strong inclination: *audax*, daring (*audēre*); *mordax*, biting; *furax*, thievish; *fallax*, deceitful.

5. **ŭlus**; as *bibŭlus*, fond of drinking; *sedulus*, zealous.

6. **ŭus**; as, *assiduus*, constant, unremitting.

§ 182.

Denominative Adjectives (*adjectiva denominativa*) are mostly derived from substantives; in a few instances only, from adverbs of time, and from adjectives; they have the following endings:

1. **ĕus** denotes the *material; aureus*, of gold, golden; *ferreus*, *argenteus:* where the material is wood, **neus** or **nus** is the ending; as, *quernĕus*, *quernus*, oaken; *Cedrinus*, cedar; *faginus*, beechen; *adamantinus*, adamantine; *crystallinus*, crystalline.

2. **acĕus** and **icius**; *chartaceus*, paper; *latericius*, brick.

3. **icus**; *bellicus*, relating to war; *domesticus*, belonging to the house, household; *Africus*, African; *Persicus*, Persian; *Socraticus*, Socratic. (*Pudicus*, modest, from *pudet*).

4. **ālis** and **āris** (the latter only in such words as contain an **l**); *mortālis*, mortal; *regalis*, kingly; *militāris*, martial; *consularis*, *vulgaris*, *popularis*.

5. **ilis**; as, *virilis*, manly; *hostilis*, hostile.

6. **ius**; as, *imperatorius*, belonging to a general; *sororius*, sisterly; *patrius*, fatherly; *regius*, kingly; *Corinthius*, Corinthian; *Lacedaemonius*, Lacedæmonian.

7. **inus**, in *names of animals* and also other living beings; as, *anserinus*, belonging to a goose; *vitulinus*, of a calf (*caro vitulina*, veal); but *bubŭlus*, of an ox; *suillus*, of a hog; *ovillus*, of a sheep. *Divinus*, divine; *femininus*, female. *Matutinus*, morning, early; *vespertinus*, of evening; but *pristinus*, previous; *crastinus* of to-morrow; also in names of places,

Latinus, from *Latium*, Latin; *Tarentinus*, Tarentine (*Iugurthinus*, Jugurthine).

8. **ānus,** in describing *locality; montānus*, belonging to mountains, mountainous; *urbānus*, of a city; *Romānus*, Roman; *Troianus*, Trojan; *Thebanus*, Theban (*Ciceronianus*, Ciceronian; *Sullanus*, belonging to Sulla; *quotidianus*, daily; *meridianus*, noonday).

9. **ārius,** denotes *trade, profession; coriarius*, the tanner (*corium*, leather); *statuarius* (*i. e.*, *homo*), sculptor; *ars statuaria*, the art of sculpture; (*gregarius* and *gregalis*, belonging to the herd, common; *auxiliarius* and *auxiliaris*, auxiliary).

10. **ivus,** *tempestivus*, seasonable, early; *aestivus*, summer; *captivus*, captured.

11. **ernus,** *paternus*, fatherly; *maternus, fraternus;* to denote time, *hibernus*, wintery; *hodiernus*, of to-day; *hesternus*, of yesterday; *aeternus*, eternal; *diurnus*, daily; *nocturnus*, nightly; *diuturnus*, lasting.

12. **itimus** (*itŭmus*), *legitimus*, lawful; *finitimus*, neighboring; *maritimus*, belonging to the sea (*legitŭmus*, etc.).

13. **ester,** *campester*, level, belonging to a plain; *pedester*, on foot; (*paluster*, marshy; *coelestis*, heavenly; *agrestis*, rustic).

14. **ensis,** refers to a *place; forensis* (*forum*), belonging to a market; *Atheniensis*, Athenian; *Karthaginiensis*, Carthaginian; *Cannensis*, belonging to Cannae.

15. **ōsus,** denotes *abundance; animosus*, full of courage, spirited; *saxosus*, rocky; *periculosus*, dangerous; *bellicosus*, warlike.

16. **ulentus,** denotes *plenty; opulentus*, mighty, wealthy (*opes*, resources); *pulverulentus*, dusty; but **olentus,** in *violentus*, vehement; *sanguinolentus*, bloody; *vinolentus*, drunk with wine.

17. **ātus,** means supplied with; *barbatus*, bearded; *calceatus*, wearing shoes, shod; but *auritus*, having ears; and thus for all words in **is**; as, *crinitus, pellitus; cornūtus*, horned.

18. **stus** (properly **tus**), marks how qualified; *molestus*, troublesome; *venustus*, comely; *honestus, scelestus, onustus, robustus.*

19. Besides the derivations of proper names under 3, 6, 7, 8, 14, the following are also found: **ēus**; as, *Pythagorēus*, Pythagorean; **ās,** *Arpinas*, belonging to Arpinum; likewise, *nostras*, gen. *ātis*, of our country, our countryman; *vestras, cuias;* **aeus,** *Smyrnaeus*, of Smyrna.

20. Adjectives derived from other adjectives are only **diminutives** with the usual endings (§ 179, 2); as, *parvŭlus*, very small; *aurĕolus*, finely gilt, golden; *tenellus*, very delicate; *maiuscŭlus*, somewhat larger, rather large. From *benus* (*bonus*) *benulus* whence *bellus*, pretty, and *bellŭlus; paucus* has *paucŭli*, (plural only); in the singular, *paulus*. and thence *paulŭlus*.

§ 183.

The VERBAL VERBS (*verba verbalia*) are divided into four classes.

1. **Frequentatives** (*verba frequentativa*). They denote the frequent repetition of an action, or an increase of the action expressed by the primitive verb (*verba intensiva*). They all belong to the first conjugation, and are formed:

a. From verbs of the first conjugation, by changing **ātum** of the supine into **ito**; as,

clamo — *clamātum* — *clam***ito,** I shout *often* or *loud.*
rogo — *rogātum* — *rog***ito,** I ask often.
volo — *volātum,* — *vol***ito,** I fly to and fro.

b. From verbs of the second and third conjugations, by changing **um** of the supine into **o**; as,

habeo — *habitum* — *habit***o,** I dwell (have often).
cano — *cantum* — *cant***o,** I sing often, loud.
volvo — *volūtum* — *volūt***o,** I roll about.
pello — *pulsum* — *puls***o,** I batter.

Stand isolated: *salto,* I dance, from *salire,* to jump; *dormito,* I am sleepy, from *dormire.*

Remark, moreover: *agito,* from *ago; sciscitor,* I inquire after, from *scisco;* from *dico* is formed *dicto,* and thence *dictito.*

2. **Desideratives** (*verba desiderativa*), which express a desire. They are formed from the supine by changing **um** into **ūrio**; as,

Esurio, I desire to eat, I am hungry, from *edo, esum.* They all belong to the fourth conjugation, and have neither perfect nor supine.

3. **Inchoatives** (*verba inchoativa,* cfr. § 129). They end in **asco** when derived from verbs of the first; **esco,** of the second; **isco,** of the third and fourth conjugations.

4. **Diminutives** (*verba diminutiva*) end in **illo, illāre**; as, *conscribillo, conscribillāre,* I scribble together.

§ 184.

DENOMINATIVE VERBS (*verba denominativa*) end in *āre, ēre, ire;* only a few inchoatives follow the third (§ 131). Those of the first and fourth conj. are mostly transitive; those in *ēre,* intransitive.

liberāre, to free;	*canēre,* to be gray (*canus*).
vulnerare, to wound;	*florēre,* to bloom (*flos*).
mollire, to soften;	*lucēre,* to shine (*lux*).
finire, to finish;	*frondēre,* to be in leaf (*frons*).
vestire, to clothe;	*mitescěre,* to grow mild (*mitis*).
albēre, to be white (*albus*).	*ignescěre,* to take fire (*ignis*).

2. Many deponents are formed from substantives and from a few adjectives. They express being that which the noun denotes; as, *aemulor*, I am an *aemulus*, rival, I rival; *furor*, I am a *fur*, steal; *dominor*, I lord over; *laetor*, I rejoice; cfr. § 102.

NOTE.—For the derivation of adverbs, see § 158.

§ 185.

FORMATION OF WORDS BY COMPOSITION.

1. The latter word in composition is the basis or fundamental word, and determines the meaning; the former only modifies and limits the meaning; thus *agricŏla*, farmer, one who takes care of land; *agrum colens*.

2. In composition the former element appears only in its *root-form*. When a second component begins with a consonant the tie-vowel **I** (rarely **ŏ** or **ŭ**) generally serves to bind the elements together; as, *arm-***I***-ger*, armor-bearer (*quadr-***u***-pes*, four-footed; *sacr-***o***-sanctus*, inviolable); but *magn-animus*, noble-minded.

3. If the former element is a preposition, its final consonant is assimilated to the subsequent consonant; thus, *i***m***-pono*, instead of *i***n***-pono; a***t***traho* for *a***d***traho, a***u***fero* for *a***b***fero; e***f***ficio* for *e***x** *ficio*.

4. Besides the ordinary prepositions, there are some which are never used by themselves, but occur only in compound words (*praepositiones inseparabiles*).

Prefixes: **amb,** around, about; **com, con, co** (from *cum*), with, together; **dis, di,** denoting separation; **rĕ** (*red*), again, back; **sē,** aside. Add **in,** meaning **un, in,** with adjectives (unworthy, infirm).

5. The latter element sometimes undergoes slight changes; as, *perf***i***cio*, I complete, from *f***a***cio; inermis*, unarmed, from *arma; accūso*, I accuse, from *causa; suffōco*, I stifle, from *fauces; illīdo*, I strike heavily against, from *laedo; insulsus*, unsalted, from *salsus*.

NOTE.—In the assimilation of prepositions, the following rules are to be observed:

a. All prepositions remain unchanged before vowels and **h,** but *com* and *circum* sometimes drop the **m**; as, *coeo, coopto, circueo, circuitus* (also *circumeo* and *circumitus;* but *comĕdo* and *comitor*. However, only **ab** before vowels (never *a* or *abs*), **ex** (never *e*); *pro* before vowels inserts the euphonic **d**; as, in *prodeo*. Exceptions, *prout, proinde, proavus*.

b. **ad,** before *i*, (*j*), *v*, *m*, is unchanged; *adiicio, adveho, admiror;* before other consonants it is generally assimilated; as, *accedo, affero, acquiro;* instead of *adnosco* (*adgnosco*) always *agnosco;* for *adspicio, adscendo, adsto*, also *aspicio, ascendo, asto*. Meaning *to, near, at*.

c. **ob,** unchanged; before *c*, *f*, *p*, assimilated; *oblino;* but *occido offero*, *oppono;* (**obs** in *obsolesco*, and *ostendo* for *obstendo*). Meaning *against*, *down*.

d. **per,** unchanged, except in *pellicio* and *pellucidus*. Meaning *through* (often intensive).

e. **trans,** unchanged; however, *trado*, *traduco*, *traiicio* are more frequent than *transdo*, &c. Otherwise always *trans;* as, *transmitto* (rarely *tramitto*); always *transpono*. Meaning *over*, *across*.

f. **a, ab, abs;** before *m* and *v* always **a**; thus, *amitto*, *avello;* before *c* and *t* always **abs**; as, *abscondo*, *abstineo;* before vowels and most consonants, **ab**; thus, *abduco*, *abiicio;* but *aufugio*, *aufero*, and *afui*, rather than *abfui;* before *p*, only **as** (from *abs*), *asporto*, carry away. Meaning *from*, *away*.

g. **e, ex;** before vowels and *c*, *p*, *q*, *s*, *t* always **ex**; before *f*, it is assimilated into **ef;** before all other letters **e**; *excedo*, *exsto*, *extraho*, *effero*, (*extuli*, *elatum*), *ebibo*, *edo*, *emitto*. Meaning *out of* (sometimes only intensive).

h. **in,** generally unchanged; as, *incido*, *induco*, etc., but assimilated before *l* and *r;* as, **il***lido*, **ir***rumpo;* **im** before *b*, *m*, *p;* as, **im***bibo*, **im***mitto*, **im***pono;* for *innosco* (*ingnosco*), *ignosco*. Meaning *in*, *into;* also **un, in** (negative); as, *irritus*, *impurus*.

i. **sub,** unchanged, but usually assimilated before *c*, *f*, *p*, and *g*, *m*, *r;* as, *subdo*, *subluo;* *succurro*, *sufficio*, *suppono*, *suggero*, *summoveo*, *surripio*. However, **sus** (*subs*) in *suscipio*, *sustineo*, etc. (**su**-*spiro* for *sus-spiro*, *suspicor*). Meaning *under*, *from under* (sometimes it lessens or weakens the meaning).

k. **com,** always before *b*, *m*, *p;* before vowels, **co**; as, *coalesco*, *cohaereo*. **Com** only in *comedo*, *comes*, *comitium*, *comitor*. Assimilated before *l* and *r;* as, *colligo*, *corrodo;* before other consonants, **con**; as, *concilium*, *condo*

l. **dis,** unchanged before *c*, *p*, *q*, *t*, and also *s*, when followed by a vowel; as, *disputo*, *dissolvo;* assimilated before *f*, **dif***fero* (*distuli*, **di***latum*); **di** everywhere else, *diduco*, *diruo*, *disto* (*dirimo* from *dis* and *emo*).

m. **rĕ,** unchanged; *removeo*, *reduco;* before vowels always **red**, **red***arguo*, *redeo*, likewise *reddo*. *Rĕfert*, he carries back; but *rēfert*, from *res* and *fero*, it concerns.

n. **sē,** unchanged; *sēduco;* but **sēd***itio* (*ire*); **sobrius**, sober, for *se-ebrius;* **socors**, heartless.

§ 186.

I. ADVERBIAL COMPOUNDS, (*composita adverbialia*); in which the adverb, as modifying element, belongs to the basis:

inter*rex*, regent.
con*discipulus*, schoolmate.
co*gnomen*, surname.
in*eptus*, unfit (*aptus*).
cis*alpīnus*, cisalpine.
per*brĕvis*, very short.
prae*clarus*, very renowned.
dis*par*, unequal.
dis*similis*, unlike.
in*dignus*, unworthy.
male*dicus*, reviling.
brevi*lŏquus*, speaking briefly (for *breviter loquens*).
sub*molestus*, rather annoying.

Con*vŏco*, summon.
co*ĕo*, go together.
com*ĕdo*, consume.
amb*io*, go around.
am*plector*, embrace.
dis*curro*, run about.
dis*cindo*, tear.
di*rumpo*, break.
di*mitto*, send away.
rĕ*pello*, drive back.
rĕ*vertor*, return.
rĕd*eo*, return.
rĕ*pugno*, fight against.
sē*dūco*, lead away.
sē*iungo*, sever (unbind).
dē*dūco*, lead astray.
de*spēro*, despair.
prō*fugio*, escape.
prōd*eo*, come forth.
sub*iicio*, submit.
sus*cipio*, undertake.
suc*cēdo*, follow.
ad*miror*, wonder at.
ar*rideo*, smile at.
al*lŏquor*, address.
circum*do*, surround.
circu*eo*, go around.
ob*rēpo*, steal upon.
oc*curro*, meet.
op*pōno*, oppose.
oc*cīdo*, strike down (*caedo*).
oc*cĭdo*, sink (*cado*).
per*dūco*, carry through.
per*doceo*, teach thoroughly.
trans*iicio*, / **trā***iicio*, } throw over, cross.
trā*do*, surrender.
ā*mitto*, lose.
ab*do*, hide.
abs*tineo*, refrain (*teneo*).
ex*pōno*, explain.
ē*bibo*, drink out.
in*fundo*, pour in.
im*pono*, place upon.
ir*rumpo*, break into.
il*lābor*, fall upon.

§ 187.

II. COMPOUNDS BY CONSTRUCTION, in which the oblique case is considered dependent on the basis:

armiger, armor-bearer (*arma gerens*).
artifex, artist (*artes faciens*).
particeps, partaking (*partem capiens*).
tubicen, trumpeter (*tubā canens*).

tibicen, flute-player (for *tibiicen*, *tibia canens*).
agricŏla, farmer (*agrum colens*).
fratricidium, brother's murder (*fratris caesio*).
ignivŏmus, spitting fire (*ignem vomens*).
honorificus, honorable (*honorem faciens*).
animadverto, notice (*animum adverto*).
aedifico, build (*aedes facio*).
gratificor, oblige (*gratum facio*).
belligĕro, carry on war (*bellum gero*).

Here may also be added the so-called compounds, in which fully declined elements are joined together; as, *respublica*, for which also *res publica* is found; thus also, *iusiurandum*, oath; *tresviri*.

In the foregoing both words are declined; as, *reipublicae*, *iurisiurandi*, *triumvirum*. So also *senatūsconsultum*, decree of the senate; *populiscitum*, decree of the people. Remark *resque publica*, *senatusque consultum*.

NOTE.—Verbs compounded with verbs. In these compounds **facio** is the basis or fundamental word in the composition; as, *arĕfacio*, to dry, from *arēre*, to be dry, and *facio;* cfr. §144, 2. The remaining compounds of *facio*, become *ficio*, when the former element is a preposition § 120, 3), but *fico* or *ficor*, when a noun is the first element; as, *magnifico*, *aedifico*, *gratificor*, *testificor*.

§ 188.

III. POSSESSIVE COMPOUNDS: (*composita possessiva*):

magnanimus, noble-minded (*magnum animum habens*).
quadrŭpes, four-footed (*quattuor pedes habens*).
capripes, goat-footed (*caprae pedes habens*).
affinis, bordering.
concors, united, same mind.
discors, disunited, divided.
triceps, three-headed (*tria capita habens*).

Words of this class compounded with *a*, *de*, *ex*, *in*, *se*, have through these particles a privative meaning.

amens, senseless, } *i. e.*, *mentem non habens*, *sine mente*.
demens, foolish, }
decŏlor, colorless (*colorem non habens*, *sine colore*).
expers, destitute, (*partem non habens*, *sine parte*).
exspes, hopeless
informis, shapeless, ugly.
infāmis, notorious.
inermis, unarmed.
iners, inactive.
securus, careless.

PART II.

SYNTAX.

CHAPTER XXXII.

SENTENCES. AGREEMENT OF THEIR PARTS.

§ 189.

I. 1. A **sentence** is a thought expressed in words.

Every sentence necessarily contains two parts: a *Subject* and a *Predicate.* The **Subject** is that of which something is affirmed; the **Predicate**, that which is affirmed of the subject.

2. Both the subject and the predicate may be *Simple* or *Complex* or *Compound.* They are:

Simple, when not modified by any other word or phrase (grammatical subject or predicate).

Complex, when modified by some other word or phrase (logical subject or predicate).

Compound, when there are two or more simple or complex subjects or predicates.

3. The **Subject** may be modified by *Adjuncts* (adjectives, genitives), or by *Appositions* or by *Adverbial Modifications* (adverbs, prepositions with their respective cases, or cases alone).

The **Predicate** may be modified by its *Object* and by *Adverbial Modifications.*

4. The *subject* as well as the *modifiers* in a sentence may be resolved into **dependent clauses**, as; Tuus amor *mihi gratus est* = quod me amas, *mihi gratum est. Agnoscimus* diligentiam vestram = *agnoscimus. vos* diligentes esse. Bonum *regem omnes*

amant = *Regem*, qui bonus est, *omnes amant. Legati missi sunt* ad res repetendas = ut res repeterent. Such clauses are then called, according to the part of sentence represented by them, Subject, Object, Adjunct, or Adverbial Clauses.

5. A sentence is either **simple** or **compound.**

A *simple* sentence contains **one proposition.** A *compound* sentence contains **two** or **more** propositions connected together. These propositions are called *members* or *clauses;* these clauses are either *independent* (coördinate) or *dependent* (subordinate). The independent clause, from which another depends, is, with regard to this, called the *principal* or *leading* sentence.

6. All **principal clauses** are coördinate; the dependent clauses are subordinate to the principal, but may be coördinate among themselves.

7. **Dependent** are: *a*) the *conjunctive* clauses (§ 165); *b*) the *indirect* questions (§ 176, 263); *c*) the *relative* clauses (§ 257).

II. 1. The **subject** of a sentence is either a *substantive*, or a word or phrase used as a substantive. It is always in the *nominative case.*

2. The **predicate** is either a *verb* or a *noun* (any declinable word), with a *verb*, as *copula.*

3. In every sentence the predicate must agree as closely as possible with the subject:

a. The *verb*, as predicate, agrees with the subject always in *person* and *number.*

b. The *adjective* or *participle*, as predicate, agrees with the subject always in *number*, *case*, and *gender.*

c. The *substantive*, as predicate, agrees with the subject always in *case*, and, as far as possible, also in *number* and *gender.*

Experientia docet. Varietas delectat. Virtus manet, divitiae pereunt. Aves volant, pisces natant. Tu doces, nos discimus.

Animus hominis est immortalis, corpus est mortale. Flos est caducus. Divitiae sunt incertae.

Usus est optimus magister. Vita rustica parsimoniae magistra est. Leo est rex animalium. Aquila est regina avium.

Indus est omnium fluminum maximus. Probus invidet nemini. Multi semper volunt, nunquam faciunt. Duo cum faciunt idem, non est idem. Errare humanum est. Nemo nascitur doctus. Nemo fit casu bonus.

Roma a Romulo condita est. Thebae ab Alexandro dirutae *sunt.* Africa *est* nutrix *leonum.* Athenae *omnium artium* inventrices *fuerunt.*

1. If the subject is a personal pronoun, it is omitted in Latin, as the termination of the verb sufficiently indicates the person; *Homines* sumus, *errare* possumus. Only in case of an emphasis, and especially of an antithesis, must the pronoun be expressed; Ego *credo*, tu *dubitas.*

2. If the predicate noun is a variable substantive (§ 4, 5), it must always agree with the subject; as, *Flos est* nuntius *veris. Ciconia est* nuntia *veris.* Only when the subject is neuter, the predicate noun retains the masculine gender. Tempus *est* optimus magister.

In other cases, the agreement is impossible. *Roma erat* lumen *orbis terrarum. Captivi militum* praeda fuerunt. *Athenae* clarissima urbs *Graeciae* fuerunt (or *fuit*).

Sometimes the neuter of an adjective is used as a substantive and remains as the predicate: Turpitudo peius *est quam dolor* (a greater evil). Mors *omnium rerum* extremum *est* (§ 237, 4).

3. The copula *est* or *sunt* is often omitted, especially in short, pithy sayings, as proverbs, etc. *Quot capita, tot sententiae. Suus cuique mos* (*sunt, est*). With a participle and adjective the infinitive *esse* is also omitted sometimes; but *erat, sit,* etc., are seldom omitted.

4. *Construction according to sense.* Sometimes the predicate agrees with the subject, not as to its form, but as to its sense and meaning:

a) With collective nouns in the singular, the predicate may be in the plural. Multitudo *hominum* concurrerunt (also *concurrit*). Pars *perexigua, duce amisso, Romam* inermes delati sunt (or *inermis delata est*).

b) With *millia* and *capita* the predicate is often in the masculine gender. *Sex* millia *hostium* caesi *sunt.* Capita *coniurationis securi* percussi *sunt.*

c). With *partim — partim,* meaning *alii — alii* or *alia — alia,* the predicate takes the gender of *alii,* etc. Partim *e nobis* timidi *sunt,* partim *a re publica* aversi. *Bonorum* partim necessaria *sunt,* partim non necessaria.

5. The verb *esse* sometimes takes an adverb as adjunct (not as predicate) as: *Hostes* prope sunt. *Patria est, ubicunque* bene est. Sic est *vita hominum.* Ita sum. *Deus* semper fuit *et* semper erit.

6. Sometimes the predicate verb agrees with the predicate noun instead of agreeing with the subject, especially when the verb stands nearer to the former: *Non omnis error stultitia* dicenda est.

7. You may say: *nos* instead of *ego*, *noster* instead of *meus*, but never *vos* instead of *tu*. Historians, especially when speaking of soldiers, often use the singular instead of the plural; as: *miles*, *Romanus*, *Volscus* for *milites*, *Romani*, *Volsci*.

§ 190.

1. When there are *two* or *more subjects* in a sentence, the predicate is put in the plural. As to person, the predicate is in the *first person*, when there is among the subjects a pronoun of the first person; in the *second*, when there is a pronoun of the second and none of the first person.

Romulus et Remus Romam condiderunt. *Si* tu *et mater tua* valetis, *bene est; ego et pater tuus* valemus.

2. When the subjects are *names of persons* of the *same gender*, the predicate-noun takes the gender of the subjects; when the subjects are of *different gender* the predicate noun is in the masculine, and, of course, in the plural.

Veneno absumpti sunt *Hannibal et Philopoemen. Iuno et Minerva Troianis* inimicae erant. *Pater mihi et mater* mortui sunt.

3. When the subjects are *inanimate beings* of the *same gender*, the predicate-noun sometimes agrees with the subjects in gender; but generally it stands in the neuter plural. In case of *different gender*, the predicate stands always in the neuter plural.

Grammatice quondam et musice iunctae fuerunt. *Honores et victoriae* fortuita sunt. *Stultitia et temeritas et iniustitia et intemperantia* fugienda sunt.

1. When the several subjects form in sense a *unit* or *whole*, the predicate stands in the *singular*. Religio et fides anteponatur *amicitiae*. Senatus populusque Romanus decrevit.

2. Often, however, the predicate agrees only with one subject, usually the nearest, and is understood with the others. Homerus fuit *et Hesiodus ante Romam conditam. Brachia modo atque* humeri liberi *ab aqua erant.* Visae *nocturno tempore* faces *ardorque coeli.*

3. You can say: *Ipse dux* cum *aliquot principibus* capitur, but also, capiuntur, § 189, II., 4.

§ 191.

1. The *adjective*, both as attribute and as predicate agrees with its substantive in *gender*, *number* and *case* (*in genere, numero et casu*).

Mala societas *deprāvat* bonos mores. Bella civilia *sunt* nefaria. *Hominis utilitati* agri omnes *et* maria *parent*, (also, *et* omnia maria).

2. The same is the case with every *pronoun*, *participle* and *numeral* connected with a substantive.

Hi viri *doctissimi sunt*. Acti labores *iucundi sunt*. Coniunctae vires *plus valent*. Duas aures *habemus et* unum os.

3. The *pronoun* (without a substantive) agrees with its *antecedent* in *number* and *gender*, but its case depends on the construction of the clause to which it belongs.

Dolores, quos *Deus dat, utiles sunt;* huic *credamus*, hunc *veneremur*. *Agricola serit* arbores, quarum *fructus ipse numquam adspiciet*. *Socrates succubuit* odio *malorum*, in quod *sine sua culpa inciderat*.

1. When the English *that* or *this* points to a thought (not to a word), the demonstrative pronoun in Latin agrees with the predicate noun. Ista *quidem vis est* = *this* is violence, indeed. Isti *sunt fructus negligentiae*. Haec *fuga est, non profectio*. Hic *murus ahenẹus esto: Nil conscire sibi, nulla pallescere culpa!*

2. When the pronoun is connected with a *predicate noun*, it generally agrees with it. *Epicurus* (hoc *enim vestrum* lumen *est*) *istud negat*. *Thebae*, quod *Boeotiae* caput *est*, *in magno motu erant*. *Animal hoc plenum rationis*, quem *vocamus hominem* (seldom, quod *vocamus hominem*).

3. The *relative pronoun* is often construed according to the sense (§ 189, II., 4). *Caesar equitatum praemittit* qui videant. Concerning *Ego*, qui *vidi*, I, who have seen, cfr. § 288, 4.

4. As the *adjective*, *pronoun*, etc., so also a *substantive* can be added as an attribute to another *substantive in the same case*. *Antiochia* urbs, the city of Antioch; *Tarquinius* rex, King Tarquin.

This attributive substantive, when it takes the place of an abridged sentence, is called *apposition*.

Apposition is twofold:

a. Relative, when it stands for a relative clause; as, *Alexander*, rex Macedŏnum, *Babylone mortuus est*, for, *qui rex Macedonum erat.*

b. Adverbial, when it stands for an adverbial clause. *Cato* senex *litteras Graecas didicit*, for *cum senex esset*, when he was.

5. The *apposition* agrees with its substantive *always* in *case*, and, as far as possible, also in *number* and *gender* (§ 189, II, 2).

Marcus Tullius Cicero, clarissimus orator *Romanorum*, *ab Antonio occisus est. Pythagoras*, vir sapientissimus, *maxime commendabat frugalitatem*, genitricem *virtutum.*

Alexander adolescens *Philippo patri successit. Appium Claudium* senem *omnes verebantur.*

Athenae, urbs clarissima *Graeciae. Tempus, optimus* magister. *Memoria, omnium rerum* thesaurus.

1. The predicate agrees, also, in this case, always with the real subject of the sentence. *Tullia, deliciae nostrae, munusculum tuum* flagitat. Only with *names of cities* the predicate often agrees with the apposition: *Coriŏli*, oppidum *Volscorum*, captum est.

2. The apposition and the pronoun also admit sometimes a construction according to sense (§ 189, II, 4). *Concursus* populi, mirantium, *quid rei esset* (as if *hominum* stood in place of *populi*). *Veiens bellum ortum est*, quibus *Sabini arma coniunxerant* (Veientium *quibus*). *Ex eo numero* qui sunt (for *eorum*). *Amicitia est ex eo* genere, quae *prosunt.* Concerning the apposition with a relative, cfr. § 238, 5.

3. The apposition to a possessive pronoun takes the *genitive* construction according to sense. *Nomen* meum absentis *tibi honori fuit.* Likewise, emphatically, *meum ipsius, tuum unius* (§ 210, 3).

4. When the apposition expresses a comparison, the English *as* or *like* must be rendered by *ut* or *tanquam. Aegyptii canem et felem* ut *deos colunt. Cicero haec cecinit* ut *vates.*

6. In English the *neuter* of adjectives and pronouns is often used in the *singular*, whilst the *plural* must be used in Latin. *Omnia*, all (all things); *haec*, this (these things).

The *plural* must be used when *several single things* are meant, the *singular*, when only *one.*

Omnia praeclara rara (*sunt*), all that is excellent is rare; *i. e., omnes res praeclarae.* Omnia, quae *videmus, a Deo* creata sunt

Nostra *etiam* vestra sunt. Multa *a multis hominibus* narrantur, quae vera *non sunt.*

But: *Epaminondas pro patria mortuus est:* hoc *ei* decorum fuit.

7. Say: *Hostes* terga *verterunt*, not *tergum*, the enemy turned the back. *Cn. et P. Scipiones*, Cneius and Publius Scipio. *Catones*, men like Cato.

CHAPTER XXXIII.

THE USE OF CASES.—THE NOMINATIVE.

§ 192.

1. The **subject** of every sentence is in the *nominative* (in answer to the question, *who?* or *what?*).

2. *Verbs* with *two* nominatives.—The predicate noun is in the nominative with the following verbs:

a. The verbs of being, becoming, appearing: *sum*, I am; *fio*, *evādo*, *exsisto*, I become, exist; *nascor*, I am born; *maneo*, I remain; *videor*, I seem; *appareo*, I appear; *morior*, I die.

Nemo fit *casu* bonus. *Nemo* nascitur doctus. *Puerorum amicitiae* stabiles manere *non possunt*. *Sol* maior appāret *quam luna*.

b. The passive verbs of calling, naming: *appellor*, *dicor*, *nominor*, *vocor*.

Apud Lacedaemonios ii, *qui amplissimum magistratum gerunt*, nominantur senes. *Cicero* pater *patriae* appellatus est. *Iustitia erga deos* religio dicitur, *erga parentes* pietas.

c. The passive verbs meaning, to be regarded, considered, nominated, chosen, elected; as, *putor*, *habeor*, *iudicor*, *existimor*, I am regarded, considered; *creor*, *eligor*, I am elected; *fio*, *efficior*, I am made; *declaror*, I am declared; *renuntior*, I am proclaimed.

Multi putantur docti, *qui non sunt*. *Post Romulum Numa Pompilius* rex creatus est. *Hannibal a militibus* dux est factus. *Cicero ab universo populo* consul declaratus erat. Consul *omnibus centuriis Sulla* renuntiatus est.

3. This *double nominative* remains with those verbs also, when they stand in the infinitive, as the object of an incomplete verb. Such *incomplete* verbs are: *possum, volo, cupio, debeo, audeo, scio, disco, coepi, pergo, desino,* etc. § 269, 3.

Beatus esse *sine virtute nemo* potest. *Cato* esse *quam* videri bonus malebat. *Omnes improbi* miseri putari debent. *Oracula evanuerunt, postquam homines minus* creduli esse coeperunt.

4. Note the *personal* construction of *videri*, to seem:

Instead of the English, it seems that I am, thou art, etc., say in Latin always: *videor esse, videris esse,* etc.

Videor aegrotus *esse:* It seems that I am sick. Videbar *aegrotus esse,* it seemed that I was, etc., § 273. Likewise, videbaris *aegrotus esse,* it seemed as though you were sick.

5. The same *personal* construction obtains with *dicor* (*perhibeor, putor, trador, feror*), I am said, it is said, reported, etc., that.

Tu verus *patriae* dicĕris *esse* pater. *Aristīdes omnium* iustissimus traditur fuisse. *Xanthippe, uxor Socratis,* morosa *fuisse* fertur. *Veteres Germani* fortissimi *fuisse* feruntur (*dicuntur,* etc.)

6. The English indefinite, *one, they, people* (French, *on,* German, *man*) is rendered in Latin:

a. By the third singular passive: *Rex laudatur,* they (people) praise the king (strictly, the king is praised); *laudāris,* people praise you; *laudati sumus,* they have praised us.

b. By the third person plural active or deponent: *Regem* laudant, they praise the king. In this way are often used: *dicunt, tradunt, ferunt,* they say, relate; *vocant,* people call: *putant,* one believes. *Vulgo* admirabantur *Pompeium,* people admired Pompey. § 268.

c. By the first person plural active or deponent, if the speaker includes himself: *Facile* credimus, *quod* optamus, one believes easily, what one wishes (we easily believe what we wish). Admiramur, *quae non intelligimus.*

d. Note.—Cavendum *est,* one must beware; *virtutem auro non* emes, you will not buy virtue for gold; *dicas, one* would say; *putares, one* could have thought (§ 248, 3, *a*).

CHAPTER XXXIV.

THE ACCUSATIVE.

§ 193.

The **Object-Accusative.** All *transitive* verbs have the object of their action in the *accusative* (in answer to the question, *whom?* immediate object).

Most verbs that are active transitive in English are also transitive in Latin.

Deus mundum *creavit.* Artificem *commendat opus. Boni cives* bonum regem *amant. Scipio vicit* Hannibalem. *Virtus* nullam mercedem *postulat.*

These sentences may, without change of meaning, be expressed in the passive voice: *Mundus a Deo* creatus est. *Bonus rex* amatur *a bonis civibus* (§ 220, 3).

§ 194.

Though, on the whole, the verbs that are transitive in English are so, also, in Latin, there are, nevertheless, many *transitive* verbs in Latin whose corresponding verbs in English are either used both ways, as *transitive and intransitive*, or *only intransitive*, or as a *verb with a preposition.*

Such are:

deficio, tr., I leave, forsake; int., I am wanting in.
effugio, tr., I escape; int., I flee from.
sequor, sector, tr., I follow; int., I come or go after.
imitor, tr., I imitate, copy; int., I try to be like.
adūlor, tr., I flatter; int., I fawn upon one.
aequo, I am equal to.
aemulor, tr., I emulate; I vie with.

Fortes *fortuna* adiŭvat. Bonos *numquam honestus sermo* deficiet. Mortem effugere *nemo potest. Gloria* virtutem *tanquam umbra* sequitur. *Beneficio provocati nonne* imitari agros fertiles *debemus, qui plus efferunt, quam acceperunt? Tum senatores* plebem adulari *coeperunt. Quis cursu* equum aequare *poterit? Quod me* Agamemnonem aemulari *putas, falleris.*

1. The compounds of these verbs govern the accusative likewise as, *consequor*, I reach, require, come up with; *prosequor*, I accompany, I go with; only, *obsequor*, I obey, governs the dative. Also *adulor* and *aemulor* govern sometimes the dative, but *blandior* always. *Aequare*, meaning, to make equal to, stands with the accusative and the dative; as, *urbem solo aequare*, to make the city level with the ground (to raze it). *Aequiparare* (seldom used), to reach, to be equal to, takes always the accusative.

2. Say: *deficere animo*, to lose courage; *deficere a re publica*, to fall away from the state; *deficere ad hostem*, to go over to the enemy. *Effugere ex manibus* = to flee from one's hands; *effugere manus*, to avoid one's grasp; *fugere aliquem*, to shun some one; *fugere* ab *aliqua re*, to flee from something.

3. Some intransitive verbs take an object-accusative of a word of the same stem, when joined to an adjective: *miseram vitam vivere; eosdem cursus currere* (*servitutem servire*, emphatic).

4. Some verbs, especially such as express a disagreeable *sensation* or *affection*, sometimes govern the accusative in Latin, although they are intransitive: *casum amici dolere*, to feel sorry over a friend's misfortune; *horrere mortem*, to be afraid of death, to dread it. In a similar way: *Sitire sanguinem*, to thirst after blood; *crocum olere*, to smell of saffron; figuratively, *malitiam olere*, to smell of malice; *ridere aliquem*, to laugh at one. With *desperare*, to despair of, you may say, *desperare aliquid*, *de aliqua re*, and *alicui rei*, to despair of something.

5. Also with some other intransitive expressions the accusative of a pronoun in the neuter gender is used, whilst a substantive would have to stand in another case: Istud *magnopere* lactor, for *ista re*, of that I am very glad. Hoc *tibi* auctor sum, for *huius consilii*, § 198, 3, I give you this counsel.

§ 195.

Many *intransitive verbs of motion*, when compounded with prepositions, become transitive, and consequently govern the accusative. This is always the case with the prepositions, *circum*, *per*, *praeter* and *trans: circumfluo*, I flow around; *percurro*, I run through; *praetereo*, I pass over; *transeo*, I cross over.

Spartam *Eurōtas amnis* circumfluit. *Cupiditates omnium* mentes pervagantur. *Sententiae saepe acutae non acutorum hominum* sensus praetervŏlant. *Peccare est tanquam* transire lineas.

NOTE 1.—Also, *supergredi* and *supervadere* take the accusative. *Adire aliquem*, to address one (with a petition or question); *aggrĕdi aliquem*, to attack one; *convenire aliquem*, to meet one; *inire societatem*, to form an alliance; *inire magistratum*, to enter upon an office; *inire consilium*, to form a plan; *adire hereditatem*, to take possession of an inheritance; *obire negotium*, to manage a business; *obire diem* or *diem supremum*, to die; *transire* (*excedere*) *modum*, to exceed the bounds (but *excedere* ex urbe or *urbe*, to leave the city); *subire periculum*, to undergo a danger.

NOTE 2.—Say *anteire, antecedere, praecedere* alicui and aliquem, *excellere* ceteris (dative) and inter ceteros. Also *praestare* alicui, seldom, *aliquem*.

NOTE 3.—Besides the verbs of motion, the following are to be remembered as transitive in composition: *alloqui*, to address one (speak to one); *allatrare*, to bark at one; *obsidere*, to besiege (lie around); *oppugnare*, to fight, resist one; *expugnare*, to take (by storm).

§ 196.

1. The *impersonal verbs*, expressing a *disagreeable* feeling (§ 154, 2), *pĭget, pŭdet, poenitet, taedet*, and *mĭseret*, take the *person* (that feels) in the accusative; the *object* (that causes the feeling), in the genitive, or, if a *verb*, in the infinitive.

Piget me *stultitiae meae*, I am disgusted with, grieved at my folly. *Pudeat* te *tuae negligentiae*. Be ashamed of thy negligence. *Nunquam primi consilii* deum *poenituit*. *Taedet* me vitae. Eorum nos *magis miseret, qui misericordiam nostram non requirunt, quam qui illam efflagitant*. *Non* me *poenitet* vixisse.

NOTE.—Instead of the genitive, the accusative is used with the neuter of a pronoun. *Sapiens nihil facit*, quod *eum poenitere possit* (instead of *cuius rei*, § 194, 5).

2. *Decet*, it becomes, is becoming, and *dedĕcet*, it is unbecoming, take the accusative of the person (§ 154, note 3).

Candida pax homines, *trux* decet *ira* feras. Oratorem dedecet *irasci*. Parvum *parva* decent.

3. *Fallit, fugit, praeterit me*, it escapes me, my memory; *iuvat, delectat me*, it gives me pleasure, delight.

§ 197.

DOUBLE ACCUSATIVE. Many verbs govern a double accusative, one of the object, the other of the predicate, viz.:

1. Those which signify to name, call, choose, proclaim.

2. Those signifying to take, give, acknowledge as, show, prove.

3. Those signifying to consider, reckon, declare.

The passive of these verbs takes the double nominative (§ 192).

1. Hence we say: *vocare (appellare, dicere, nominare) aliquem patrem*, to call one father; *facere (efficere, reddere) aliquem beatum*, or *regem*, to make one happy, or king; *creare (eligere) aliquem ducem*, to choose one for leader; *renuntiare aliquem consulem*, to proclaim one consul.

2. *Habere (sumere, dare, cognoscere) aliquem amicum*, to have one for a friend; *praestare (praebere, ostendere) se fortem*, to show one's self brave.

3. *Putare (ducere, existimare, iudicare) aliquem divitem*, to reckon one rich; *declarare aliquem hostem*, to declare one an enemy.

Romulus urbem *ex nomine suo* Romam vocavit. *Sola religio* vitam beatam facit (*efficit*, *reddit*). *Post Romulum populus* Numam Pompilium regem creavit. Ciceronem *universus populus* consulem declaravit. *Natura homini praescripsit*, *ut* nihil pulchrius, *quam hominem* putaret. Praesta te eum, *qui mihi a teneris*, *ut Graeci dicunt*, *unguiculis es cognitus*.

Here belongs the phrase, *facere aliquem certiorem*, to inform one, with the genitive of the thing, or with *de*; as *Patrem consilii mei certiorem feci* or *de consilio meo*. In the passive voice, *reddi* means only, to be given back (not, to be made) *fieri* or *effici*, to be made; *haberi*, only, to be held, considered; *habere aliquem pro hoste;* also, *pro nihilo putare* (seldom *nihil putare*).

§ 198.

DOUBLE ACCUSATIVE OF THE OBJECT:

1. *Doceo* (*edoceo*), I teach; *celo*, I conceal from, take the person and the thing in the accusative.

Philosophia, nos multas res docuit. Ciceronem *Minerva* omnes artes edocuit. *Non* te celavi hunc sermonem.

NOTE.—As we say, *doceo te Latinam* linguam, so also, *doceo te Latine* loqui, I teach you to speak Latin (the infinitive, as object). Doctus litteris *Graecis* (seldom *litteras Graecas*), learned in Greek literature. *Docere aliquem* de *aliqua re*, to acquaint one with something. Say, also: *celare aliquem* de *aliqua re*, to keep one in ignorance of something. In the passive only *celor* de hac re, not, hanc rem.

2. *Posco* (*reposco*) and *flagito*, I demand, ask urgently, take the thing demanded in the accusative, and the person of whom it is demanded, either in the accusative or in the ablative, with *a*, or *ab*; thus, *poscere* or *flagitare aliquem aliquid* or *aliquid ab aliquo*, to demand something of some one.

Nulla salus bello, pacem te poscimus *omnes*. *Caesar* Aeduos frumentum *flagitabat*. *Nihil* a te posco. *Quid artes* a te *flagitent*, *tu videbis*.

NOTE 1.—*Postulare*, to beg, pray; *petere*, to petition; *quaerere*, to ask, seek, never take the accusative of person. Hence, *postulare aliquid* ab aliquo; *petere aliquid* ab aliquo; *quaerere* ex (ab) aliquo, to ask one. *Amicus* ab amico *nihil* postulabit, *nisi quod honestum est*. *Athenienses* a Lacedaemoniis *auxilium* petierunt. Quaesivi ex patre, *quid facerem*.

Oro and *rogo*, I pray, beseech, generally take only one accusative, either that of the person or that of the thing; however, sometimes both accusatives are used.

Iugurtha Metellum *per legatos* pacem oravit. Deos vitam roga *et* salutem.

NOTE 2.—If the person is in the accusative, the thing is generally expressed by a clause with *ut* or *ne* (§ 250, 275). Sometimes the person is not expressed, but understood: *Legatos ad Caesarem miserunt, qui rogarent* auxilium, who were to ask for help.

3. Many transitive verbs, especially those of *asking*, *admonishing*, take a double accusative, one of the person, the other, of the thing, when the latter is a pronoun in the neuter; as, *hoc te interrogo* or *rogo*, this I inquire of you; *illud te oro* or *rogo*, that I ask of you. *Istud te hortor*, *cogo*, I exhort, force, you to this; *id unum te moneo* or *admoneo*, of this one thing I remind you.

Hoc te *primum* rogo *ne animum demittas*. Pusionem *quendam Socrates apud Platonem* interrogat quaedam *geometrica*. *Saepe non audimus ea*, quae *ab natura* monemur.

NOTE 1.—Otherwise we say: *interrogare aliquem* de *aliqua re*, to ask some one about something. In official language, *interrogare sententias*, means, to solicit (canvass) votes; *rogatus* or *interrogatus sententiam*, being asked one's vote.

NOTE 2.—Say: *Caesar* exercitum Ligerim *traducit* and *trans Ligerim*; the same with *traiicio*, *transmitto*, *transporto*.

§ 199.

ACCUSATIVE OF EXTENT. The accusative is used to express the measure of extent, both of time and space, in answer to the question, *how long? how old? how far? how broad? how deep? how high?*

Duodequadraginta annos *tyrannus Syracusanorum fuit Dio-*

nysius, quum quinque et viginti annos *natus* (old) *dominatum occupavisset. A recta conscientia* transversum unguem *non oportet discedere* (not a finger's breadth). *Milites aggerem, latum* pedes trecentos, *altum* pedes octoginta *exstruxerunt. Perpetuae fossae*, quinos pedes *altae* (deep) *ducebantur.*

1. Instead of *quinque annos*, for five years, you may also say, *per quinque annos*, during five years. *Quinque horis*, during five hours.

2. *Puer novem annorum*, a boy of nine years; *puer novem annos natus*, a boy nine years old; *annum agens nonum*, in his ninth year; *plus novem annos natus*, more than nine years old. § 226, 1.

3. A millibus *passuum* duobus, at a distance of two miles. Aequo spatio or aequum spatium *abesse*.

§ 200.

CONSTRUCTION OF THE NAMES OF TOWNS:

1. When asking, *where to? whither?* the names of towns are always put in the *accusative* without preposition. *Romam*, to Rome; *Karthaginem*, to Carthage. Accusative of motion towards.

With names of other places, use the accusative with *in*, though poets often use the accusative alone.

2. When asking, *from where? whence?* all names of towns are put in the *ablative* without preposition. Hence, *Romā*, from Rome; *Babylone*, from Babylon.

With names of other places, generally *ex*, with abl. § 282.

3. In answer to the question, *where?* the names of towns in the singular of the first and second declensions are put in the *genitive;* whereas those of the plural, and all those of the third declension are put in the *ablative* without preposition; therefore: *Romae*, at Rome; *Corinthi*, at Corinth; *Athenis*, at Athens (also, from Athens); *Delphis*, at Delphi (also, from Delphi); *Babylone*, at Babylon (also, from Babylon).

With other names, generally *in*, with abl. § 283.

The names of small islands are construed like the names of towns; as, *Delum*, to Delos; *Deli*, in or on Delos; *Delo*, from Delos.

Demaratus, Tarquinii regis pater, Tarquinios Corintho *fugit. Ut* Romae *consules, sic* Karthagine *quotannis bini reges creabantur. Talis* Romae *Fabricius, qualis* Athenis *Aristides fuit.*

Aeschines orator Athenis *cessit et* Rhodum *se contulit.* Romā *legati* Athenas *missi sunt. Alexander Magnus* Babylone *mortuus est.* Ephesi *templum Dianae erat.* Delphis *erat oraculum Apollinis. Conon plurimum* Cypri *vixit.*

Ad Brundisium, near Brundisium (in its neighborhood); *e. g., pugnatum est* or *venit*, into its neighborhood. *Caesar a Gergovia discessit*, from the neighborhood of Gergovia. *Omnis ora* a *Salonis* ad *Oricum* (direction and extent). Ad urbem *esse*, to be in the neighborhood of Rome. *Cypri*, at Cyprus; in *Cypro* (*insula*), on the island of Cyprus.

§ 201.

1. The words *domus* and *rus* follow the construction of names of towns. Thus, without prepositions:

*dom***um**, *home* (homeward).	*rus*, *into* the country.
*dom***o**, *from* home.	*rur***e**, *from* the country.
*dom***i**, *at* home.	*rur***i**, *in* the country.

Domus retains this construction when connected with a *possessive pronoun* or a *genitive* (possessive): *domi meae*, in my home; *tuae, suae*, etc. Domi *Caesaris*, in, at Caesar's house (home), seldom *in domo Caesaris; domi eius*, in his house. But with other adjectives, *in* or *ex* must be used; in illa *domo*, in *domum* celebrem, ex amplissima *domo*.

In case there are several persons, home is then *domos: domibus*, from home; *domos iverunt*, they went home; *domibus venerunt*, they came from home.

2. A similar construction obtains with *humi*, on the ground; with *belli* and *militiae*, in connection with *domi;* as, *domi belique*, at home and in the war; *domi militiaeque*, at home and in the field.

Cicero senex multum ruri *vivebat.* Domum *redibo; libentissime sum* domi meae. *Nos* humi *strati haec suspicere non possumus. Caesaris virtus* domi militiaeque *cognita est.*

3. The names of countries and large islands are used with prepositions: *In Italiam*, to Italy; *in Sicilia*, in Sicily; *ex Britannia*, from Britain. The preposition is seldom omitted.

NOTE 1.—When *urbs* or *oppidum*, without an adjective, is placed as attribute before the name of a town, it always takes the preposition *in* or *ex;* in oppidum *Gades*, into the city of Gades; in *urbem Romam*, into the city of Rome; in *oppido Cittio;* ex *urbe Alexandria.* In connection with *totus*, say, totā *Romā*, in all Rome; also, *totā domo.* § 238, 1.

Note 2.—*Urbs* or *oppidum*, joined to an adjective and used in apposition *after* the name of a city, generally takes the preposition *in* or *ex*. But, without the preposition, also, in answer to the question, *Where?* it is always put in the ablative, even though the name of the city be in the genitive. *Demaratus se contulit* Tarquinios, *in urbem Etruriae florentissimam.* Tusculo, *ex clarissimo municipio.* *Archias natus est* Antiochiae, celebri *quondam urbe*, or, *in celebri urbe* (never *urbis*).

§ 202.

Accusative in Exclamations. The *person* or *thing* that excites the feeling is put in the accusative (either with or without *heu* or *o*).

Me miserum! Heu me miserum! O wretched me! *O hominem infortunatum!* O unfortunate man! *O fallacem* hominum *spem fragilemque fortunam!*

1. When a person is addressed (the second person), the *vocative* is used. The interjections, *vae* and *hei*, are followed by the *dative;* as, *Vae victis!* Woe to the vanquished! *Hei mihi misero!* With *ecce* and *en*, lo! behold! the *nominative* is used, and also the *accusative;* En *vobis* iuvenis or iuvenem! Behold the youth!

2. The accusative of the neuter of the pronoun is sometimes used in a loose way, instead of another case; thus, *homo* id *aetatis*, for, ea *aetate*, a man of this age. Hoc unum *laetor*, over that one thing I rejoice, for, *hac una re.* Quid *tibi auctor sim*, what shall (may) I advise you. But only: pacis *tibi auctor sum.* Cfr. § 194, 5; 198, 3.

3. Concerning the accusative with prepositions, cfr. §§ 161 and 163; on the Greek accusative, cfr. § 226, 3.

CHAPTER XXXV.

THE DATIVE.

§ 203.

1. The Dative of Advantage (*dativus commodi*). This dative is used in answer to the question, *whom? to whom? for whom?* with many adjectives and verbs.

Adjectives signifying necessary, useful, agreeable; fit, suitable, like, easy, convenient; near, friendly, faithful, known; fair, equal, etc.; as, *necessarius* (*necesse, opus*), *utilis, gratus, iucundus, aptus, commodus, idoneus, fidus, aequus, aequalis, amicus, similis, propinquus, finitimus, facilis, notus, par, molestus, acerbus, consentaneus*, etc., besides their contraries.

Verbs; as, *prosum*, *placeo*, *obtempero*, *oboedio*, *fido*, *impero*, *indulgeo*, *ignosco*, *ministro*, *faveo*, I favor, etc. *Dicto audiens sum imperatori*, I obey the general's command (two datives).

Some adverbs also take the dative; as, *convenienter* naturae *vivere*.

Apes parent reginae *suae*. *Is qui imperat* aliis, *serviat ipse* nulli cupiditati. Patriae *deesse* aliis *turpe*, *Camillo etiam nefas est*. *Mors similis est* somno. *Quod* tibi *utile est*, mihi *iucundum erit*. *Vir bonus est*, *qui* prodest, quibus *potest*, *nocet* nemini.

2. The dative is used in answer to the question, *for whom?* *for whose benefit* or *disadvantage?*

Non scholae *sed* vitae *discimus*. *Non* nobis solis *nati sumus*, *sed etiam* patriae *et* civibus nostris. *Charondas et Zaleucus* civitatibus suis *leges scripserunt*.

NOTE 1.—The adjectives *similis*, similar; *proprius*, proper, peculiar; *affinis*, akin; *vicinus*, near, are also followed by the genitive: he is my peer (equal), always in the gen., mei *similis est*. *Utilis*, *aptus*, *idoneus*, generally take *ad* and *acc.*, in answer to the question, *to*, *for what?* ad *nullam rem* utilis, aptus, etc. *Propior* and *proximus* may take the dative, the accusative, and the ablative with *a*: *propior* urbi, urbem and ab urbe.

NOTE 2.—*The* ETHICAL DATIVE. *Hic tu* mihi *pacis commoda commemoras*, and still you talk to me of the advantages of peace! It is often impossible to render this dative in English.

NOTE 3.—We can only say, communicare *aliquid* cum *aliquo* (not *alicui*), to communicate something to some one (literally, to share with some one). *Dux victoriae gloriam* cum *legionibus* communicavit. *Consilia nostra* communicamus cum *amicis*. *Iubere* and *vetare* do not take the dative, but the accusative and infinitive (§ 194).

NOTE 4.—When *for* expresses protection or substitution it is always rendered by *pro*, § 164, 10.

§ 204.

The following verbs govern the dative:

> *mĕdeor*, *persuādeo*, *nūbo*, *văco*, *stŭdeo*,
> *maledīco*, *parco*, *supplīco*, *obtrecto*, and *invīdeo*.

medeor, I heal.

persuadeo, I persuade, convince.

nubo, I marry (*viro*, a husband).

vaco, I am at leisure (*alicui rei*, for something, I devote myself to it; but *vacare aliqua re*, to be free from something).

maledico, I chide, upbraid.

studeo, I strive after, endeavor.

parco, I spare.

supplīco, I entreat.

obtrecto, I belittle.

invīdeo, I envy.

Medici medentur morbis, *philosophia* medetur animis. Tibi persuade, *virtutem esse summum bonum.* *Venus* nupsit Vulcano. Philosophiae *semper* vaco. *Omnes homines naturā* libertati student. *Frustra* maledices fortunae. Tempori parce. Caesari *pro te libentissime* supplicabo. Obtrectare alteri *nihil utilitatis habet.* *Vir probus* invidet nemini.

1. In *changing* the verb into the *passive* voice, the *dative* must always remain; the verb is put in the third person singular; as: *Mihi persuadetur,* I am being persuaded, convinced; *mihi persuasum est,* I am convinced. The person that acts may be added in the *ablative* with *a;* tuae laudi invidetur *a multis,* your praise is envied by many (you are envied by many for the praise you get). *Invidere* alicui *laudem,* to envy one (on account of) his praise; also, *invidere* laudi alicuius; *invidere* aliqua re, is found in later writers.

2. Some verbs have a *different meaning* according as they govern the dative (dat. of advantage) or the accusative.

Metuo or *timeo te,* I fear you, am afraid of you; *tibi,* for you, am anxious about you.

Caveo te or *a te,* I am on my guard against you; *tibi,* I take care of you.

Consulo te, I consult you; *tibi,* I consult your interests. Also, I advise you, i. e., *suadeo tibi.*

Convenio te, I visit; *convenit mihi tecum de . . .,* or, *res mihi convenit tecum,* I agree with you about; *convenire alicui ad,* in rem, to suit.

Cupio te, I want you; *cupio tibi,* I wish you well.

Prospicio or *provideo periculum,* I foresee the danger; *tibi,* I provide for you; *provideo* or *prospicio frumentum,* I furnish (supply with) grain.

Tempero and *moderor aliquid,* I arrange something; *tempero mihi* (*irae meae*), I check, control myself (my anger); *tempero a lacrimis,* I abstain from tears.

§ 205.

The Dative with Compounds. Verbs compounded with the prepositions, *ad, ante, con, in, inter, ob, post, prae, sub, super,* often govern the dative instead of repeating the preposition.

Natura sensibus adiunxit *rationem.* *Virtutes animi* bonis *corporis* anteponuntur. *Hannibal* Romanis *magnum terrorem* iniecit. Consiliis *interdum* obstat *fortuna.* *Hannibal* Alexandro Magno *non* postponendus *est.* *Animus* praepositus *est* corpori. Succumbere doloribus *miserum est.*

Parva magnis *saepe rectissime conferuntur.* *Nasus quasi murus* oculis interiectus *est.* *Sunt quaedam sidera, quae* infixa coelo *non moventur et* suis sedibus *inhaerent. Neque deesse neque* superesse rei publicae *volo* (I will not survive the republic).

NOTE 1.—In English, of course, the objective case is often governed directly by the verb, often by the preposition corresponding to the Latin; as, *arridet mihi*, he smiles upon me; *senectus obrēpit adolescentiae*, old age creeps upon, overtakes youth.

NOTE 2.—Often the preposition is repeated, especially *ad*, *con*, and *in*. *Macedones* ad *imperium Graeciae* adiunxerunt *Asiam*. *Romani non* conferendi *sunt* cum *Graecis*. In *philosophia magna* inest *vis virtutis* (*inesse* nearly always with *in*). *Interesse alicui rei*, means, to be present at something; but, *interest inter*, there is a difference between. Adsum in *senatu*, I am *present;* adsum amicis, I *assist* my friends. A kindred preposition is sometimes substituted; as, *incumbere* ad *aliquid*, and, in *aliquid*, to apply one's self to something. Obversari ante *oculos*, obiicere contra *impetum hostium* (*ob*, however, is never repeated).

§ 206.

The verbs, *circumdo*, *dono*, *induo*, *adspergo*, *macto*, *exuo*, and a few others, admit a *double construction;* either:

1. The *dative* of the *person* (or the thing treated as a person) and the *accusative* of the *thing;* or,

2. The *accusative* of the *person* and the *ablative* of the *thing* (in answer to the question, *With what?*); *donare* alicui pecuniam, to give money to some one; *donare* aliquem pecuniā, to present one with money.

Circumdo,	1. I put around;	2. I surround, enclose with.
dono,	1. I give;	2. I present with.
induo,	1. I put on;	2. I clothe.
adspergo,	1. I sprinkle at;	2. I besprinkle.
macto,	1. I slay, immolate;	2. I honor with sacrifice.
exuo,	1. I take off;	2. I divest, rob.

Semiramis Babylonem condidit murumque urbi circumdedit. *Deus* animum corpore circumdedit. Ciceroni *populus Romanus* immortalitatem donavit. *Atticus* Athenienses omnes frumento donavit. *Hostium* legiones Telluri *ac* diis manibus mactabo. *Barbari* deos *puerorum* extis mactare *solebant*. *Sapientia* vanitatem exuit mentibus. *Caesar* hostes armis exuit.

Sometimes also, *intercludere alicui commeatum*, and *aliquem commeatu*, and *a commeatu*, to cut off one's supplies; *impertire alicui aliquid* and *aliquem aliqua re*, to confer something upon somebody

§ 207.

DATIVE OF POSSESSOR. *Esse*, with *dative* of the person, is often equivalent to the English, I have. Mihi sunt *libri*, i. e., *habeo libros*.

Homini *cum deo similitudo* est. *Iam Troicis temporibus* erat *honos* eloquentiae. *Nulla* est voluptati *cum honestate coniunctio*.

1. To express a *mutual relation*, we say: est *mihi* cum *aliquo amicitia* (not *habeo amicitiam*). Sunt mihi *inimicitiae* cum *malis*. Tecum mihi *res est*. *Omnia* mihi cum *amicis communia sunt*.

2. Patri *est*, the father *has*; patris *est*, it *belongs* to the father. Of *mental* qualities, we say: *esse* or *inesse in aliquo*. In *patre est summa comitas* (also *pater est summa comitate*, § 225).

3. Say: Mihi est *nomen* Ferdinandus and Ferdinando, my name is Ferdinand; seldom *Ferdinandi*. With *nomen dare* use the accusative: *Parentes* ei *nomen dederunt Fridericum* (also *Friderico*). In the passive: *Inditum* ei *est nomen* Fridericus (*Friderico*).

§ 208.

A *double dative*, one of end or purpose and a dative of advantage, is used with the following verbs:

1. *Esse* and *fieri*, to be, serve, bring, afford.

2. *Tribuere*, *vertere*, *dare*, *ducere*, *habere*, to reckon, to give, to hold.

3. *Venire*, *dare*, *mittere*, *relinquere*, etc., in their usual meaning, to express the *end or purpose* for which.

Hoc mihi commodo est, this *is to* my advantage; *alicui contemptui esse*, to be an object of derision, contempt, to some one. *Alicui* aliquid *dedecori tribuere*, *vertere*, *dare*, *ducere*, *habere*, to hold something a disgrace to some one. *Alicui auxilio venire* (*proficisci*), to come (go) to one's aid; *alicui aliquid dono dare* (*mittere*), to give (send) one something as a present.

Crudelitas omnibus hominibus odio est, *probitas et clementia* amori. *Tua salus* mihi curae *est*. *Nolito* tibi laudi ducere *quod* aliis vitio vertisti. *Hortensius nunquam bello civili interfuit; hoc* illi tribuebatur ignaviae. *Virtus sola* nemini dono *datur*. *Mille Plataeenses* Atheniensibus auxilio *venerunt* (*missi sunt*).

1. *Usui esse*, to be of use; *admirationi esse*, to be admired; *habere aliquem ludibrio*, to hold one in derision; *habere aliquid religioni*, to scruple about something, to hold it sacred; *diem dicere colloquio*, to appoint a day for an interview; *receptui canere*, to sound a retreat. Here the dative of the thing stands alone.

2. The purpose or design is seldom expressed by a predicate-accusative; *Iovi coronam* donum *mittunt*. But with personal nouns, the purpose, for which, must be expressed by the accusative after the verbs, *dare*, *mittere*, *habere*, etc. Amicum *meum tibi* comitem dabo, I will give you my friend for companion (§ 197).

§ 209.

Sometimes the dative is used in the passive, instead of *ab* with the ablative; as, *Honesta* bonis viris, *non occulta quaeruntur*, honest, not secret things, are sought by good men. This dative must be used with the participle future passive. Mihi *faciendum est*, it has to be done *by me*, I must do (not *a me*); but, a me tibi *respondendum est*, I must answer you.

CHAPTER XXXVI.

THE GENITIVE.

§ 210.

A SUBSTANTIVE, limiting another word in answer to the question, *Whose? Of whom? Of which? Of what?* is put in the *genitive* case. It is of a double kind:

1. The SUBJECTIVE GENITIVE (*genitivus subiectivus*), in answer to the question, *Whose?* to denote the person who, as the subject, has or does something; *amor patris*, the father's love (*pater amat*); *studium adolescentis*, the study of the youth (*adolescens studet*).

The subjective genitive most commonly denotes the possessor (author) (*genitivus possessivus*); as, *Domus* Caesaris; *pericula* belli. The writings of Cicero, *scripta Ciceronis*; a part of Epirus, *pars Epiri*. Likewise, a letter *from* you, *epistola* tua (§ 236, 4).

2. The OBJECTIVE GENITIVE (*genitivus obiectivus*), in answer to the question, *What kind of?* to denote the thing which is the object of an action; as, *amor* patriae, the love of one's country, or for one's country (*patriam amat civis*); *studium* veritatis, love of truth, zeal for the truth (*veritati studet vir bonus*).

Timor hostium, fear of enemies; *cupiditas* gloriae, desire for glory; *odium* hominum, hatred of men; *fiducia* virium, confidence in strength.

Molesta est cura rerum alienarum. *Iucunda est* memoria praeteritorum malorum. *Memoriam* vestri *semper retinebo. Habenda est* ratio *non* sua *solum* (instead of *sui*, cfr. 3), *sed etiam* aliorum.

1. The objective genitive is in English generally *expressed by prepositions;* as, of, for, after; these may be retained in Latin, when the object is a person or a thing considered as a person; as, *Tuus* erga or in *patriam amor*, thy love *of* country; *odium* adversus *homines* (but not *amor* in *litteras*).

2. We say: *Nomen regis*, the king's name, and also, the name or title of king. Likewise, *nomen carendi*, the word "to want;" *opus Academicorum;* the work "*Academica*"; *flos* rosae, the flower rose (a rose); *familia* Scipionum, the *Scipio* family.

3. The *possessive pronouns* stand generally for the subjective genitive; as, *amor* meus *erga* te (*ego amo*): but *amor mei* is objective, love for me; *misericordia vestri*, compassion for you. *Iniuria tua*, however, may be both subjective, the wrong you do; and objective, the wrong done to you. Emphatically: *tua* ipsius *soror*, your own sister; *vestra omnium salus*, the welfare of all of you, *mea* unius (*solius*) *opera*. Construction according to sense, § 191, 5, 3.

4. We say only, *Leges Spartiatarum duriores sunt quam Atheniensium*, or *quam leges Atheniensium*, than those of the Athenians; never *quam eae Atheniensium*. In the way of contraction, we find: *Quae tam excellens virtus in ullis fuit, ut sit* cum maioribus nostris *comparanda*, for *cum virtute maiorum nostrorum*, with that of our ancestors.

5. *Habitabat rex* ad Iovis Statoris, supply *templum*. *Ptolemaeus Lagi*, *i. e.*, *filius*. *Terentia* Ciceronis, *i. e.*, *uxor*.

§ 211.

Descriptive Genitive (*genitivus qualitatis*). The genitive of a substantive with an adjective, is used to mark a *quality* or *property*.

This genitive may be connected with a substantive immediately as *attribute*, or with *esse* as *predicate*.

Tarquinius fratrem habuit Aruntem, mitis ingenii *iuvenem. Athenienses belli duos duces deligunt, Periclem*, spectatae virtutis *virum et Sophoclem, scriptorem tragoediarum. Titus* tantae *fuit* liberalitatis, *ut nihil cuiquam negaret.*

A man of talent, *homo* magni ingenii (also, *vir* summo ingenio, abl. qual., § 225), never without an adjective; likewise, eiusmodi *res*, such things; *puer* novem annorum; *fossa* quindecim pedum. But oftener, *tridui* via, *i. e.*, *via trium dierum*.

§ 212.

The genitive is used to express the whole to which either something belongs as a part, or of which it is composed; hence in two ways:

1. The Partitive Genitive (*genitivus partitivus*), which is used with numerals, pronouns, comparatives, and superlatives.

Nemo discipulorum, none *of the* scholars; *multi discipulorum*, many of the scholars; *quis vestrum?* which of you, among you; *Maior fratrum*, the older of the (two) brothers; *optimus omnium*, the best of all.

Quis, aliquis, quidam, quisquam, uter, alter, neuter, uterque, alteruter; aliquot, solus, nullus, nonnulli, multi, pauci, nemo, hic, ille, etc.

Multae istarum arborum *mea manu satae sunt. Hem! nos homunculi indignamur, si* quis nostrum *interiit. Excellentissimi Persarum reges Cyrus et Darius fuerunt*, quorum prior *apud Massagetas in proelio cecidit. Socrates* omnium sapientissimus *oraculo Apollinis iudicatus est.*

1. We must distinguish between *hic discipulus*, and *hic discipulorum; multi milites* and *multi militum*. *Uterque* takes only a *substantive* in the same case as itself; *uterque frater, utrique consuli;* but a *pronoun* always in the *genitive; eorum uterque, quorum utrique, utrumque nostrum.*

2. We say: Indus *est omnium fluminum* maximus (not, *maximum*), when the subject stands first; but, Velocissimum *omnium animalium est* delphinus, when the superlative with the paritive genitive stands first.

3. Instead of the genitive, *ex*, with the *ablative*, is often used; sometimes also, *inter*, with the *accusative*, but never *a* or *ab*. But, *Unus ex tribus; unus de multis*, is always used, unless *alter* follow; often, however, *quorum* unus, *alter*, etc.; for *sui* always *ex se; multos ex se miserunt.*

4. With *numerals*, we often use in English the genitive of a pronoun, where not a *part*, but *all*, are meant; in this case, the genitive cannot be used in Latin. *Causa cadunt, qui aliter existimant;* quos *video esse* multos, *sed imperitos*, of whom, I see, there are many (not *quorum*). Vos *praesertim cum tam* pauci sitis, as there are so *few of you* (not *vestrum*); *volui esse quam coniunctissimos. Trecenti iuravimus*, three hundred *of us* have sworn (we are three hundred that have sworn). Take notice of the *person* used.

5. Sometimes the partitive genitive is governed by *adverbs;* Omnium virtutum maxime *laudamus iustitiam.*

2. Genitive of Quantity (*genitivus quantitatis* or *generis*): it is used with substantives or with the neuter of adjectives and pronouns taken substantively, as also with adverbs of quantity.

Multitudo hominum, a mass of people; *modius tritici,* a bushel of wheat; *quinque pondo auri,* five pounds of gold. *Multum pecuniae,* much money; *satis eloquentiae, sapientiae parum,* enough of eloquence, little wisdom; *aliquid temporis,* some time; *nihil prudentiae,* no prudence.

Acervus, copia, cohors, grex, mo nultitudo, numerus, pars, pondus, talentum, turma, vis.—Multum, plus, plurimum, paulum, minus, minimum, quantum, nimium; hoc, illud, istud, id, idem, quod, quid, aliquid, quidquid, quidquam; nihil, satis, parum, nimis, abunde, etc.

The neuters used substantively are joined only in the *nominative* and *accusative* to a *genitive;* as, *multum auri,* but, *cum multo auro* (never *auri*).

Multi modii salis *simul edendi sunt, ut amicitiae munus expletum sit. Mundus* animorum consentientium multitudine *completus est. Potest quidquam absurdius esse, quam quo* minus viae *restat, tanto* plus viatici *quaerere? Iustitia* nihil *expetit* praemii, nihil pretii. *Nemo nostrum ignorat,* quid consilii *ceperis.*

1. Nearly equivalent are *quid consilii* and *quod consilium; nihil praemii* and *nullum praemium. Multum pecuniae* and *magna pecunia.*

2. The *genitive singular neuter* of adjectives of the *second declension* is used in the same way; thus, *tantum mali,* so much evil; *aliquid novi,* something new; *nihil pulchri,* nothing fine. But with adjectives of the *third declension* the *nominative* remains; *aliquid dulce,* something sweet; *nihil memorabile,* nothing remarkable; *nihil melius,* nothing better; *nihil eminens,* nothing eminent. But when two adjectives are joined, thus, *aliquod* novi *ac* memorabilis, and *aliquid* memorabile *ac* novum.

3. Similar genitives with *adverbs of place:* ubi *terrarum,* where in the world? *eo* or *huc arrogantiae,* to that height of impudence.

§ 213.

The Objective Genitive (*genitivus obiectivus*) with *adjectives.* Adjectives denoting desire, knowledge, participation, memory, certainty, fear, guilt, plenty, and the contrary, govern the *genitive.*

Avidus pecuniae, desirous of money (money-seeking); *rei militaris peritus,* skilled in warfare; *beneficii memor,* mindful of a benefit; *rationis particeps*, possessed of (partaking of) reason; *mentis compos*, having the use of reason; *gaudii plenus*, full of joy. Likewise, *cupidus*, longing for; *studiosus*, eager; *conscius*, conscious; *ignarus*, ignorant; *imperitus*, inexperienced; *rudis*, unskilled; *immĕmor*, unmindful; *fecundus*, *ferax*, *fertilis*, fertile; *sterilis*, barren; *expers*, devoid; *impos*, incapable; *pauper*, *inops*, poor; *inanis*, empty, etc.

Multi contentionis *sunt* cupidiores, *quam* veritatis. *Pythagoras* sapientiae studiosos *appellavit philosophos*. *Sapiens homo ac* multarum rerum peritus *ad res iudicandas requiritur*. *Nihil quod* animi rationisque expers *est*, *generare ex se potest animantem* compotemque rationis. *Humana omnia* plena *sunt* errorum. *Omnes* immemorem beneficii *oderunt*. *Papirii aetas* ferax virtutum *fuit*.

1. *Refertus*, full, usually takes the ablative: *vita undique* referta bonis. So also sometimes the other adjectives denoting *plenty* or *want*, § 229.

2. A kind of Greek genitive is sometimes used by poets and later authors: anxius *animi*; integer *vitae scelerisque* purus; *dubius viae*; *insuetus laboris*. But also in good prose we find *pendere animi*, to be in suspense; but in the plural only, *pendere animis*.

§ 214.

The Objective Genitive with *Participles*. Some present participles of transitive verbs govern the *genitive*, when denoting not so much a single action, as rather an *habitual quality*; *amans gloriae*, glory-loving, fond of glory.

Romani semper appetentes gloriae *fuerunt*. *Epaminondas adeo fuit* veritatis diligens, *ut ne ioco quidem mentiretur*.

Patiens frigoris, one that *can bear* the cold; *patiens frigus*, one that *actually* bears it. In the latter example, the cold is felt; in the former, though it be cold, still it is not felt.

§ 215.

1. The Possessive Genitive (*genitivus possessivus*) in the predicate of a sentence, with *esse* and *fieri*. With *esse* and *fieri*, the genitive of a noun is used to express property, characteristic quality, peculiarity, business, duty, distinctive mark, etc., some thing is or becomes.

Divitias sine divitum esse (let the rich have their riches); *tu virtutem praefer divitiis*. *Omnia, quae* mulieris fuerunt, viri fiunt *dotis nomine.* Cuiusvis hominis est *errare*, nullius, *nisi* insipientis, *in errore perseverare.* Sapientis iudicis est, *semper quid lex et religio cogat cogitare.* *Ut res adversas, sic secundas immoderate ferre* levitatis est.

2. Instead of the *genitive* of a personal pronoun (*mei*, *tui*, etc.,) the *neuter possessive* is always used; as, *meum est*, it is my duty; *vestrum est*, it is your duty.

Si cuiusquam, *certe* tuum *est*, *nihil praeter virtutem in bonis ducere.* Nostrum est *ferre modice populi voluntates.*

NOTE 1.—*Esse* may be omitted; as, *sapientis iudicis*, or *meum videtur*, *putatur*, *manet*, it seems to be the part of a wise judge, it seems to be my duty, etc.

NOTE 2.—Like *fieri*, so also *facere* is used with the possessive genitive. *Totam Galliam* suae potestatis fecit, he brought the whole of Gaul under his power.

NOTE 3.—*Hoc dicere* arrogantis *est*, characterizes a class of *people*; *hoc dicere* stultum *est*, characterizes an *action*.

§ 216.

The OBJECTIVE GENITIVE with *verbs of memory.* Verbs of reminding, remembering and forgetting, generally govern the *genitive.*

1. *Admoneo*, *commoneo*, *commonefacio aliquem* alicuius rei, I remind one of something.

2. *Memini* and *reminiscor*, I remember; *recordor*, I recollect; *obliviscor*, I forget; also, *venit mihi in mentem* alicuius, somebody (or something) comes to my mind. Some of these verbs take sometimes the *accusative* or the *ablative* with *de.*

1. *Res adversae* admonent religionum. *Grammaticos* officii sui commonemus. *Nemo est in Sicilia*, *quin* tui sceleris *ex illa oratione* commonefiat.

2. *Animus* meminit praeteritorum, *praesentia cernit*, *futura praevidet.* *Proprium est stultitiae*, *aliorum vitia cernere*, oblivisci suorum. *Homo improbus ipse certe aliquando agnoscet et cum dolore* recordabitur flagitiorum suorum. Venit mihi Platonis in mentem. Recordor memoriam *pueritiae* ultimam. *Libenter* beneficia memini, obliviscor iniurias.

With *admoneo* only: hoc *te admoneo*; multa me *admonuit*, not *huius*, *multorum* (§ 202, 2). Likewise, hoc *te moneo*, or, de hac re (not the genitive). *Obliviscor* takes the *person* always in the *genitive; recordor*, always in the *ablative* with *de* (the *thing* mostly in the *accusative*). *Memini* patrem, I remember my father *yet; memini* patris, I *think* of him just now, or I mention him.

NOTE.—Concerning the objective genitive, with *piget*, *pudet*, etc., cfr. § 196.

§ 217.

GENITIVE OF CRIME (*genitivus criminis*). With *legal terms* of accusing, condemning, and acquitting, the *crime*, and sometimes also the *penalty*, is put in the (objective) *genitive*.

Accusare, *incusare*, *arguere*, *insimulare*, to accuse; *arcessere*, *postulare*, *reum facere*, to summon, to arraign; *coarguere*, *convincere*, to convict; *damnare*, *condemnare*, to condemn; *absolvere* (*liberare*) to acquit; *capitis reus*, condemned to death, accused of a capital crime.

Miltiades proditionis accusatus *et*, *quamquam* capitis absolutus, *tamen pecunia multatus est*. *Socrates a iudicibus* capitis damnatus *est*. *Cicero Verrem* avaritiae coarguit. *Caelius iudex* absolvit iniuriarum *eum*, *qui Lucilium poëtam in scena nominatim laeserat*.

1. With *damnare*, the *penalty* is expressed; capitis (also *capite*) *damnatus*, sentenced to death; *quanti*, to how much; *dupli*, to the double. But *specified sums of money* are put in the *ablative;* decem millibus *aeris damnatus est* (§ 248, 2). *Other penalties* are expressed by the verb *multare*, always with the *ablative* (never *damnare*); pecunia *multare*, to condemn to a fine; *exilio*, to exile; *morte*, to death.

2. The word *crimen* stands, with the verb *accusare*, in the *ablative; accusabo te* eodem crimine (not *criminis*).

3. *Accusare aliquem repetundarum* and *de repetundis*, of extortions; *parricidii* and *de parricidio*, of parricide; only *de vi* (*vis* has no genitive); inter *sicarios*, of assassination. *Condemnare aliquem* ad *bestias*, in *metalla*. In common language (not legal), it is mostly, *accusare* (*incusare*) negligentiam *alicuius*, to accuse one of negligence.

§ 218.

GENITIVE OF PRICE (*genitivus pretii*). The *price* or value of a thing (*how much? how dear?*) is generally expressed by the *genitive* of adjectives of quantity.

1. With the verbs, to estimate, to be worth, to be considered, all *adjectives* expressing the *value* are in the *genitive;* as, magni *duco*, *puto*, *facio*, *aestimo*, and *pendo*, I esteem, appreciate

highly; pluris *sum*, I am worth more; maximi *fio, habeor*, I am esteemed very highly.

Likewise, *permagni, plurimi, parvi, minoris, minimi, tanti, quanti* (never *multi*, but *magni;* never *maioris*, but *pluris;* seldom *nihili*).

Voluptatem virtus minimi facit. *Agere considerate* pluris est, *quam cogitare prudenter. Sapientis viri est, opes atque divitias et quae sunt generis eiusdem* parvi ducere. *Auctoritas regis* magni habetur.

2. With the verbs, to buy, to sell, to cost, to rent, etc., only the four *comparative* adjectives, *tanti, quanti, pluris, minoris,* are used in the *genitive* to denote the *price;* all *other adjectives* and all *substantives* are used in the *ablative* (§ 222). Tanti *hunc hortum emi*, I have bought this garden for *so much*. But, parvo *eum emi*, I have bought it cheap (for little); also, *magno, plurimo, minimo, vili, nihilo, duobus talentis eum emi.*

Emere, to buy; *vendere*, to sell; *venire*, to be for sale; *redimere*, to buy back; *constare*, to cost; *conducere*, to hire; *locare*, to let; *licere*, to be for sale.

Vendo meum frumentum non pluris, *quam ceteri, fortasse etiam* minoris. *Homo cupidus hortulos* tanti *emit*, quanti *venditor voluit. Hortos istos emamus vel* magno, *si* parvo *non possumus. Te* redimas *captum quam queas* minimo, *si nequeas* paululo, *at* quanti *queas.*

Hunc hominem flocci (*nauci, pili, assis*) *non facio*, I do not care a straw for this man (I don't consider him worth that!). *Tanti est*, it is worth while.

§ 219.

With *interest*, it is of interest, of importance, it concerns, the *person* is put in the *genitive: patris interest*, it is of interest to the father, it concerns, etc. If the person is a personal *pronoun*, we always use the *abl. fem. posses.* instead of the *gen. pers. pron.*; not *mei interest*, but *meā, tuā, suā, vestrā interest*, etc.

The same ablative is used with *refert*, it concerns; *nostrā refert*, it concerns us; *refert* takes the genitive very seldom.

Natura corvis et cornicibus, quorum *id nihil* interest, *vitam diuturnam, hominibus*, quorum *maxime* interfuit, *exiguam vitam dedit. Caesar dicere solebat, non tam* sua, *quam* rei publicae interesse, *ut valeret.*

Vestra *nihil* refert, *victum esse Antonium.* Tua *quod nil* refert, *percontari desinas.*

1. *That which interests*, concerns one, matters to one, is not expressed by a *substantive*, but by a *clause*, either with *ut* or with the *accusative* and *infinitive* (§ 270), or with an *indirect question. In omnibus novis conjunctionibus multum interest, qualis primus aditus sit*, the first appearance is of high importance.

2. To express *how much* it interests, concerns, matters, etc., we find:

a. The adverbs: *magnopere, valde, vehementer, magis, maxime, parum, minus, minime.*

b. The *accusatives: multum* (*non multum*, little), *plus, plurimum, tantum, quantum, minimum, nimium, nihil, aliquid, quid?*

c. The *genitives: magni, pluris, tanti, quanti, parvi* (little).

3. The *object* or *end* for which it is important, is expressed by the *accusative* with *ad;* as, *maxime* ad salutem *omnium* interest, *ut omnes legibus obediant.*

CHAPTER XXXVII.

THE ABLATIVE.

§ 220.

The *Ablative* expresses various relations which are in English generally expressed by prepositions.

1. Ablative of Instrument (*ablativus instrumenti*). The ablative without preposition is used to express the *means* or *instrument.* Question, *by what means? wherewith? Oculis cernimus*, we see with our eyes.

Sol luce *sua cuncta illustrat.* Dente *lupus*, cornu *taurus petit. Benevolentiam civium* blanditiis *et* assentando *colligere turpe est.*

Note 1. When *persons* are the *means* or *instrument* (question, *by whom? through whom?* the *accusative* with *per* is always used: *per legatos eum certiorem facit; per me* (or *mea opera*) *factum est.* To denote *accompaniment* of persons or things (question, *with whom? with what?*) *cum* is used: cum patre *profectus sum*; *cum rege locutus sum; cum magno damno abiit; cum gladio, cum magna pecunia venit* (but, *hunc agrum magna pecunia emi*).

NOTE 2. The following may also be considered an *ablative of means*: *tenere se castris*, to stay in the camp; *recipere aliquem tecto*, to receive one under one's roof. But in a figurative sense, only *recipere aliquem in amicitiam.*

2. ABLATIVE OF INANIMATE AGENT (*ablativus rei efficientis*). The ablative without a preposition is used with passive and intransitive verbs to denote the thing by which anything is effected. (Question, *whereby? by what?*)

Boni nullo emolumento *impelluntur in fraudem, improbi saepe* parvo. *Trahimur omnes* studio *laudis et optimus quisque maxime* gloria *ducitur. Corpora iuvenum firmantur* labore. Concordia *parvae res crescunt*, discordia *maximae dilabuntur.*

3. ABLATIVE OF LIVING AGENT (*ablativus auctoris*). With passive verbs the *person* who is the *author* of an action is put in the *ablative* with *a* or *ab.*

Roma a *Romulo, Alexandria* ab *Alexandro condita est. Alexander* ab *Apelle potissimum pingi et* a *Lysippo fingi volebat.*

Natus, ortus, genitus (born, descended from) take the name of the father or mother in the *ablative*, without preposition; however, *ex* is sometimes used. *Quod ex nobis natos appellamus liberos, idcirco Cerere nati appellati sunt Liber et Libera;* but with regard to more remote ancestry, we find *oriundus* or *ortus a claris maioribus*, descended from renowned ancestors. *Naturā*, by nature (as inanimate cause); *a natura*, from nature (as a person). In the sentence, *per quos et a quibus homines occisi sunt? a* denotes the authors, *per* the actual doers as the tools of the former.

§ 221.

ABLATIVE OF CAUSE (*ablativus causae*). The *ablative* without preposition is used to express the *cause for which* or *motive through which* something is done.

Most generally this ablative is used with substantives expressing *feeling* or *emotion*; as, *dolore, ira, studio, odio, metu, timore, cupiditate, avaritia, spe, misericordia, benevolentia, amore, taedio, mollitia.* In English, *through, with, for.*

Multi metu *mortis vim tormentorum pertulerunt. Nimio* gaudio *paene desipiebam. Multi officia deserunt* mollitia *animi. Nolito putare, me* oblivione *tui rarius ad te scribere. Regale civitatis genus non tam regni, quam regis* vitiis *repudiatum est.*

2. The ablative of cause is most frequently used with verbs and adjectives denoting feeling or emotion. (Question, *on what account? for what? at what?*)

Thus, *dolere*, *maerere*, *laborare*, *gaudere*, *laetari*, *delectari*, *exsultare*, *gloriari*, *triumphare*; *laetus*, *anxius*, *contentus*, satisfied with; *fretus*, trusting in, and the corresponding verbs, *nitor*, *fido*, *confido*, I trust in, *aliqua re*, something; (*fido*, *confido*, also with dative, I place trust in; and *diffido alicui*, I mistrust one).

Omnes boni interitu *suorum* maerent. Diversis duobus vitiis, avaritia *et* luxuria, *civitas Romana* laborabat. *Delicto dolere, correctione gaudere oportet. Nulla re tam laetari soleo, quam meorum officiorum conscientia. Contentum suis rebus esse maximae sunt certissimaeque divitiae. Haec ad te scripsi: fretus conscientia benevolentiae tuae. Quis poterit aut corporis firmitate aut fortunae stabilitate confidere?*

1. *Odio*, through hatred; but better, *odio permotus*. In the same way, *amore ductus*, *cupiditate impulsus*; *ira incensus* or *inflammatus*; *ardens odio*; *flagrans cupiditate*; *timore* or *timore permotus*, through fear; *prae timore*, for fear. *Meā causā*, for my sake; *meā ipsius causā*, for my own sake (§ 238, 9); *tuā*, *suā*, etc., *causā*. *Ea de causa* (or, *ob eam causam*), on that account; *amicorum causa* (*gratia*), for the sake of my friends (§ 164, 15, 4) (*causa* and *gratia* always after the dependent word). *Consilio Themistoclis*, by the advice of Themistocles; *iussu consulis*, by command of the consul; *iniussu populi*, without the people's will; *mandatu meo*, by my direction; thus also, *monitu*, *permissu*, etc.

2. *Laborare ex capite*, to have a headache; so also, *ex dentibus*, *ex intestinis*, *ex pedibus*. *Gloriari de aliqua re* and *in aliqua re*; *se iactare*, nearly always, *in aliqua re*, to boast of a thing; sometimes, however, *iactare aliquam rem*, instead of *se iactare in aliqua re*.

§ 222.

Ablative of Price (*ablativus pretii*).—The *substantive* denoting the *price* at which something is bought or valued, is put in the *ablative*.

When the price is expresed by an adjective, after verbs of valuing, the gen. is used; after those of buying or selling, the abl. and gen. § 218.

Otium non gemmis *neque* purpura *venale* (*est*) *neque* auro. *Viginti* talentis *unam orationem Isocrates vendidit. Darius mille talentis percussorem Alexandri emere voluit.*

Quanti habitas? how much rent do you pay? *Parvo*, cheap; *duodecim thaleris*, twelve dollars; *duobus millibus nummum*, 2,000 sesterces.

§ 223.

The adjectives *dignus* and *indignus*, worthy and unworthy, always govern the *ablative* (concerning *dignus qui*, cfr. § 258).

Excellentium civium virtus imitatione, *non* invidia digna *est. Nihil magno et praeclaro viro dignius placabilitate et clementia. In summa difficultate nulla vox audita est populi Romani* maiestate indigna.

The verb *dignor*, I deign, consider worthy, and am considered worthy, also governs the ablative. *Res dissimiles saepe consimili laude dignantur.*

§ 224.

Ablative of Manner (*ablativus modi*).—To denote manner we use:

1. The *ablative* without a preposition with words that express *manner* and *way;* as, *hoc modo, hac ratione*, in this manner; *Graeco more*, after the Greek manner; *pecudum ritu*, after the manner of animals; *nostra consuetudine, hac lege; certis conditionibus*, under certain conditions.

2. The *ablative*, with *cum*, is used with all other words which are *not limited* by an adjective; *cum diligentia*, with diligence, *i. e., diligenter; cum fide*, with faithfulness; *cum voluptate*, with pleasure; *cum ignominia*, with shame.

Also *per* with the accusative; as, *per dedecus*, with shame, in shame.

3. The *ablative* is used either *with or without* the preposition *cum*, when the word is modified by an adjective; as, *magna* cum *diligentia*, and *magna diligentia; incredibili cum celeritate* and *incredibili celeritate*.

Quid aliud est, gigantum modo *pugnare cum diis, nisi naturae repugnare? Beate vivere et honeste, id est* cum virtute *vivere. Is cultus deorum est optimus, ut eos semper* pura mente *veneremur. Albucium cum multa venustate risit Lucilius.*

1. *Iure* (with reason), rightfully; *iniuriā* (without reason), unjustly; *ratione et via*, with method and reason; *voluntate* (*sponte*), voluntarily; *silentio*, silently; *ordine*, in good order. Nouns expressing a disposition of mind, even when joined to an adjective, are used without *cum; aequo animo; hoc consilio; ea mente. Per vim*, in a violent way; *vi*, by force; *per ludum*, in a playful manner; *specie*, under the color of; *per speciem*, on pretence.

4. To denote an article of dress, *cum* may be added or left out; as, *sedebat cum tunica pulla; sedebat pulcherrimo vestitu.* To denote a part of the body, *cum* is not used. *Nudo capite incessit.* *Cum ferro*, with the sword (in hand); *ferro*, with the sword (ablative of instrument); *ferro ignique*, with fire and sword.

§ 225.

ABLATIVE OF QUALITY (*ablativus qualitatis*).—The ablative of a substantive with an adjective is used to express a *quality*.

This ablative is used both as predicate and as attribute.

Agesilaus statura *fuit* humili *et* corpore exiguo. *Cato in omnibus rebus singulari fuit prudentia et industria.* *Aristoteles, vir summo ingenio, prudentiam cum eloquentia coniunxit.*

The *descriptive genitive* (§ 211) may be used instead of the *ablative of quality*, except when parts of the body are described; hence only, *Britanni* capillo *sunt* promisso. When a numeral takes the place of the attributive adjective the genitive only is used; as, *classis* trecentarum navium.

§ 226.

ABLATIVE OF LIMITATION (*ablativus limitationis*).—The ablative without preposition is used in order to express a *limitation of the judgment*, by indicating the measure according to which the judgment is to be applied. (In English generally, *with regard to, as to, in*).

Multi utilitate *officium dirigunt magis, quam* humanitate. *Sunt quidam homines non* re, *sed* nomine. *Magnos homines* virtute *metimur, non* fortuna. *Socrates omnium eruditorum testimonio, philosophorum omnium facile fuit princeps.* *Mea quidem sententia paci semper consulendum est.*

1. Here belongs, *maior natu*, older; likewise, *maximus natu; minor natu; minimus natu;* but, *Cyrus Maior*, *Scipio Maior*, without *natu*. *Claudus altero pede;* lame of one foot.

2. *Mea sententia, meo iudicio*, in my opinion, judgment; *ex (mea) sententia*, according to my wish; *numero quinque*, five in number; *genere*, by race; *natione Gallus*, by nation a Gaul.

3. Poets use an accusative of limitation, after the Greek manner, (*accus. Graecus*); as, *longam vestem indutus*, instead of *longa veste; os humerosque Deo similis;* instead of *ore humerisque.* *Feminae Germanorum nudae erant brachia et lacertos.*

§ 227.

Ablative of Comparison (*ablativus comparationis*).—The ablative is used after an adjective in the *comparative* degree instead of *quam*, with the nominative or the accusative; thus, *filius* patre *maior est*, for *filius maior est* quam pater.

Patria mihi vita mea *multo est* carior. *Nihil est* amabilius virtute. *Vilius argentum est* auro, virtutibus *aurum*. *Lacrimā nihil citius arescere dicunt*. *Recte auguraris, nihil abesse a me longius crudelitate*. *Quem auctorem locupletiorem Platone laudare possumus?*

1. This ablative *cannot* be used when it would render the meaning doubtful. *Germani graviores hostes sustinuerunt*, quam Romanos; not *Romanis*, which would mean *quam Romani*. Often: *hoc* or *quo nihil vidimus indignius*. *Scipio Punici belli perpetrati, quo nullum neque maius neque periculosius Romani gessere, unus praecipuam gloriam tulit;* than which the Romans waged none, either greater or more perilous.

2. *Minus*, *plus* and *amplius* (also *longius*) when joined to words of number and measure usually drop *quam*, without any further change; as, *Plus pars dimidia ex quinquaginta millibus hominum caesa est* (seldom *quam pars* or *parte*). *Milites Romani plus dimidiati mensis cibaria ferebant*. *Minus duo millia hominum ex tanto exercitu effugerunt*.

In the phrase, *Caesar* opinione *celerius advenit*, *opinione* may be explained either as standing for *quam opinio* advenit, or as *quam opinio* erat (*est*, *fuit*). In the same manner we often say; *plus aequo; solito magis; spe citius* or *serius*, etc. *Multi plus aequo in amicitiam congerunt*.

§ 228.

Ablative of Measure (*ablativus mensurae*).—The *measure* by which a thing or an action surpasses another, is expressed by the *ablative;* as, *multo melior*, by far better.

This ablative is principally used with *comparatives*, *superlatives* and *verbs* having a comparative meaning; as *malle*, *antecellere*, *praestare*, *superare*, *postponere*, etc. *Multo meo iudicio stare malo, quam reliquorum omnium*, I will by far rather.

Hibernia dimidio minor *est*, *quam Britannia*. *Diogenes disputare solebat*, quanto *regem Persarum vitā fortunāque superaret*. (*Ego*) Tanto pessimus *omnium poëta* quanto *tu* optimus *omnium patronus*.

1. *Quo — eo*, the — the; *quanto — tanto:* quo *quisque est doctior*, eo *est nequior;* *the* more learned he is, *the* more wicked is he; which may also

be expressed thus: *doctissimus quisque nequissimus:* or, *ut quisque est doctissimus, ita est nequissimus.*

2. With the above mentioned verbs (except *malle*) the adverbial forms *longe, multum, tantum* may also be used; this, however, seldom occurs with comparatives; with the superlatives *longe* is generally used.

§ 229.

Ablative of Plenty (*ablativus copiae*).—Verbs denoting plenty or want, filling, furnishing with or depriving, govern the *ablative.*

Abundare, redundare, affluere, to abound in; *carere,* to miss, to be wanting; *vacare,* to be free from; *egere,* to be in need of; *indigere,* to want, need; *implere, complere, refercire,* to fill; *privare, orbare, spoliare,* to rob, deprive; *nudare,* to divest.

Germania Galliaque abundant rivis et fluminibus. *Monitio* acerbitate carere *debet. Quid affere consilii potest, qui ipse* eget consilio? *Gravius est spoliari fortunis, quam non augeri dignitate. Deus bonis omnibus explevit mundum, mali nihil admiscuit.*

Here belongs the expression, *afficere aliquem aliqua re;* as, *Poena eos affecit,* he punished them; *magno me dolore affecisti,* you have caused me great sorrow. Also, *praeditus,* endowed with; as, *Virtute qui praediti sunt, soli sunt beati.*

Indigere, when it means to stand in need of, takes the genitive; as, *Consilii tui indigeo,* I need your advice. *Interdicere,* to exclude, forbid, *alicui aliqua re;* seldom *interdicere alicui aliquid. Ciceroni aqua et igni interdictum est,* Cicero was exiled. *Lapidibus (lacte, sanguine) pluit,* it has rained stones.

§ 230.

Ablative with opus est, there is need. After the impersonal *opus est* the *thing* is put in the *ablative;* the *person,* that needs, may be added in the *dative.* Mihi opus *est* libris: I need books.

Opus est may, however, be construed personally (except in negative sentences); then the thing needed stands as subject in the *nominative. Mihi opus sunt* libri (*opus,* an indecl. subst.).

Multis non duce *tantum* opus est, *sed* adiutore *et* coactore. Dux *nobis et* auctor *opus est* (or *duce, auctore*); but negatively, only nihil *opus est* duce; quid *opus est* exemplo? *Themistocles celeriter*, quae opus erant *reperiebat*.

Hence only; *quantum opus est, multa opus sunt* (the neuter of the adjective; never *quanto, multis*, even in negative and interrogative sentences).

§ 231.

The five deponents, *fruor, fungor, potior, utor, vescor*, take their object in the *ablative*.

Frui otio, to enjoy leisure; *fungi munere*, to discharge an office, perform a function; *potiri imperio*, to obtain the supreme command; *uti ratione*, to use reason; *vesci carne*, to eat meat. Thus also their compounds, *perfruor, defungor, abutor*, etc.

Commoda, quibus utimur, *lucemque*, qua fruimur, *spiritumque, quem ducimus, a deo nobis dari videmus. Nemo parum diu vixit, qui virtutis* functus est munere. *Imperator* urbe potitus *est. Numidae plerumque* lacte *et* ferina carne vescebantur.

Rerum (not *rebus*) *potiri*, to have supreme power. *Facili me utetur patre*, he will find in me a kind father; *utor eo doctore*, I have him for teacher.

§ 232.

Ablative of Separation. *Verbs* which denote a separation take the *thing* in the *ablative* with or without the preposition *a*, or *ex;* but the *person* always with the preposition *ab* (question, *from where? from whom? from what?*).

Arcere, to keep off; *expellere*, to banish; *desistere*, to leave off; *deterrere*, to deter; *excedere*, to depart; *liberare*, to free; *abstinere*, or *abstinere se*, to abstain.

Apud Germanos quemcunque mortalium arcere tecto *nefas habetur. Tarquinius Superbus* urbe expulsus est. *Homines* ab iniuria *natura non poena* arcere *debet. Hannibal* ex Italia decedere *coactus est. Themistocles Graeciam servitute liberavit. Post mortem animus a corpore liberatus erit.*

2. The adjectives *alienus*, strange, averse; *purus* and *immunis*, pure; *liber*, free; *vacuus*, devoid, free from, take the *ablative* with or without *ab;* thus, *curis vacuus*, free from cares; *ab exercitationibus vacuum tempus*, a time without exercise (practice).

Animus per somnum curis vacuus *est. Artibus variis ita eram deditus, ut ab exercitationibus nullus tamen dies vacuus esset. Avaritia* aliena est a bono viro.

1. *Abdicare se dictatura*, to resign (lay down) the dictatorship; *aliquem tribu movere*, cast one out from the tribe.

2. *Prohibere hostem a rapinis*, or *rapinis*, to thwart in his robberies, and *prohibere rem publicam a periculo* or *periculo*, to save the state from danger. Likewise, *defendere ab iniuria*, (never the ablative alone), to defend against injustice; *defendere iniuriam*, to ward off an injury (never *ab* or ablative).

3. Verbs compounded with *se* and *dis* have nearly always *a* or *ab*: *secerno, sepăro, seiungo*, I separate; *disto, differo*, I differ; *distinguo, discerno*, I distinguish.—Mostly also, *aliēno*, I estrange, *abhorreo*, I shrink from, *a scelere*, the crime. Instead of *dissentire ab aliquo*, to disagree with one, *dissentire cum aliquo*, can be said.

§ 233.

Ablative of Place (*ablativus loci*). The answer to the question, *where?* is put in the *ablative* with *in*. But the word *locus*, and any substantive joined to *totus*, always stand in the *ablative* without a preposition.

Omnibus locis *virtus coli potest. Tyriorum coloniae paene* toto orbe *terrarum diffusae sunt.*

Hoc loco, in this place; *opportuno loco*, in a favorable place; *loco, suo loco* (rarely *in loco*) in the right place; *parentis loco* or *numero esse alicui*, to be a father to one; *toto mari*, over the whole ocean; *tota Italia*, in all Italy, etc. *Terra marique* (also *et mari et terra*), by sea and land; but *in mari*, in the sea; *in terra*, on the land; *dextrā*, on the right; *sinistrā*, on the left. *Hoc libro disputatur de officiis*, refers to the contents of the book; *in hoc libro*, marks particular passages.

2. The ablative without preposition is used to mark the *line* or *direction* in which motion takes place.

Demonstrabo iter; Aureliā viā *profectus est. Lapis cadens* recta linea *deorsum fertur.*

Qua, which way; *hac, eā, recta*, this, that, straightways. *Portā Collinā*, through the Colline gate; also, *per portam Collinam. Dextra parte*, on the right side, *side* taken as a direction; *in dextra parte*, taken as a point.

§ 234.

Ablative of Time (*ablativus temporis*).—The ablative without a preposition answers the question, *when?* as, *hoc tempore*, at this time; *hieme*, in winter; *nocte* or *noctu*, by night; *occasu solis*, at sunset; *luce*, by day.

Roma condita est anno septingentesimo quinquagesimo tertio *ante Christum natum. Virtus* nullo tempore *relinquenda est.* Qua nocte *Alexander natus est*, eādem *templum Dianae Ephesiae deflagravit.*

1. *Hoc tempore*, at this time; *in hoc tempore*, at this crisis; *extrema pueritia*, at the close of boyhood; but, *in pueritia, in vita. Initio, principio* (seldom with *in*), at the beginning; *ab initio, a principio*, from the beginning. *Luculli adventu*, on the arrival of Lucullus; *comitiis*, at the elections; *ludis, contionibus, bello*, in the time of, (but *in bello*, in the war).

2. The length of time within which something is done is expressed by the ablative: as, *Agamemnon cum universa Graecia vix decem annis unam urbem cepit* (also *intra decem annos*). With a numeral adverb *in* is added; *bis in die*, twice a day; *ter in anno*, three times in the year.

2. The ablative preceded or followed by *ante, post*, denotes *how long* before or after; as, *tribus annis ante* (*post*), or *tribus ante* (*post*) *annis*, three years ago (after); *paulo ante*, shortly before; *multo post*, long after.

Themistocles fecit idem, quod viginti annis ante *fecerat Coriolanus. Corpus Alexandri* paucis post annis *Alexandriam translatum est. Numa Pompilius permultis annis ante fuit, quam Pythagoras.*

1. Here *ante* and *post* are adverbs, and the ablative is rather that of measure than of time; (§ 228.) *Ante* (*post*) *tres annos*, or *ante* (*post*) *tertium annum*, are the same as, *tribus ante* (*post*) *annis.* When *quam* follows, it may be joined to *ante* and *post;* as, *Panaetius triginta annis vixit, postquam libros de officiis edidit. Post* is sometimes omitted after the ablative; as, *hoc factum est tertio anno, quam Aristides mortuus erat.* But in such instances the relative may be used instead of *quam;* as, *Mors Roscii quadriduo, quo is occisus est, Chrysogono nuntiatur.*

2. Three years ago (to-day) is, in Latin, *ante tres annos*, or *abhinc tres annos*, or *abhinc tribus annis*, seldom *ante hos tres annos.*

§ 235.

1. Concerning the *ablative with prepositions*, cfr. § 162, 163.

2. The verbs *ponere, collocare*, to put, place (also, *locare, statuere, constituere, considere*) take the ablative with *in*, though they imply motion, not r st.

Plato animi principatum, id est rationem, in capite *sicut* in arce posuit. *Herculem hominum fama* in concilio *deorum* collocavit.

1. *Ponere* and *collocare* are always constructed as implying rest in a place, not motion to a place. Hence: *Ubi, hic, ibi, Romae fortunas meas posui.*

2. *Advenire*, to arrive; *convenire*, to meet together; *cogere*, to assemble; *nuntiare*, to announce; *abdere*, to conceal, take *in* with the accusative. *Graeci in Isthmum convenerunt*, the Greeks met on the Isthmus. *Romam nuntiatum est*, it was announced in Rome. Likewise, *quo, huc, illuc, eo convenerunt. In silvas se abdiderunt;* but only, *abditus in silvis.*

CHAPTER XXXVIII.

PECULIARITIES OF SYNTAX.

IDIOMS OF ADJECTIVES AND PRONOUNS.

§ 236.

ADJECTIVES.

In Latin an *adjective* is often placed in *apposition*, where in English we employ an *adverb*, or an adverbial clause (preposition and noun): such are,

1. Many participial adjectives; as, sciens *calumniatus est*, he has slandered *knowingly*.

Thus: *absens*, in one's absence; *praesens*, in (my) presence; *ignorans, insciens* (*ignarus, nescius*), unwittingly; *occultus*, secretly; *mortuus*, after (one's) death; *vivus*, alive; *tacitus*, in silence, silently.

Hortensium vivum *amavi, Crassum non odi* mortuum. *Natura ipsa de immortalitate animorum* tacita *iudicat.*

2. The comparatives and superlatives denoting place; superior *stabat lupus*, higher up stood the wolf.

Thus: *inferior, prior, propior, extremus, infimus, primus, princeps.* Likewise, *medius, unus, solus, totus,* (*omnis, universus*), *frequens, creber, assiduus, rarus.*

Caesar constituerat, prior *proelio non lacessere. Philosophiae nos nunc* totos *tradimus. Roscius* assiduus *ruri vixit.*

3. The adjectives and participles of feeling; as, *laetus, libens, sobrius, invitus, trepidus,* etc.

Socrates venenum laetus *et* libens *hausit.* Soli *hoc contingit sapienti, nihil ut faciat* invitus, *nihil* coactus.

The adjective here always refers to the subject; but if the predicate is to be modified, then the adverb must be used; *sciens calumniatus est; scienter calumniatus est.*

4. Adjectives derived from proper nouns: *Hercules Xenophonteus*, the Hercules of Xenophon; *pugna Leuctrica, Marathonia, Cannensis*, the battle of Leuctra, etc. *Cimon Atheniensis*, Cimon of Athens, (the Athenian).

Epistola mea, my letter, and a letter from me. If the predicate is modified, the preposition must be used: *Lacedaemonii a Thebanis pugna ad Leuctra victi sunt.*

§ 237.

Other Peculiarities in the Use of Adjectives:

1. An adjective is seldom joined immediately to a proper noun. *Pompeius*, vir clarissimus, the renowned Pompey (not *clarus Pompeius*). *Socrates*, homo sapientissimus; *Corinthus*, urbs opulentissima.

But *Corinthus sola; universa Graecia; omnis Gallia; cuncta Italia; tota Asia; noster ille Ennius; Cicero meus; Sulla Felix; Pompeius Magnus; Scipio Maior*, these are considered as a single name.

2. Words like *former, first, last, alone, only, self*, are sometimes expressed by an *adverb*, but oftener by an *adjective* (§ 236, 2), which then takes the case of the supposed or expressed antithesis; as, *hoc tu mihi* primum *dixisti* (scil. postea *negasti*) *hoc* tu *mihi* primus *dixisti* (scil. *postea* frater tuus); *hoc tu* mihi primo *dixisti* (scil. *postea fratri tuo*). *Sibi* ipse *omnia licere putat* (scil. *ceteri non putant*); sibi ipsi *omnia licere putat* (scil. *ceteris non putat*).

Homo non sibi *se* soli *natum meminerit, sed* patriae, *sed* amicis. *Non egeo medicina; me* ipse *consolor.*

3. The superlative of adjectives of place is often used in Latin, where in English a *substantive* or an *adverb* of similar meaning is employed: *in summo monte*, on the top of the mountain; *in media urbe*, in the middle of the city. So also with regard to time: *prima nocte*, at the beginning of the night; *prima luce*, at day-break; (*primo die*, on the first day;)

extremo anno, at the end of the year; *novissimum agmen*, the rear guard.

4. As in English, so also in Latin, *adjectives* are sometimes used as *substantives: bonum*, the good; *malum*, the evil; *verum*, the truth. *Aequalis*, the equal; *adversarius*, the adversary; *socius*, the ally.

1. Neuters of this kind are almost exclusively only the adjectives of the second declension, especially when used in the genitive: *nihil boni*, nothing good; *natura iusti et aequi mater est* (§ 212, 2, 2), but adjectives of the third declension, rarely; as, *turpe*, the ugly thing. Plural, *bona*, *mala*, *turpia*, good, bad, shameful things or actions. *Verum* or *vera dicere*, to tell the truth (not *veritatem*).

2. To denote persons, most adjectives are used as substantives in the plural only; in the singular, *vir* or *homo* is added. *Docti* or *homines docti*, learned men, or the learned; but *homo doctus*, a learned man; *doctissimi* or *homines doctissimi*, the most learned men; *homo vere doctus*, a really learned man. Thus also, *boni*, *mali*, *probi*, *improbi*, *prudentes*, *divites*, *pauperes; mei*, *tui*, *nostri*, *Stoici*, *Graeci*, etc. *Amicus*, *affinis*, *aemulus*, *cognatus*, *familiaris*, *necessarius*, *peregrinus*, *propinquus*, *vicinus* are very often used in the singular as substantives; also a few others, especially in contrasts. *Plurimum interest inter doctum et rudem.*

3. Adjective substantives take *nemo* for no one, *quisquam*, any one (never *nullus*, *ullus*); thus, *nemo doctus*, no learned man; *nemo Romanus*, no Roman; *si quisquam sapiens hoc dixisset*, if any wise man had said this.

5. In comparing *two adjectives* both are often put in the *comparative* degree; as, *pestilentia* minacior *fuit*, *quam* periculosior, the pestilence was more threatening than dangerous (but also, *magis minax quam periculosa*).

So also with adverbs: *Romani bella fortius semper, quam felicius gesserunt*, more bravely than successfully, or, with greater valor than success.

§ 238.

Pronouns.

1. The English, *and that too*, *and that indeed*, are expressed in Latin by *et is*, *et is quidem*, *atque is*, *isque* (*nec is*, and that not indeed).

Homo memoriam habet, et eam *infinitam*, *rerum omnium*. *Uno* atque eo *facili proelio hostes caesi sunt*. *Annum iam audis Cratippum* idque *Athenis*.

Haec locutus est, he spoke as follows (not *sequentia*); *Platonis illud*, that saying of Plato.

2. The Relative Pronoun is often used differently from the English:

a. The relative is used after *idem* for the English *as*. *Servi* iisdem *moribus esse solent*, quibus *dominus* (as the master; also *atque*, § 170, 2).

b. For the English, *so called*, we say in Latin, *qui vocatur* (*vocabatur*, *dicebatur*), or *quem vocant* (*vocabant*, *dicebant*). *Vestra*, quae *dicitur*, *vita mors est*, your so-called life is death.

For *above mentioned* never *supra dictus*, but *quem supra dixi*, *commemoravi*; and, in the same way, *quem paulo post commemorabo*.

c. To express the English, *considering*, according to, in accordance with, the *relative* is used in the following and similar phrases: *Spero te*, quae *tua prudentia et temperantia est*, *iam valere*, considering your prudence, in accordance with your prudence, as may be expected from your prudence. Also, pro *tua prudentia*.

3. The *demonstrative* is often omitted before a relative or put after the relative clause, in which latter case a substantive belonging to the demonstrative, is placed in the relative clause.

Num vir bonus emet denario, quod *sit mille denarium* (*id quod*)? *Male se res habet*, *quum* quod *virtute effici debet*, id *tentatur pecunia*. Quam *quisque norit* artem, in hac *se exerceat*. Qua nocte *Alexander natus est*, eadem *templum Dianae Ephesiae deflagravit*.

4. When the *relative* as *subject* refers to a personal pronoun of the first person the verb of the relative clause is also in the *first person*; if it refers to the second person, the verb is put in the second person (§ 191, 3, 2).

Non sum is consul, *qui nefas esse* arbitrer *Gracchos laudare*. *Vos*, *qui* adfuistis, *totam rem narrare poteritis*.

5. If the *relative* refers to a substantive in *apposition*, then this substantive is transferred to the relative clause. Cato, a man, whose authority surpassed that of all the rest, etc.; thus, *Cato*, qui vir *auctoritate omnes superabat* (never, *Cato vir*, *qui*). *Nihil cognovi ingratius*; *in* quo vitio *nihil non inest mali*.

Oppius curat negotia Rufi, quo equite *Romano ego familiarissime utor.*

6. The *relative* pronoun is often used, instead of *hic* or *is* with *et*, *nam*, *enim*, *sed*, *autem*, to connect sentences.

Perobscura est quaestio de natura deorum; quae (for *sed ea*) *ad agnitionem animi pulcherrima est. Illa Stoicorum de se opinio firma in Rutilio et stabilis inventa est.* Qui (for *nam is*) *cum innocentissimus in iudicium vocatus esset, oratorem adhibere noluit.*

A similar construction of *qui* is very frequent, as, *qui cum*, *qui ut*, *qui postquam* and other conjunctions. But if *qui* serves to connect two sentences it can never be followed by *autem*, *enim* or *vero*.

7. The *reflexive* pronoun *sui*, *sibi*, *se*, and the *possessive*, *suus*, have the following peculiarities:

a. The *reflexive* is used in all sentences, without exception, when the pronoun of the third person refers to the *subject* of the *same* sentence.

Caesar se *ad* suos *recepit. Homo placabilis facile ignoscit iniurias* sibi *illatas.*

b. The *possessive*, *suus*, is also generally used when the pronoun refers not indeed to the subject, but to *some other noun* of the *same* sentence. *Puer columbam cepit in nido* suo, in its nest (*eius*, less correct).

Suus must be used in case of emphasis; as, *his own;* also with *quisque;* moreover, always, *sui*, his, their friends, possessions, etc.

Caesarem etiam sua *natura mitiorem facit. Hannibalem* sui *cives e civitate eiecerunt. Desinant insidiari domi* suae *consuli. Scipio Syracusanis* suas *res restituit.* Suis *flammis delete Fidenas.* Sua quemque *fraus et* suus *terror maxime vexat*, suum *quemque scelus agitat amentiaque afficit.* Sui cuique *mores fingunt fortunam.* Suum cuique *tribue. Conserva tuis* suos.

NOTE. But when the pronoun is not emphasized, *eius* may be used. *Deum agnoscis ex operibus eius.* Sometimes *eius* must be used, in order to avoid ambiguity: *Accipiter columbam cepit in nido eius*, because *sus* would refer to the hawk's own nest. *Huic Caesar pro eius virtute atque in se benevolentia maiorum locum restituerat.*

c. The *reflexive* is used in all *infinitive* and *subjunctive* clauses, that are intrinsically dependent, provided the pronoun refers to the subject of the *principal sentence.*

Intrinsically dependent clauses are those which contain a thought or sentiment, etc., of the leading subject in the principal sentence (not a simple statement of the speaker or writer). Such clauses are the accusative with the infinitive; subjunctive clauses (*ut*, *ne*, *quo*, *quominus*, *quin*); relative clauses expressing the thought of another (§ 261), and indirect questions. Clauses expressing simply effect or consequence and all indicative dependent clauses are only extrinsically dependent.

Sentit animus se sua *vi*, *non aliena moveri*. *Ariovistus respondit*, *quod* sibi (him) *Caesar* denuntiaret, se (that he) *Aeduorum iniurias non neglecturum: neminem* secum *sine* sua *pernicie contendisse*. *Romani a Prusia petebant*, *ne inimicissimum* suum (their) secum (with himself) *haberet* sibique (to them) *dederet*.

1. When the pronoun refers to a word which is not the grammatical, but the logical subject of the principal sentence, the reflexive is used. *Faustulo spes fuerat* (*Faustulus speraverat*) *regiam stirpem apud se educari*.

2. In subjunctive clauses, expressing only effect or consequence, *eius*, *ei*, *eum*, etc., are used, not *sui*, *sibi*, *se*; as, *Epaminondas erat disertus*, *ut nemo Thebanus* ei *par esset eloquentia* (§ 275, 2).

3. The reciprocal one another, each other, is generally rendered by *inter se*. *Veri amici non solum colent* inter se *ac diligent*, *sed etiam verebuntur*. *Haec* inter se *repugnant*. *Alter alterum colit*, the one honors the other; *alius alium colit*, one honors this one, another that one. *Civis civem trucidabat*; *miles militi obstrepebat*.

8. The *possessive*, his, hers, theirs, is expressed in Latin by *suus*, only when it refers to a noun of the same sentence (or to the subject of the leading sentence). When it refers to a noun in some other (coördinate sentence), the genitive, *eius*, *eorum*, *earum*, must be used.

Multi cives interfecti eorumque *bona publicata suut*. *Omitto Isocratem discipulosque* eius. *Quoquo se verterint Stoici*, *iaceat necesse est omnis* eorum *sollertia*.

9. The *possessives* are often omitted when the sense will easily supply the omission: as, *Patrem amisi* (scil. *meum*); *fratrem tibi reddidi* (scil. *tuum*); *parentes carissimos habet* (scil. *suos*). But *patrem* meum *occidisti*; *fratrem* tuum *amamus*. Meum ipsius (*tuum ipsius*, *suum ipsius*, *nostrum ipsorum*, *ipsarum*) *patrem*, my *own* father, to strengthen the emphasis.

Suo loco, in the right place; *Cicero omnes honores suo anno cepit* (as soon as he had reached the legal age); *meo iure*, with my full right; *tuo*, etc., *iure*, never *pleno iure*.

CHAPTER XXXIX.

USE OF THE TENSES.

§ 239.

1. The tenses in Latin are used, on the whole, in the same way as those of the English verb.

The *principal tenses* (*tempora absoluta*) are the Present, Perfect and Future; the *relative tenses* (*tempora relativa*) are the Imperfect, Pluperfect and Future Perfect. These latter are used only when reference to the time of another action is to be expressed.

2. The PRESENT denotes the present time. It expresses actions that are done now, or generally, or at all times.

Lego *hunc librum; gaudio* afficior, *dum* lego. *Quotidie aliquid* scribo. *Tempestas* nocet *frugibus. Deus mundum* conservat.

The present tense is sometimes used to denote *past* events; 1, *historical* present (§ 242); 2, with the conjunction *dum* (§ 245).

§ 240.

The PERFECT is used to express an action as entirely past, either in relation to the present time or without relation to any other time.

1. The *perfect definite*, or present perfect (*perfectum logicum*) is used to express that a past action is, in its relation to the present time, completely finished.

Mundus a Deo creatus est. *Virtutem ne de facie quidem* nosti. *Disertissime Romuli nepotum, quot sunt, quotque* fuere, *M. Tulli!* Fuimus *Troes*, fuit *Ilium et ingens gloria Teucrorum.* (The same as in English.)

2. The *historical perfect* (*perfectum historicum*) denotes a past event without any reference to the time of any other action. It is the English past tense.

Miltiades brevi tempore barbarorum copiis disiectis loca castellis idonea communivit; *multitudinem, quam secum duxerat, in agris* collocavit *crebrisque excursionibus* locupletavit. *Regulus in senatum* venit, *mandata* exposuit; *sententiam ne diceret* recusavit; *reddi captivos* negavit *esse utile.*

§ 241.

The IMPERFECT is used, to denote a past action as existing at the same time with another past action.

1. The *imperfect* is especially used to denote by its *tense-form* the continuation of the action in past time.

Regulus Karthaginem rediit. Neque vero tum ignorabat, *se ad exquisita supplicia proficisci; sed iusiurandum servandum* putabat. *Mos* erat *patrius Academiae adversari omnibus in disputando.*

In the sentence, *Semper mos fuit Academiae adversari omnibus in disputando*, the duration in the past is also expressed, but by *semper*, not by the tense-form *fuit.*

2. To express that a past action was often repeated; to denote custom, manner or habit.

Ut Romae consules, sic Karthagine quotannis annui bini reges creabantur. *Hortensius nullum* patiebatur *esse diem, quin aut in foro diceret aut meditaretur extra forum.*

3. To narrate circumstances accompanying the principal action; to introduce descriptions, digressions, etc. The principal action stands in the *perfect.*

Caesar Alesiam circumvallare instituit. *Ipsum* erat *oppidum in colle summo, cuius radices duo duabus ex partibus flumina* subluebant; *ante id oppidum planities* patebat; *reliquis ex partibus colles oppidum* cingebant.

Compare: *Aequi se in oppida receperunt murisque se tenebant. Conticuere omnes intentique ora tenebant.*

§ 242.

In *animated narration:*

1. The present indicative (historical present) is often used instead of the imperfect or the historical perfect.

Caesar ea, quae sunt usui ad armandas naves, apportari iubet.

Ipse in Illyricum proficiscitur, *civitatibus milites* imperat *certumque in locum convenire* iubet.

2. The *present infinitive* (historical infinitive) is used instead of the imperfect in lively descriptions.

Nondum fuga certa, nondum victoria erat; tegi *magis Romanus, quam* pugnare; *Volscus* inferre *signa,* urgere *aciem, plus caedis hostium* videre *quam fugae.*

§ 243.

The PLUPERFECT is used, to express that a past action was already completed before another past action took place.

Pausanias eodem loco sepultus est, quo vitam posuerat.

1. In modifying clauses, the pluperfect is often used in Latin where we use the imperfect in English; as, *Verres quum rosam viderat tum ver incipere arbitrabatur* (when he saw). *Caesar quum in Galliam venisset* (came), *magna difficultate afficiebatur.*

2. In letters the perfect or imperfect is often used instead of our present, and the pluperfect instead of our perfect. The writer adapts his tenses to the time of the reader.

Nihil habebam quod scriberem; neque enim novi quidquam audieram, et ad tuas omnes epistolas rescripseram pridie, I have nothing to write; I have heard nothing; I answered all your letters yesterday. *Scripsi ad te ante lucem,* I write. But, *Si vales, bene est; ego valeo. Maximi te semper et feci et facio.*

§ 244.

1. The FUTURE is used, to express that an action will be done at a future time: *omnes* moriemur; *cras Romam* proficiscar.

2. The *future perfect* is used, to express that a future action will have been completed before another future action. *Quum Romam* venero, *statim ad te scribam.*

3. In English the *present* is often used for the future and future perfect; and the *perfect* for the future perfect; but in Latin *that tense* must be used which corresponds exactly with the *time* in which an action is done. *Faciam, si* potero, if I can. *Ut sementem* feceris (as you sow), *ita metes.*

Naturam si sequemur *ducem, nunquam aberrabimus. De Karthagine vereri non ante* desinam, *quam illam excisam esse cognovero. Qui Antonium* vicerit, *is bellum confecerit* (conquers, finishes).

Note. Sometimes the future takes the place of the imperative. *Si quid novi acciderit, facies, ut sciam* (§ 265, 1).

§ 245.

Various *conjunctions* have in Latin an unmistakable influence on the choice of the tenses.

1. *Dum*, whilst, is generally used with the present.

In the meaning of *so long as*, *dum* is also followed by the imperfect or perfect.

Dum *haec in colloquio* geruntur, *Caesari nuntiatum est, equites Ariovisti propius accedere.* Dum *ea Romani* parant consultantque, *iam Saguntum summa vi oppugnabatur.*

Catilina metuendus erat tam diu, dum urbis moenibus continebatur.

2. Conjunctions meaning *as soon as*, take the perfect indicative in a narration. They are: *simulac* or *simulatque*, as soon as; *posteaquam* or *postquam*, after; *ut*, *ut primum*, *ubi*, *ubi primum*, *quum*, *quum primum*, as, as soon as, when. In English we use the pluperfect and imperfect.

Simulac *Verri occasio* visa est, *consulem deseruit.* Postquam *Xerxes in Graeciam* descendit, *Aristides in patriam restitutus est.* *Pompeius* ut *equitatum suum pulsum* vidit, *acie excessit.* Ubi *de Caesaris adventu Helvetii certiores* facti sunt, *legatos ad eum miserunt.*

1. The historical present is sometimes used instead of the historical perfect. *Quae ubi Romam* nuntiantur, *senatus extemplo dictatorem dici iussit.*

2. To express repeated actions, also in this case, the imperfect or pluperfect is used instead of the perfect; as, *Alcibiades* simulac *se* remiserat, *neque causa* suberat, *quare animi laborem perferret*, *dissolutus reperiebatur* (whenever, as soon as).

3. When clauses with these conjunctions refer to the present time, even then the perfect is used in Latin (the present in English). *Simulatque* increpuit *suspicio tumultus, artes illico nostrae* conticescunt. *Quum fortuna reflavit, affligimur.* Likewise with *is qui* and words compounded with *cunque*. *Quocunque adspexisti* (you look) *tuae tibi occurrunt iniuriae, quae te respirare non sinunt.*

4. The conjunctions *simulac*, *postquam*, etc., require the future perfect when the thought refers to future time (§ 244, 3). *Me sapientia, simulatque ad eam confugero, in libertatem vindicabit.*

5. *Postquam*, later, after, when a long or definite space of time inter-

sence, so that there is no immediate succession of actions, takes the pluperfect; as, *Hannibal anno tertio, postquam domo profugerat, cum quinque navibus Africam accessit.*

§ 246.

Sequence or Succession of Tenses (*consecutio temporum*). In intrinsically dependent clauses (§ 238, 7, c) the tense (of the subjunctive) depends upon the tense of the principal sentence. This dependence or succession of tenses (*consecutio temporum*) is regulated by the following rules:

1. If the *verb* of the *principal* sentence is in the present tense, or one of the futures, the verb in the *dependent* clause must be in the present, perfect or future (subjunctive); as,

Audio quid facias, quid feceris, quid facturus sis; audiam and *audivero quid facias, feceris, facturus sis.*

Quid est, Catilina, quod te iam in hac urbe delectare possit, *in qua nemo* est *extra istam coniurationem perditorum hominum, qui te non* metuat, *nemo qui non* oderit? *Num, quae tempestas* impendeat, *vates melius* coniiciet, *quam gubernator? Epicurus dicit, omnium rerum, quas ad bene beateque vivendum sapientia comparaverit, nihil esse iucundius amicitia. Morati melius erimus, quum didicerimus, quae natura desideret. Agamemnon non dubitat, quin Troia brevi sit peritura.*

2. If the *verb* of the *principal* sentence is in the imperfect or pluperfect, the verb of the *dependent* clause must also be in the imperfect or pluperfect (subjunctive); as,

Audiebam, audiveram, quid faceres, fecisses, facturus esses.

Unum illud semper extimescebam, *ne quid turpiter* facerem *vel iam* fecissem. *Libertas ut laetior* esset, *regis superbia* fecerat.

3. If the *verb* of the *leading* sentence is a historical perfect (English past tense), the verb of the *dependent* clause must be in the imperfect or pluperfect (subjunctive).

Caesar audivit, quid Galli facerent, fecissent, facturi essent.

Regulus iuratus missus est *ad senatum, ut, nisi* redditi essent *Poenis captivi nobiles quidam,* rediret *ipse Karthaginem.*

4. Even if the *verb* of the *principal* sentence is in the perfect definite (present perfect), the *dependent* clause has the verb mostly in the imperfect or pluperfect, rarely in the present or perfect (subjunctive).

Audivi quid faceres, fecisses, facturus esses, seldom *quid facias, feceris, facturus sis.*

Haec, non ut vos excitarem, locutus sum, *sed ut mea vox officio functa consulari* videretur. *Ad eamne rem vos* delecti estis, *ut eos* condemnaretis, *quos sicarii iugulare non* potuissent? *Membris utimur prius, quam* didicimus, *cuius ea utilitatis causa* habeamus (*didicimus*, i. e., *scimus*).

1. Clauses of purpose, interrogative and relative clauses are mostly always rendered by the imperfect and pluperfect (subjunctive) after a perfect definite. *Hoc dixi ut scires;* rarely, *ut scias.* But when a consequence or result is to be expressed, the present and perfect subjunctive are more common; because,

2. In clauses of consequence or result (with *ut*, so that, cfr. 249, 1, 2), the tense is entirely independent of the verb in the principal sentence. Therefore, in a clause of consequence, the tense is always that which would be used, if the clause were a leading sentence. *Verres Siciliam ita* perdidit, *ut ea restitui in antiquum statum non* possit; even, *Ardebat Hortensius cupiditate dicendi sic, ut in nullo unquam flagrantius studium* viderim. *In eam rationem vitae nos res ipsa deduxit, ut sempiternus sermo hominum de nobis futurus sit.* Compare: *Ita nati sumus, ut inter omnes esset societas quaedam* (object of our existence), and, *Ita nati sumus, ut inter omnes* sit *societas quaedam* (consequence of our existence).

3. A historical present may be followed by any tense of the subjunctive. *Helvetii legatos ad Caesarem mittunt, qui dicerent, sibi esse in animo iter per provinciam facere; rogare, ut id sibi facere liceat.*

4. If a clause be dependent on the infinitive, supine, gerund, participle, adjective or substantive, the verb of the clause must conform itself to the tense for which the infinitive, supine, etc., stand. *Cato mirari se aiebat, quod non rideret haruspex, haruspicem quum vidisset* (= *mirabatur*). *Miserunt Delphos consultum, quidnam facerent de rebus suis* (= *consuluerunt*). *Constitit rex, incertus, quantum esset hostium. Explicavi sententiam meam, et eo quidem consilio, tuum iudicium ut cognoscerem.*

5. A hypothetical thought, which, as leading or independent sentence, is stated in the imperfect subjunctive, always preserves the same tense, even when it is made to depend on a present or future. *Honestum tale est, ut vel si ignorarent id homines, sua tamen pulchritudine* esset *laudabile. Omnia sic erunt illustria, ut ad ea probanda totam Siciliam testem adhibere* possem.

6. The future subjunctive is often replaced by other forms:

a. The present or perfect subjunctive are used for either future when the reference to future time is already plain from some other future word in the sentence. *Affirmo tibi, hoc si mihi contingat* (*contigerit*) *magnopere me gavisurum.* (Of course: *Affirmabam tibi, hoc si mihi contingeret* [*contigisset*] *magnopere me gavisurum.*) *Affirmo tibi, naturam si sequaris ducem, nunquam te aberraturum* (not *si secuturus sis*).

b. If the verb has no future subjunctive (in the passive and in verbs without supine) a circumlocution with *futurum sit* (*esset*) *ut*, is employed whenever the future is not otherwise expressed. *Non dubito, quin futurum sit, ut huius te rei poeniteat. Non dubitabam, quin futurum esset, ut Pompeius a Caesare vinceretur.*

CHAPTER XL.

USE OF THE INDICATIVE.

§ 247.

I. The INDICATIVE is the mood of knowing and asserting.

1. The *indicative* is used, to express by a simple *assertion* that which is known.

Virtus manet, *divitiae* pereunt. *Veni, vidi, vici. Veniet hora mortis.*

2. The *indicative* is used in such conditional sentences as are, in reality, positive assertions (without the least uncertainty, § 248, 3, c).

Si Deus est, *sempiternus* est.

3. The *indicative* is used in *direct questions* which require a positive answer.

Suntne *miseri, qui mali* sunt? (Ans., *Sunt*). *Infelix* est *Fabricius, quod rus suum fodit?* (Ans., *Non est*).

II. The Latin makes use of the *indicative* where the English idiom has the *potential* form, as follows:

1. I must, should, could, would, might; it would be just, right, useful, necessary, better, difficult, etc., are rendered in Latin by the indicative present, when they are not accompanied by a conditional clause.

Possum *persequi multa oblectamenta rerum rusticarum, sed ea ipsa, quae dixi, sentio fuisse longiora.* Animadvertendum est *diligentius, quae natura rerum sit,* (we) must consider more attentively.

Longum est, it would take too long; *difficile est*, it would be difficult, too difficult.

2. I should have, could have, would have, ought to have, it would have been right, are put in the imperfect or perfect (also pluperfect) indicative. This occurs when there is a question of events which did not take place, but which should have taken place.

Contumeliis onerasti eum, quem patris loco colere debebas, whom you *should have* (ought to have) honored, but did not. *Perturbationes animorum* poteram *morbos appellare; sed non conveniet ad omnia. Aut non suscipi bellum* oportuit *aut geri pro dignitate populi Romani et perfici quam primum* oportet. *Plato philosophos ne ad rem publicam quidem accessuros putat, nisi coactos;* aequius *autem* erat, *id voluntate fieri.*

a. In a similar manner, *arbitrabar*, I would, should have thought; *nunquam putavi*, I would never have believed. *Ingenii magni est non committere, ut aliquando dicendum sit: Non putaram.*

b. The participle in *urus* takes *eram* and *fui*, even when a conditional clause is added. *Aratores agros relicturi* erant, *nisi Metellus litteras misisset* (they would have left). *Hos viros testes citaturus* fui, *si tribuni me triumphare prohiberent* (I should have).

3. With *paene* and *prope*, nearly, almost, the perfect indicative is used in Latin, where, in English, the potential mood is generally used. *Brutum non minus amo, quam tu; paene dixi, quam te* (I might almost say, I had almost said). *Prope oblitus sum, quod maxime fuit scribendum.*

4. *Pronouns* and *relative adverbs* made general by being *doubled*, or by assuming the suffix *cunque*, take the indicative.

Quisquis, whosoever; *quotquot*, how many soever; *quamquam*, although; *quicunque, quantuscunque, quocunque, utcunque, ubicunque*, etc.

Quidquid *in me* est *excultarum virium, tibi debetur. Virtutem qui adeptus erit*, ubicunque erit *gentium, a nobis diligetur. Quoscunque de te queri audivi, quacunque ratione potui placavi.*

5. The *disjunctive* conditional clauses, with *sive — sive*, be it — be it, whether — or, have the *indicative* in Latin.

Mala et impia consuetudo est contra deos disputandi, sive *ex animo id* fit, sive *simulate. Veniet tempus mortis et quidem celeriter, et sive* retractabis, *sive* properabis; *volat enim aetas.*

CHAPTER XLI.

USE OF THE SUBJUNCTIVE.

§ 248.

The *subjunctive* is the mood of *desire*, *supposition*, *possibility* and *doubt*. Whatever we express by the subjunctive, we do not maintain nor assert, but we wish or suppose it, we consider it possible or doubtful.

I. The Subjunctive in Principal Sentences.

1. The *subjunctive* is used:

a. To express a *wish* (*coniunctivus optativus*); as, Sis *felix*, may you be happy!

Valeant *cives mei;* sint *incolumes*, sint *florentes*, *sint beati;* stet *haec urbs praeclara mihique patria carissima! Curio causam Transpadanorum aequam esse dicebat; semper autem addebat:* Vincat *utilitas rei publicae. Potius* diceret (should have said) *non esse aequam*, *quia non utilis esset rei publicae. Quod dubitas*, ne feceris. Ne sim *salvus*, *si aliter scribo ac sentio.*

b. To express an *entreaty* or a *command* mildly (*coniunctivus hortativus*); as, *Oremus*, let us pray!

The negative particle with the optative and hortative subjunctive is *ne* (not *non*).

Imitemur *maiores nostros;* meminerimus, *etiam adversus infimos iustitiam esse servandam!* Ne credamus *vanis opinionibus.*

1. To express the wish more forcibly, *utinam* is joined to the subjunctive (§ 254, 1); with an entreaty the subjunctive stands alone.

2. In asseverations, the first person of the subjunctive is often found; as, *Sollicitat, ita vivam, me tua valetudo*, as I live, your state of health troubles me. *Ita vivam, ut maximos sumptus facio.*

2. The *subjunctive* is used to express *concession* or *supposition* (*coniunctivus concessivus*).

***Ut* is often added to this subjunctive; negative particle, *ne* (§ 249, 3 and 250, 1).**

Naturam expellas *furca, tamen usque recurret.* Fuerint *cupidi,* fuerint *irati,* fuerint *pertinaces: sceleris vero crimine, furoris, parricidii, liceat Cn. Pompeio mortuo, liceat multis aliis carere.*

3. The *subjunctive* denotes *possibility* and *doubt.* It is used:

a. To express a *judgment* in a milder form, not as a thing *that is,* but that *may be* (*coniunctivus potentialis*); the negative particle is *non.*

The perfect in the potential subjunctive has often the same force as the English present; and the imperfect in Latin is always used where in English we employ the pluperfect potential.

Roges *me, qualem deorum naturam esse dicam; nihil fortasse* respondeam. *Forsitan* quaeratis, *qui iste terror sit et quae tanta formido. Omnibus fere in rebus, quid non sit, citius, quam quid sit,* dixerim.

Crederes, you would have believed; *putares, diceres. Isti mirandum in modum (canes venaticos diceres) ita odorabantur omnia et pervestigabant.*

b. In *doubtful questions,* called also questions of appeal (*coniunctivus dubitativus*); negative particle, *non.*

It is either a subjunctive of wavering purpose (akin to the *coniunctivus hortativus*); as, *quo fugiam?* Whither shall I flee? or a subjunctive of doubtful possibility (like the potential subjunctive).

Quo me vertam? *quid* faciam? *quod auxilium* implorem? *Quem* vocet *divum* (= *deorum*) *populus auxilio?*

Quis dubitet, *quin in virtute divitiae sint? Ego tibi* irascerer, *mi frater? ego tibi* possem *irasci? ego te videre* noluerim? Putaresne (would you have believed) *unquam accidere posse, ut mihi verba deessent?*

Here also the imperfect is used, as under *a.*

c. In *conditional* clauses that are *uncertain* and *unreal* (*coniunctivus hypotheticus* or *condicionalis*); negative particle, *non.*

In hypothetical sentences, the present and perfect subjunctive represent the supposition as *possible* though uncertain (not at all improbable); the imperfect and pluperfect represent it as contrary to fact (unreal) both in the leading sentence and dependent clause. The former is the potential subjunctive, the latter the hypothetical subjunctive.

Aequabilitatem vitae servare non possis, *si aliorum virtutem imitans* omittas *tuam. Nunquam Hercules ad deos* abisset, *nisi eam sibi viam virtute* munivisset. *Si* constitueris, *te cupiam advocatum in rem praesentem esse venturum, atque interim graviter aegrotare filius* coeperit: *non* sit *contra officium, non facere, quod dixeris. Si Roscius has inimicitias cavere* potuisset, viveret.

The present and perfect subjunctive serve particularly to introduce an example as illustration. Sometimes conditional sentences are expressed by the indicative with *si*, etc.; as, *Si vales, bene est. Nunquam laberis, si te audies* (§ 247, I, 2). *Velim*, I should wish (and really do wish); *vellem*, I should have wished (under certain circumstances, but actually I do not wish).

§ 249.

II. The Subjunctive with Conjunctions.

Ut, ne, quin, quominus, and *quo*,
And *licet, quasi, dummodo*,
And *o si, ac si, modo, dum*,
With *quamvis, utinam*, and *quum*
(Whene'er the cause it does denote)
Must go with the subjunctive mode.

O si and *utinam* are not properly conjunctions, but rather particles expressing a wish. They stand only in principal sentences.

Ut governs the subjunctive:

1. When it means *that, in order that*, to express purpose.
2. When it means *so that*, to express a result or consequence (§ 275).
3. When it means *though, although*, to express a supposition or concession (§ 248, 2).

Esse oportet, ut *vivas, non vivere*, ut *edas. Tanta vis probitatis est*, ut *eam etiam in hoste* diligamus. Ut desint *vires, tamen est laudanda voluntas.*

§ 250.

1. **Ne** governs the subjunctive, and means:

a. That not, in order that not, lest, to denote purpose.

b. Though not, to denote a supposition (§ 248, 2).

Nemo prudens punit, quia peccatum est, sed ne *peccetur.* Ne *sit* (though pain may not be) *summum malum dolor, malum certe est.*

Instead of *ne*, we often find *ut ne*, especially with *quis, quid. Iustitiae primum munus est, ut ne cui quis noceat.*

2. *That not* is rendered by *ut non:*

a. When it expresses simply a *result* or *consequence.*

b. When the negative particle *non* belongs only to *one* word of the sentence.

Quis est tam miser, ut non *dei munificentiam senserit?* *Tune Catilinam exire patiēre,* ut *abs te* non *emissus ex urbe, sed immissus in urbem esse videatur?*

When two negative clauses of purpose are joined together, the second is connected by *neve* (= *et ne; neque* = *et non*). *Hoc te rogo, ne demittas animum, neve te obrui magnitudine negotii sinas.*

3. After verbs of fearing, *that* is rendered by *ne*, and *that not* by *ut.*

Here the dependent clause is conceived as a wish, and the *thing wished* or desired is expressed by *ut*, with the subjunctive; the thing which is *not wished*, by *ne.* We find also *ne non* for *ut.*

Words of fear are, *timeo, metuo, vereor,* I fear; *timor, metus,* the fear; *periculum est,* there is danger; also, *caveo,* I am on my guard; *terreo* and *deterreo,* I deter.

Timebam, ne *evenirent ea, quae acciderunt. Omnes labores te excipere video;* timeo, ut *sustineas. Animi conscientia improbi semper sunt in* metu, ne *aliquando poena afficiantur. Adulatores si quem laudant,* vereri *se dicunt,* ut *illius facta verbis consequi possint.*

1. *That not* must be expressed by *ne non* (never *ut*): (1) when *vereor, timeo,* etc., are preceded by *non*; (2) when the negation belongs only to a *single* word of the sentence.

Non *vereor,* ne *tua virtus opinioni hominum* non *respondeat. Veremur, ne forte* non aliorum *utilitatibus,* sed *propriae laudi servisse videamur. Vereor dicere,* I hesitate to say; *non vereor dicere,* I do not hesitate to say; these are nearly the same as *non dubito dicere* (§ 252, II).

2. The *future* is never used after verbs of fearing. *I fear that he will come,* must be translated, *Timeo,* ne veniat (not *venturus sit*). *Timebam, ut veniret,* I feared that he would not come (not *venturus esset*). The tenses after verbs of fearing are the present and imperfect subjunctive.

§ 251.

Quo, as conjunction (= *ut eo*), governs the subjunctive:

1. When it means *that by which, that by this means, in order that.*

2. In the expression *non quo*, not as if, and *non quo non*, not as if not; *non quod* is also used for *non quo*, and *non quod non* for *non quo non*, or if a negation precedes, *non quin*.

In funeribus a Solone sublata est celebritas virorum ac mulierum, quo *lamentatio* minueretur. *Legem brevem esse oportet*, quo *facilius ab imperitis* teneatur.

Non soleo temere disputare contra Stoicos; non quo *illis admodum* assentiar; *sed pudore impedior. De consilio meo ad te*, non quo *celandus* esses, *nihil scripsi; sed quia communicatio consilii quasi quaedam admonitio videtur esse officii.* Non *tam ut prosim causis elaborare soleo, quam ut ne quid obsim;* non quin *enitendum* sit *in utroque; sed tamen multo est turpius oratori, nocuisse causae, quam non profuisse.*

Also: *non eo quo*, *non idcirco quod*, not because, not as if on that account.

§ 252.

I. **Quin** can be used only after *leading negative* sentences; it governs the subjunctive, and is used for:

1. *Qui non*, or *quod non*, who not, or that not.
2. *Ut non*, that not, but that, without.

Est fere nemo quin *acutius atque acrius vitia in dicente, quam recta videat* (there is scarcely any one *that* does *not* see). Nihil *est*, quin *male narrando* possit *depravari.* Quis *est* (= *nemo est*) quin cernat, *quanta vis sit in sensibus?*

Hortensius nullum *patiebatur esse diem*, quin *aut in foro* diceret *aut* meditaretur *extra forum* (on which he did not speak, § 260, note 2). *Nunquam tam male est Siculis, quin aliquid facete et commode dicant. Nunquam accedo, quin abs te abeam doctior* (but I depart).

Instead of *quin* we may say *qui non*, *quod non* or *ut non;* the feminine *quae non* is nearly always retained: as, *Nulla tam detestabilis pestis est*, quae non *homini ab homine nascatur.*

II. *Quin* is used after negative expressions implying doubt, uncertainty, omission and the like (*quin non*, that not). The English is *that* or *to.*

Non dubito quin, I do not doubt that; *non dubium est, quin*, there is no doubt that; *non multum abest quin*, not much is wanting that; *non (vix, aegre) abstineo quin*, I cannot (can hardly) refrain from; *praetermittere non possum*, or *facere non possum quin*, I cannot avoid, or I cannot help (doing).

Homines etiam quum taciti quid optant, non dubitant, quin *dii illud* exaudiant. *Dubitandum non est*, quin *nunquam* possit *utilitas cum honestate contendere*. *Prorsus* nihil *abest*, quin sim *miserrimus*. *Facere non possum, quin quotidie litteras ad te mittam*. *Non possumus recusare*, quin *alii a nobis dissentiant*.

But when (*non*) *dubito* signifies I (do not) hesitate, scruple, it generally takes the infinitive. *Non dubito sapientem solum* dicere *beatum*. Likewise, *dubito num*, I doubt whether; *dubito utrum—an*, whether—or. *Dubito an* is also used, but in an affirmative sense, while *dubito num* is generally used in a negative sense. (Cfr. § 176, note 3, d).

§ 253.

Quominus (that thus the less = *ut eo minus*) *that not*, governs the subjunctive and is used after verbs of hindering, opposing, and the like.

Impedire, prohibere, officere, obstare, to hinder, to prevent; *obsistere*, to oppose; *deterrere*, to deter; *recusare*, to refuse.

Aetas non impedit, quominus *agri colendi studia* teneamus *usque ad ultimum tempus senectutis*. *Isocrati*, quominus haberetur *summus orator, non officit, quod infirmitate vocis* ne *in publico* diceret, impediretur. *Quid* obstat, quominus *Deus beatus* sit?

Instead of *quominus* we may use *ne*, and if a negation precedes, *quin*. *Impedior animi dolore, ne de huius miseria plura dicam*. *Prohibere* very often takes the infinitive. *Non ignobilitas sapientem beatum esse prohibebit* (cfr. § 269).

§ 254.

Utinam expresses a wish, Oh, that! Oh would that! It is used with the present or perfect subjunctive when the fulfilment of the wish is conceived as possible; and with the imperfect and pluperfect when impossible. (*O si*, if only.)

Utinam *modo conata efficere* possim! Utinam *illud* ne *vere* scriberem! *Utinam ego natus non essem!*

O mihi praeteritos referat si Iuppiter annos!

2. *Quasi, ac si, tamquam, velut, velut si*, as if, govern the subjunctive. The *tense* depends upon that of the *principal* verb (§ 246).

Stultissimum est, in luctu capillum sibi evellere, quasi *calvitio maeror* levetur. *Sequăni absentis Ariovisti crudelitatem*, velut si *coram* adesset, *horrebant.*

3. **Dummodo** (whilst only) *if only, if but*, or simply *dum*, or *modo*, governs the subjunctive. When joined with a negation, it becomes *dummodo ne, dum ne*, or *modo ne* (for the tense, cfr. § 248, 3, c).

Nonnulli recta omnia et honesta negligunt, dummodo *potentiam* consequantur. *Manent ingenia senibus*, modo permaneat *studium et industria. Sit summa in iure dicundo severitas*, dummodo *ea* ne varietur *gratia, sed* conservetur *aequabilis. Mediocritas* (*in puniendo*) *placet Peripateticis, et recte placet;* modo ne laudarent *iracundiam.*

4. *Nedum*, not to say, not to mention — that (or *ne* alone) governs the subjunctive.

Vix in ipsis tectis frigus vitatur; nedum *in mari et in via* sit *facile abesse ab iniuria temporis.*

5. *Quamvis* (*quantumvis, quamlibet*) and *licet*, although, how ever much, govern the *subjunctive.*

Licet is used only with the present or perfect.

Quod turpe est, id quamvis occultetur, *tamen honestum fieri nullo modo potest.* Licet *ipsa vitium* sit *ambitio, frequenter tamen causa virtutum est.*

Quamquam, although, governs the indicative (§ 247, 4). *Etsi* and *etiamsi* follow the construction of *si* (§ 248, 3, c). Sometimes *quamquam* and *etsi* have the meaning of meanwhile, nevertheless, still (§ 172).

§ 255.

1. **Dum, donec, quoad,** with the meaning of *whilst, as long as*, govern the *indicative;* with the meaning of *until*, they govern the *subjunctive*, when the sentence expresses a *purpose;* the *indicative*, when it simply states an *actual* fact.

Cato, quoad vixit, *virtutum laude crevit. Iratis aut subtrahendi sunt ii, in quos impetum conantur facere*, dum *se ipsi* colligant; *aut rogandi orandique sunt, ut, si quam habent ulciscendi vim, differant in tempus aliud,* dum defervescat *ira. Ea vero continebis,* quoad *ipse te* videam. *Epaminondas ferrum usque eo in corpore retinuit,* quoad renuntiatum *est, vicisse Boeotios.*

In narration, several writers use *donec* in the sense of *as long as*, with the imperfect subjunctive.

2. *Antequam* and *priusquam*, before, take the imperfect and pluperfect in the *subjunctive* only; the perfect in the *indicative* only; the *present* either in the indicative or subjunctive.

Aristides interfuit pugnae navali apud Salamina, quae facta est, priusquam *poena exsilii* liberaretur. *Saepe magna indoles virtutis,* priusquam *rei publicae prodesse* potuisset, *exstincta fuit. Civitas Atheniensium* antequam delectata est *hac laude dicendi, multa iam memorabilia effecerat.* Priusquam incipias, *consulto, et ubi consulueris, mature facto opus est.* Antequam *de re publica* dicam, *exponam breviter consilium profectionis meae.*

§ 256.

I. **Quum** governs the *subjunctive* in four instances:

1. *Quum,* denoting *cause,* in the sense of *since* (*quum causale*).

Quum sint *in nobis consilium, ratio, prudentia, necesse est, deos haec ipsa habere maiora.* Quum *Athenas* sis profectus, *inanem redire turpissimum est.*

2. *Quum,* denoting *concession,* though, although (*quum concessivum*).

Hoc ipso tempore, quum *omnia gymnasia philosophi* teneant, *tamen eorum auditores discum audire quam philosophum malunt. Phocion fuit perpetuo pauper,* quum *divitissimus esse* posset.

3. *Quum,* denoting *opposition,* though, whilst (*quum adversativum*).

Homines quum *multis rebus infirmiores* sint, *hac re maxime bestiis praestant, quod loqui possunt. Nostrorum equitum erat quinque millia numerus,* quum *hostes non amplius octingentos equites* haberent.

4. *Quum,* in *narration* (*quum narrativum*), governs the imperfect and pluperfect subjunctive in the sense of *when,* to express the connection between historical facts.

Epaminondas quum vicisset *Lacedaemonios apud Mantineam atque ipse gravi vulnere exanimari se* videret, *quaesivit, salvusne esset clipeus.*

II. **Quum** (*cum*) governs the *indicative* also in four cases:

1. *Quum*, denoting *time* merely (*quum temporale*), in the sense of when, while, and determining the time of an event; it is often preceded by *tum, eo die, eo tempore.*

Regulus tum, quum *vigilando* necabatur, *erat in meliore causa, quam si domi periurus consularis remansisset. Ligarius* eo tempore *paruit*, quum *parere senatui necesse* erat. Quum *Caesar in Galliam* venit, *alterius factionis principes erant Aedui, alterius Sequani.*

2. *Quum*, denoting *repetition* (*quum iterativum*), as often as, as soon as.

Qui non defendit iniuriam neque propulsat a suis, quum potest, *iniuste facit.* Quum *recte navigari* poterit, *tum naviges.* Quum *ver esse* coeperat, *dabat se Verres labori atque itineribus.*

3. *Quum*, denoting *coincidence* (*quum additivum*), when, while; in the *apodosis*, it adds something unexpected to a previously mentioned circumstance.

In such cases, *quum* takes the perfect in a *narration*, but the imperfect in *descriptions*. The *protasis* is usually in the imperfect or pluperfect and rendered more forcible by *vix, aegre, iam, nondum*; and the *apodosis* with *quum*, strengthened by *interea, repente, subito.* *Quum* is often equivalent to *et tum.*

Evolarat iam *e conspectu fere fugiens quadriremis*, quum etiamtum *ceterae naves uno in loco* moliebantur. *Hannibal* iam *scalis* subibat *muros Locrorum*, quum repente *patefacta porta Romani* erumpunt (historical present for perfect).

4. *Quum*, explanatory (*explicativum*), takes the present and perfect indicative in the sense of *eo quod*, in as much as, while.

If this *quum* is connected with an *imperfect* or *pluperfect* it governs the subjunctive.

De te, Catilina, quum quiescunt, *probant;* quum patiuntur, *decernunt;* quum tacent, *clamant. Praeclare facis*, quum *Luculli memoriam* tenes. *Catulus cepit magnum suae virtutis fructum*, quum *omnes una prope voce* "*in ipso vos spem habituros esse*" dixistis.

NOTE. Sometimes, however, notwithstanding the above rules, the subjunctive, particularly the imperfect and pluperfect, occurs: Quum *in hus duci debitorem* vidissent, *undique convolabant* (as often as).

§ 257.

III. THE SUBJUNCTIVE IN RELATIVE CLAUSES.

1. *Relative clauses* require the subjunctive when they express: *a.* an *effect* or *consequence*; *b.* an *intention* or *purpose.*

The relative is then equivalent to *ut* with a demonstrative; thus, *qui* = *ut ego, ut tu, ut is; cuius* = *ut mei*, etc.; *cui* = *ut mihi*, etc.; also, *ubi* = *ut ibi, unde* = *ut inde.*

Innocentia est affectio talis animi, quae noceat *nemini. Nulla gens tam fera, nemo omnium tam immanis est*, cuius *mentem non* imbuerit *deorum opinio. Non sumus ii*, quibus *nihil verum esse* videatur, *sed ii*, qui *omnibus veris falsa quaedam adiuncta esse* dicamus.

Multi eripiunt aliis, quod *aliis* largiantur. *Homini natura rationem dedit*, qua regerentur *animi impetus. Verba reperta sunt, non* quae impedirent, *sed* quae indicarent *voluntatem.*

Non sum is *consul*, qui *nefas esse* arbitrer, *Gracchos laudare.*

Too great to (greater than that) is *maior quam ut;* however *maior quam qui* may be used, but always with the subjunctive. *Famae ac fidei damna maiora sunt, quam quae aestimari possint. Maior sum, quam cui possit fortuna nocere.*

§ 258.

2. After *dignus, indignus, aptus* and *idoneus* the English infinitive is rendered by *qui* with the *subjunctive* (§ 223, 288).

Qui modeste paret, videtur dignus *esse*, qui *aliquando imperet. Academici mentem volebant rerum esse iudicem: solam censebant* idoneam, cui crederetur. *Nulla mihi videbatur* aptior *persona*, quae *de senectute* loqueretur, *quam Catonis.*

§ 259.

3. The *relative clause*, when it expresses a *reason* or *cause*, takes the subjunctive; *qui* is then equivalent to *quum ego, quum tu*, etc.

O fortunate adolescens, qui (= *quum tu*) *virtutis tuae Home rum praeconem* inveneris! *O magna vis veritatis, quae contra hominum calliditatem facile se per se ipsam* defendat!

§ 260.

4. *Relative clauses* require the subjunctive whenever the *relative* refers to an *omitted*, or to a *negative* or *interrogative* word; especially after those general and indefinite expressions: *est qui, sunt qui* (there are men who), *inveniuntur* or *reperiuntur qui; nemo est qui; non est* or *nihil est quod; quis est qui? quid est quod?* etc.

The relative clause here specifies the class referred to by the indefinite subject. The word *talis* or *eiusmodi* may be supplied here.

Sunt, qui *una animum et corpus occidere* censeant. Qui *se ultro morti* offerant, *facilius* reperiuntur, *quam* qui *dolorem patienter* ferant. Nemo *est orator*, qui *se Demosthenis similem esse* nolit. Nullum *est animal praeter hominem*, quod *habeat notitiam aliquam dei.* Quis *est*, qui *non* oderit *protervam adolescentiam?* Quae *latebra est, in* quam *non* intret *metus mortis?* Quotusquisque *est*, qui *optimi cuiusque hominis auctoritatem magni* putet? *Non* est, quod *te* pudeat *sapienti assentiri.* Quid *est*, cur *virtus ipsa per se non* efficiat *beatos?* Nihil *habeo*, quod *accusem senectutem* (I have no reason why).

1. When a substantive or a numeral is added to *sunt* the indicative may be used. Multi *sunt, qui dicunt* or *dicant.*

2. After negative expressions the imperfect is used in Latin where in English the pluperfect is generally used. *Polycrati* nihil *acciderat, quod* nollet (that he would not have wished). Nemo *inventus est tam impudens, qui istud* postularet (that would have asked).

§ 261.

5. *Relative clauses* take the *subjunctive* when they express the *thought* or *opinion* of *another* (not the opinion of the author).

The use of *quod*, because, with the subjunctive is common in such clauses.

Recte Socrates exsecrari eum solebat, qui *primus utilitatem a iure* seiunxisset. *Aristides nonne ob eam causam expulsus est patria*, quod *praeter modum iustus* esset? *Socrates accusatus est*, quod corrumperet *iuventutem et novas superstitiones* induceret. *Bene maiores nostri accubitionem epularem amicorum*, quia *vitae coniunctionem* haberet, *convivium nominarunt.*

NOTE.—*Hic quum Hannibalis permissu exisset de castris, rediit paulo post*, quod *se oblitum nescio quid* diceret, instead of *quod oblitus esset;* often also with *dicere, putare, arbitrari*, etc.

§ 262.

6. All *subordinate* relative *clauses* require the subjunctive when they form an *essential* part in the statement of a thought expressed by the infinitive or the subjunctive.

Grave est homini pudenti petere aliquid magnum ab eo, de quo *se bene meritum* putet. *Socrates dicere solebat, omnes in eo*, quod scirent, *satis esse eloquentes. Tanta in Hortensio memoria erat, ut*, quae *secum* commentatus esset, *ea sine scripto iisdem verbis redderet*, quibus cogitavisset.

1. In a similar manner, the subjunctive is used, not only in relative clauses, but also in other dependent clauses, especially in the indirect discourse (*oratio obliqua*) (cfr. § 277, 3).

2. Sometimes relative clauses are joined to an infinitive or subjunctive clause, without being essential parts of the same, but are rather inserted parenthetically, and may be omitted without destroying the sense. But then the indicative is used. *Caesar Helvetios in fines suos*, unde erant profecti, *reverti iussit.* When Caesar continues: *Per exploratores certior factus est, ex ea parte vici*, quam *Gallis* concesserat, *omnes noctu discessisse*, he considers, as reports of the scouts, only the words, *ex ea parte vici omnes noctu discesserunt.* But the indicative is often retained when the relative clause is only an explanation or circumlocution for a single word; as, *ii qui audiunt*, for *auditores; ii qui praesunt*, higher magistrates; *ea quae importantur*, exports; *ea quae scimus*, our knowledge.

§ 263.

IV. THE SUBJUNCTIVE IN INDIRECT QUESTIONS.

In indirect questions the verb is always in the *subjunctive* (§ 176, note 2).

Dubito, num *idem tibi, quod mihi, suadere* debeam? (Direct: *Num suadere* debeo?) *Non recordor*, unde ceciderim, *sed unde* surrexerim? (*Unde cecidi? unde surrexi?*) *Quaeritur, naturā* an *doctrinā* possit *effici virtus? Saepe ne utile quidem est scire*, quid *futurum* sit. Qualis sit *animus, animus ipse nescit.*

Incertum est, quo *te loco mors* exspectet. *Permultum interest*, utrum *perturbatione aliqua animi*, an *consulto* fiat *iniuria*. Sitne *malum dolor*, necne, *Stoici viderint*.

NOTE 1.—Questions in the indicative mood are always to be considered as direct questions, though they may seem to be indirect. *Dic quaeso:* Num *te illa* terrent, *triceps Cerberus*, *Cocyti fremitus*, *travectio Acherontis?* It might be, *Dic quaeso*, *num te illa terreant*, etc. *Vide! Quam conversa res est.*

NOTE 2.—Expressions like *nescio quis*, *nescio quomodo*, are sometimes used parenthetically, and do not imply a question; then, the indicative is, of course, retained. *Minime assentior iis, qui istam* nescio quam *indolentiam magnopere laudant. Sed* nescio quomodo inhaeret *in mentibus quasi saeculorum quoddam augurium futurorum.* In a similar way, expressions like *mirum quantum*, *nimium quantum*, are often equivalent to *plurimum* (wonderfully much), and then have the indicative. *Id* mirum quantum (*plurimum*) *profuit ad concordiam civitatis. Sales in dicendo nimium quantum valent.* But, of course: *Id mirum est quantum profuerit ad concordiam.*

NOTE 3.—*Indirect questions* must be carefully distinguished from *relative clauses.* The former are always transformed from direct questions; the latter always admit a demonstrative with the relative. *Elige*, utrum *tibi commodum* sit, choose which of the two is suitable to you. When you are in *suspense* about that which is really comfortable or suitable: *Utrum tibi commodum est*, *elige;* for, *id elige*, choose that which is suitable when you are no longer in suspense, but are sure of that which is suitable. So also: *Dic*, quid *sentias*, say what you think (give your opinion); *dic*, quod *sentis*, say what (that which) you think. *Nihil est in* (*Q. Maximo*) *admirabilius*, *quam* quo modo *mortem filii* tulit; i. e., *quam is modus quo tulit.*

NOTE 4.—Sometimes two questions are converted into one. *Considera*, quis quem *fraudasse dicatur* (who and whom?). *Quaerere debetis*, uter utri *insidias fecerit* (which of the two to the other).

CHAPTER XLII.

USE OF THE IMPERATIVE.

§ 264.

1. THE IMPERATIVE expresses a *command* (prayer, advice, or exhortation).

2. If the command is to be executed *immediately*, the imperative *present* is used; if *at a later time*, the *future* imperative.

3. The *future* imperative is used especially in maxims, rules of conduct, legal phrases and contracts.

Si quid in te peccavi, ignosce. Vale! vive *felix!* Ignoscito *saepe alteri, nunquam tibi. Cras* petito, *dabitur; nunc* abi. *Quum valetudinis tuae rationem habueris*, habeto *etiam navigationis. Consules summum ius* habento; *nemini* parento, *illis salus populi suprema lex* esto.

1. Always: *scito*, *scitote*, know (never *sci* or *scite*); thus also, *memento*, *mementote*.

2. To soften the expression, the imperative is often followed by *quaeso*, *quaesumus*, I, we, pray; *sis* (*si vis*, § 141, note) *sodes* (*si audies me*), if you please; *dum*, well. *Refer animum*, sis, *ad veritatem*. *Agedum* or *agitedum*, well, come on! *iteradum*, please, repeat.

3. In animated discourse the imperative takes sometimes the place of a conditional clause. *Iracundus non semper iratus est;* lacesse, *iam videbis furentem* (= *sed si eum lacessiveris*) provoke him, and you will soon see. (Never *et* in Latin.)

§ 265.

A *prohibition* or *negative command* is, in the language of the *law* and of *poets*, expressed by *ne* with the *imperative;* in ordinary *prose* always by *noli* with the *infinitive*.

Hominem mortuum in urbe ne sepelito neve urito. *Tu* ne cede *malis, sed contra audentior* ito. Nolite *putare homines consceleratos terreri Furiarum taedis ardentibus*. Noli oblivisci, *te Ciceronem esse*. Nolite *id* velle, *quod fieri non potest*.

1. Instead of *noli* with the infinitive, *cave* with the subjunctive or *ne* with the subjunctive or *non* with the future may be used. *Cave festines*, do not hurry; *ne* feceris (seldom *ne facias*), do not do it; *non facies*, do not do it. Poets say: *fuge quaerere* instead of *noli quaerere*.

2. Other paraphrases of the *imperative* are: fac *animo forti* sis, be of good cheer; *fac ut valeas*, farewell! *fac ne quid omittas*, do not forget anything; *cura ut valeas*, take care of your health.

CHAPTER XLIII.

USE OF THE INFINITIVE.

§ 266.

THE INFINITIVE is used partly as *subject*, partly as *object*. Irasci *non decet*, to get angry is not becoming; peccare *nolo*, I do not wish to sin.

Bene sentire *recteque* facere *satis est ad bene beateque vivendum*. Invidere *non cadit in sapientem*. *Docto et erudito homini* vivere *est* cogitare.

Vincere *scis*, *Hannibal; victoria* uti *nescis*. *Spartae pueri* rapere *discunt*. *Magistri te Latine* loqui *docuerunt*. Beatus esse *sine virtute nemo potest*. *Cato* esse, *quam* videri, *bonus malebat*. *Cives Romani omnia* perpeti *parati erant*.

1. When the *subject* of the *infinitive* is added, it is always in the *accusative*. Deum *esse*, that a God exists; Caesarem *venire*, that Cæsar comes.

2. When a *predicate noun* is added, this also is always in the *accusative*, if the infinitive itself is the *subject* of the sentence: *Deum esse* sapientissimum *facile intelligitur*. But, if the infinitive be the *object*, the *predicate noun* is put in the nominative case when it refers to a nominative, but in the accusative case, when it refers to an accusative; as, *Caesar Romae* primus *esse voluit*, Cæsar wished to be the first at Rome (because *primus* refers to *Caesar*); but, *Caesar se Romae* primum *esse voluit* (because *primum* refers to *se*), Cæsar wished that he (himself) should be the first at Rome (cfr. § 192, 3).

3. The infinitive as object with the predicate noun in the *nominative*, provided both members have the *same subject*, follows the verbs *volo*, *nolo*, *malo*, *cupio*, *scio*, *disco*, *statuo*, *decerno*; also, *audeo*, *studeo*, *incipio*, *pergo*, *desisto*, *consuesco*, etc., (§ 269).

4. In the best prose only one adjective, *paratus*, ready, takes the infinitive. But the poets, imitating the Greek idiom, make the infinitive follow many other adjectives; as, *cedere nescius*, *cantare peritus*, *avidus committere pugnam*, etc.

§ 267.

The *infinitive* with its *subject* in the *accusative* forms what is called the *accusative* with the *infinitive* (*accusativus cum infinitivo*).

This construction drops the English *that*, puts the *subject* in the accusative case and the *verb* in the infinitive mood. *Esse*, and verbs with the double nominative, likewise take the predicate noun in the accusative (cfr. § 192).

Deum esse (that there is a God) *certum est.* Deum esse bonum *scimus omnes. Putavi*, te *hoc* dicere, *dixisse*, *dicturum esse*, *dicturum fuisse* (that you said, had said, would say, would have said).

1. The *phrase* expressed by the accusative with infinitive is considered as *one thought* or idea, and sometimes as *object* for the accusative, sometimes as *subject* for the nominative; also for any other case, though more rarely.

2. When the subject is an *indefinite person*, the subject accusative is omitted; as, Contentum esse *suis rebus, maximas sunt certissimaeque divitias* (to be satisfied, etc.). *Hesiodus eadem mensura* reddere *iubet* (that one should return), *qua acceperis, aut etiam maiore, si possis.*

§ 268.

The *accusative* with the *infinitive* is the *object* of verbs of perceiving and saying (*verba sentiendi* and *dicendi*), to express that something *exists* or *happens*.

They are: *video, audio, sentio, animadverto, opinor, puto, credo, iudico, censeo, suspicor, perspicio, comperio, intelligo, scio, nescio, ignoro, memini, recordor, obliviscor, disco, accipio, spero, despero, concludo;* also, *dico, narro, trado, prodo, nego, fateor, scribo, doceo* (I teach, assert), *nuntio, affirmo, declaro, ostendo, demonstro, perhibeo, promitto, polliceor, minor, simulo, dissimulo.* The expression, *aliquem certiorem facio*, and nouns like *opinio, spes, nuntius*, etc., with or without a verb (*habere, excitare, capere, affere*, etc.).

When these verbs are used in the passive voice, the *accusative* with *infinitive* becomes of course the *subject. Humana omnia caduca esse facile intelligitur.*

Lapidum conflictu atque tritu elici ignem videmus. *Ego ne* utilem *quidem* arbitror esse *nobis futurarum rerum* scientiam. *Tantum quisque laudat, quantum* se posse sperat *imitari.* Platonem ferunt (= *dicunt*) *primum de animorum aeternitate* sensisse *idem, quod* Pythagoram (scil. *sensisse ferunt*). Concede, nihil esse bonum, *nisi quod honestum sit; concedendum est, in virtute sola positam esse beatam vitam. Aristoteles* docet, Orpheum *poëtam nunquam* fuisse (§ 198, 1).

1. *Persuadeo*, I convince, takes the accusative with infinitive; but *persuadeo*, I persuade, has *ut. Pater persuasit mihi, hoc verum esse*, and *persuasit mihi, ut hoc facerem.* The former shows that something *exists* or *takes place;* the latter, that something *should* take place. *Censeo*, I believe, has only the accusative with the infinitive; as, *Aristoteles* omnia moveri *censet.* But *censeo*, I advise or resolve, when followed by the *active*, always takes *ut;* however, when followed by the *passive*, it has the accusative with the infinitive joined to the participle in *ndus. Senatus* censuit, ut *Caesar Aeduos* defenderet. *Ceterum* censeo, *Karthaginem esse* delendam. Several of the above verbs take *ut* according to the above distinction; as, *Philosophia nos* docuit, ut *nosmet ipsos* nosceremus. Compare, *Scripsit mihi*, licere *sibi venire*, and, ut liceret *sibi venire.*

2. After the verbs, to hope, swear, promise, threaten (*sperare, iurare, polliceri, promittere, spondere, vovere, minari, minitari*), the *present infinitive* is generally used in English, to express an action done by the *same subject;* but, in Latin, the accusative with future infinitive, must be used (§ 244, 8). *Spero* me *mox* rediturum esse, I hope to return soon, or, that I shall soon return. Likewise, *spero*, te *mox rediturum. Pollicetur* (*iurat*), se *hoc* facturum *esse*, he promises to do it. *Milites minantur*, se *esse* abituros, threaten to depart. Concerning the reflexive, see § 238, 7. The omission of the reflexive, as well as the use of the present infinitive, is rare; as, *Pollicentur obsides dare*, instead of *se daturos esse;* but, in the meaning, to believe, *spero* takes sometimes the *present* or *perfect. Te mihi et* esse *amicum spero et semper* fuisse (§ 274, 4, note).

3. It is said of Pythagoras that he had come, is rendered in Latin, *Pythagoram* dicunt (*tradunt, ferunt*) *venisse* (never, *de Pythagora dicunt eum venisse*). Achilles of whom it was believed that he was the son of a goddess; or, who was, as people believed, the son, is, in Latin, *Achilles*, quem putabant *esse deae filium. Cicero*, quem scimus *patrem patriae nominatum esse. Brutus*, cuius patrem *esse Caesarem dicebant. Errare te* verisimile est, you probably err. *Patrem* spero *mox* rediturum *esse. Ciceronem* constat *eo tempore consulem fuisse*, Cicero was, as is well known, etc. *Quo cruciatu* censemus *Dionysium illum angi solitum?* The same with *puto, videor.*

4. *He, she, it, his*, etc., in connection with the accusative and infinitive, are always rendered by *sui, sibi, se, suus*, when the pronoun refers to the subject of the *principal* sentence. Ariovistus *dicebat, neminem sine sua pernicie* secum *contendisse* (§ 238, 7, c.)

§ 269.

The *accusative* with the *infinitive* is the *object* of such verbs as denote a *wish*, or *permission*, and their contraries (*verba voluntatis*).

These verbs are, *volo, nolo, malo, cupio, studeo; iubeo, veto, prohibeo; cogo, sino, patior*. But *opto, postulo, peto, permitto, concedo*, etc., prefer *ut* (§ 275, 1).

1. When *both members* have the *same subject*, the infinitive alone is more generally used with *volo* and *malo* (§ 266, 3). *Prohibeo* takes also *quominus* (§ 253).

Ego me Phidiam esse mallem, *quam vel optimum fabrum lignarium. Mos est hominum, ut* nolint eundem *pluribus rebus* excellere. *Aristoteles versum in oratione* vetat esse, numerum *iubet. Hortensius nullum* patiebatur esse diem, *quin aut in foro diceret aut meditaretur extra forum. Germani* vinum *ad se* importari *omnino non* sinunt.

2. *Iubeo te* audire, I command you to hear; *iubeo te* audiri, I command (others) to hear you. *Vetuit eum venire*, he forbade him to come; *vetuit eum ligari*, he forbade (others) to bind him. But when *iubeo* is followed by a passive, it has the meaning, to suffer, to cause; as, *Iussit eum occidi*, he caused him to be killed, ordered him to be killed. This may also be rendered by the simple *occidit eum. Archipiratam securi percussit* (cfr. § 281, 3, note).

3. But, *impero tibi, ut hoc facias;* however, with the passive, *impero hoc fieri; imperavit eum interfici*, seldom *ut interficeretur*.

4. *Volo, nolo, malo*, also take the subjunctive without *ut; malo te sapiens hostis metuat, quam stulti cives laudent.*

§ 270.

The *accusative* with *infinitive* is used as SUBJECT in three cases:

1. With many *impersonal verbs:*

Appāret, elūcet, constat, fugit me, oportet (opus est, necesse est), decet, dedĕcet, licet, placet, convĕnit, iuvat, condūcit, expĕdit, interest; refert (piget, pudet, poenitet, taedet).

Leges *ad salutem civium* inventas esse constat. Narrationem oportet *tres* habere *res*, *ut brevis*, *ut aperta*, *ut probabilis sit*. *A deo* necesse est mundum regi. *Omnibus bonis* expedit salvam esse rem publicam. *Ut* equos *ad cursum*, aves *ad volatum*, *sic* homines apparet natos esse *ad cogitandum*.

2. With *neuter adjectives* and *est:*

Apertum est, manifestum est, perspicuum est, verum est, verisimile est, par est, aequum est, rectum (*pulchrum, iustum, honestum, grave, facile, difficile, iniquum, molestum*, etc.) *est*.

Aliud est *iracundum* esse, *aliud iratum*. *Scipio* nihil difficilius esse *dicebat*, *quam* amicitiam *usque ad extremum vitae diem* permanere.

3. With substantives and *est:*

Tempus est, facinus est, scelus est, magna laus est, opinio est, spes est.

Facinus est vinciri civem *Romanum*. Tempus *est* nos *de illa perpetua iam*, *non de hac exigua vita* cogitare.

1. *Necesse est*, *oportet* and *licet* may, instead of the accusative with infinitive, also take the subjunctive without *ut*. *Necesse est hoc facias* or *te hoc facere*.

2. When *licet* has the person in the *dative*, then the predicate noun of the infinitive is also in the *dative*. *Licuit esse* otioso *Themistocli*. *Mihi* negligenti *esse non licet*.

3. *Interest* and *refert* may also have *ut* instead of the accusative with infinitive. *Magni mea interest*, ut *te videam*.

§ 271.

The *accusative* with *infinitive* is used as an *indirect* or more remote *object* with verbs of *emotion* and *feeling* (*verba affectuum*).

Such verbs are: *gaudeo, laetor, glorior, miror, admiror, doleo, angor, sollicitor, indignor, queror, aegre* (*moleste, graviter*) *fero*. *Quod* may be used instead of the accusative with infinitive (cfr. § 276).

Gaudeo, *id* te *mihi* suadere, *quod ego mea sponte feceram*. *Minime* miramur, te *tuis praeclaris operibus* laetari. *Virtutes noli vereri ne* querantur, se esse relictas.

§ 272.

The *accusative* with *infinitive* is used as an *expression* of astonishment or complaint; or as an impassioned question (sometimes *ne* is appended).

Me *non* esse *cum bonis!* I not to be on the side of the good! *Ita* comparatam esse *hominum* naturam, *aliena ut melius videant et diiudicent, quam sua!* Tene *hoc* dicere, *tali prudentia praeditum!*

Ut is similarly used. *Tu* ut *unquam te* corrigas! That you should ever amend! With the infinitive, *credibile est*, may be understood; and *postulandum est*, with *ut*.

§ 273.

1. The *Nominative* with the *Infinitive*. The passives, *videor, dicor, putor, iubeor, sinor, vetor, perhibeor, arguor;* as also, *traditur, fertur, feruntur*, are, in good prose, always used personally and construed with the nominative and infinitive (§ 192, 4, 5).

Hoc fecisse dicor, they say that I have done this (not, *dicitur* me *hoc fecisse*); *hoc fecisse* diceris; *hoc* facere iussus sum; *tu hoc dixisse* perhiberis.

2. In the same way, are often construed, *nuntior, existimor, iudicor;* sometimes also, *negor, memoror, scribor, cognoscor, perspicior, intelligor, audior, demonstror, ostendor, reperior;* still the latter more commonly have the *impersonal* construction, together with accusative and infinitive.

Non ita generati a natura sumus, ut ad ludum et iocum facti *esse* videamur. Romulus *Amulium regem* interemisse fertur. Luna *solis lumine* collustrari putatur. *Lycurgi temporibus* Homerus fuisse traditur. Tyndaridae fratres *non modo* adiutores *in proeliis, sed etiam* nuntii *victoriae* fuisse perhibentur. *Non fecisti, quod* facere iussus es. *Acta* agere vetamur *vetere proverbio.*

1. The impersonal construction and the accusative with infinitive of the verbs under No. 1 is very rare. Dicitur, *eo tempore* matrem *Pausaniae* vixisse. It should, however, be used when both the principal verb and the infinitive are formed by means of a participle. Hence, *Athenae conditae* esse putantur; but only, *Athenas conditas esse putatum* or *putandum est.*

2. But if, after a sentence personally construed with *dicitur, videtur*, etc., the *infinitive* construction is continued in several successive sentences, the accusative with the infinitive must be used in the latter. *Ad Themistoclem* quidam doctus homo accessisse dicitur *eique artem memoriae* pollicitus esse *se traditurum*. *Quum ille quaesisset, quidnam illa ars efficere posset*, dixisse illum doctorem, *ut omnia meminisset*. *Et ei* Themi-

stoclem respondisse, *gratius sibi illum esse facturum, si se oblivisci, quae vellet, quam si meminisse docuisset.*

3. *Consiliis, ut* videmur (it seems), *bonis utimur.*

§ 274.

The different *tenses* of the infinitive are used in Latin as in English. However, the following peculiarities must be remarked:

1. The *present*, *perfect*, or *future infinitive* is used after any tense of the principal sentence, according as *the time to be expressed* is present, past, or future, with regard to the action of the principal sentence.

Dicunt (*dicent*, *dixerint*) *eum* venire, *venisse*, *venturum esse*, that he comes, has come, will come. Dicebant *eum* venire, *venisse*, *venturum esse*, that he was coming, had come, would come; also, dicunt or *dicebant eum* venturum fuisse, he would have come.

2. With *memini*, I remember, past events which *I have witnessed* are often expressed by the *present infinitive.*

Memini, *Catonem mecum et cum Scipione* disserere. *Metellum* memini *puer bonis* esse *viribus extremo tempore aetatis* (*disserebat; erat*).

3. Instead of *hoc fieri volo*, I wish this to be done, we often find, *hoc factum* (*esse*) *volo*, I would like to have this done.

4. Many verbs have *no supine* and hence also no infinitive future, active or passive; then the circumlocution *futurum esse ut* or *fore ut* is used. This is also common with other verbs; as, *Scio*, futurum esse (or *fore*), ut *omnes hoc* discant, or *ut hoc ab omnibus* discatur, I know that all *will learn* this, that this *will be learned* by all.

Video, te velle in coelum migrare, et spero, fore, ut contingat *id nobis.* *Clamabant homines,* fore, ut *ipsi sese dii immortales* ulciscerentur. *Plerique existimabant,* futurum esse, ut *oppidum* amitteretur.

The infinitives *posse*, *velle*, *nolle*, *malle*, are generally used as future infinitives without *fore ut.* *Spero, me hoc perficere* posse.

§ 275.

It is not always easy to determine when the English "*that*" is to be expressed in Latin by the accusative with infinitive, or by the subjunctive with *ut* or *quod*. We, therefore, add a few rules on the use of *ut* and *quod*.

The word *that* must be rendered by *ut* in two instances (§ 249).

1. When *that* denotes a purpose, and is equivalent to *in order that*.

A *purpose* is contained in verbs and expressions which signify to advise, cause, beg, exhort (warn), strive, obtain; *suadeo, praecipio, mando; facio, efficio, perficio; oro, rogo, precor, postulo, opto*, also *permitto* and *concedo; moneo, hortor, commoveo; nitor, contendo, peto, curo, operam do, id ago; impetro, assequor, adipiscor*, etc.

Idcirco amicitiae comparantur, ut *commune commodum mutuis officiis gubernetur. Temperantia sedat appetitiones et* efficit, ut *hae rectae rationi pareant.* Impetrabis *a Caesare*, ut *tibi abesse liceat et esse otioso. Natura* fert, ut *eis faveamus, qui eadem pericula, quibus nos perfuncti sumus, ingrediantur. Magnopere te* hortor, ut *orationes meas studiose legas. Omne animal se ipsum diligit et* id agit, ut *se conservet. Phaëton* optavit, ut *in currum patris tolleretur. Qui stadium currit*, eniti *debet et* contendere, ut *vincat*.

2. When *that* denotes a consequence, or is used after words which contain the particle *so* or *such*, it must be rendered by *ut;* as, *ita, sic, eiusmodi, adeo, tantopere, tantus, talis, tam* and *is* = *talis*.

A consequence or result is expressed by *fit* (future infinitive, *fore*), *accidit, contingit, evenit*, it happens, occurs (= *efficitur*); also by, *restat, relinquitur, reliquum est, superest, sequitur, proximum est, extremum est, prope est, longe abest, lex est, mos est* or *moris est, consuetudo est; hac lege, hac condicione*.

Talis *est ordo actionum adhibendus*, ut *omnia in vita sint apta inter se et convenientia.* Fieri *potest*, ut *recte quis sentiat et id, quod sentit, polite eloqui non possit. Plerisque* accidit, ut *praesidio litterarum diligentiam in perdiscendo remittant. Temporibus persaepe* evenit, ut *utilitas cum honestate certet.* Restat, ut *doceam, omnia, quae sunt in hoc mundo, hominum causa facta esse.* Reliquum est, ut *certemus officiis inter nos. Vetus* est lex *illa iustae veraeque amicitiae*, ut *idem amici semper velint*.

1. Especially in short sentences *ut* (*ne*) is sometimes omitted. *Cave ignoscas*, do not forgive; *fac animo forti* sis or ut sis; *sine te* exorem (§§ 265, 2, 269, 4; 270, 3, 1).

2. REMARK: *Tantum abest ut . . . ut*, to be so far from . . . that. *Tantum abest, ut nostra miremur, ut nobis non satisfaciat ipse Demosthenes*, we are so far from admiring our own productions that even Demosthenes does not satisfy us. *Philosophia tantum abest, ut digne laudetur, ut a multis etiam vituperetur*, far from being praised by all, philosophy is even blamed by many.

3. *Efficere*, in the sense of, to prove, generally takes the accusative with infinitive; but sometimes also, *ut*. *Plato* efficit, animos *hominum* esse *immortales*.

4. With a passive infinitive, we say, *Plato a Deo* aedificari *mundum* facit, Plato assumes that the world is built by God. But the active participle is also used after *facio* in the same case. *Xenophon Socratem disputantem facit*, he makes Socrates maintain, introduces Socrates as maintaining. Likewise with deponents, *Quae est Socratis oratio, qua Plato eum facit usum apud iudices!*

§ 276.

That is expressed by *quod* in four cases:

1. After *est* with a noun, *quod* is used to signify the *fact that*, the *circumstance that*.

In fabrica mundi nihil maius est, quam quod ita cohaeret, ut nihil cogitari possit aptius. Magnum beneficium est naturae, quod necesse est mori.

2. *Quod* is placed at the beginning of sentences with the meaning, *if*, *that*.

Quod *nos in Italiam salvos venisse gaudes, perpetuo gaudeas velim.* Quod *me Agamemnonem aemulari putas, falleris.*

3. When the conjunction *that* is explanatory and refers to a preceding demonstrative, *quod* is used.

Hoc uno *praestamus vel maxime feris*, quod *exprimere dicendo sensa possumus. Qui benigniores sunt, quam res patitur, in eo peccant*, quod *iniuriosi sunt in proximos.*

4. *Quod* is used, when the conjunction *that* denotes a reason or cause, especially after verbs of *feeling* or *emotion*, and after words which give outward expression to feeling. It is then generally equivalent to *because* (§ 271).

Quod is used after verbs which give outward expression to feeling:

such as, *accuso, reprehendo, vitupero, gratias ago, gratulor, laudo, damno;* also, *indignor, misereor.*

Cato mirari *se aiebat* quod *non rideret haruspex, haruspicem quum vidisset.* Quod *spiratis*, quod *vocem mittitis*, quod *formas hominum habetis*, indignantur. *Praeclare in epistola quadam Alexandrum filium Philippus* accusat, quod *largitione benevolentiam Macedonum consectetur. Magna diis immortalibus* habenda est gratia, quod *hanc pestem effugimus.* Gratulor *tibi*, quod *te provincia decedentem summa laus prosecuta est.*

1. However, after the verbs of feeling the accusative with infinitive is also used (§ 271).

2. *Nisi quod, praeterquam quod*, unless, except that.

3. *Accedit quod*, but also *accedit ut*, in addition, moreover.

§ 277.

On the Indirect Discourse (Oratio Obliqua).

The indirect discourse, is that which in form and conception is made to depend on some other idea. *Tu venisti*, you have come, is direct discourse (*oratio recta*); *dico te venisse*, I say that you have come, is indirect discourse. However, by indirect discourse is commonly meant the narrative or historical form of a previously spoken discourse. For this latter the following rules will hold.

1. All *leading* sentences of the *direct discourse* that express a narration or assertion, are, in the *oratio obliqua*, put in the *accusative* with *infinitive.*

2. The *leading* sentences of the *direct discourse* that express a command, wish or question, are, in the *oratio obliqua*, put in the *subjunctive* imperfect (pluperfect).

3. All *dependent clauses* are, in the *oratio obliqua*, expressed by the *subjunctive* (imperfect or pluperfect).

4. The *pronouns* of the first person in the *direct discourse* become, in the *oratio obliqua*, *reflexive* pronouns (*sui, sibi, se, suus*, seldom *ipse*) § 238, 7, c.

The *second person* of the direct discourse becomes, in the *oratio obliqua*, generally *ille*, sometimes *is;* the *third person*, on the contrary, generally *is*, sometimes *ille.*

In consilio Aeduorum Dumnorix dixerat, sibi a *Caesare regnum civitatis* deferri (*oratio recta.* mihi defertur). *Consules scripta ad Caesarem mandata remittunt, quorum haec erat summa: Caesar in Galliam* reverteretur, *Arimino* excederet, *exercitus* dimitteret (*oratio recta*, revertere, excede, dimitte). *Ei legationi Ariovistus respondit:* "*Si quid* ipsi (for *sibi*) *a Caesare opus esset, sese ad eum venturum fuisse; si quid ille se vellet, illum ad se venire oportere. Praeterea se neque sine exercitu in eas partes Galliae venire audere, quas Caesar possideret, neque exercitum sine magno commeatu in unum locum contrahere posse; sibi autem mirum videri, quid in sua Gallia, quam bello vicisset, aut Caesari aut omnino populo Romano negotii esset.*"

1. Sometimes the form of a question is used instead of the negative form, then the accusative with infinitive is used. *Tribuni militum nihil temere agendum existimabant;* "quid *enim* esse levius aut turpius, *quam auctore hoste de summis rebus capere consilium?*" as much as, *nihil enim esse levius.*

2. Relative clauses are, in the *oratio obliqua*, expressed by the accusative with infinitive when *qui* stands for *et is*, *unde* for *et inde*, etc. *Res defertur, esse civem Romanum, qui se Syracusis in lautumiis fuisse quereretur;* quem *iam* ingredientem *navem* retractum esse et asservatum (for *et eum*).

3. When the indirect discourse depends on a *historical present*, the present subjunctive may be used instead of the imperfect subjunctive (§ 246, note 3). But in the course of a long, indirect discourse, the present subjunctive is also allowed, by way of exception, after a historical perfect.

CHAPTER XLIV.

USE OF THE PARTICIPLES.

§ 278.

1. PARTICIPLES are adjectives in form and inflection, but they govern the case of their verb.

2. Some *perfect passive participles* have, besides the *passive*, also an *active* meaning:

cenatus, dined, and one that has dined.
iuratus, sworn, and one that has sworn.
potus, drunk, and one that has drunk.
pransus, breakfasted, and one that has breakfasted.

NOTE.—The perfect participles passive of some verbs, especially intransitives, have become simple adjectives, but with an active meaning. Thus, *consideratus*, deliberate; *profusus*, extravagant, lavish; *falsus*, false, deceitful. Of intransitives, *adultus*, grown up; *concretus*, dense (grown together); *coniuratus*, conspiring; *consuetus*, accustomed; *deflagratus*, burned down; *nupta*, married; *obsoletus*, obsolete; *praeteritus*, past. *Adultus sum*, I am grown up; *adolevi*, I have grown up.

3. Many *perfect participles* of *deponent* verbs have, besides the active, also a passive meaning; as,

Comitatus (accompanying and accompanied), *complexus, confessus, dimensus, ementitus, expertus, interpretatus, meditatus, pactus, partitus, populatus, testatus.*

4. Many *perfect participles* of deponent and semi-deponent verbs are used with the meaning of a present participle Thus, always *ratus* and *solitus* (never *rens*, seldom *solens*); often, also *fisus, diffisus, veritus;* sometimes, *ausus, gavisus*, etc. *Caesar* veritus, *ne hostes effugerent, duas legiones, in armis excubare iubet.*

5. The *perfect participle passive* of some verbs, with *habeo, mihi est, teneo* is often used as a more forcible expression for the perfect indicative active.

Siculi meam fidem spectatam *iam* habent *et diu* cognitam (*spectaverunt, cognoverunt*). Statutum *iam* habeo, *quid mihi agendum putem. Senatum* inclusum *in curia* habuerunt (they kept). Mihi *Siculorum causa* suscepta est.

Mihi persuasum est or *persuasum habeo* (never *mihi*), I am convinced.

§ 279.

1. *Participles* are used far oftener in Latin than in English; they often take the place of *relative* and of *subordinate* clauses.

2. There are two kinds of participial constructions.

a. The *attributive*, when the participle is an attribute or in apposition to some word of the principal sentence.

b. The *absolute*, when the participial sentence does not refer to any word of the principal sentence, hence altogether independent of the principal sentence (§ 283).

3. The *attributive* participial construction is thus arranged: The relative or the conjunction is omitted; the finite tense is changed into the corresponding participle, and is made to agree in gender, number, and case, with the word to which it refers.

§ 280.

1. The *participle* supplies the place of a *relative clause* (for *qui*, *quae*, *quod* with a finite tense).

Est enim lex nihil aliud, nisi recta et a numine deorum tracta ratio, imperans *honesta*, prohibens *contraria* (i. e. *quae imperat, prohibet*). *Misericordia est aegritudo ex miseria alterius, iniuria* laborantis. *Pater filio vitam dedit* perituram; *sunt divitiae certae, perpetuo* mansurae. *Pisistratus Homeri libros*, confusos *antea, sic disposuisse dicitur, ut nunc habemus.*

2. When the *relative* in English has a *demonstrative* for its antecedent, the latter must be omitted in the participial construction (§ 281, 4, note 1).

Verum dicentibus *facile credam*, I shall easily believe those that tell the truth (never iis *verum dicentibus*). *Male* parta *male dilabuntur.* Imperaturus *omnibus eligi debet ex omnibus.*

§ 281.

The *participle* takes the place of an *adverbial* clause. The participle is then equivalent to a conjunction.

1. *Present participle*—equivalent conjunctions, *while*, *when.* Ego *recreavi afflictos animos bonorum, unumquemque* confirmans, excitans (i. e. dum *confirmo, excito*). *M'. Curio, ad focum* sedenti (i. e. dum *sedet*) *magnum auri pondus Samnites quum attulissent, repudiati sunt. Mundum efficere* moliens *deus terram primum ignemque iungebat* (i. e. quum *moliretur*).

2. *Perfect participle*—equivalent conjunctions, *after*, *when.* Dionysius *tyrannus, Syracusis* expulsus, *Corinthi pueros docebat* (i. e. *postquam expulsus est*). *Pleraeque scribuntur orationes,* habitae *iam, non ut habeantur* (*postquam habitae sunt*). *Hostes, hanc* adepti *victoriam, in perpetuum se fore victores confidebant* (i. e. *quum adepti essent*).

3. *Final participle* (expressing purpose) only in the future active or passive—equivalent conjunctions, *in order that*, *in order to.*

Ad prima signa veris Hannibal in Etruriam ducit, eam quoque gentem aut vi aut voluntate adiuncturus (i. e. *ut adiungat*).

Alexander Hephaestionem *in regionem Bactrianam misit, commeatus* paraturum (i. e. *ut* or *qui pararet*).

Demus nos *philosophiae* excolendos *patiamurque sanari* (i. e. *ut excolamur*). *Antigonus* Eumenem *mortuum propinquis eius* sepeliendum *tradidit. Hi* ossa *eius in Cappadociam ad matrem* deportanda curarunt (i. e. *ut sepeliretur, ut deportarentur*).

The use of this future participle passive is very common, especially with *dare, tradere, mandare, mittere, relinquere, proponere, accipere, conducere, locare*, and, in particular, *curare*; as, *Fabricius perfugam* reducendum *curavit ad Pyrrhum* (took care to have him brought back; caused him to be led back).

4. Sometimes the participles of all the three tenses may be resolved into *if* (conditional participle), *because* (causal participle, *although* (concessive participle).

Non potestis, voluptate omnia dirigentes (i. e. *si dirigitis*), *aut tueri aut retinere virtutem.* Quis *potest, mortem* metuens (i. e. *si metuit*), *esse non miser? Ne mente quidem recte uti possumus, cibo vinoque* completi (*quum completi sumus*). *Dionysius tyrannus, cultros* metuens (i. e. *quia metuebat*) *tonsorios, candente carbone sibi adurebat capillum. Risus interdum ita repente erumpit, ut eum* cupientes (i. e. *quamvis cupiamus*) *tenere nequeamus. Herculem Germani*, ituri (i. e. *quum ituri sunt*) *in proelium, canunt.*

1. If the participle takes the place of a *conjunction* (but not of a relative, § 280, 2), the demonstrative may be retained. *Quid posset* iis *esse laetum, exitus suos* cogitantibus (i. e. *si cogitarent*).

2. The verbs *to see* and *to hear* have three kinds of construction: 1. *Vidi eum currere*, I saw that he ran. 2. *Vidi eum quum curreret*, I saw him, when, as, while he ran. 3. *Vidi eum currentem*, I saw him running. So also: 1. *Audivi eum dicere*, I heard that he said. 2. *Audivi eum quum diceret*, I heard him when, or, as he said. 3. *Audivi eum dicentem*, I heard him saying.

§ 282.

Besides the above participial sentences, we may add:

1. The *copulative participle*, the participle equivalent to *and*.

Grues, quum loca calidiora petentes *mare transmittunt, trianguli efficiunt formam* (i. e. *petunt et transmittunt*). *Sunt sidera, quae* infixa *coelo non moventur* (i. e. *quae infixa sunt et non moventur*). *Manlius Torquatus Gallum in conspectu duorum exercituum* caesum *torque spoliavit* (i. e. *cecīdit et*).

2. The *negative participle* (*i. e.*, the participle with a negation) is very often equivalent to *without* (and a participial noun).

Epicurus non erubescens (without blushing) *omnes voluptates nominatim prosequitur. Nihil feci iratus, nihil impotenti animo, nihil* non *diu* consideratum *et multo ante* meditatum (without having considered), cfr. § 283, note 2.

Without, and a participial noun, is sometimes expressed by *ut non. Multi malunt existimari boni viri*, ut non *sint* (without being such), *quam esse*, ut non *putentur*. If another *negation* precedes, *quin* may be used for *ut non* (§ 252).

3. The *substantive participles*. The passive participle is often used in Latin where the English idiom requires a participial noun, or a verbal noun with *of*.

Lacedaemoniis nulla res tanto erat damno, quam disciplina *Lycurgi, cui per septingentos annos assueverant*, sublata (as the abolishing of the constitution). *Poena* violatae religionis (of violating) *iustam recusationem non habet. Homerus fuit et Hesiodus ante Romam* conditam (before the building of Rome). *Ab* oppugnanda *Neapoli Hannibalem absterruere* conspecta *moenia*, Hannibal was deterred from besieging Naples by the sight of the walls.

1. In a similar way, the participle is to be translated, when modifying the *predicate* of a sentence. *Omne malum* nascens *facile opprimitur;* inveteratum *fit plerumque robustius*, every evil is easily checked in the beginning (at its birth); it generally grows stronger by age. *Qui erant cum Aristotele, Peripatetici sunt dicti, quia disputabant* inambulantes *in Lyceo*, because they had discussions on their walks in the Lyceum. Also, *Valet apud nos clarorum hominum et bene de re publica meritorum memoria, etiam* mortuorum (even after their death, § 286).

2. Many of the participial clauses in § 281 can be translated by verbal substantives with prepositions.

§ 283.

Ablative Absolute (*ablativus absolutus* or *consequentiae*).

1. The attributive participial construction, instead of the adverbial clause, can be used only when *some* word of the *principal* sentence is the *subject* of the *clause*. The subject of the

clause must occur in some form or other in the principal sentence, not, however, necessarily as subject.

2. But when the *subject* of the dependent *clause* does *not* occur at all in the principal sentence, the absolute participial construction, i. e., *ablative absolute* is used.

The construction of the ablative absolute consists in omitting the conjunction (when, whilst, etc.) and putting the subject of the dependent clause with its predicate in the ablative. If the predicate is a verb, it is put in the corresponding participle; the copula is rejected.

Tarquinio regnante *Pythagoras in Italiam venit* = quum Tarquinius regnaret, when or whilst Tarquin was king, in or during the reign of Tarquin. Mortuo Traiano *Hadrianus imperator factus est* = *postquam Traianus mortuus est*, after or when Trajan had died, after the death of Trajan.

Maximas virtutes iacēre omnes necesse est, voluptate dominante (= *quum* or *si voluptas dominatur*). Reluctante naturā *irritus labor est* (= *si natura reluctatur*). *Artes innumerabiles repertae sunt*, docente naturā. Pietate *adversus deos* sublata *fides etiam et societas generis humani et una excellentissima virtus, iustitia, tollitur*. Regibus exterminatis *libertas in re publica constituta est*. Causā *morbi* inventā *medici curationem esse inventam putant*. Perditis rebus *omnibus tamen ipsa virtus se sustentare potest* (= *etiamsi res omnes perditae sunt*).

1. The conjunctions, *quamquam* and *etsi*, are sometimes retained by the side of the ablative absolute; as, *Augustus Neapolim traiecit*, quamquam morbo variante.

2. When the perfect participle requires *ab eo, a se*, to complete the sense, it is better translated by the active; as, *Antonius, repudiata* (i. e., *a se*) *sorore Octaviani, Cleopatram uxorem duxit*, Antony, the sister of Octavius, having been put away (by him), etc., or, Antony having put away the sister, etc.; or, after Antony had put away —, he married. But *ab eo, a se* must *never* be expressed after the participle. *Xerxes, rex Persarum, terror ante gentium*, bello *in Graecia infeliciter* gesto, *etiam suis contemptui esse coepit*. *Natura dedit usuram vitae, tamquam pecuniae*, nulla praestituta die, without determining the day (limit), § 282, 2.

3. Sometimes a whole clause takes the place of a subject-ablative. *Alexander*, audito Darium movisse *ab Ecbatanis, fugientem insequi pergit*. *i. e.*, after he had heard; strictly, after it had been heard, that Darius had

moved, etc. Such isolated ablative participles are especially, *audito, cognito, comperto, nuntiato, edicto, explorato. Auspicato*, after taking the auspices; *inauspicato*, without taking the auspices; *summoto*, after room had been made.

§ 284.

Instead of a *participle* various substantives and adjectives may be used in the construction of the *ablative absolute*.

1. *Verbal substantives* which denote the *acting person;* as, *dux, comes, adiutor, auctor*, etc.; thus, *naturā duce = quum natura dux est*, when nature is the guide, under the guidance of nature; *patre comite*, in the company of the father; *deo adiutore*, with the help of God; *auctore Caesare*, upon the advice of Cæsar.

2. *Substantives* describing a person according to age, dignity or office; as, *puer, iuvenis, senex, rex, consul, praetor, dictator;* thus, *me puero = quum ego puer essem*, in my boyhood; *te adolescente*, in thy youth; *Cicerone consule = quum Cicero consul esset; Romulo rege.*

3. *Adjectives: deo propitio = si deus propitius est*, with God's mercy; *invitā Minervā*, against the will of Minerva (without skill); *coelo sereno*, with a clear sky, when the sky is clear; *patre ignaro*, without the father's knowledge.

Quod affirmate et quasi deo teste *promiseris, id tenendum est.* Sapientia praeceptrice *in tranquillitate vivi potest.*

Caninio consule *scito neminem prandisse; nihil* eo consule *mali factum est. Eius orationis epilŏgus tanto in honore*, pueris nobis, *erat, ut eum etiam edisceremus.*

Romani Hannibale vivo *nunquam se sine insidiis futuros arbitrabantur.* Sereno *quoque* coelo *aliquando tonat. Nonne* simillimis formis *saepe dispares mores sunt et* moribus simillimis *figura dissimilis est?*

CHAPTER XLV.

USE OF THE ERUND.

§ 285.

1. The *gerund* is, in form, the neuter of the future participle passive in the four oblique cases. It has, however, always an *active meaning* and *governs* the *case* of its verb.

2. When the verb governs the *accusative*, the gerund is generally changed into the future participle passive, the accusative is put into the case of the gerund, while the gerund itself becomes participle future passive, and agrees with the object noun in gender, number and case.

Thus, instead of *consilium* condendi urbem, we generally say: *consilium* condendae urbis, the plan for building a city; instead of *tempus accommodatum* demetendo fructus, generally: *demetendis fructibus*, the season suitable for gathering fruits; instead of *ad levandum fortunam* only *ad levandam fortunam*. The change has always to be made when the *gerund* is connected with a *preposition*.

1. The participle in *ndus* of the intransitives, *utor*, *fruor*, *fungor*, *potior*, *vescor*, is used in the same way. *Ad perfruendas voluptates* instead of *ad perfruendum voluptatibus*. But in the nominative it is used impersonally: Utendum *est viribus*, not *utendae sunt vires*, one must use his strength. *Suo cuique consilio utendum est.* But: *Omnia bona* utenda *ei ac* possidenda *tradidit.*

2. Sometimes the gerund with an accusative remains unchanged; always, when the accusative is a *neuter pronoun*; as, *studium* illud *videndi*, not *illius videndi*, because it would be doubtful, whether *illius* stands for *illum* or *illud*. Moreover, only, *cupiditas* plura *cognoscendi*. But even where there is no ambiguity this construction is found, however, only when the gerund is in the genitive or dative, or in the ablative without preposition.

§ 286.

The *genitive* of the gerund is used in answer to the question *what kind*, *of what*, after substantives and adjectives which govern the genitive (§ 210, 2; 213). Thus, *ars dicendi*, the art of speaking, oratory, like *ars orationis; cupidus regnandi*, desirous of ruling (*cupidus regni*).

The substantives most common with this construction are: *ars, causa, consilium, consuetudo, cupiditas, difficultas, facultas, genus, libido, modus, occasio, potestas, ratio, scientia, spes, studium, tempus, vis, voluntas.* Especially frequent is the ablative *causā* with the gerund in *di* to denote a purpose (for the sake of): *regnandi causā, venandi causā* (also *gratiā*). For adjectives of this kind see § 213.

Ut quisque optime dicit, ita maxime dicendi difficultatem *pertimescit. Male fecisti, quod cum* spe vincendi *simul abiecisti* certandi cupiditatem. *Nihil Xenophonti tam regale videtur, quam* studium agri colendi. *Vestis* frigoris depellendi causa *reperta est. Pythagoreorum more* exercendae memoriae gratia, *quid quoque die dixerim, audierim, egerim, commemoro vesperi.*

Epaminondas studiosus *erat* audiendi. *Multae res oratorem ab* imperito dicendi *ignaroque distinguunt. Multi propter gloriae cupiditatem cupidi sunt* bellorum gerendorum.

1. We often find, *Eius* mos *est omnibus* adversari (*ut adversetur*), in answer to the question, What is his custom? (*adversari*, subject; *mos*, predicate). But, *mos omnibus adversandi turpis est*, in answer to, What kind of custom? Likewise, *tempus est, consuetudo est, consilium est.*

2. Remark, *me, te, se, nos, vos conservandi causa*, to save me, thee, etc.; or, *mei, tui*, etc., *conservandi causa*, in which construction *conservandi* is never put in the *feminine* or in the *plural*. *Regina* sui conservandi *causa urbem reliquit* (not *conservandae*). *Principes* sui conservandi *causa profugerunt. Nostri conservandi causa urbe excessimus.*

3. Sometimes a genitive plural is found with the genitive of the gerund. *Agitur, utrum Antonio facultas detur agrorum suis latronibus condonandi*, for *agros condonandi*, or *agrorum condonandorum.*

4. Sometimes the genitive of the gerund is used with or without *esse*, to express purpose or tendency. *Naves deiiciendi operis*, ships (built, used) for the destruction of the work. *Haec prodendi imperii Romani, tradendae Hannibali victoriae sunt.*

§ 287.

The *dative* of the *gerund*, in answer to the question, *to whom, for whom?* is used especially in three cases:

1. With the adjectives, *utilis, idoneus, aptus, habilis, bonus, accommodatus, par*, and their contraries.

Aqua nitrosa utilis *est* bibendo (better, *ad bibendum*). *Ver tanquam adolescentiam significat ostenditque fructus futuros; reliqua tempora* demetendis fructibus *et* percipiendis accommodata *sunt.*

2. With the verbs, *praeesse, operam dare, laborem impertire, diem dicere, locum capere, satis esse,* also *esse* alone, in the sense of, to serve, to be suitable.

However, instead of the dative of the gerund, it is more usual to put the accusative with *ad*, especially after adjectives (§ 288, 1), or else a clause of purpose with *ut* or *qui* (§ 258).

Tune, Eruci, praeesse agro colendo *flagitium putas? Neque mihi licet neque est integrum, ut meum laborem hominum* periculis sublevandis *non impertiam.*

3. The dative of the gerund also stands after certain official names, to denote their object (*for what?*); *e. g., triumvir coloniae deducendae,* a triumvir for leading away a colony.

Decemviros legibus scribendis *creavimus. Valerius consul comitia* collegae subrogando *habuit.*

Solvendo non est, he is not able to pay; *scribendo adfuit*, he was present at the writing (as a witness).

§ 288.

The *accusative* of the gerund is used only after some prepositions:

1. Very frequently after *ad*, to denote *tendency* or *purpose.*

2. Sometimes with *in;* seldom with *ob, inter;* still more rarely with *ante, circa.*

Ut ad cursum equus, ad arandum *bos,* ad indagandum *canis, sic homo ad duas res,* ad intelligendum *et* ad agendum *natus est. Breve tempus aetatis satis longum est* ad *bene beateque* vivendum. *Natura animum ornavit sensibus,* ad res percipiendas *idoneis. Ipsa utilitatis magnitudo homines impellere debet* ad suscipiendum *discendi iuris* laborem. *Boum terga non sunt* ad onus ferendum *figurata.*

Dubitabitis, quin tantum boni in rem publicam conservandam conferatis? Mores puerorum se inter ludendum simplicius detegunt.

1. As we say, idoneus *ad percipiendas res*, so also, *aptus, accommodatus,*

utilis, docilis, habilis, bonus, take *ad* with the gerund. Likewise, *res facilis, difficilis ad intelligendum; verba ad audiendum iucunda.*

2. The poets use the infinitive instead of *ad* with the gerund. *Proteus pecus egit altos* visere *montes*, for *ad visendos montes; ut viseret montes.*

§ 289.

The *ablative* of the gerund is used:

1. As ablative of instrument (*with what? by what?*).

2. After the prepositions, *ab*, *de*, *ex*, and *in*.

Hominis mens discendo *alitur et* cogitando. *Omnis loquendi elegantia augetur* legendis oratoribus et poëtis. *Homines ad deos nulla re propius accedunt, quam* salutem *hominibus* dando (or *salute danda*, § 285, 2).

Aristotelem non deterruit a scribendo *Platonis magnitudo. Multa* de *bene beateque* vivendo *a Platone disputata sunt. Ex providendo appellata est prudentia.* In voluptate spernenda *virtus vel maxime cernitur. Multa sunt dicta ab antiquis de* contemnendis rebus humanis.

CHAPTER XLVI.

USE OF THE SUPINE.

§ 290.

1. The *supine* in **um** has an *active* meaning, and *governs* the *case* of its verb; the *supine* in **u** has a *passive* meaning and *never* governs a case.

2. The supine in *um* is used with verbs of *motion*, to express the purpose or end to which the motion is directed. *Cubitum ire*, to go to sleep; *exploratum* or *speculatum mittere*, to send to reconnoitre.

Legati ab Roma venerunt, questum iniurias *et ex foedere res* repetitum. *Fabius Pictor Delphos* missus est, sciscitatum, *quibus precibus deos placare possent.*

1. *Cur te is perditum?* Why do you want to go to ruin? (to ruin yourself?) *Nuptum dare*, to give in marriage.

2. Compare the following constructions of clauses of purpose: *Legati Delphos missi sunt*

1. *Consultum Apollinem.*
2. *Ut* or *qui consulerent Apollinem.*
3. *Ad consulendum Apollinem.*
4. *Apollinem consulendi causa* or *Apollinis consulendi causa.*
5. *Apollinem consulturi* (seldom).

§ 291.

The Supine in *u* is used after a few *adjectives* and *three indeclinable* substantives. *Res facilis cognitu,* easy to know, to be known.

Adjectives with the supine in *u: facilis, difficilis, honestus, incredibilis, iucundus, memorabilis, optimus, proclivis;* sometimes also, *dignus, indignus, mirabilis, utilis;* the three substantives: *fas, nefas, opus.*

The most common *supines* in *u* are: *dictu, factu, auditu, cognitu, aditu, visu;* seldom: *inventu, memoratu, intellectu,* etc.

Quod optimum factu *videbitur, facies. Humanus animus cum alio nullo, nisi cum ipso deo, si hoc* fas *est* dictu, *comparari potest. Quid est tam* iucundum cognitu *atque* auditu, *quam sapientibus sententiis gravibusque verbis ornata oratio?*

Either: *Haec res facilis est dictu* or *ad dicendum,* or *hanc rem facile est dicere.*

CHAPTER XLVII.

RULES AND DIRECTIONS FOR THE CONSTRUCTION OF SENTENCES.

I. ARRANGEMENT OF WORDS.

§ 292.

1. The Latin admits of far greater variety in the arrangement of words (*ordo verborum*) than the English. But with all this freedom and variety there are certain general laws of arrangement which must be observed.

2. We must distinguish, in general, a twofold arrangement of words:

a. The Grammatical.

b. The Rhetorical.

The former considers the words in their *grammatical* character and in their relation to each other, as parts of speech and as parts of a sentence.

The latter refers more to the *intrinsic* and *extrinsic* value and weight of the words in conveying the *meaning* of the sentence.

With regard to both it is important to notice the *prominent* or *emphatic places* of the sentence; these are always the *beginning* and the *end;* but the former more so than the latter; any intermediate place is less *significant.* Sol *omnia luce sua* illustrat. *Sol* and *illustrat* occupy the emphatic places.

§ 293.

The fundamental principle of the grammatical arrangement is the following:

The more important a word is grammatically, the more prominent also the place which it should occupy. Hence the arrangement in a simple sentence will naturally be, that the *subject* and the *predicate* occupy the *emphatic* places; the subject the *first* place, the predicate the *last;* all *modifiers* stand between the two. *Cicero rediit. Cicero revocatus est. Cicero in Italiam rediit.* Cicero *a civibus suis Romam* revocatus est.

§ 294.

1. The *modifiers of the subject,* and of every substantive, in general, follow the subject or the substantive. If the thought implies a close connection, the modifiers are placed nearer the substantive.

Modifiers of nouns: 1. Adjective; 2. Genitive; 3. Adverbial modification; 4. Apposition.

Imago pulchra *Athenis collocata erat;* — *imago* pulchra Minervae *Athenis collocata erat;* — *imago* pulchra Minervae ex aere *Athenis collocata erat;* — *imago* pulchra Minervae, ex aere, opus Phidiae, *Athenis collocata erat.*

2. The *modifiers* of the *predicate* precede the predicate.

The modifier which in the thought or proposition is most intimately connected with the predicate stands next to it. Hence the order to be observed: 1. The direct object (accusative); 2. The indirect object (any oblique case); 3. The adverbial modification; 4. The adverb.

Pater librum *donavit*—*pater* filio suo librum *donavit*—*pater* magno cum gaudio filio suo librum *donavit*—*pater* hodie magno cum gaudio filio suo librum *donavit*.

This arrangement may, however, be varied in various ways.

§ 295.

In dependent and subordinate *clauses*, conjunctions and relatives are placed before the *subject*, therefore at the beginning of the sentence.

Thus always, *nam*, *namque*, *etenim*, *sed*, *verum*, *at*, *sin*, *quare*, *quamobrem*, *dummodo;* also (unless an inversion be necessary for some rhetorical reason) *quum*, *ut*, *ne*, *quin*, *quominus*, *dum*, *quoniam*, *quia*, *quam*, *si*, *nisi*, *etsi*, *etiamsi*, *quamquam*, *quamvis*, *licet;* *itaque*, nearly always in Cicero; *tamen*, varies.

Never at the beginning, but only after some emphasized word can we use *enim*, *vero*, *autem*, *quoque*, *quidem;* *igitur* is seldom found in the first place.

§ 296.

The strict adherence to grammatical arrangement may place the important word of the sentence in the background, and also give rise to a succession of words and sounds displeasing to the ear. The principles of the *Rhetorical* arrangement remedy this twofold defect:

1. By placing the *important* word of the sentence in the most *prominent* place (this is called the *Logical* arrangement); 2, by disposing the words in such a manner as to please the ear (the *Rhythmic* arrangement).

§ 297.

According to the first principles of the rhetorical arrangement, those words occupy the most prominent position in the sentence, which are the most important in the expression of the thought. This especially happens in *contrasts*.

Dicebat *melius*, *quam* scripsit *Hortensius*. Because *dicebat* is the most important word; *scripsit*, being next in importance, holds the second place, after the conjunction. It would be incorrect to say, *Dicebat melius quam Hortensius scripsit;* though it would be correct, according to grammatical arrangement, to say, *Hortensius melius dicebat quam scripsit.*

§ 298.

The *modifiers* of the subject may, for the sake of greater *emphasis*, be placed before it.

Humana *figura*, contrasted with *aliae figurae* (*e. g.*, *bestiarum*); but, figura *humana*, contrasted with *animus humanus.*

Caesaris *sapientia*, contrasted with aliorum *sapientia;* sapientia *Caesaris*, with fortitudo, etc., *Caesaris.*

But if the *emphasis* falls on two words grammatically connected, one is placed at the beginning, the other at the end of the sentence. This arrangement makes them more conspicuous.

Tantam *ingenuit animantibus conservandi sui natura* custodiam.

§ 299.

When *contrasted* words are in the same member of the sentence, they are usually placed *side by side*, in order that the contrast may more effectually appear. But when they belong to different members, the arrangement follows the general rule, which is sometimes also the case when there is only a single member.

Cur igitur victus est (*a Milone Clodius*)*?* *Quia non semper* viator *a* latrone, *nonnunquam etiam* latro *a* viatore *occiditur quia*, *quamquam* paratus *in* imparatos *Clodius*, *tamen* mulier *inciderat in* viros. *Ex* falsis verum *effici non potest.* Errare *mehercule malo cum Platone*, *quam cum istis* vera sentire. Milvo *est quoddam quasi naturale bellum cum* corvo.

§ 300.

When the *same word* (in a different form) is repeated, and also when words, similar in sense or derivation, occur in the same member of the sentence, they should not be separated from each other.

Aliis aliunde *periculum est. Nulla* virtus virtuti *contraria est. Sublato* tyranno tyrannida *manere video. Sequere, quo* tua te *virtus ducit.*

§ 301.

When a *contrast* is expressed by *pairs or couples* of words, the two words of each pair that express the contrast most forcibly are placed by the side of each other, the remaining two at the beginning and end. Grammarians call this *chiasmus*, from the form of the Greek X.

Vir specie *quidem* puerili, senili *vero* prudentia. Ratio *nostra* consentit, repugnat oratio.

§ 302.

In many expressions and phrases custom has established a certain order which must be observed. The following rules will serve as a guide.

1. In joining a *noun* (especially a proper name) and an *attribute* together, the noun usually stands first; as, *Cicerone consule.* But custom requires *urbs Roma*, as Rome is the *urbs* by excellence.

2. In joining an *adjective* (participle, numeral) to a *noun*, the noun likewise is placed first. The rhetorical arrangement, however, often varies this order.

a. If an *adjective* belongs to *two substantives*, it is placed either before or between them; as, *haec forensis laus et industria*, or *vir et consilii magni et virtutis.*

b. But if the *adjective* stands *after the last substantive* it belongs *generally* — if it stands *immediately before* it, it belongs *always* to this substantive alone. *Agri et omnia maria* means only, the lands and all the seas; *agri et maria omnia* generally means the same.

c. If *two* adjectives belong to *one substantive*, they are placed either *grammatically*, both after the substantive; as, *Senatum* afflictum *et* abiectum *excitavi;* or *rhetorically*, both before the substantive; as, egregia *et* praeclara *indoles;* or one precedes the substantive, the other with a conjunction follows it; as, effrenata *libido et* indomita (never *effrenata et libido indomita*).

3. When a *genitive* and *noun* are joined together, the *latter* is placed *first.* However, owing to the rhetorical arrangement, variations are very frequent. When the genitive refers to two nouns it follows the rule laid down for the adjective under *a.*

Caesaris *virtus ac prudentia. Virtus* Caesaris *ac prudentia. Virtus ac prudentia* Caesaris; but not *virtus ac Caesaris prudentia.* The same with: *Ciceronis et Caesaris orationes.*

4. But if *one* of the *two genitives* depending on a noun is subjective and the other objective, the former is placed before the noun; the latter may be placed either after the subjective genitive or after the noun.

Theophrasti orationis *ornamenta.* Siculorum *spes exigua* reliquarum fortunarum. Atheniensium populi *potestatem* omnium rerum.

§ 303.

Notice the following points:

1. The demonstrative pronoun stands generally before the noun; hoc *tempus;* illo *tempore;* ista *causa.*

Ille, meaning *he, the well known, famous*, etc., is generally put *after*, or in complex expressions, *between* the adjective and the substantive. *Ex Ponto Medea* illa *profugisse dicitur. Magnus* ille *Alexander.*

Ipse, in connection with another pronoun, stands commonly *after* it: sua ipsi *frumenta corrumpunt; hoc ipsum, illud ipsum*, etc.

2. The relative *qui* stands always in the *first place;* prepositions alone are placed before the relative; as, *propter quem; a quo; de quorum fide dubitabat.*

When two relatives must be placed beside each other, that one holds the first place, which refers to some previous expression; as, *Epicurus non satis politus est iis artibus*, quas qui *tenent, eruditi appellantur.*

3. For the position of *quisque* see § 68, note 4.

§ 304.

1. The *prepositions* stand immediately *before the cases* they govern; only *tenus*, *versus* (*causā*, *gratiā*) stand after them.

2. However, the *pronoun*, either relative or demonstrative, may sometimes be placed *before* the preposition; as, *res* qua *de agitur;* quem *contra dicit; dies* quam ante; *hunc post; quem propter; si quos inter.* But when the pronoun is joined to a noun, a monosyllabic preposition only can, in good prose, be placed between the pronoun and the noun; as, *qua* in *urbe; ista* in *re; quibus* de *rebus; hanc* ob *rem; quam* ad *scientiam*, also *ad quorum scientiam; cuius* cum *moribus*, or *cum cuius moribus.* The pronoun *is*, alone, follows the preposition always; as, *ob* eam *rem*, *cum* ea *cura; ab* eo *homine; de* is, however, an exception; as, *ea de causa; iis de rebus.*

3. The *adjective* when *emphasized* is often placed before the preposition; as, *magna* cum *cura; tanto* in *honore.* But Cicero and Cæsar always place *medius* after the preposition; as, *in* medio *mundo; in colle* medio.

§ 305.

Prepositions are seldom separated from their cases. They may, however, be separated from them by:

1. A *genitive;* as, *de* doloris *terrore.* Propter Hispanorum, *apud quos consul fuerat*, iniurias.

2. *Enclitics*, such as, *que*, *ve; de que re publica.* By the conjunctions *autem*, *enim*, *vero*, etc., but only with prepositions governing the accusative; as, *post* enim *Chrysippum; praeter enim tres disciplinas.*

3. *Adverbs*, when the word governed by the preposition is a participle or a gerund; *ad* bene beateque *vivendum; de* praeclare *gestis a te rebus* — *ex* ante *convecta copia.*

Two prepositions must never be together in Latin; as, cum ex *Graecia profectis militibus*, but cum *militibus* ex *Graecia profectis;* neither can any case, except the genitive, separate the preposition and the word which it governs. Every preposition must have its own case, hence two prepositions cannot govern one and the same case; never, therefore, say, *per et propter se*, but *per se et propter se.*

§ 306.

Conjunctions generally keep their grammatical position at the beginning of the sentence. However, *quum*, *ut*, *ne*, *dum*, *quia*, etc., are often preceded by a relative, a demonstrative, or any other word strongly emphasized, provided the principal sentence follows the dependent clause with its conjunction.

Quae quum ita sint, *Catilina, perge quo coepisti.* Id ille ut *audivit, domum reverti noluit. Naturam* si *sequemur ducem, nunquam aberrabimus.*

§ 307.

With respect to the particles, we may remark, that:

1. *Non*, when it belongs to a *single* word of the sentence, always stands immediately before it; as, non te *reprehendo, sed fortunam;* but if the negative word belongs to the whole proposition, *non* stands before the *verb*, and more particularly before the finite verb, if an infinitive depends on it; as, *cur tantopere te angas, intelligere sane* non possum. But if the negative is to be emphasized, it is placed at the beginning of the sentence; as, non *de improbo, sed de callide improbo quaerimus.* Instead of *non dico*, *nego* is generally used; negavit *eum adesse*, he said that he was not there.

2. *Etiam*, *adeo*, *praeterea*, *porro*, are *seldom* put after the word or thought to which they belong; *tantum* and *demum* nearly always, *quidem* always. But if there is a *pronoun* in the sentence, *quidem* is attracted to it and placed after it, though the sense or emphasis would require another arrangement.

Tibi persuade, esse te quidem *mihi carissimum, sed multo fore cariorem;* instead of *esse quidem te*, or *carissimum quidem te esse.*

§ 308.

In some phrases, custom has established a certain order; as,

1. The ablatives, *opinione*, *spe*, *aequo*, *iusto*, *solito*, *dicto*, when joined to a comparative, are regularly placed before the comparative; as, *opinione melius*, *dicto citius.* Livy, however, has *magis solito*, *longius solito*, etc.

2. The *vocative* is, in Latin, not placed at the beginning of the address, but is inserted after some other word and most generally just after the *pronoun or verb* of the person addressed. *Multa mihi necessario, iudices, praetermittenda sunt,* Judges, I necessarily, etc. *Quousque tandem abutere, Catilina, patientia nostra,* Cataline, how long, etc.

3. In *letters,* the writer puts in the first place his own name, then either the salutation, *S. D.* (*Salutem Dico* or *Dicit*), or the name of the person addressed in the dative; *Cicero Ap. Pulchro, ut spero, Censori S. D.* A simple *S* (*Salutem*) always after the dative, is used in more familiar correspondence; *Cicero Attico S.* Sometimes even *S.* is omitted; *Cicero Domitio.*

Rarely *S. P. D.* or *S. P.* (*Salutem Plurimam Dicit*); but, if used, it stands always after the dative.

4. *Place* and *date* of letters are written only at the end; and first the date, then the place (from which); *Valete.* Pridie Kalendas Maias, Brundisio.

When *D.* or *Data* (*sc. epistola,* not *dabam* or *dedi*) is added, it is placed before the *date; Vale.* Data *Nonis Martiis, ex castris Taricheis.*

5. *Inquam* is placed after one or more of the words quoted; if a subject is added to the verb, its position is after *inquam;* as, *Est vero,* inquam, *notum signum. Mihi vero,* inquit Cotta, *videtur.*

6. The following are idiomatic expressions:

Terra marique; ferro ignique (or *ferro atque igne*); *ferro flammaque* (or *flamma ac ferro*); *domi militiaeque; pace belloque; velis remisque; equis virisque,* with might and main; *ultro citroque; quod ad rem attinet* (never *ad rem quod attinet*).

§ 309.

The Romans considered the rhythmic arrangement of sentences of great importance and always endeavored, as well by the choice of single words (*sonus* or *vocum suavitas*) as by the position of the words (*numerus*), to produce the greatest euphony. *Duae sunt res, quae permulceant aures,* sonus *et* numerus.

It would, therefore, be very inelegant Latin:

1. If a number of *monosyllables,* or a number of *polysyllables*

of the same *cadence* or inflection of voice, were made to follow each other; as, *Cur tu in hac re te non debere cedere crederes?* The rhythmus would be much improved by the following disposition of the words: *Cur tu cedere in hac re non debere te crederes?* The sentence, *Ista pugna Caesar multos Gallos vicit atque cepit*, is devoid of all euphony. To avoid the monotony of the dissyllables, other words must be chosen; thus, *Isto proelio Caesar multos Gallos devicit atque cepit.* Sentences like the following should be avoided: *Romani Germanos hucusque invictos vicerunt*, or *Africanus Numantinos gloriose resistentes superavit.*

2. If many words beginning and ending with a vowel be put together; as, *cui ea omnia accepta ille esse putabat* — or words containing the same or nearly the same consonants; as, *Rex Xerxes; ars studiorum; ingens est stridor.*

3. If words of similar ending follow each other; as, *Horum duorum fortissimorum virorum; Quidquid fit, id puter non concedet.*

§ 310.

1. The *rhythmic* arrangement of the sentence (*numerus*) engaged the special attention of the ancients. They compared the sentence in prose with the verse in poetry, and required the same melody and rounding of the period in the former as in the latter. However, they carefully avoided making of this rhythm a perfect verse. Hence, Cicero says, *Versus in oratione si efficitur coniunctione verborum, vitium est.*

2. Particular attention was given to the termination of sentences (*clausula*). Cicero recommends as termination especially the *creticus* (— ⏑ —) even twice or thrice repeated, and preceded by the *Paeon primus* (— ⏑ ⏑ ⏑). But an hexametrical close was most carefully avoided; hence the frequent *mihi crede* instead of *crēdĕ mĭhī;* never close with *ēssĕ vĭdētur.* The first oration of Cicero against Catiline may serve as model, both for the rhythmus and the termination of sentences (*clausula*).

CHAPTER XLVIII.

II. ON THE CONNECTION OF SENTENCES AND THE CONSTRUCTION OF COMPOUND SENTENCES.

§ 311.

The Romans were very careful to leave sentences or members unconnected, as rarely as possible. The links or hinges to make this connection of the sentences were, 1. the *relative;* 2. the *negative* conjunction *neque* (*nec*).

The *relative* was very often used where we use in English the demonstrative, either alone or with *and, but, for;* (*qui = et is, is autem; quo = et eo, eo autem.* See § 238, 6.)

Cum Pompeio nullis in aliis nisi de re publica sermonibus versatus sum: quae *nec possunt scribi, nec scribenda sunt* (i. e. *ea autem*). *Illa Stoicorum de se opinio firma in Rutilio et stabilis inventa est.* Qui quum *innocentissimus in iudicium vocatus esset, oratorem adhibere noluit* (i. e. *nam is*).

§ 312.

From this tendency to connect sentences by relatives, arose the use of *quod* before certain conjunctions, merely as a copulative. In English we may either omit it altogether, or render it by *nay, now, and, but.* It is most frequent before *si* and its compounds *nisi, etsi;* we also find, *quod quum, quod ne, quod quoniam, quod quia, quod ubi, quod utinam, quod simulatque,* in some writers also *quod ut.*

Incumbe toto animo in eam rationem, ut eos, quos tuae fidei senatus populusque Romanus commisit, diligas et omni ratione tueare. Quod si *te sors Afris aut Hispanis praefecisset, immanibus ac barbaris nationibus, tamen esset humanitatis tuae consulere eorum commodis et saluti servire* (and if *fate,* etc.).

§ 313.

The *negative* connection by means of *neque* for *et* with a negative word is very common in Latin; as, *neque unquam* instead of *et nunquam*. At the beginning of a sentence *neque* often takes the place of *non*, hence always *neque vero;* nearly always *neque tamen;* mostly *neque enim;* often, however, *non enim.*

Rutilius huic humilitati vel mortem anteponendam esse dicebat. Neque vero *hoc solum dixit, sed ipse et sensit et fecit.*

§ 314.

Whilst short, simple sentences are one of the characteristic features of the English language, we find the Latins very much given to the construction of long, well-rounded compound sentences or *periods* (*periodus*). In such a period there are at least two members. Quintilian says: *Habet periodus membra minimum duo; medius numerus videntur quattuor; sed recipit frequenter et plura.* — No precise rules can be given as to the construction of such periods; the following rules, however, may serve as a guide.

§ 315.

When the *leading* sentence and the *dependent* clause have *several* parts in *common*, the *latter* are placed first, then follows the dependent clause, and finally the remainder of the leading sentence.

Stultitia, *etsi adepta est quod concupivit, nunquam se tamen satis consecutam putat.* Alexandrum omnes, *ut maxime metuerunt, item plurimum dilexerunt.*

§ 316.

When the leading sentence and the dependent clause have no parts in common, that word of the principal sentence is placed before the dependent clause, which would stand at the beginning, if the principal sentence were unaccompanied by a clause.

Insidiatores, *postquam in eum locum agmen pervenit, decepti ordine atque vestitu, in eum faciunt impetum qui suppositus erat.*

§ 317.

All *dependent* clauses are, in the construction of *periods*, placed *before* the *leading* sentences. The relative clauses, however, are generally put before the demonstrative pronoun referring to the relative.

Si *mihi republica bona frui non licuerit, at carebo mala.* Quum *tempus necessitasque postulat, decertandum manu est. Socrates hanc viam ad gloriam proximam et quasi compendiariam dicebat esse, si quis id ageret, ut* qualis *haberi vellet* talis *esset.*

§ 318.

1. Great care must be taken to allot each dependent clause its proper place. The *order* is determined, in the narrative or historical style, by the *time* in which the circumstances or facts, related in the clauses, succeed each other.

Darius, quum *ex Europa in Asiam* rediisset, hortantibus *amicis ut Graeciam redigeret in suam potestatem, classem quingentarum navium comparavit.* It would be wrong to say, *Darius,* hortantibus *amicis ut redigeret in suam potestatem,* quum *ex Europa in Asiam,* etc., because the advice of his friends was subsequent to his return from Asia.

2. If the order of the dependent clauses is not determined by the succession of external circumstances, the place of the clause may be designated by the *connection of the thoughts,* or by a word of the principal sentence which points to the clause, or lastly by any circumstance which draws the attention to the clause.

3. When there are several clauses, great care is necessary to avoid *harshness* and *monotony.* This can be easily done by the use of conjunctions, participles and the ablative absolute, which give variety as well as harmony to the period.

Numitor, *inter primum tumultum hostes invasisse urbem atque adortos regiam* dictitans, quum *pubem Albanam in arcem praesidio armisque obtinendam* avocasset, postquam *iuvenes perpetrata caede pergere ad se gratulantes* vidit: *extemplo* advocato consilio *scelera in se fratris, originem nepotum, ut geniti, ut educati, ut cogniti essent, caedem deinceps tyranni seque eius auctorem* ostendit.

§ 319.

In a succession of dependent clauses, the *verbs,* especially, if they have the same terminations, should not be placed too near each other. The following sentence is a violation of this rule.

Quum expediti utrimque ad occupandos super urbem tumulos processissent, pari ferme intervallo ab iugo, quod capiendum erat, quum inter se conspecti essent, constiterunt, nuntios in castra remissos, qui quid sibi, quando praeter spem hostis occurrisset, *faciendum* esset, consulerent, *quieti opperientes.*

§ 320.

Symmetry of construction, in the members of the period, adds very much to its beauty. Thus:

Etsi vereor, iudices, ne turpe sit, pro fortissimo viro dicere incipientem timere, minimeque deceat, quum T. Annius ipse magis de rei publicae salute quam de sua perturbetur, me ad eius causam parem animi magnitudinem afferre non posse: tamen haec nova iudicii forma terret oculos, qui, quocunque inciderunt, veterem consuetudinem fori et pristinum morem iudiciorum requirunt.

CHAPTER XLIX.

FIGURES AND TROPES.

§ 321.

1. CERTAIN deviations from the regular form, construction or signification of words are called *figures;* they are either *grammatical* or *rhetorical.*

2. The principal grammatical figures are:

Ellipsis, pleonasm, enallage and *hyperbaton.*

3. **Ellipsis** is the omission of some word or words in a sentence; as, *Aiunt* scil. *homines. Quid multa?* scil. *dicam. Darius Hystaspis* scil. *filius.*

Ellipsis includes *asyndeton, zeugma, syllepsis* and *prolepsis.*

4. **Pleonasm** is using a greater number of words than is necessary to express the meaning; as,

Sic ore locuta est; casu et fortuito; prudens sciens.

Pleonasm includes *polysyndeton, hendiadys* and *periphrasis.*

5. **Enallage** is the substitution of one part of speech for

another, or of one grammatical form for another; as, *populu-late rex* (for *regnans*) a people of extensive sway.

Enallage includes *antimerīa, heterosis, antiptosis, synĕsis* and *anacoluthon.*

6. **Hyperbăton** is a transposition in the usual order of words or clauses. *Praeter arma nihil erat super* (*superat*), nothing remained except their arms.

Hyperbăton includes *anastrŏphe, hystĕronprotĕron, synchĕsis, tmĕsis* and *parenthĕsis.*

§ 322.

FIGURES OF RHETORIC OR TROPES.

A rhetorical figure is a mode of expression different from the direct and simple way of expressing the same idea. It is called *trope;* it turns a word from its original and customary meaning.

The principal tropes are:

1. **Metaphor,** which indicates the resemblance of two objects by applying the name, attribute or act of one directly to the other. *Ridet ager,* the field smiles; *aetas aurea,* the golden age.

2. **Metonymy,** by which we put the cause for the effect or the effect for the cause; as, *cedant arma togae,* for *cedat bellum paci.*

3. **Synedoche,** the use of a part for the whole, or of the whole for a part; of the special for the general, or of the general for the special; of the singular for the plural, or of the plural for the singular; as, *In vestra tecta* (*domos*) *discedite. Armato milite* (*militibus*) *complent.*

4. **Irony,** by which we mean quite the contrary of what we say: *A quo repudiatus ad sodalem tuum, virum optimum, M. Marcellum demigrasti.*

5. **Hyperbole,** which represents things as greater or less, better or worse than they really are: *Ventis et fulminis ocior alis.*

In order to obtain a more exact knowledge of these, as well as of the other figures and tropes, it is necessary to refer to a book of Rhetoric.

PART III.

PROSODY.

CHAPTER I.

OF THE LENGTH AND SHORTNESS OF SYLLABLES.

§ 323.

Syllables are long or short, either by the nature of the vowel they contain, or they become long by their short vowel being followed by two or more consonants, that is, by their position. We shall first speak of the natural length and shortness of vowels.

§ 324.

1. All diphthongs are long, and also all those single vowels which have arisen from the contraction of two into one; such as, *cōgo* (from *coăgo*), *mālo* (from *măvŏlo*), *tibīcen* (from *tibiicen* and *tibia;* but *tubĭcen*, from *tuba*), *bīgae* (from *biiugae*), *būbus* and *bōbus* (from *bŏvibus*), and so also *dīs* for *diis*, and *nīl* for *nihil*.

Note.—The preposition *prae* is commonly short, when compounded with a word which begins with a vowel; *e. g.*, *Ovid*, *Metam.*, vii, 181, *Quos ubi viderunt praeacutae cuspidis hastas.*

2. A vowel is short when it is followed by another vowel (*vocalis ante vocalem brevis est*); as, in *dĕus*, *filĭus*, *pĭus*, *rŭo*, *corrŭo;* and, as *h* is not considered a consonant, also in such words as *trăho*, *contrăho*, *vĕho*, and *advĕho*.

Note 1.—The e in the termination of the genitive and dative of the fifth declension is long when it is preceded by a vowel, as in *diēi*, *speciēi*.

Note 2.—All the genitives in ius have the i commonly long. The poets, however, use the i in *illius*, *istius*, *ipsius*, *unius*, *totius*, *ullius*, and *utrius*, sometimes as a long, and sometimes as a short vowel; but *alius*, being a contraction for *aliius*, can never be made short.

NOTE 3.—The verb *fio* has the i long, except when an r occurs in it. *Ovid, Trist.*, 1, 8, 7, *Omnia iam fient, fieri quae posse negabam.*

NOTE 4.—Greek words retain their own original quantity, and we therefore say *āēr, ēos* (ἠώς); *Amphion, Agesilāus*, and *Menelāus*. The e and i in the terminations *ea* and *eus*, or *ia* and *ius*, therefore, are long when they represent the Greek εια and ειος (the Romans, not having the diphthong ει in their language, represent the Greek ι sometimes by e and sometimes by i; but these vowels, of course, are always long); *e. g.*, *Galatēa, Medēa, Aenēas, Darius, Iphigenia, Alexandria, Antiochia, Nicomedia, Samaria, Seleucia, Thalia, Arius, Basilius, nosocomium;* and the adjectives, *Epicurēus, Pythagorēus, spondēus*, and the like. But when the Greek is εα or ια, the e and i are short, as in *idĕa, philosophia, theologia*.

§ 325.

USAGE (*auctoritas*) alone makes the vowel in the first syllable of *māter, frāter, prāvus, māno* (I flow), *dīco, dūco, mīror, nītor, scrībo, dōno, pōno, ūtor, mūto, sūmo, cūra*, etc., long; and short, in *păter, ăvus, cădo, măneo, grăvis, rĕgo, lĕgo, bĭbo, mĭnor, cŏlo, mŏror, prŏbo, dŏmus, sŏno, sŏror*, and others. It must be presumed that the student makes himself acquainted with the quantity of such words as these by practice; for rules can be given only with regard to derivatives. It must further be observed that the i in the following words is long: *formīca, lectīca, lorīca, vesīca, urtīca, hemīna, resīna, sagīna, salīva, castīgo*, and *formīdo*.

§ 326.

DERIVATIVE words retain the quantity of their root, as in declension and conjugation; thus, the a in *ămor* and *ămo* is short, and therefore also in *ămoris, ămat, ămabam, ămavi*, etc., except when the consonants after the vowel of the root produce a difference. *New* words, formed from roots or stems, likewise retain the quantity; as, from *ămo, ămor, ămicus, ămabilis;* from *lux, lūcis — lūceo, lūcidus;* from *māter — māternus, mātertera;* and from *fīnis — fīnio, fīnitio, fīnitimus*, etc.

§ 327.

With regard to conjugation, however, the following rules also must be observed:

1. The *perfect* and *supine*, when they consist of two syllables, and the tenses formed from them, have the first syllable long,

even when, in the present tense, it is short; *e. g.*, *vĭdeo, vīdi; fŭgio, fūgi; lĕgo, lēgi; lēgisse, lēgeram*, etc. (except, however, when one vowel stands before another, in which case the general rule remains in force; as, in *rŭo, rŭi, dirŭi*), *vĭdeo, vīsum; mŏveo, mōtum, mōtus, mōturus.*

Seven dissyllable *perfects*, however, and *nine* dissyllable *supines*, together with their compounds, make their penultima short; viz., *bibi, dĕdi, fĭdi* (from *findo*), *stĕti, stiti, tŭli*, and *scidi* (from *scindo*), and *dătum, rătum, sătum, ĭtum, lĭtum, cĭtum, quĭtum, sĭtum*, and *rŭtum*. *Sisto* makes its supine *stătum*, whence *stătus, a, um*, and the compounds *adstitum, destitum, restitum.*

2. *Perfects* which are formed by reduplication; as, *tundo, tŭtŭdi; cano, cĕcĭni; pello, pĕpŭli*, have the first two syllables short; but the second sometimes becomes long by position; as, in *mordeo, mŏmordi; tendo, tĕtendi.* *Caedo* retains the long vowel in the syllable which forms the root, *cecīdi;* whereas, *cādo*, in accordance with the rule, has *cĕcĭdi.*

3. The perfect *posui* and the supine *positum* have the o short, although in *pono* it is long.

§ 328.

With regard to declension, we must notice:

1. The exception that the words, *lār, pār, sāl*, and *pēs*, shorten their vowel throughout their declension; *sălis, pĕdis*, etc.

2. The terminations *ilis* and *bilis* have the i short when they make derivatives from verbs, but long when from substantives; *e. g.*, *facilis, docilis*, and *amabilis*, but *civilis, hostilis, puerilis, senilis*, etc.

§ 329.

Compound words retain the quantity of the vowels of their elements; thus, from *ăvus* and *nĕpos* we make *abăvus* and *abnĕpos;* from *prāvus, deprāvo;* from *prŏbus, imprŏbus;* from *iūs* (*iūris*) *periūrus;* from *lĕgo* (I read) *perlĕgo;* and from *lēgo* (I despatch) *ablēgo, delēgo, collēgo.* Even when the vowel is changed, its quantity remains the same; *e. g.*, *laedo, illīdo; caedo, incīdo; aequus, inīquus; fauces, suffōco; claudo, reclūdo.*

1. We may, therefore, infer from compounded words the quantity of those of which they consist; *e. g.*, from *adōro, admiror* and *abūtor* we conclude that *oro, miror* and *utor* have the first syllable long; and from *commŏror* and *desŭper* that the first syllable in *moror* and *super* is short.

2. But there are some exceptions, and the following compounded words change the long vowel into a short one: *deiĕro* and *periĕro*, from *iūro; causidicus, fatidicus, maledicus, veridicus* from *dicere; agnitus* and *cognitus* from *nōtus; innŭb(us), -a,* and *pronŭb(us), -a,* from *nūbo.*

3. In respect to composition with *prepositions,* it is to be remarked that prepositions of one syllable which end in a vowel are long, and those which end in a consonant are short: *dēduco, ăboleo, pĕrimo;* but the **o** (for *ob*) in *ŏmitto* is short. **Pro,** in Latin words is long; *e. g., prōdo, prōmitto;* but in many it is short; *prŏfugio, pronĕpos, prŏfiteor.* **Se** and **di** (for *dis*) are long; the only exceptions are *dĭrimo* and *dĭsertus.* **Re** is short; it is long in the impersonal verb *rēfert.*

CHAPTER LI.

FINAL SYLLABLES.

§ 330.

MONOSYLLABIC WORDS.

In regard to the quantity of *final syllables,* the following special rules must be observed:

1. All *monosyllables* ending in a vowel are long, except the particles which are attached to other words: *quĕ, vĕ, cĕ, nĕ, tĕ* (*tutĕ*), *pse* (*reapsĕ*), and *ptĕ* (*suoptĕ*).

2. Among the monosyllables ending in a *consonant,* the *substantives* are long; as, *sōl, vēr, fūr, iūs;* and all those are short which are not substantives, as, *ŭt, ĕt, nĕc, ĭn, ăn, ăd, quĭd, quŏt.* The following substantives, however, are short: *cŏr, fĕl, mĕl, vĭr* and *ŏs* (gen. *ossis*). Some words, on the other hand, are long, although they are not substantives; as, *ēn, nōn, quīn, sīn, crās. plūs, cūr* and *pār,* with its compounds, and also the adverbs in *ic* or *uc,* as *sīc, hīc, hūc.*

The monosyllabic forms of declension and conjugation follow the general rules about the quantity of final syllables, and *dās, flēs* and *sols,* accordingly, are long, while *dăt*, *flĕt* and *scit* art short; *hīs*, *quōs*, *quās* are long, like the terminations *ōs* and *ās* in declension (§ 332). So, also, the ablative singular *hōc* and *hāc*. The nominative *hic* and the neuter *hoc*, on the other hand, although the vowel is naturally short, are commonly used as long. The abridged imperatives retain the quantity of the root, so that *dīc* and *dūc* are long, while *făc* and *fĕr* are short.

§ 331.

FINAL SYLLABLES IN WORDS OF TWO OR MORE SYLLABLES:

I. Such as Terminate in a Vowel.

1. **A** is short in nouns, except in the ablative singular of the first declension and in the vocative of Greek proper names in *as* which belong to the first or third declension; *e. g.*, *Aeneā*, *Pallā*. **A** is long in verbs and indeclinable words, such as *amā*, *frustrā*, *ergā*, *anteā* and *posteā* (except when separated into *post ea*); except, *ită*, *quiă*, *eiă*, and the imperative *pută* in the sense of "for example." In the indeclinable numerals, as *triginta* and *quadraginta*, the *a* is sometimes long and sometimes short.

2. **E** is short, as in *patrĕ*, *currĕ*, *nempĕ;* but long in the ablative of the fifth declension and in the imperative of the second conjugation. Adverbs in *e*, formed from adjectives of the second declension, are likewise long, as *doctē*, *rectē;* also, *ferē*, *fermē* and *ohē* (but *benĕ* and *malĕ* are always short).

3. **I** is long. The *i* is common or doubtful in *mihi*, *sibi*, *ibi* and *ubi;* in compounds we usually find *ibĭdem*, and always *ubīque*, whereas in *ubĭvis* and *ubĭnam* the *i* is always short. In *uti* for *ut*, the *i* is long, but in the compounds *utĭnam* and *utĭque* short.

4. **O** is common in the present tense of all the conjugations, and in the nominative of the third declension, as in *sermo*, *virgo*. But *o* is long in the second declension, as in *lectō*, and in adverbs formed from nouns and pronouns by means of this termination; *e. g.*, *vulgō*, *falsō*, *paulō*, *eō*, *quō* and also *ergō*, *iccircō*, *quandō* and *retrō*.

5. **U** is always long, as in *diū*, *vultū*, *cornū*.

6. **Y**, in Greek words, is always short.

§ 332.

II. Such as Terminate in a Consonant.

All final syllables ending in a consonant are short, and special rules are required only for those ending in the sibilant **s**.

1. **As** is long in Latin words, with the exception of *anăs, anătis;* but the Greek nominatives in *as*, which make their genitives in *αδος*, and in Latin in *adis*, such as *Ilias, Pallas*, and the Greek accusatives plural of the third declension, are always short, as in *heroăs*.

2. **Es** is long; *e. g., amēs, legēs, audiēs, patrēs*. But Latin nominatives in *es*, which increase in the genitive, and have their *penultima* short, are themselves short; *e. g., milĕs, militĭs; segĕs, segĕtis* (except *abiēs, ariēs, pariēs, Cerēs*, and the compounds of *pēs*); the preposition *penĕs* and the second person of the compounds of *sum*, *ĕs; e. g., abĕs, potĕs;* but the *ēs* (for *edis*) from *edo*, is long.

3. **Is** is generally short, but long in all the cases of the plural, as *armīs, vobīs, omnīs* (accusative for *omnes*); in the second person singular of verbs whose plural is *ītis*, that is, in the fourth conjugation, and in *possīs, velīs, nolīs, malīs* and *vīs* (thou wilt) with its compounds, such as *mavīs, quivīs, quamvīs*.

Us is short in verbs and nouns, except monosyllables, but long in the genitive singular, in the nominative and accusative plural of the fourth declension, and in the nominatives of the third, which have *ū* long in the genitive, as *virtūs, ūtis; palūs, ūdis*.

5. **Ys**, in Greek words, is short, as *Halўs, Tethўs, chlamўs*.

§ 333.

Syllables (as was remarked in § 328) may become long by their vowel being followed by two or more consonants, that is, by their *position*.

X and z are accounted as two consonants.

1. A *position* may be formed in three ways:

a. When a syllable ends in two or three consonants, as in *ex, est, mens, stirps*.

b. When the first syllable ends in a consonant and the second begins with one, as in *ille, arma, mentis, in nova*.

c. When the first syllable ends in a vowel, and the one following begins with two consonants.

2. By the first and second kinds of position, a syllable which is naturally short becomes long.

Exceptions to this rule occur only in the comic poets, who frequently neglect position, especially that of the second kind.

3. In the third kind of position (made by two consonants beginning the syllable after a vowel), we must distinguish as to whether it occurs within a word or between two words, and whether the consonants are mutes with a liquid (*muta cum liquida*) or not. Within a word, a syllable ending in a short vowel is regularly made long, when it is followed by two consonants, or *x* and *z*, as in *aptus*, *factus*, *axis;* but when the first consonant is a mute and the second a liquid (which is called *positio debilis*), they make the vowel only common, according to the pronunciation in prose. Thus, we may pronounce either *cerĕbrum*, *lugŭbris*, *mediŏcris*, *intĕgri*, or *cerēbrum*, *lugūbris*, *mediōcris*, *intēgri*. Ovid, for example, says: *Et primo similis volŭcri, mox vera volūcris.* (*Metam.* xiii, 607.)

4. Between two words the vowel is rarely lengthened, except in the *arsis* of a verse. The last syllable of a word thus remains short; *e. g.*, in Horace, at the beginning of a hexameter: *quem mală stultitia aut;* or at the end: *praemiă scribae.* An instance in which the vowel is lengthened by the accession of the *arsis* occurs in Virgil, *Bucol.* iv, 51. *Terrasque tractusque maris coelumque profundum.*

5. Qu is not accounted as two consonants, for *u* is not a true consonant, though we usually pronounce it as such. But *j* alone is sufficient to make position, because this consonant was pronounced double (in early times it was also written double); *e. g.*, *major* like *maiior*, and, in like manner, in *ēius* and *Trōia*. In the compounds of *iugum* alone, it does not lengthen the preceding vowel, as *biiugus*, *quadriiugus*.

CHAPTER LII.

VERSIFICATION.

§ 334.

Syllables are combined into certain metrical groups called **feet, and** feet, singly or in pairs, are combined into verses.

The most common metrical feet are:

1. ⏑ –́, *iambus* iambic; as, *rĕgūnt*, *grăvī*, *pătēs*.
2. –́ ⏑, *trochaeus* (*chorēus*), trochee; as, *mātrĕ*, *rēbŭs*, *fōrtĭs*.
3. – –, *spondēus*, spondee; as, *mātrēs*, *aūdāx*, *vōbīs*.
4. –́ ⏑ ⏑, *dactylus*, dactyl; as, *ōmniă*, *mātribŭs*, *aūdiăt*.
5. ⏑ ⏑ –́, *anapaestus*, anapaest; as, *dŏmĭnō*, *fŭgiūnt*, *bŏnĭtās*.

⏑ ⏑, *pyrrhichius*, pyrrhic; ⏑ ⏑ ⏑, *tribrachys*, tribrach; ⏑ – ⏑, *amphibrachys*, amphibrach; ⏑ – –, *bacchius*; – – ⏑, *palimbacchius* (antibacchius); – ⏑ –, *creticus* (*amphimacer*), cretic; – – –, *molossus*. There are, besides, sixteen compound feet of four syllables.

§ 335.

1. In every verse the long and short syllables vary according to a fixed law; the simple and constantly recurring combination of long and short syllables in a verse are called feet.

2. The movement and melody of a verse constitute what is termed *Rhythm*. It is the effect produced by the variation of sounds according to a fixed rule; the variation of sounds consists in the *raising* (*arsis*) and *sinking* (*thesis*) of the voice in the delivery of the verse.

The arsis is marked by ′ (the *ictus*); the thesis is either not marked at all, or else by ‵. Examples of rising rhythm are, ⏑ –́, ⏑ ⏑ –́; of falling, –́ ⏑, –́ ⏑ ⏑.

3. A short syllable in a verse is considered as the standard; the portion of time consumed in pronouncing the same is called **mora.** A long syllable has two *moras*. Hence, a long syllable may be put instead of two short syllables, and *vice versa*.

4. At the end of every verse a short pause must be made, even when the punctuation does not point it out; hence, the last syllable may be either long or short. In a long verse, there is also, within the same, a slight pause or rest, but always at the **end** of a word. If this pause falls within a metrical (verse) foot, it is called **Caesura,** but when at the end of a foot it is termed **Diaeresis,** or incision.

5. The caesura is called *strong* when it immediately follows the arsis: as

Incidit in Scyllam ‖ *qui vult vitare Charybdim:*

weak, when it falls within the thesis; as,

Obstupuit simul ipse, ‖ *simul percussus Achates.*

6. In the recitation or delivery of a Latin verse, the **elision** must be observed. When a word ends with a **vowel** or **m**, and the succeeding word begins with a *vowel* or *h*, the first and last syllable of both words are in the delivery contracted into one (the final syllable is dropped or elided); thus, *sapere aude*, read *saper'aude; improvisi aderant, improvis'-aderant; orandum est, ut sit mens sana in corpore sano*, read *orand'est* or *orandum'st san'in;* likewise, *homo est*, either *hom'est* or *homo'st.* But if the two words stand in different lines, no elision takes place, except in very rare cases (*versus hypermeter*, § 337, 5).

§ 336.

Among the most frequent Latin verses, may be reckoned the Iambic Senarius, the Hexameter, and the Pentameter.

The Iambic Senarius (senos *iambos continens, versus* senarius) consists of six Iambics. It is also called Iambic Trimeter (*trimeter iambicus*) because every two feet (a dipody) form a measure; so that the whole verse consists of three measures or dipodies. The caesura falls usually after the first thesis of the second dipody (after the fifth half-foot), sometimes after the second thesis of the second dipody (after the seventh half-foot).

Scale of the pure Iambic Senarius:

⏑ –́ ⏑ –́ | ⏑ ‖ –́ ⏑ –́ | ⏑ –́ ⏑ –́

Bĕā́tŭs ĭ́l | *lĕ* ‖ *quí prŏcŭ́l* | *nĕgṓtĭī́s.*

However, the pure Senarius is, in general, rare; all poets use it with the following licenses:

a. A *long* syllable may take the place of one short syllable at the beginning of every dipody.

b. *Two short* syllables may take the place of every long syllable, except the *last.*

c. One short syllable may always replace the last long syllable.

Scale of the modified Senarius (*Iambic Trimeter*).

⏒ –́ ⏑ –́ | ⏒ –́ ⏑ –́ | ⏒ –́ ⏑ –́

⏒ ⏑́⏑ ⏑ ⏑́⏑ | ⏒ ⏑́⏑ ⏑ ⏑́⏑ | ⏒ . ⏑ ⏑́

Some poets, particularly Phaedrus, take still greater license: for they employ a long syllable instead of a short one everywhere, except in the last foot; thus,

⏓ –́ – –́ | ⏓ –́ – –́ | ⏓ –́ ⏑ ⏒

and then each long syllable may again be converted into two short syllables. The verse is then apparent only by the *arsis*, which is more marked in the first original long syllable of every dipody, but less so in the second.

Aesŏpus aúc | tor ‖ quám ma | téri | am rēppĕrĭt,
Hanc ĕgŏ polí | vi ‖ vérsibŭs | senáriis,
Duplĕx libél | li ‖ dŏs est, quŏd | risŭm mŏvĕt,
Et quŏd prudĕn | ti ‖ vitam cón | siliŏ mŏnĕt.
Calúmniă | ri ‖ sí quis aŭ | tem vŏlŭĕrit,
Quod ărborĕs | loquăntur ‖ nŏn | tantŭm fĕras:
Fictis iocă | ri ‖ nŏs meminĕ | rit făbŭlis.

§ 337.

The Hexameter (*versus heroicus*) consists of six dactyls: each of these is counted as a measure. The last dactyle, however, lacks one syllable. But two short syllables may always be exchanged for a long syllable: this, however, is very rare in the fifth foot.

The principal *caesurae* of the Hexameter are:

1. After the arsis of the third foot; scale:

– ⏖ – ⏖ – ‖ ⏖ – ⏖ – ⏑⏑ – ⏓

Rēgiă, | crēdĕ mi | hi ‖ rēs | ĕst sŭc | cŭrrĕrĕ | lăpsis.

2. After the first short syllable of the third foot, (the trochaic *caesura*); scale:

– ⏖ – ⏖ – ⏑ ‖ ⏑ – ⏖ – ⏑⏑ – ⏓

Ōdē | rúnt pĕc | cárĕ ‖ bŏni vir | tútis ămórĕ.

The thought is, sin is avoided, by the good, out of love for virtue; do not avoid it therefore through fear of punishment. Hence the *caesura* comes necessarily after *peccare* not after *boni.*

3. After the arsis of the fourth foot, sometimes with a secondary *caesura* after the arsis of the second foot; scale:

– ⏖ – | ⏖ – ⏖ – ‖ ⏖ – ⏑⏑ – ⏓

Quid rĕ | fĕrt, ‖ mŏr | bo an fŭr | tis ‖ pĕrĕ | ămnĕ ră | pinis?

4. The verse becomes animated and lively by the use of many dactyls, while it is rendered grave and solemn by several spondees, but particularly when the fifth foot is a spondee (*versus spondiacus*).

Quădrŭpĕdăntĕ pŭtrĕm sŏnitŭ quătit ŭngŭlă cămpŭm.
Illi intĕr sēsē măgnă vi brăchiă tŏllŭnt.
Cónstitit ătque oculis Phrўgia agmină circŭmspĕxit.

3. Example of a *versus hypermeter* (§ 335, 6).

Omnia Mercurio similis vocemque coloremque
Et crines flavos et membra decora iuventae.

§ 338.

1. A verse is termed *Pentameter*, because the number of its syllables forms five feet. Properly speaking it consists of six dactyls, but the thesis in the third and sixth (both short syllables) are suppressed. Hence after the arsis, which is left over from the third foot, there is a strong pause (here a Diæresis); this divides the verse into two nearly equal parts. The first part allows a spondee instead of a dactyl, the second never; scale:

–́ ⏖ –́ ⏖ –́ | –́ ⏑⏑ –́ ⏑⏑ –́

Iā́m tĕ́tĭgĭt sū́mmōs | *vḗrtĭcĕ Rṓmă dĕṓs.*

2. The *Pentameter* occurs only as a sequence to the *Hexameter*. This union is called *Distichon* (distich) or elegiac verse.

Principiis obsta! Sero medicina paratur,
Quum mala per longas convaluere moras. —
Donec eris felix, multos numerabis amicos;
Tempora si fuerint nubila, solus eris. —
Laudat alauda deum, dum sese tollit in altum;
Dum cadit in terram, laudat alauda deum.

CHAPTER LIII.

SHORT VIEW OF THE LYRIC METRES OF HORACE.

§ 339.

I. The shorter Asclepiadēan system consists of four short Asclepiadēan verses; thus,

–́ – | –́ ⏑ ⏑ – | –́ ⏑ ⏑ | –́ ⏑ ⏓
–́ – | –́ ⏑ ⏑ – | –́ ⏑ ⏑ | –́ ⏑ ⏓
–́ – | –́ ⏑ ⏑ – | –́ ⏑ ⏑ | –́ ⏑ ⏓
–́ – | –́ ⏑ ⏑ – | –́ ⏑ ⏑ | –́ ⏑ ⏓

I : 1. III : 30. IV : 8.

The choriambics express something grand; the even movement of the verse implies great confidence and strong conviction.

II. The first Asclepiadean stanza in which the Glyconic verse alternates with the shorter Asclepiad; thus,

–́ – | –́ ⏑ ⏑ | –́ ⏑ ⏓
–́ – | –́ ⏑ ⏑ – ‖ –́ ⏑ ⏑ | –́ ⏑ ⏓
–́ – | –́ ⏑ ⏑ | –́ ⏑ ⏓
–́ – | –́ ⏑ ⏑ – ‖ –́ ⏑ ⏑ | –́ ⏑ ⏓

I : 3, 13, 19, 36. III : 9, 15, 19, 24, 25, 28. IV : 1, 3.

III. The second Asclepiadean stanza consists of three short Asclepiads and a Glyconic verse; thus,

–́ – | –́ ⏑ ⏑ – ‖ –́ ⏑ ⏑ | –́ ⏑ ⏓
–́ – | –́ ⏑ ⏑ – ‖ –́ ⏑ ⏑ | –́ ⏑ ⏓
–́ – | –́ ⏑ ⏑ – ‖ –́ ⏑ ⏑ | –́ ⏑ ⏓
–́ – | –́ ⏑ ⏑ | –́ ⏑ ⏓

I : 6, 15, 24, 33. II : 12. III : 10, 16. IV : 5, 12.

IV. The third Asclepiadean stanza in which a Pherecratian verse is substituted for the third Asclepiad in the preceding stanza: thus,

–́ – | –́ ⏑ ⏑ – ‖ –́ ⏑ ⏑ | –́ ⏑ ⏓
–́ – | –́ ⏑ ⏑ – ‖ –́ ⏑ ⏑ | –́ ⏑ ⏓
–́ – | –́ ⏑ ⏑ | –́ ⏒
–́ – | –́ ⏑ ⏑ | –́ ⏑ ⏓.

I : 5, 14, 21, 23. III : 7, 13. IV : 13.

V. The greater Asclepiadean system consists of four greater Asclepiads: thus,

–́ – | –́ ⏑ ⏑ – ‖ –́ ⏑ ⏑ – ‖ –́ ⏑ ⏑ | –́ ⏑ ⏓
–́ – | –́ ⏑ ⏑ – ‖ –́ ⏑ ⏑ – ‖ –́ ⏑ ⏑ | –́ ⏑ ⏓
–́ – | –́ ⏑ ⏑ – ‖ –́ ⏑ ⏑ – ‖ –́ ⏑ ⏑ | –́ ⏑ ⏓
–́ – | –́ ⏑ ⏑ – ‖ –́ ⏑ ⏑ – ‖ –́ ⏑ ⏑ | –́ ⏑ ⏓

I : 11, 18. IV : 10.

§ 340.

VI. The Sapphic Stanza consists of three smaller Sapphics with an Adonic as the fourth verse; thus,

–́ ⏑ – –̀ | –́ ‖ ⏑ ⏑ | –́ ⏑ – ⏒
–́ ⏑ – –̀ | –́ ‖ ⏑ ⏑ | –́ ⏑ – ⏒
–́ ⏑ – –̀ | –́ ‖ ⏑ ⏑ | –́ ⏑ – ⏒
–́ ⏑ ⏑ | –́ ⏒.

This metre is grave and solemn, and particularly adapted to invocations and prayer.

I : 2, 10, 12, 20, 22, 25, 30, 32, 38.
II : 2, 4, 6, 8, 10, 16.
III : 8, 11, 14, 18, 20, 22, 27.
IV : 2, 6, 11.

Carmen saeculare.

VII. The greater Sapphic stanza, in which the Aristophanian verse alternates with the greater Sapphic.

–́ ⏑ ⏑ | –́ ⏑ – ⏓
–́ ⏑ – –̀ | –́ ‖ ⏑ ⏑ – | –́ ⏑ ⏑ | –́ ⏑ – ⏓
–́ ⏑ ⏑ | –́ ⏑ – ⏓
–́ ⏑ – –̀ | –́ ‖ ⏑ ⏑ – | –́ ⏑ ⏑ | –́ ⏑ – ⏓

I : 8.

§ 341.

VIII. The Alcaic stanza is composed of two verses of eleven syllables, one of nine syllables, and one of ten syllables; they are all Alcaics; thus,

⏓ | –́ ⏑ – ⏓ ‖ –́ ⏑ ⏑ | –́ ⏑ ≚
⏓ | –́ ⏑ – ⏓ ‖ –́ ⏑ ⏑ | –́ ⏑ ≚
⏓ | –́ ⏑ – ⏓ | –́ ⏑ – ⏓
–́ ⏑ ⏑ | –́ ⏑ ⏑ | –́ ⏑ – ⏓

This metre is lively and energetic, and well suited to encourage, to challenge, to advise and to cheer up.

The first line consists of two halves, the third verse is a doubling of the first half, while the fourth is an amplification of the second half. For the Catalectic in the first and second verse, answers to the omission of an entire double Trochee in the fourth line.

The Alcaic stanza resembles a composition in which after the musical idea has stamped itself on the ear by repetition, it is resolved into its elements and more fully carried out.

This is the favorite metre of Horace, and he uses it not less than thirty-seven times.

I : 9, 16, 17, 26, 27, 29, 31, 34, 35, 37.
II : 1, 3, 5, 7, 9, 11, 13, 14, 15, 17, 19, 20.
III : 1, 2, 3, 4, 5, 6, 17, 21, 23, 26, 29.
IV : 4, 9, 14, 15.

§ 342.

IX. The first Archilochian stanza in which there is an alternation of (dactylic) Hexameter and the shorter Archilochian verse: thus,

–́ ⏔ | –́ ⏔ | –́ ‖ ⏔ | –́ ⏔ | –́ ⏑ ⏑ | –́ ⏓
–́ ⏑ ⏑ | –́ ⏑ ⏑ | ⏓
–́ ⏔ | –́ ⏔ | –́ ‖ ⏔ | –́ ⏔ | –́ ⏑ ⏑ | –́ ⏓
–́ ⏑ ⏑ | –́ ⏑ ⏑ | ⏓

IV : 7.

The four Archilochian stanzas are all expressive of sad and gloomy thoughts.

X. The second Archilochian stanza consists of the (dactylic) Hexameter and Iambic Elegiac verse; thus,

–́ ⏔ | –́ ⏔ | –́ ‖ ⏔ | –́ ⏔ | –́ (⏔) | –́ ⏓
⏓ –́ ⏑ – | ⏓ –́ ⏑ ⏒ . –́ ⏑ ⏑ | –́ ⏑ ⏑ | ⏒

The Iambic Dimeter is inserted without any connection between the two members of the preceding stanza.

Epode 13.

XI. The third Archilochian stanza consists of the Senarius or Iambic Trimeter and the Iambic Elegiac verse; thus,

⏓ –́ ⏑ – | ⏓ ‖ –́ ⏑ – | ⏓ –́ ⏑ ⏓
–́ ⏑ ⏑ | –́ ⏑ ⏑ | ⏒ . ⏓ –́ ⏑ – | ⏓ –́ ⏑ ⏒

Epode 11.

XII. The fourth Archilochian stanza alternates the greater Archilochian verse with a verse of Iambic character; thus,

–́ ⏔ | –́ ⏔ | –́ ‖ ⏔ | –́ ⏑ ⏑, –́ ⏑ – ⏑ – ⏓
⏓ | –́ ⏑ – ⏓ ‖ –́ ⏑ – ⏑ – ⏓
–́ ⏔ | –́ ⏔ | –́ ‖ ⏔ | –́ ⏑ ⏑, –́ ⏑ – ⏑ – ⏓
⏓ | –́ ⏑ – ⏓ ‖ –́ ⏑ – ⏑ – ⏓

I : 4.

§ 343.

XIII. The Almanic stanza in which the (dactylic) Hexameter alternates with a Catalectic Dactylic Tetrameter; thus,

–́ ⏔ | –́ ⏔ | –́ ‖ ⏔ | –́ ⏔ | –́ (⏔) | –́ ⏓
–́ ⏔ | –́ ⏔ | –́ (⏔) | –́ ⏓
–́ ⏔ | –́ ⏔ | –́ ‖ ⏔ | –́ ⏔ | –́ (⏔) | –́ ⏓
–́ ⏔ | –́ ⏔ | –́ (⏔) | –́ ⏓

I : 7, 28. *Epode* 12.

§ 344.

XIV. The Senarius or Iambic Trimeter, with only slight variations is employed as in the following scale,

⏒ –́ ⏑ – | ⏒ ‖ –́ ⏑ – | ⏒ –́ ⏑ ⏓

Epode 17.

XV. The Iambic stanza consists of the Senarius or Iambic Trimeter and the Iambic Dimeter; thus,

⏒ –́ ⏑ – | ⏒ ‖ –́ ⏑ – | ⏒ –́ ⏑ ⏓
⏒ –́ ⏑ – | ⏒ –́ ⏑ ⏓

Epodes 1–10.

This is properly the metre of the Epodes. The abrupt closing is well adapted to make the language keen and pointed.

XVI. The first Pyth-iambic stanza consists of the (dactylic) Hexameter and the Iambic Dimeter. It is termed pythic because the Pythoness delivered the oracles in this metre.

–́ ⏔ | –́ ⏔ | –́ ‖ ⏔ | –́ ⏔ | –́ ⏑ ⏑ | –́ ⏒
⏓ –́ ⏑ – | ⏒ –́ ⏑ ⏓

Epodes 14, 15.

XVII. The second Pyth-iambic stanza is composed of the (dactylic) Hexameter and the Senarius or Iambic Trimeter; thus,

–́ ⏔ | –́ ⏔ | –́ ‖ ⏔ | –́ ⏔ | –́ ⏑⏑(–) | –́ ⏓
⏑ –́ ⏑ – | ⏑ ‖ –́ ⏑ – | ⏑ –́ ⏑ ⏓

Epode 16.

§ 345.

XVIII. The Trochaic stanza (of Hipponax) in which a Catalectic Trochaic Tetrapody is substituted in the second verse of the fourth Archilochian stanza; thus,

–́ ⏑ – ⏑ | –́ ⏑ ⏒
⏒ | –́ ⏑ – ⏒ ‖ –́ ⏑ – ⏑ – ⏓
–́ ⏑ – ⏑ | –́ ⏑ ⏒
⏒ | –́ ⏑ – ⏒ ‖ –́ ⏑ – ⏑ – ⏓

II : 18.

§ 346.

XIX. The rising Ionic system; thus,

⏑ ⏑ ´– – | ⏑ ⏑ ´– –
⏑ ´– – | ⏑ ⏑ ´– –
⏑ ⏑ ´– – | ⏑ ⏑ ´– – | ⏑ ⏑ ´– – | ⏑ ⏑ ´– –
⏑ ⏑ ´– – | ⏑ ⏑ ´– ⏓

III : 12.

APPENDIX.

CHAPTER LIV.

THE ROMAN CALENDAR.

§ 347.

1. The first day of every month is called **Kalendae** (*Calendae*, *K.*, or *Kal.*), *Calends;* in March, May, July, and October, the fifteenth day is called **Idus,** *Ides;* the seventh, **Nonae,** *Nones* (from *nonus*, because counting backward, it is nine days from the Ides). In the other *eight* months the *Ides* fall on the thirteenth and the *Nones* on the fifth day.

2. The *name* of the *month* is always joined as adjective to these three words, and to express a date, the *ablative* is used; thus, *Kalendis Ianuariis*, the first of January; *Nonis Ianuariis*, the fifth of January; *Idibus Ianuariis*, the thirteenth of January; *Kalendis Octobribus*, first of October; *Nonis*, *Idibus Octobribus*, seventh, fifteenth of October.

3. The eve of the Calends, Nones, and Ides, was always expressed by *pridie* with the accusative (the day after, sometimes by *postridie*, with accusative); as, *pridie Kalendas Apriles*, thirty-first of March; *pridie Idus Septembres*, twelfth of September (*postridie Nonas Maias*, eighth of May).

4. To express any of the other days, count how many days it is before the next Calends, Nones, or Ides, taking care to include the starting and concluding days, so that from the third to the seventh there are five days; from the nineteenth of May to the first of June, fourteen days. Hence the third of March is *dies quintus ante Nonas Martias;* nineteenth of May, *dies quartus decimus ante Kalendas Iunias.* But, instead of saying, *die quinto ante Nonas Martias*, third of March, and *die quarto decimo ante Kalendas Iunias*, an abridgment and transformation is very common; as, *ante diem quintum Nonas Martias* (*a. d. V. Non. Mart.*), *ante diem quartum decimum Kalendas Iunias* (*a. d. XIV. Kal. Iun.*); or, by omitting *ante;* thus, *quinto Nonas Martias* (*V. Non. Mart.*) *quarto decimo Kalendas Iunias* (*XIV. Kal. Iun.*)

5. Calendar for the Year.

Our Date.	I. March, May, July, and October (31 Days).	II. January, August, and December (31 Days).	III. April, June, September, and November (30 Days).	IV. February (28 Days).
1	Kalendis Martiis.	Kalendis Ianuariis.	Kalendis Aprilibus.	Kalendis Februariis
2	a. d. VI. Nonas Martias.	a. d. IV. Nonas Ianuar.	a. d. IV. Nonas April.	a. d. IV. Non. Febr.
3	a. d. V. " "	a. d. III. " "	a. d. III. " "	a. d. III. " "
4	a. d. IV. " "	pridie " "	pridie " "	pridie " "
5	a. d. III. " "	Nonis Ianuariis.	Nonis Aprilibus.	Nonis Februariis.
6	pridie " "	a. d. VIII. Idus Ianuar.	a. d. VIII. Idus April.	a. d. VIII. Id. Febr.
7	Nonis Martiis.	a. d. VII. " "	a. d. VII. " "	a. d. VII. " "
8	a. d. VIII. Idus Martias.	a. d. VI. " "	a. d. VI. " "	a. d. VI. " "
9	a. d. VII. " "	a. d. V. " "	a. d. V. " "	a. d. V. " "
10	a. d. VI. " "	a. d. IV. " "	a. d. IV. " "	a. d. IV. " "
11	a. d. V. " "	a. d. III. " "	a. d. III. " "	a. d. III. " "
12	a. d. IV. " "	pridie " "	pridie " "	pridie " "
13	a. d. III. " "	Idibus Ianuariis.	Idibus Aprilibus.	Idibus Februariis.
14	pridie " "	a. d. XIX. Kal. Februar.	a. d. XVIII. Kal. Maias.	a. d. XVI. Kal. Mart.
15	Idibus Martiis.	a. d. XVIII. " "	a. d. XVII. " "	a. d. XV. " "
16	a. d. XVII. Kal. Apriles.	a. d. XVII. " "	a. d. XVI. " "	a. d. XIV. " "
17	a. d. XVI. " "	a. d. XVI. " "	a. d. XV. " "	a. d. XIII. " "
18	a. d. XV. " "	a. d. XV. " "	a. d. XIV. " "	a. d. XII. " "
19	a. d. XIV. " "	a. d. XIV. " "	a. d. XIII. " "	a. d. XI. " "
20	a. d. XIII. " "	a. d. XIII. " "	a. d. XII. " "	a. d. X. " "
21	a. d. XII. " "	a. d. XII. " "	a. d. XI. " "	a. d. IX. " "
22	a. d. XI. " "	a. d. XI. " "	a. d. X. " "	a. d. VIII. " "
23	a. d. X. " "	a. d. X. " "	a. d. IX. " "	a. d. VII. " "
24	a. d. IX. " "	a. d. IX. " "	a. d. VIII. " "	a. d. VI. " "
25	a. d. VIII. " "	a. d. VIII. " "	a. d. VII. " "	a. d. V. " "
26	a. d. VII. " "	a. d. VII. " "	a. d. VI. " "	a. d. IV. " "
27	a. d. VI. " "	a. d. VI. " "	a. d. V. " "	a. d. III. " "
28	a. d. V. " "	a. d. V. " "	a. d. IV. " "	pridie " "
29	a. d. IV. " "	a. d. IV. " "	a. d. III. " "	
30	a. d. III. " "	a. d. III. " "	pridie " "	
31	pridie " "	pridie " "		

CHAPTER LV.

ROMAN WEIGHTS, MONEY AND MEASURES.

§ 348.

1. A Roman pound (*libra*, *pondo*) weighed about 11¼ ounces. As a whole or unit it was called *as*. Fractions of the pound (*as*) are *uncia* = $\frac{1}{12}$; *sextans* = $\frac{1}{6}$; *quadrans* = $\frac{1}{4}$; *triens* = $\frac{1}{3}$; *quincunx* = $\frac{5}{12}$; *semis* = $\frac{1}{2}$; *septunx* = $\frac{7}{12}$; *bes* (gen. *bessis*) = $\frac{2}{3}$; *dodrans* = $\frac{3}{4}$; *dextans* (*decunx*) = $\frac{5}{6}$; *deunx* = $\frac{11}{12}$.

2. The most ancient Roman money was of copper (*aes*, *aeris*), and it was computed by pounds, **asses**; thus, *duo asses*, *tres asses*. When the amount was large, the word *asses* was omitted, and *aeris* used in its stead; *e. g.*, *centum millia aeris*, 100,000 pounds of copper. The most ancient *asses* (*asses liberales*, full, also *aes grave*) were worth $0.88; but when silver was more common, the copper *as* became lighter, and about 250 B. C. was worth only $0.06; about 217 B. C., $0.03; about 191 B. C., $0.01½.

After the introduction of silver money, about 268 B. C., sums of money are reckoned by sesterces. The sesterce (*sestertius*) was a silver coin equivalent to 2½ *asses* (whence the sign of a *sestertius*, *HS*, from *LLS*, *i. e. libra libra semis*) worth $0.03¾. Two sesterces make one *quinarius* (5 *asses*); two *quinarii* one *denarius* (10 *asses*) about $0.15.

Gold coins were very scarce before the emperors. An *aureus* (scil. *nummus*) was equal to 25 *Denarii*, worth about $3.75.

The greatest sums were also computed in sesterces, hence *nummus* standing alone is always a *sestertius*. One thousand sesterces, is *mille sestertii*, or more commonly *mille sestertium* (genitive plural like *mille passuum*); 2000 sesterces, *duo millia sestertium*; 3000 sesterces, *tria millia sestertium*. But another substantive was soon formed, **sestertium** (genitive *i*., neuter), which expressed a sum of 1000 sesterces, about $37.50 (but this did not exist as a coin). Hence *duo sestertia* is the same as *duo millia sestertium*, 2000 sesterces. Distributive numbers are also very frequently used, as *bina sestertia*, *terna sestertia*, *centena sestertia*, 100,000 sesterces. A million sesterces is in full, *decies centena millia sestertium* (genitive plural of *sestertius*) or simply *decies centena* (omitting *millia sestertium*). But here again the use of the substantive *sestertium* is very frequent to express millions, which is, however, only used in the singular; and when joined to numeral adverbs means not 1000 but 100,000 sesterces; thus, *sestertium decies* 1,000,000; *sestertium vicies* 2,000,000.

The Attic *talent* has 60 *minae*, one *mina* is 100 *drachma*; one *drachma* is 4½ sesterces, about $0.16⅞; one *mina* is 450 sesterces, equivalent to $16.88; one *talent* is 27,000 sesterces, in value $1012.

3. The Roman foot (**pes**) is divided into sixteen inches (*digitos*); it is 8 lines shorter than our foot, and is equal to 11.6 inches. The span (*palmus*) = 4 *digiti*; the ell (*cubitus*) = 1½ feet; the pace (*passus*, double step) = 5 feet; the rod (*decempeda*) = 10 feet. The *iugerum*, a surface measure, is 240 feet long by 120 wide, or 28,800 square feet.

On the public highways there was, at every 1,000 paces, a milestone (*lapis* or *milliarium*, *scil. marmor*), this distance forms the Roman mile (*mille passuum*), equal to 5,000 Roman feet or ⅕ of a geographical mile. *Ad quintum lapidem*, at the fifth milestone, *i. e.*, five miles from the city; likewise, *ad tertium milliarium*, three miles from Rome.

4. The *amphora* (*quadrantal*), about a cubic foot, equivalent to nearly 7 gallons wine measure. It contains 2 *urnas*, 3 *modios*, 8 *congios*, or 48 *sextarios*; a *sextarius* is a little more than a half-pint.

CHAPTER LVI.

THE MOST COMMON ABBREVIATIONS.

§ 349.

NAMES. — A., *Aulus.* — App., *Appius.* — C. or G., *Caius* or *Gaius.* — Cn. or Gn., *Cneius* or *Gnaeus.* — D., *Decimus.* — K., *Caeso.* — L., *Lucius.* — M., *Marcus.* — M'., *Manius.* — Mam., *Mamercus.* — P., *Publius.* — Q. or Qu., *Quintus.* — S. or Sex., *Sextus.* — Ser., *Servius.* — T., *Titus.* — Ti. or Tib., *Tiberius.*

OFFICIAL OR LEGAL DESIGNATIONS. — A. d., *ante diem.* — Aed., *Aedilis.* — C., Cal., or Kal., *Kalendas.* — Cos., *Consul;* Coss., *Consules.* — Des., *designatus.* — D., *Divus.* — Eq. Rom., *Eques Romanus.* — F., *filius.* — Id., *Idus.* — Imp., *Imperator.* — Leg., *Legatus,* or legio. — N., *nepos.* — Non., *Nonae.* — O. M., *Optimus Maximus.* — P. C., *Patres conscripti.* — P. R., *Populus Romanus.* — Pr., *Praetor.* — Praef., *Praefectus.* — Proc., *Proconsul.* — Pont. Max., *Pontifex Maximus.* — Quir., *Quirites.* — Resp., *Respublica.* — S., *Senatus.* — S. C., *Senatus consultum.* — Tr. Pl., *Tribunis plebis.* — S. P. Q. R., *Senatus Populusque Romanus.* — Q. B. F. F. S., *Quod bonum faustum feliaque sit.*

IN LETTERS. — S., *Salutem.* — S. P., or S. D., or S. P. D., *Salutem plurimam*, or *Salutem dico* (or *dicit*), or *Salutem plurimam dico.* — S. V. B. E. E. V., *Si vales, bene est; ego valeo.* — S. V. V. B. E. E. V., *Si vos valetis*, etc. — D., *Data.*

OTHER ABBREVIATIONS WHICH WERE ADOPTED LATER. — A., *anno.* — a. c., *anni currentis.* — a. pr., *anni praeteriti.* — A. M., *anno mundi.* — A. u. c., *anno urbis conditae.* — A. Chr., *anno Christi.* — a. Chr. n., *ante Christum natum.* — Ictus., *Iurisconsultus.* — L. s., *Loco sigilli.* — M. S., *manuscriptus* (*sc. liber*). — c., *caput.* — cf., *confer* or *conferatur.* — i. e., *id est.* — h. l., *hoc loco.* — l. c. or l. l., *loco citato* or *laudato.* — p. or pag., *pagina.* — sc. or scil., *scilicet.* — sq. or seq., *sequens.* — v., *versus.* — v. or vid., *vide* or *videatur.*

INDEX.

The Figures denote the Sections, Subdivisions, and Notes.

A.

O.

P.

Q.

T.